ANIMALIBUS VOL. 5
OF ANIMALS AND CULTURES

Nigel Rothfels and Garry Marvin,
GENERAL EDITORS

ADVISORY BOARD:
Steve Baker (*University of Central Lancashire*)
Susan McHugh (*University of New England*)
Jules Pretty (*University of Essex*)
Alan Rauch (*University of North Carolina at Charlotte*)

Books in the Animalibus series share a fascination with the status and the role of animals in human life. Crossing the humanities and the social sciences to include work in history, anthropology, social and cultural geography, environmental studies, and literary and art criticism, these books ask what thinking about nonhuman animals can teach us about human cultures, about what it means to be human, and about how that meaning might shift across times and places.

OTHER TITLES IN THE SERIES:
Rachel Poliquin, *The Breathless Zoo:
Taxidermy and the Cultures of Longing*

Joan B. Landes, Paula Young Lee, and
Paul Youngquist, eds., *Gorgeous Beasts:
Animal Bodies in Historical Perspective*

Liv Emma Thorsen, Karen A. Rader, and
Adam Dodd, eds., *Animals on Display:
The Creaturely in Museums, Zoos, and Natural History*

Ann-Janine Morey, *Picturing Dogs, Seeing
Ourselves: Vintage American Photographs*

Animal
Companions

Pets and Social Change in
Eighteenth-Century Britain

Ingrid H. Tague

The Pennsylvania State University Press
University Park, Pennsylvania

Library of Congress Cataloging-in-Publication Data

Tague, Ingrid H., 1968– , author.
    Animal companions : pets and social change in
eighteenth-century Britain / Ingrid H. Tague.
        pages   cm — (Animalibus)
Summary: "Explores how thinking about pets in eighteenth-
century Britain reflected and influenced the great social and
cultural debates of the day, including struggles over gender,
race, class, and national identity"—Provided by publisher.
Includes bibliographical references and index.
ISBN 978-0-271-06588-5 (cloth : alk. paper)
ISBN 978-0-271-06589-2 (pbk. : alk. paper)
    1. Pets—Social aspects—Great Britain—History—
18th century.
    2. Human-animal relationships—Great Britain—
History—18th century.
    3. Pet owners—Great Britain—History—18th century.
I. Title. II. Series: Animalibus.

SF411.36.G7T34   2015
636.088'70941—dc23
2014041903

Title page illustration: Joshua Reynolds, *Mrs. Abington as Miss
Prue in "Love for Love" by William Congreve,* 1771 (detail). Yale
Center for British Art, Paul Mellon Collection.

For ANNEMARIE *and* BERKLEY TAGUE

Contents

LIST OF ILLUSTRATIONS ~ *ix*

ACKNOWLEDGMENTS ~ *xiii*

Introduction ~ *1*

1 The Material Conditions of Pet Keeping ~ *14*

2 Domesticating the Exotic ~ *50*

3 Fashioning the Pet ~ *91*

4 A Privilege or a Right? ~ *138*

5 Pets and Their People ~ *174*

EPILOGUE ~ *229*

NOTES ~ *235*

BIBLIOGRAPHY ~ *269*

INDEX ~ *283*

Illustrations

1   George Morland, *Selling Guinea Pigs,* ca. 1789. Yale Center for British Art, Paul Mellon Collection.   *25*

2   Henri Merke, after Thomas Rowlandson, *Cries of London. No. 1: Buy a Trap, a Rat Trap, Buy My Trap,* ca. 1799. Courtesy of the Lewis Walpole Library, Yale University, 799.01.01.03.   *27*

3   T. L. Busby, *Dogs Meat,* ca. 1800. Courtesy of the Lewis Walpole Library, Yale University, 800.00.00.67.   *39*

4   Brass dog collar inscribed "Stop me not but let me jog for I am S. Oliver's Dog. Bicknell," eighteenth century. Trustees of Leeds Castle Foundation.   *41*

5   Leather and silver dog collar, eighteenth century. Trustees of Leeds Castle Foundation.   *42*

6   *Lady Fashion's Secretary's Office, or Peticoat Recommendation the Best,* 1772. Courtesy of the Lewis Walpole Library, Yale University, 772.00.00.15+.   *43*

7   Charles Grignion, after John Collet, *January and May,* 1771. Courtesy of the Lewis Walpole Library, Yale University, 771.04.16.01+.   *45*

8   *Cobler's Hall,* ca. 1793. Courtesy of the Lewis Walpole Library, Yale University, 778.00.00.07.2+.   *46*

9   William Hogarth, *The Graham Children,* 1742. National Gallery, London. © National Gallery, London / Art Resource, New York.   *47*

10   Gérard Jean Baptiste Scotin II, after Gravelot, *Chimpanzee,* 1738. The British Museum. © The Trustees of the British Museum. All rights reserved.   *51*

11   *Animated Nature, or Lady en Famille,* 1786. Courtesy of the Lewis Walpole Library, Yale University, 786.02.20.02.   *93*

12 Joseph Wright of Derby, *Dressing the Kitten*, ca. 1768–70. Kenwood House, London. © English Heritage. *99*

13 *Lady All-Top*, 1776. Courtesy of the Lewis Walpole Library, Yale University, 776.05.15.01. *103*

14 *The Cork Rump or Chloe's Cushion*, 1776. Courtesy of the Lewis Walpole Library, Yale University, 776.11.19.01. *104*

15 *The Supplemental Magazine*, 1786. Courtesy of the Lewis Walpole Library, Yale University, 786.01.01.05+. *105*

16 John Goldar, after John Collet, *The Canonical Beau, or Mars in the Dumps*, 1768. Courtesy of the Lewis Walpole Library, Yale University, 768.10.25.01+. *109*

17 Joshua Reynolds, *Mrs. Abington as Miss Prue in "Love for Love" by William Congreve*, 1771. Yale Center for British Art, Paul Mellon Collection. *111*

18 Philip Dawe, *A New Fashion'd Head Dress for Young Misses of Three Score and Ten*, 1777. Courtesy of the Lewis Walpole Library, Yale University, 777.05.08.01+. *113*

19 James Roberts, *The Happy Consultation, or Modern Match*, 1769. The British Museum. © The Trustees of the British Museum. All rights reserved. *115*

20 John Pettit, *Old Maids at a Cat's Funeral*, 1789. Courtesy of the Lewis Walpole Library, Yale University, 789.04.10.01. *117*

21 Thomas Rowlandson, *Virginia*, 1800. Courtesy of the Lewis Walpole Library, Yale University, 800.08.15.03+. *119*

22 P. Crotchet, after Daniel Dodd, *Grown Ladies Taught to Dance*, 1768. Courtesy of the Lewis Walpole Library, Yale University, 768.01.01.04+. *121*

23 *Boarding School Education, or The Frenchified Young Lady*, 1771. Courtesy of the Lewis Walpole Library, Yale University, 771.10.19.01.2+. *123*

24 *A New Academy for Accomplishments*, 1778. The British Museum. © The Trustees of the British Museum. All rights reserved. *124*

25 Charles White, after Captain Minshull, *The Macarony Dressing Room*, 1772. Courtesy of the Lewis Walpole Library, Yale University, 772.11.09.01+. *126*

26 *Which Is the Man,* 1786. Courtesy of the Lewis Walpole Library, Yale University, 786.05.30.06. *127*

27 James Caldwall, after Michel Vincent Brandoin, *The Macarony Brothers,* 1772. Courtesy of the Lewis Walpole Library, Yale University, 772.07.25.01.1. *130*

28 After John Collet, *Summer,* ca. 1779. Courtesy of the Lewis Walpole Library, Yale University, 779.01.01.04+. *143*

29 William Hogarth, *First Stage of Cruelty,* 1751. Courtesy of the Lewis Walpole Library, Yale University, 751.02.01.03.1+, box 200. *154*

30 George Morland, *The Miseries of Idleness,* before 1790. Scottish National Gallery. *160*

31 Henry Kingsbury, after John Kitchingman, *The Beggar and His Dog,* 1775. The British Museum. © The Trustees of the British Museum. All rights reserved. *169*

32 Thomas Gainsborough, *Pomeranian Bitch and Puppy,* ca. 1777. Tate. © Tate, London, 2015. *184*

33 *The Rival Favourites,* 1788. Courtesy of the Lewis Walpole Library, Yale University, 788.02.04.03+. *186*

34 *Pretty Miss a Sleep,* 1771. Courtesy of the Lewis Walpole Library, Yale University, 771.10.03.04. *188*

35 *Preserving the Young,* ca. 1793. Courtesy of the Lewis Walpole Library, Yale University, 793.00.00.73. *189*

36 *Miss Thoughtful,* 1775. Courtesy of the Lewis Walpole Library, Yale University, 775.06.20.01+. *191*

37 John Dixon, after Thomas Gainsborough, *Henry Scott, 3rd Duke of Buccleuch,* 1771. National Portrait Gallery. © National Portrait Gallery, London. *196*

38 Henry Raeburn, *Boy and Rabbit,* ca. 1814. Royal Academy of Arts, London. *199*

Acknowledgments

Writing can often feel like a lonely and isolated process—until we remember how many people have helped us through the loneliness and isolation. In the years it has taken to produce this book, I have acquired many debts. The time and money to research and write are precious, and I am grateful to the University of Denver for both, in the form of two sabbaticals, a Faculty Research Fund grant, and a Professional Research Opportunities for Faculty grant. I have also drawn on divisional and departmental financial support. Much more important, I have been lucky to have enormously supportive colleagues. During most of the time that I worked on this project, I was serving as department chair; it is because of my fellow faculty members that the role felt like a privilege rather than a burden. I owe a special debt to Susan Schulten, not only for being such a wonderful friend and colleague, but also for her willingness to step into the role of chair and allow me to step down. As always, help from the University of Denver's librarians has been invaluable. This book would not have been possible without their efforts to get me the sources I needed; my thanks in particular to Carrie Forbes, Peggy Keeran, and Michael Levine-Clark. David Cox served as my summer research assistant; I both appreciate and am sorry for the hours he spent ruining his posture and his eyesight as he scrolled through endless reels of microfilm.

Support from beyond the University of Denver has been equally important. I am grateful to the Animalibus series editors, Garry Marvin and Nigel Rothfels, for their interest in this project. Kendra Boileau at Penn State Press has offered valuable support and has dealt patiently with my queries; she and the anonymous readers for the Press helped make this a better book. The Lewis Walpole Library of Yale University provided a Visiting Research Fellowship that enabled me to spend a month in the library's amazing archives. Maggie Powell, Sue Walker, and the rest of the staff made me feel at home from the beginning, and I benefited enormously from their wealth of knowledge. I am grateful as well for permission from the Walpole Library to use so many of its images in this work. Across the Atlantic, the staff of the British Library and the British Museum Prints and Drawings study room were, as ever, helpful and patient; without their assistance, I would have missed a great deal of valuable material. Tori Reeve of Leeds Castle graciously allowed me access to the castle's collection of dog collars while it was off display, as well as providing images. I had useful exchanges with Christopher Plumb (by e-mail and in person), and I am thankful to him for sending me a copy of his unpublished doctoral dissertation. Portions of chapters 2 and 4 appeared in "Companions, Servants, or Slaves? Considering Animals in Eighteenth-Century England," *Studies in Eighteenth-Century Culture* 39 (2010): 103–22; another part of chapter 4 is drawn from sections of "Eighteenth-Century English Debates on a Dog Tax," *Historical Journal* 51, no. 4 (2008): 901–20.

Other support was less formal but no less important: Luc Beaudoin, Helen Berry, Tim Harris, Susannah Ottaway, and Dror Wahrman provided encouragement and helpful feedback through the long years that I worked on this project. Peter and Cheryl Tague frequently housed and fed me in London during the initial research for this book, and at the end they provided much-appreciated hospitality once more, this time in New York. Both also contributed directly to my research: Cheryl first alerted me to the existence of a dog collar museum at Leeds Castle; Pete took me on a memorable visit to the Hartsdale Pet Cemetery. The last acknowledgments are, as usual, reserved for the greatest debts. Through no fault of his own, Paul Dewen lived with this book for a decade. He bore with my long absences as I visited archives, and he coped admirably with my all too frequent bouts of anxiety, panic, and despair. I owe him more than I can say, but at least I know how lucky I am.

Many years ago, when I was working on my doctoral dissertation, I tried to find something about my research on elite women that might entertain my mother. I began telling her stories about Lady Isabella Wentworth, an eccentric old woman who kept multiple dogs, a parrot, and a monkey. "Forget aristocrats," my mother declared during one of these conversations; "just write about pets." Although I did finish the project on aristocratic women, her suggestion stuck with me. Let this be a warning to parents everywhere: your children really do listen to you, and they may even follow your advice. She and my father suffered more than

anyone else from the effects of that careless joke. They allowed themselves to be taken on lengthy excursions so that I could follow up on
sources; they never complained when our visits to art exhibitions were
hijacked by my fascination with the tiny doghouse or even tinier songbird
in the corner of a picture; and they managed to seem genuinely interested
as I rehashed my ideas and my dilemmas, both personal and professional.
It is a poor form of repayment to impose yet more pets upon them, but
this book is for them—"dearest and best of parents," as Lady Wentworth
would say—with all my love.

In a cemetery in Hartsdale, New York, sits a monument to three beloved family members who died in the 1970s. All three were in their early teens, and the inscription on their common headstone speaks of the grief of their "Mommy" and "Daddy." But these were not three human children; they were dogs named Lynett, Bizet, and Chou-Chou, and they lie interred in America's oldest pet cemetery. The cemetery, which was founded in 1896 (and officially incorporated in 1914), now contains close to eighty thousand pets, mostly dogs and cats, and is still in active use today.[1] The inscription for Lynett and her "siblings" is typical: "Here sleep my most precious possessions who have given us love, happiness, and companionship in past years. Now they are gone forever. Now we remain lonely." In these sentences, we see the fundamental paradox of modern pet keeping: a deep emotional attachment to individuals who provide the great gifts of "love, happiness, and companionship" and whose loss means loneliness, and, simultaneously, an awareness that those individuals are "possessions." How can we love a possession? How can a society decide that animals must not receive the privilege of burial among humans, and yet also decide that some are worthy of a cemetery of their own? And how do we choose which animals are thus singled out?

Pets are so ubiquitous in Britain and America today that it can be difficult to imagine that there was ever a time when they were seen as unusual. In our world of specialized accessories, food, and even hotels for pets, when a story of an abandoned or abused animal is an easy way for the local news to tug on our heartstrings, a failure to love animals can seem like a sign of cold-heartedness—a warning sign that a person may not be capable of loving another human, either. And yet we continue to treat pet animals in ways that are completely distinct from our treatment of humans. We may talk of our "fur babies," but local laws require that dogs be kept on leads, entire breeds considered dangerous can be banned from cities, and, most strikingly, many pet owners agree about the necessity of spaying and neutering their animals.[2] For all that we love our pets, we treat them in ways that would never be acceptable in treating other human beings. And the legal perspective is stark: pets are the property of humans.[3] We may think of ourselves as "Mommy" or "Daddy" to our pets, but they remain distinct from our human children. This book explores the development of modern pet keeping and its attendant paradoxes in a time before the creation of the first pet cemetery, before pet supplies became a multimillion-dollar industry, before towns began to pass ordinances defining pets as "companion animals" and their human owners as "guardians." During the eighteenth century, when pet keeping was first becoming a widespread phenomenon in Britain, many people were horrified by what they saw as a wasteful extravagance. Material and emotional resources that should have been devoted to humans, in this view, were diverted to the care of creatures that God had intended to serve humans as labor or food. Pet keeping was at best a useless luxury; at worst, it was actually sinful. Yet throughout the century, pet keeping became more commonplace, and by 1800 attitudes had changed so much that many people had come to regard the love of pets as a sign of moral virtue rather than corruption. One goal of this book is to explain why that transformation occurred. More than that, however, I aim to explore the role of pets in helping eighteenth-century Britons think through the major problems of their day.

My central argument is that pets, being neither fully human nor fully part of the natural world—part of a household yet distinct from its human inhabitants—offered a unique opportunity for eighteenth-century Britons to articulate their view of what it meant to be human and what their society ought to look like. This was a period when such questions took on special urgency. It saw the growth of a strong state government, supported through a sophisticated economic system of credit and debt and a greatly expanding overseas empire. Having begun to break out of the Malthusian cycle of dearth and famine, Britain became the wealthiest nation in Europe, with newly widespread disposable income and unprecedented access to consumer goods of all kinds. Closely connected with these material changes was the Enlightenment, with its implications for contemporary understanding of religion, science, and non-European cultures. All of these transformations generated both excitement and anxiety, and they were reflected in debates over the rights and wrongs of human-animal relationships. Pets were both increasingly visible indicators of spreading prosperity and catalysts for debates about the morals of the radically different society emerging in this period.

In order to understand the spread of pet keeping, it is helpful first to explore the meaning of the term "pet." The word itself is relatively new; the *Oxford English Dictionary*'s first citation that refers to an animal comes from 1539, when it meant a "cade lamb"—one reared by hand in the house. The word derives from Scottish Gaelic, and the OED notes that the use was primarily confined to Scotland, northern England, and northern Ireland. This was the same definition that Samuel Johnson provided in his 1755 dictionary. This early meaning suggests two key characteristics of the modern pet: it is tame, and it lives in the house. Yet a lamb reared by hand is clearly not the same thing as a pet dog or cat in our current sense, and it is significant that the word "pet" was rarely used during the early modern period. The OED's first citation of a source that refers specifically to "an animal (typically one which is domestic or tame) kept for pleasure or companionship" comes from Richard Steele's *Tatler* in 1710. Steele describes an old woman who had "transferred the amorous Passions of her first Years to the Love of Cronies, Petts and Favourites," which were various animals. But Steele's use of the term relies primarily on another, older definition of "pet" as "favorite," with the strongly negative connotation of a person who was favored unfairly. When people in the early modern period referred to "pets," they most often did so in this derogatory sense. This meaning survives today in our concept of the "teacher's pet"—and, of course, the modern notion of a "pet" incorporates the idea as well: a pet is an animal that has been singled out for special treatment. The word "pet" in the modern sense, combining favoritism and domesticity, did not come into common usage until the nineteenth century, and I contend that this lack reflects the relative absence of pet keeping in early modern society. The phenomenon had to exist before a term developed for it. Occasional references in the late eighteenth century suggest that its usage was gaining popularity during this period, as pet keeping entered the mainstream; for example, a popular children's book from the 1790s called a woman who kept a cat "Mrs Petlove."[4]

The OED's definition is a useful starting point, but I want to draw attention to more specific characteristics of the modern pet. Keith Thomas has suggested three defining features of a pet: it is kept in the house; it is given a special name (often a human one); and it is never eaten.[5] Yi-Fu Tuan, in *Dominance and Affection*, takes a different approach and emphasizes the power relations at the heart of pet keeping; he argues that a pet is "a diminished being" and "a personal belonging, an animal with charm that one can take delight in, play with, or set aside, as one wishes." Tuan thus stresses that humans such as women, children, and especially slaves can be pets.[6] Tuan's insight into the unequal power relations inherent in pet keeping is an important one, and I will return later in this work to the parallels between animals and slaves—parallels of which eighteenth-century observers were well aware. But for the purposes of this book, I want to keep the meaning of "pet" specifically related to animals, and I will emphasize two defining characteristics of the pet: it lives in the domestic space, and its primary purpose for humans is entertainment and companionship. While it is certainly true that people had for a very long time experienced strong emotional ties to animals like horses and hunting dogs, their utility and their exclusion from the house placed them in a separate category. As we will see, those emotional bonds were not seen as problematic in the way that, for example, a woman's affection for her lapdog was. This differentiation between working animals and pets was, moreover, one that was widely recognized in the eighteenth century. Oliver Goldsmith thus followed tradition in categorizing dogs according to their service to humans, from turnspits to hunting dogs, and in simply dismissing breeds like lapdogs as "useless."[7] Although Goldsmith and his contemporaries recognized that many people kept dogs purely as pets, they regarded the practice as pointless, if not downright immoral and wasteful.

More recent work on pets and pet keeping has further developed our understanding of the roles pets play in human life. Marc Shell, for instance, argues that pets are defined by their boundary crossing: their human owners see them as simultaneously part of the family and not part of the family, and as simultaneously human and nonhuman. Shell suggests that the pet fulfills an important role in enabling people to consider how they define human identity and how they structure ideas of kinship.[8] I argue throughout this book that it was precisely this liminal status that made pets so intriguing and so problematic in eighteenth-century Britain. In a society committed to interwoven hierarchies based on birth, title, wealth, gender, and race, and that struggled to maintain order within those hierarchies in a rapidly changing world, the fluid identity of pets played into many other anxieties. Yet, ironically, by the end of the century that same fluidity became a great asset, as more and more people hoped for the possibility of breaking down the boundaries between humans and the natural world.

Erica Fudge has also done much to theorize human-animal relationships, and in her book *Pets* she makes the important point that animals have too often been seen as filling a gap in modern life—that they are perceived to be compensations or substitutes for something that their human owners should be able to find in other humans but cannot. Thus pet keeping has sometimes been portrayed as a result of modern urbanization or industrialization and their concomitant problems of alienation.[9] While, as I will argue, the spread of pet keeping is indeed related to the material changes brought on by increased wealth and consumerism, Fudge's point that pets should not be seen purely as compensation for some sort of absence or failure is a crucial one to keep in mind.[10] But the criticisms of pet keeping that she addresses have their roots in eighteenth-century responses to the spread of keeping pets, and thus understanding those responses can shed light on the persistence of such views today.

The idea that pets somehow fill a void created by modern social conditions reflects a common belief that pet keeping did not emerge as a widespread practice until the nineteenth century. Existing scholarship on the history of pets and pet keeping supports this view; the works of Kathleen Kete for France, Harriet Ritvo for Britain, and Katherine Grier for the United States all focus on the nineteenth century as the period in which pet keeping took off.[11] In part, this scholarly bias reflects the widespread association, also posited by Keith Thomas, between the rise of pet keeping and the rise of the urban middle class.[12] But there are two obvious problems with that association. For one thing, it is clear that pet keeping existed (especially among the elite) long before the eighteenth century.[13] Moreover, studies of other cultures have shown that pet keeping occurs all over the world and does not require Western values or urbanization.[14] Discussion of the rise of pet keeping sometimes seems to echo the old debates about "the rise of the middle class," with claims for its emergence traced ever further back in time. Nevertheless, I contend that pet keeping does not take the same form, or hold the same meaning, across all periods or cultures, any more than practices such as marriage or child rearing do. This book thus recognizes the importance of growing prosperity among the middle ranks as a factor encouraging the acquisition of pets across a much wider segment of society, yet it also seeks to interrogate the retrospective association between middle-class values and pet keeping—the assumption that pet keeping is an inherently "bourgeois" phenomenon. Instead, I hope to situate thinking about pets in a broader context of social, economic, and cultural change, understanding class as one important factor among many affecting ideas about human-animal relations in the period.

Although recent scholarship specifically related to the history of pet keeping focuses primarily on the nineteenth century, the eighteenth century as well as the rest of the early modern period has proved fruitful territory for scholars in the field of animal studies.[15] Erica Fudge's groundbreaking work has helped put animals at the center of our understanding of Renaissance culture, while others have drawn attention to the importance of animals in Enlightenment thinking.[16] Like Fudge, many of these scholars rely heavily on literary sources, from treatises on "wild children" to the Houyhnhnms and Yahoos of *Gulliver's Travels*. Another fruitful avenue of exploration, more rooted in social history, has focused on exotic imports.[17] All of these works have done much to further our understanding of the role of animals in eighteenth-century culture. The humble house cat or dog, however, has received comparatively little attention. Yet ordinary pets like these formed the basis of much eighteenth-century thinking about animals, and such common animals are at the heart of this project. By emphasizing concrete social conditions, this book seeks to build on the existing literary scholarship; and by emphasizing the importance of lived experiences, it seeks to remind us that pets were not merely metaphors used to think about the world but living, breathing beings that had a direct impact on the lives of the humans with whom they interacted.

This work is thus situated within the field of animal studies, but it departs from some of the interests that have dominated that field. Thanks in part to the fact that many early voices in animal studies were motivated by an ethical concern about our treatment of animals, much work has focused implicitly or explicitly on the ethics of relations between humans and animals. As Donna Landry notes, a central aspect of animal studies has been an emphasis on the cruelty of humans toward animals and a desire to advocate a more equal relationship between humans and nonhuman species.[18] One aspect of this work has been an interest in historical debates about the boundaries between humans and nonhumans: not only attempts to define the nature of those boundaries, but also moments when such boundaries were challenged. The animal studies movement has been enormously helpful in reminding us that distinctions between humans and other species are not straightforward; they are no more natural than other ways in which people have sought to construct difference, such as race or gender norms.[19] The assumption behind much of this work is that recognizing that the animal-human boundary is culturally constructed might in turn help break down notions of human superiority and thus lead to improved treatment for animals. And it is certainly true that even a cursory examination of early modern ideas about animals reveals the differences between what were then considered "obvious" or "natural" categories and those employed today: witness Goldsmith's classification of dogs according to their utility. My primary interest is not, however, in encouraging new attitudes toward animals today; rather, my focus is on understanding how ideas about animals have been shaped in specific ways by their specific historical contexts, and on how thinking about animals in turn helped shape other kinds of thinking at particular moments in time.

Another assumption behind much work in animal studies is the idea that contemporary problems in the treatment of animals are the result of a distinctively "modern" attitude or ideology. Some early modernists interested in animal studies have therefore suggested that the period is characterized by the development of a new commitment to a rigid human-animal divide. Laurie Shannon's recent work on early modern thinking about animals, for instance, identifies Cartesianism as marking a critical break with an earlier worldview that saw humans and animals as common members of the natural and political world. There is an appeal in the idea that recognizing, and perhaps returning to, an older notion of human-animal relations might make possible greater equality and thus better treatment of animals. My own work is informed by this sort of animal studies scholarship, and debates over the differences (if any) between humans and animals are central to this project. Part of the reason why I focus on pets is that by definition they challenge an easy distinction between humans and nonhumans. Yet my argument also questions the idea that Cartesianism or any other intellectual movement transformed early modern thinking by insisting on a radical distinction between humans and animals. Far from it: the question of the human-animal boundary remained very much an open one throughout the eighteenth century, with views ranging from a total separation between the species to an insistence on seeing humans as part of the animal world. Indeed, when eighteenth-century writers brought up Descartes, it was usually to dismiss his ideas. If some people in the period were convinced of humanity's uniqueness and superiority over all other species, this was also the moment when Linnaeus famously classified humans with other primates and even with bats.

Moreover, pets remind us that unequal power relations between humans and animals need not take the form of tyranny; it is possible both to think of animals as property *and* to recognize that they have inherent rights.[20] Vicki Hearne and Donna Haraway suggest another avenue for contemplating human-animal relations, one that sees training as beneficial to both human and pet through mutual understanding.[21] The eighteenth-century Britons who form the subject of my study did not, for the most part, think in terms of "rights" for animals, but they did struggle with the question of what they owed their pets and other animals. Eighteenth-century people accepted the idea of hierarchies in all aspects of life, among humans as well as animals, but that did not keep them from debating the nature of those hierarchies. And in a period when humans as well as animals could be property, the fundamental problem caused by loving and owning another living being took on a very different resonance than it has today. I argue that it is impossible to identify a single "modern" attitude toward animals, and that the distinctively modern phenomenon of widespread pet keeping opened up, rather than closed off, a wide range of possibilities for conceptualizing human-animal relations. To identify these possibilities is not to embrace a Whiggish notion of progress from cruelty, to humanity, and ultimately to equality; questioning boundaries between humans and animals might license cruelty (to both animals and other humans) as often as it might lead to a recognition of common rights.

Finally, this work both engages with and departs from much of the work in animal studies when it comes to the question of animal agency. The emergence of the field has led to a new awareness that human-animal relations are not merely a question of what "we" do to "them." Animals have had a significant impact on human history, and it is not coincidental that there is much overlap between the history of animals and environmental history; both areas emphasize the role of nonhuman factors in human history.[22] Nevertheless, we cannot write a history of animals in the same way that it is possible to write human history. We do not have access to animal experiences even to the extent that we have access to the experiences of the poor and illiterate, who also left no written records. We can only explain animal behavior with reference to our own, human thoughts and feelings.[23] Moreover, we must assume that, unlike even the very poor and illiterate, animals influenced human history without consciously choosing to do so. As a historian, then, I focus unapologetically on humans. I am interested in animals primarily because of their impact on human life, rather than the other way around—not because I think animals are unimportant, but because ultimately the study of history must be a study of humans. It is certainly true that focusing on animals forces us to come to terms with the instability of the category of "human." As Fudge argues, "'human' always relies upon 'animal' for its meaning."[24] This destabilization is fruitful because it undermines the assumption that we can justify our treatment of animals simply on the grounds that they are not human. But it is equally true that the historical endeavor depends on such a distinction even as we recognize its tenuousness: the history we can know and write requires access—no matter how indirect—to the motives, beliefs, and feelings of individuals in the past, which we cannot achieve with animals. This project thus inevitably relies on a fundamental divide between humans and other species even as it questions the anthropocentrism inherent in such a view.

If political and ideological agendas underlie thinking about animals today, the same was true in the eighteenth century. Each chapter of this book examines such agendas by exploring how eighteenth-century Britons used pets to engage with the defining questions of their time. Chapter 1 traces the implications of the social transformation wrought by the twin financial and consumer revolutions of the late seventeenth and early eighteenth centuries, and the concomitant growth of the British Empire. Changes in economic practices, the emergence of a consumer culture, and new arrangements of domestic space all helped make it possible to keep pets. Imperial expansion both fostered economic growth and made exotic animals much more widely available. This chapter explores the effects of such changes on the availability and cost of pets, both domestic and exotic. The new social and economic practices of the eighteenth century made pet keeping viable on a large scale; the first chapter thus establishes the background for the issues examined in the rest of the book.

The remaining chapters use the liminal status of pets, on the border between human and animal, to explore how pets encouraged the British to reconsider (or reinforce) other socially constructed boundaries. The second chapter deals most directly with the key animal studies concern of the human-animal divide, but it focuses on the implications of that question for thinking about racial boundaries. Imperial and economic growth was inextricably bound up with slavery, and this expansion forced the British to wrestle with the impact of the new animals and peoples they encountered—and sometimes subjugated—around the world. Importing exotic animals might reinforce notions of British superiority, but contact with apes and monkeys, particularly the humanoid apes, threatened to destabilize comforting notions of humanity's unique place at the top of the great chain of being. Because domestication was associated with both slavery and civilization, pets—the most extreme examples of domesticated animals—were central to debates about the benefits and problems of British social and economic organization.

Chapters 3 and 4 focus on problems closer to home. The third chapter examines the intersection of pet keeping with debates over gender and fashion, as concerns about pets mirrored other cultural anxieties. Occupying the border between humans and animals, pets also seemed to occupy the borders between masculine and feminine, individual and thing, status symbol and emotional connection. This extreme malleability led to anxieties about categorization, not just of animals but also of people. Pets were used not only to satirize fashionable femininity—and its antithesis in the form of old maids—but also to address concerns about masculinity and fashion in attacks on men such as fops or dancing masters. In chapter 4, the boundaries at issue are those in the social hierarchy of status and wealth. The central problem here is the question of which people, if any, should keep pets in a society still dealing with widespread poverty and scarcity. Wealthy pet owners could be vulnerable to criticism, portrayed as engaging in uncharitable self-indulgence; but poor people who owned pets could equally be seen as the quintessential example of the idle poor, abusing the system of poor relief and using their dogs as accomplices in poaching. Yet over time such anxieties were counterbalanced by a growing belief that perhaps all people should have the opportunity to love and care for an animal.

All of these chapters deal primarily with discussions *about* pet keeping, often in sources produced by people who neither kept nor approved of pets. The final chapter turns to the experiences of pet owners themselves, exploring how they portrayed their relationships with their animals. It builds on the change over time revealed in the previous chapter and attempts to explain that transformation in attitudes. The development of the humane movement was part of the process, but more important was the emergence of the ideals of sympathy and sensibility. Together, sensibility and sympathy gave rise to the idea that it might be possible to share feelings and experiences with all living beings, not just other humans. Thus, in their letters and portraits, pet owners began to present their affection as an ideal to emulate.

Partly because they were becoming so much more common, pets were very much on people's minds in the eighteenth century. Yet there are few sources from the period in which pets stand at the center: little was written, either fiction or nonfiction, with pets as the primary subjects; many of the material goods related to pets have disappeared, particularly those objects that were inexpensive and purely utilitarian; and the vast majority of pets never sat for portraits. Where such direct portrayals and objects survive, I make use of them. More often, however, pets remain at the margins, referred to in an offhand remark, filling empty space in a picture of humans, mentioned as a specimen in a work of natural history. This book moves pets from the margins to the center, making use of the accumulated detail to understand how people thought and talked about companion animals even when they were ostensibly thinking or talking about other things. And once we begin looking for them, pets are everywhere. I thus make use of a wide array of sources and genres: natural histories, novels, and children's literature; newspapers and periodicals; satirical prints and formal portraits; animal rights treatises and legislative debates; and the testimony of pet owners themselves. Specific kinds of animals also come to the fore in different chapters: dogs, cats, songbirds, and

monkeys all receive sustained attention because of the particularly significant roles they played in eighteenth-century thought. Different species
served different purposes, and animals that receive more or less attention
reflect those distinctions.

By employing so many different kinds of sources, moreover, I hope to
present a reasonably representative sampling of attitudes toward animals.
Hand-illustrated folio collections or full-length versions of the multivolume, erudite natural histories by the Comte de Buffon and Oliver Goldsmith, for instance, might have been accessible only to a tiny elite, but
these works were widely copied, condensed, and popularized.[25] Goldsmith himself drew heavily on Buffon, incorporating lengthy translations
of Buffon's *Natural History* into his own text, which in turn made their way
into the "common knowledge" shared by Britons about the natural world.
Even works intended for children often contained information taken
straight from these specialized works. Children's literature is useful for
other reasons as well; although many young readers may have chosen to
ignore the moralizing advice contained in stories aimed at them, the stories were designed to contain information and morals acceptable to a
broad audience. The presence of animals in so much of the literature
written for children suggests that they were perceived as helpful in moral
instruction. Similarly, images of pets in satirical prints frequently acted as
shorthand for common cultural ideas about gender and status; examining
patterns in such representations enables us to unpack the assumptions
behind them. Precisely because animals were often not the subjects under
discussion, their presence in the sources often reflects ideas or attitudes
believed to be widely shared and easily comprehensible.

Eighteenth-century Britons used pets to debate the crucial questions
of the period. Was Britain's growing wealth a sign of future happiness
and prosperity or a prelude to decadence and decline? How should society balance the benefits of imperialism and slavery against the values of
individual rights and liberty? Is it possible to identify immutable, natural
gender roles? Should social mobility be celebrated or feared? Are individual emotional relationships more important than hierarchical relationships of status and patronage? It is my contention that pets were
particularly useful in helping people think through these questions. The
dramatic transformation in the dominant social attitude toward pet keeping reflects the very real and important changes that took place over the
century. But at the same time, many of these questions, like the place of

pets themselves in society, remained unresolved. Conflicts over laws and regulations, like the hand-wringing over the expenditure wasted on cute costumes or gourmet foods, reveal that we have still not reached a consensus about the meaning and role of pets in our lives today. This book seeks to shed light on the origins of these conflicts, and to explain why they came to take the shape they have.

I ∾ THE MATERIAL CONDITIONS OF PET KEEPING

Among the many consumer delights offered in eighteenth-century London were millinery, china, furniture, plays, prints, and books—ornaments for the body, home, and mind. But the city also offered an expanding array of living consumer goods in the form of nonhuman animals. Vendors catered to aristocrats hoping to add new exotic animals to their menageries, gentry women looking for birds with festive plumage for their poultry yards, and men seeking hunting or guard dogs. They also offered pets, creatures intended for no other purpose than pleasure. Shops like the one "at the Sign of the Parrot" advertised just such a variety:

> To be SOLD,
> An uncommon good Talking Parrot, a Pair of Pintail Parroquets, some Mule Birds, Canary Birds, with a Variety of Song Birds, a beautiful Pair of the red-legg'd Partridges, all Sorts of Foreign and English Pheasants, Guinea Fowls, Pea Fowls, the large wild Turkies, the black Fowl with white Toppings, the Silk Fowl from India, small Bantams, a Pair of breeding Swans, white Muscovy Ducks, the large Roan Ducks, &c. a Pair of white Doves, Turtle-Doves, Foreign Pigeons, a Monkey from Guinea full of Tricks, likewise a very small Marmoset Monkey, a Virginia Squirrel, India Sheep and

Goats, a Boar and Sow from ditto, a remarkable large Irish Wolf Dog, small Italian Greyhound Puppies, some very small Puppies of the true King Charles's Breed, some Cocking Spaniels, the Pomerania or the Fox Dogs, &c.[1]

These shops offered everything from Irish wolfhounds to King Charles spaniels, from American squirrels to "the Silk Fowl from India," from pigs to parakeets, and they took advantage of the opportunities provided through media like newspapers to spread the word. The Parrot and businesses like it lay at the crossroads of crucial trends in the eighteenth century, including the flowering of a consumer society, the spread of the British Empire, and a fascination with the natural world characteristic of Enlightenment thought. Contact with faraway lands, containing a seemingly endless supply of novel and wonderful creatures, brought with it access to new species and the possibility of bringing those species into the home. The British had access to disposable income on an unprecedented scale: if rare parrots were out of many people's reach, almost anyone could afford a caged songbird. Keeping animals at home not only provided companionship; it also presented the opportunity to observe their behavior and describe, classify, and characterize the habits of birds and beasts. This chapter is about the forces that transformed British society and what they meant for the development of pet keeping in eighteenth-century Britain.

This period saw the development of a consumer culture around pet keeping, including the rise of specialized animal vendors and a market for pet-related products and accessories.[2] Because there was no directory of pet sellers or standard catalogue of animal pricing, however, much of the information about these developments comes from scattered references such as notices placed in newspapers.[3] Evidence from these sources is also inevitably self-limiting with regard to the class of both the people placing the ads and those likely to read and respond. The papers themselves were reasonably cheap: the *Public Advertiser* cost 2d. per issue at the start of our period and 3½d. at the end; the *Daily Advertiser* was also 2d. Moreover, many people had access to copies through coffeehouses, where they could peruse the papers or listen to them being read aloud for free. Placing an advertisement was considerably more expensive, each one costing somewhere between 2s. and 4s. This would be comparable to the cost of a dozen plates or a week's rent for a London artisan.[4] Obviously, such prices put advertisements out of reach of the poor, and thus not only were many ads placed by businesses, but the costs would also have affected the ability of pet owners to publish notices regarding lost or stolen animals. In addition, the newspapers were London-based. This chapter is heavily weighted toward London, the political, economic, and cultural center of England, and by far its largest city. Trade in animals and their associated goods was uniquely prominent there, and it is clear that most people seeking rare or unusual animals bought them in London. The absence of evidence for provincial areas makes it more difficult to generalize about the nation as a whole, although the centrality of London to the animal trade means that it influenced at least exotic animal ownership through-out Britain.

Other information about pets is visible in the surviving material culture. Dog collars, birdcages, and other animal accessories are held in museums and private collections, and they are recorded in innumerable prints and portraits. Although the high-end objects are the ones most likely to have survived, and therefore we must be careful about assuming their typicality, these objects do provide information about the kinds of goods available to pet owners in the eighteenth century. Similarly, pictures do not provide a purely objective representation of pets and their habitations, but they do reflect what artists thought would be believable to their audiences. For instance, the increasing presence of pets in domestic interiors, to the point that they were ubiquitous in happy scenes by the end of the century, suggests that pets were widely considered a central component of a cozy home, even if not everyone could actually afford them (or wanted them). Together, these disparate sources paint a picture of the material conditions of pet keeping: the social and economic changes that made it possible for large numbers of people to keep pets, how they might have obtained those animals, and how they cared for them.

Changes in financial practices were among the earliest and most significant factors in the development of Britain as a true world power. The financial revolution of the late seventeenth and early eighteenth centuries dramatically transformed credit and debt. With the establishment of the Bank of England in 1694, a formal system of public debt emerged, capable of sustaining not only the wars of the late seventeenth century but those of the eighteenth as well.[5] The bank enabled long-term borrowing by the government, which was supplemented by other means of raising money through the sale of annuities and lotteries, and, most significantly, the reform and expansion of the system of taxation.[6] This new access to funds in turn enabled the massive growth of the British state. The interconnected relationship between public debt and warfare underlay what John Brewer famously referred to as the "fiscal-military state."[7] But the growth of a stable system of public credit also fostered the development of private capital markets.[8]

Financial stability both reinforced and was bolstered by other important social changes. England had escaped from the threat of famine by the end of the seventeenth century; although periods of dearth continued (and other parts of the British Isles continued to experience famines), the English no longer faced major subsistence crises. Poverty remained a terrible burden for much of the population, but the standard of living of the entire nation improved.[9] The middling orders as a percentage of the population expanded significantly, particularly during the second half of the century, and England became increasingly urbanized, with the middle classes a large and growing segment of the new towns. These groups were crucial in the development of demand for new consumer goods and services catering to comfort, display, and pleasure—luxuries rather than necessities.[10]

One major effect of Britain's growing wealth was its impact on domestic space. Mark Girouard has traced the segregation of servants from the family in elite households at the end of the seventeenth century; kitchens, too, were moved out of the main dwelling. During the eighteenth century, great houses were thus reconfigured as spaces of sociability.[11] But changes in residential spaces were not confined to such elite buildings. Instead, there was a much broader move in this period to define specific living spaces according to their functions. Carl Estabrook, for instance, has found that ordinary residents of eighteenth-century Bristol lived in houses with separate sleeping rooms, cooking rooms, and rooms for socializing.[12] New forms of sociability, like visiting, and new forms of consumption, like drinking tea, transformed the layout of residences; parlors and dining rooms were dedicated to entertaining, and even households that could not afford to set aside rooms for visiting used creative devices like concealing beds in other furniture to create the illusion of such spaces.[13] At almost all levels of society, domestic space became increasingly divided and specialized.

The eighteenth century also saw a boom in consumerism. Although Neil McKendrick's characterization of this phenomenon as a "consumer revolution" (which he argues both predated and helped spur the more famous Industrial Revolution of the nineteenth century) has been challenged, it is clear that the nation experienced a massive increase in both the number and kinds of consumer goods in circulation.[14] In the three decades since McKendrick published his groundbreaking work, the history of consumption has become one of the biggest areas of early modern scholarship. The gendered aspects of consumption have proved especially fruitful for historians, with work on which types of consumer goods men and women were most likely to buy, and how ideas about propriety, decorum, and value shaped those purchases.[15] Whatever their motives, it is clear that more people of all classes gained access to more and different kinds of consumer goods.[16] If the wealthy were enjoying goods specially crafted for them by Wedgwood or Chippendale, those lower down the social scale were accumulating items like clocks, mirrors, and cutlery.[17] If the elite were commissioning portraits by Reynolds and Gainsborough, poorer people could cover their walls with cheap prints. If "the Quality" followed the latest French fashions, ordinary Britons also took pleasure in wearing up-to-date clothing.[18] Novel consumer goods were sought after for "the modernity, politeness, respectability, and independence they conveyed."[19] Imported commodities like tea and sugar found their way into households all over Britain, and in the process shifted from luxuries to necessities for people across the social spectrum, accompanied by specialized dishes, serving ware, tables, and new ways of socializing.[20] The complaints of social critics about servants aping their masters' manners and wearing such fashionable clothes that it was impossible to distinguish the lady from her maid were overblown, but they reflect the fact that access to consumer goods of all kinds was spreading. Some people saw these changes as symptoms of a society on the verge of collapse, as the old guarantors of hierarchy and stability vanished. For others, including thinkers like Adam Smith and David Hume, luxury was something to be celebrated because of its ability to promote commerce and thus employment and wealth.[21] Whatever their reaction, contemporaries were acutely aware that consumption was transforming their society.

The development of the fiscal-military state and the spread of consumerism were inseparable from the expansion of the British Empire and international trade in general. Over the course of the eighteenth century, Great Britain became the world's major imperial power, with territories that spanned the globe. But lands did not need to be conquered to have an impact; exploration, warfare, and trade all brought Britons into contact with people and species previously unfamiliar to them. Imports of exotic goods from Asia and the Americas created new fashions—the popularity of chinoiserie, for instance, meant that some porcelain manufacturers in China began to cater to European notions of what "Oriental" goods ought to look like, while domestic pottery imitated the "Oriental" style.[22] Not only were exotic goods imported for consumption in Britain, but British goods also made their way to foreign consumers, further fueling the home economy.[23]

All of these developments helped shape the material conditions of pet keeping in the eighteenth century. By the early years of the century, most people in England had stopped sharing their living quarters with live-stock. Creating spaces exclusively for humans meant that it became possible to designate certain animals as special by allowing them into the home rather than confining them to barns or kennels.[24] Obviously, some animals had received such special treatment long before 1700, but it was only now that such behavior became possible on a broad scale. With the assumption that humans did not routinely share space with animals came the habit of dividing even a single species, like dogs, into separate categories based on their relationship to domestic space. We can see this differentiation at work in the letters of Hester Thrale Piozzi, for instance, when she distinguishes between indoor and outdoor dogs: it is the former who are her pets, as when she tells a friend that "the *indoor* Dogs send Duty."[25] A children's story about "Cæsar and Pompey," two dogs brought up together, reflects a similar distinction. Cæsar, the good dog, wins the affection of their master, Mr. Saunders, while Pompey is mean and greedy; in return, Mr. Saunders tells Cæsar, "you shall be in future my own dog, and range about the house as you think proper." Pompey, still Mr. Saunders's property but not his "own dog," is banished to a kennel in the yard, where he is chained up.[26] Access to the home had become a privilege and, ironically, a symbol of liberty. The modern pet is as much a spatial phenomenon as an emotional one.

Britain's growing wealth also meant that more people were able to afford to purchase and care for pets, animals that consumed resources without contributing to the household economy as workers or meat. This basic financial threshold was crucial to the emergence of pet keeping on a large scale. But the spread of consumerism, I want to suggest, also made it easier for people to think about animals in terms of other kinds of consumption for pleasure. The great paradox of pet keeping, which constructs animals as simultaneously (luxury) consumer goods and family members, was intimately bound up with the spread of consumer society and all its implications. Consumerism interacted with the spread of knowledge about and interest in the natural world in a variety of ways.[27] The popularity of natural history in the period fostered a boom in sales of books on the topic, often blatantly plagiarized (Buffon and Goldsmith being the two most popular sources). These publications ranged from expensive, lavishly illustrated folios with an elite list of subscribers to cheap duodecimos for children, illustrated—if they were illustrated at all—with crude woodcuts. And the interest in natural history spread in other, surprising directions. George Edwards, who produced multiple volumes of beautiful but costly illustrations of birds and other animals, complained that "several of our manufacturers that imitate China ware, several print-sellers, and printers of linen and cotton cloths," along with periodicals, had copied his illustrations for their own use. He was frustrated not just by the theft but by the poor quality of the reproductions, which were "miserably lamed and distorted."[28] Distorted though they might have been, they helped bring awareness of exotic animals to people who would not otherwise have had access to his work. Natural history spawned trends in home décor as well, such as collecting and decorating with plants, animals, and other natural objects.[29] Horace Walpole noted the popularity of taxidermied exotic birds in 1770. "There has lately been an auction of stuffed birds," he wrote to a friend, "and as natural history is in fashion, there are physicians and others who paid 40 and 50 guineas for a single Chinese pheasant. You may buy a live one for five."[30] In this context, pets could display taste, education, and civilization in a domestic interior, just as inanimate objects did. A rare parrot might indicate both wealth and a scholarly interest in exotic fauna. A Pomeranian dog, newly available and fashionable in the eighteenth century, could signal that its owner was up to date with the latest trends. Pets were objects of affection, of course, but they said as much about their owners as any tea set or portrait.

International trade and warfare made exotic pets much more available, thanks to soldiers, sailors, and other travelers who brought back animals from far-off places in South America, Africa, and the Indies. The Seven Years' War (1756–63) was a particularly significant moment in the development of international trade in animals, thanks to the acquisition of new territories and the expansion of the East India Company—developments that were reflected in an enormous growth of offerings of exotic animals for sale.[31] Indeed, the first true pet shops—those devoted to the sale of companion animals—emerged in London during the war.[32] The sheer variety of imported animals was astonishing. Animal sellers offered creatures from all over the world; the Parrot's advertisement that begins this chapter offers "India Sheep and Goats," "Muscovy Ducks," a "Virginia Squirrel," and "a Monkey from Guinea." Canaries, no longer limited to their namesake islands, often came from the Tyrol, where they were bred in bulk. Edwards remarked on the "great numbers" of painted buntings (which he called the "painted finch") imported from North America.[33] "Virginia nightingales"—cardinals—were among the most popular birds for sale, judging from the frequency with which they appear in advertisements; undoubtedly the combination of their scarlet feathers and their song, as well as their foreign pedigree, made them particularly desirable. But it is not simply the growing number of imported animals that reveals the significance of pets in international exchange. Edwards's *Gleanings of Natural History* (1758–64) can serve as an example of how pets functioned as part of a network of knowledge about the world that relied equally on warfare, trade, patronage, and friendship. In describing the "St. Jago Monkey" or "Green Monkey," for instance, he explained that he had kept one as a pet and had also seen one "in the house of the late Duke of Richmond, at Whitehall." He added that "this sort of Monkey being pretty commonly brought into most of the maritime trading parts of Europe, it has probably been described by some former Naturalist," although he had not found such a description.[34] On another occasion, he mentioned that he owned a "Bush-tailed Monkey," a gift of "my worthy friend Capt. John Dobson, of Rotherhithe, who being Captain of a private ship of war, took it in an enemy's ship returning from the West-Indies, A.D. 1759." In a telling example of the opportunities as well as the confusion created by international travel, Edwards reported that the same monkey was "said to be a native of Surinam" despite its acquisition from a ship out of the West Indies.[35] Scholarly research, trade, and pet keeping formed a complex network of information; the pleasures of pet keeping might include the gratification of intellectual pursuits and the satisfaction of confirming Britain's power on the world stage.

All of these factors—Britain's growing wealth, the spread of consumerism, the popularity of natural history, and increasing contact with foreign lands—combined to create circumstances in the eighteenth century that were uniquely favorable to the diffusion of pet keeping. Hilda Kean has pointed out that far from vanishing from sight through the process of urbanization, animals were visible everywhere in eighteenth-century Britain.[36] Ongoing contact with animals as workers and livestock was enormously influential in thinking about animals, as she argues, but so too was the increasing visibility of animals associated with leisure, companionship, and entertainment. Later chapters will discuss how the growing visibility of pets fueled contemporary debates and anxieties about the tremendous social changes that were also taking place. First, however, let us turn to the question of how people actually acquired and cared for their animals. It is difficult to reach any firm conclusions regarding the monetary costs of eighteenth-century pet keeping; the scattered nature of the evidence makes it risky to engage in generalizations about these matters. It is possible, however, to identify some trends and patterns over the course of the century. What is clear from the surviving sources is the astonishing proliferation of animals as consumer goods, and the rise of a network of shops and manufacturers catering to the desires of pet owners.[37]

~ ~ ~

Where did pets come from? Many dogs and cats were given as gifts, and a steady supply was inevitable in a society where pets were not neutered and animals frequently roamed freely about the neighborhood.[38] It was common to request puppies and sometimes kittens when litters were expected, and "arranged matches" among favored pets also appear frequently in the sources. Horace Walpole's correspondence is filled with references to pets being offered or requested in what can seem like a vast network of circulating animals, sometimes exchanged as signs of friendship, sometimes for more mercenary reasons. Like other gifts, they were frequently used to grease the wheels of patronage. In the late 1760s, for instance, his friend Horace Mann sought Walpole's help in obtaining a pair of extremely small King Charles spaniels for an Italian courtier whose favor he was currying; Mann had heard that Walpole had such dogs, but he was mistaken, and it took Walpole, who did not own any himself, more than a year before he was finally able to send a pair.[39] When personal networks failed, it was possible to turn to advertising. Extremely small dogs were apparently both much in demand and difficult to obtain, and when individuals placed newspaper advertisements about purchasing dogs, they were often looking for such tiny dogs. One person in 1756 sought "a very small handsome Italian Grayhound Puppy, not less than six Months old."[40] Another individual wanted "*a Very Very Small*, SHORT *Nosed, Little* DOG, *of the* LAP SPANIEL *Kind*." The advertiser grumbled that she was not interested in the kinds of dogs she had already been offered, "Such a Strange Pack of Trumpery of Large, Long Nosed Mungrel Cur-Dogs, (Fitter for a Gun, or a Stable-Yard, than a Lap)."[41]

But it was not necessary to advertise or rely on friends to acquire an animal. The most common pets in the eighteenth century were caged birds, and the most common varieties of birds were native species captured in the wild. Many of the birds for sale during the eighteenth century were procured by professional bird catchers, whose methods were detailed in natural histories. Bird catchers used huge nets to capture songbirds during autumn migrations, decoying the birds with captive "callbirds." According to Thomas Pennant, it was usually "weavers and other tradesmen" from the London suburbs, especially Shoreditch, who engaged in this seasonal work. He claimed that their methods were "totally unknown in other parts of *Great-Britain*" because there was "no considerable sale for singing birds except in the *metropolis*," and the heavy equipment made it impossible for bird catchers to travel more than a few miles.[42] A bird catcher on the hunt would use "five or six *linnets* . . . two *goldfinches*, two *greenfinches*, one *woodlark*, one *redpoll*, and perhaps a *bull-finch*; a *yellowhammer*, *titlark*, and *aberdavine*" as call birds. These birds would have been subject to methods designed to induce premature molting in order to make them better and louder singers. The call birds would be placed near the nets in small cages, and their songs would lure the wild birds down toward the ground, where they could be caught in the nets.[43] Call birds were apparently highly valued by their owners; Pennant claimed that a "*call-bird linnet*" once sold for £5 10s. Not all birds were captured using this method; according to Pennant, nightingale catchers used small nets without call birds, which lowered their status with their peers. They were "considered as inferior in dignity to our bird-catchers, who will not rank with them."[44]

Professionals were also involved in the transformation of canary birds from exotic imports into common pets, thanks to the rise of large-scale breeding. In his multivolume *History of the Earth*, the most popular natural history of the period, Oliver Goldsmith noted that the name implies the bird's origin in the Canary Islands, but added, "we have it only from

Germany, where they are bred up in great numbers, and sold into different parts of Europe."[45] His discussion of canaries also reflected the popularity of breeding them at home, and he included lengthy instructions on
the best breeding practices, including how to house breeding pairs and
what sort of food they should be given.[46] Eleazar Albin went so far as to
claim that German canaries were even better than the originals, "excelling
in Handsomeness and Song those brought out of the *Canaries*."[47] A note
in the translation of Buffon's *Natural History of Birds* elaborates on the
trade in Tyrolean canaries: "The traffic in these birds makes a small article of commerce, as four Tyroleze generally bring over to England 1600
every year; and though they carry them on their backs one thousand miles,
as well as pay twenty pounds duty for such a number, yet upon the whole
it answers to sell these birds at five shillings a-piece. The chief place for
breeding Canary birds is Inspruck and its environs, from whence they are
sent to Constantinople, as well as every part of Europe."[48] The pet business was international, and commercial European trade included not only
high-end luxuries like Brussels lace and Meissen china but also songbirds.

Animals were sold by itinerant vendors, by travelers returning home
from overseas voyages, and by shops that offered living products alongside
inanimate objects. Birds were the most common pets sold by itinerant
vendors, but images of traveling puppy and monkey salesmen also survive,
and George Morland even painted a guinea pig peddler stopping at a
country cottage, to the delight of two young children (fig. 1).[49] Individuals sometimes offered single animals for sale, particularly parrots and
monkeys that had been brought back from overseas; perhaps the owners
thought better of the idea once they returned to the staid reality of life in
England. One can imagine, for instance, that the "Very fine active young
Monkey, lately brought from the East Indies," seemed like a bad idea
once its owner returned to Whitefriars.[50] The occasional parrot offered
for sale in Wapping might similarly have been a quick offer from a pass-
ing seaman.[51] Some shops that specialized in imported goods or "toys"
sold animals as part of the inventory; this was the case with a shop offering fossils, miniatures, "Carvings in Ivory, Coins, and Medals, Gold Fish,
stained Glass ancient and modern, Shells for Grottos or Flowers, a small
young Monkey, Variety of stuffed Birds."[52] In 1769, Lady Mary Coke
went aboard "an Indian Man"—a ship containing goods from the East
India Company—where she inspected a range of imported luxuries
including exotic birds; she was thwarted in her desire to buy a mynah

Fig. 1   George Morland, *Selling Guinea Pigs*,
ca. 1789. Oil on canvas, 30 × 25 in. Yale Center
for British Art, Paul Mellon Collection.

bird, which was already spoken for, but the captain gave her two smaller
"China Birds" as a present.[53]

Such ad hoc arrangements survived throughout the eighteenth century.
Increasingly, however, pets could be purchased from shops focusing on
the animal trade (fig. 2). The eighteenth century saw shops of all kinds
proliferate throughout England; in the south, the ratio of shops to people

in 1759 was 1:34.[54] Shops promoted their goods through advertisements like the ones discussed here, but also through the use of window displays and the presentation of shopping as a sociable experience.[55] London was the shopping as well as the political capital of England, leading the way in both the number of shops and the variety of goods they offered. Shops dedicated to the sale of animals were rare in the first half of the eighteenth century, but their numbers increased significantly from the middle decades on. Both native singing birds and exotics were extremely popular, and already by the early eighteenth century there was a bird market held in Covent Garden on Sunday mornings. It is not surprising, then, that one of the first kinds of establishment specializing in animal sales was the bird shop.[56] By the last quarter of the century, certain parts of London were so well known for their bird shops that a children's book could refer casually to "the Bird-Shops in Holbourn, Piccadilly, &c." selling parrots, macaws, and parakeets.[57] Symbiotic relationships among shops were also common, as in the case of the exotic birds for sale "at Mr. Tate's, at Exeter Exchange in the Strand, next Door to the Birdcage Makers."[58] In 1775, "very fine Red Birds" were offered "at Wyatt's, Turner and Cage-Maker."[59] William Pilton, "wire-worker and cage-maker" in Piccadilly, sold "Widow birds in full tail, cardinals, bluee-breasted [sic] finches, waxbills, African finches, with many other sorts."[60] Thomas Cato, another "wire-worker and bird-cage-maker," offered Essex-bred canaries along with "Breeding cages, and every convenience for breeding and keeping them."[61] The prevalence of birdcage makers and bird shops reflects their early establishment in London; at least one was operating by 1700, and Christopher Plumb has found that a few families founded successful bird-selling dynasties in the eighteenth century.[62] But bird shops could also branch out over the course of the century as demand for animals of all kinds increased; we can see the diversification at work in the animals to be

Fig. 2   Henri Merke, after Thomas
Rowlandson, Cries of London. No. 1: Buy a Trap,
a Rat Trap, Buy My Trap, ca. 1799. Etching with
aquatinted border, hand-colored, 31 × 22 cm.
Courtesy of the Lewis Walpole Library, Yale
University, 799.01.01.03. Although the rat-trap
seller is the subject of the print, the shop
appears to be selling pets.

CRIES of LONDON. N°1

Buy a Trap, a Rat Trap, buy my Trap.

sold in 1775 "at the Birdshop, in Princes-Street," which listed a wide variety of dogs, both hunting and lapdogs, for sale, before naming a few kinds of fowl as an apparent afterthought.[63] "The Poulterer's Shop in May-Fair Market" offered canaries, bullfinches, turkeys, exotic chickens, a parrot, King Charles spaniels, and a mastiff.[64]

Nor were bird shops the only ones that began offering more and more animals as both supply and demand increased in the middle years of the century. The evolution of one establishment illuminates the growing popularity of animal sales as well as the rise of specialized shops. John Tyther's shop in New Broad Street, Moorfields, began as an outlet for canes and musical instruments. His first advertisement for an animal appeared in 1753, when he offered a grey parrot, "as kind and tame a Bird as any in England." Prospective buyers were told to visit "the Cane-shop."[65] A month later, he was selling three young green parrots, "very cheap, as the Owner is going into the Country in a few Days."[66] For the next five years, he continued to sell an increasing number and variety of exotic animals, although he never completely abandoned the original business. The miscellaneous nature of his enterprise was visible in an announcement in October 1753, which presented four grey parrots and a green parrot along with "several good second-hand Spinnets, a small pretty tone Harpsichord, also a fine Starling."[67] In early 1754 he was still in this mixed business, using an advertisement to promote another grey parrot, "Two pretty-ton'd Harpsichords," "Great Choice of exceeding fine Canes, and . . . walking Sticks"—and offering to buy "rough Amber."[68] An ad in June of that year made no mention of canes or musical instruments, simply offering a grey parrot and "a large Garden Tortoise, very cheap."[69] In August 1755, Tyther ran a longer advertisement for a macaw, a variety of parrots, a mongoose, and, as an afterthought, "Great Choice of very fine long Walking Canes."[70] Two months later, he offered monkeys, a French horn, used spinets, and canes.[71] Advertisements that followed later in the year continued to emphasize exotic animals, particularly parrots, along with notices that walking canes were still available.[72] In April 1756, another ad ran for exotic birds—Tyther was apparently expanding his inventory, and was including a peacock and hen, "Virginia Nightingales" (cardinals), and a linnet, along with the usual parrots. Canes and musical instruments were not mentioned.[73] An even wider variety of birds was available from the shop in the summer, though the canes came up again, with the special mention of one that was "the finest long Cane in England."[74] More musical instruments were mentioned in July of that year; he was back to recommending harpsichords and spinets along with the birds.[75]

Although Tyther never stopped selling musical instruments (or, in all likelihood, canes) and continued to refer to his business as a cane and music shop, the animals grew throughout the 1750s from a side business to the main subjects of his advertising campaigns. Given his frequent reference to lack of space as a reason for selling musical instruments cheaply, it is even possible that the living stock was crowding out the inanimate objects. His advertisements diminished dramatically around 1760, and he seems to have shifted the focus of his business to a public house in the same location, but in 1766 he offered a grey and a green parrot along with one more bird: "A CANARY BIRD that pipes Foote's minuet in taste, bred and taught last summer by John Tyther, at the Crown, . . . who thinks it is the best bird that he ever brought up."[76] Tyther died early in 1773, and the Crown was auctioned off by his executrix.[77] Tyther remained focused throughout on birds and the occasional monkey or other small mammal; he catered to people seeking pets, not those stocking menageries on country estates. His long-running advertising campaign reveals that it was possible to make the transition into animal sales in a way that seems to have been profitable, even if it never fully replaced his original business.

Part of Tyther's success was undoubtedly due to his willingness to appeal to potential customers on different fronts, and he employed a number of enticements. He would announce when animals had been sold, ostensibly to spare buyers the effort of coming to purchase them but perhaps also to increase the sense of demand and scarcity.[78] He was quick to emphasize how docile and tractable his animals were, along with any training they had received. He even offered money-back guarantees: in October 1756 he was selling five parrots with the promise that "to prevent Trouble, the Price is marked on each Cage; the Parrots will be warranted, and changed if not liked."[79] Who could resist such an offer? While most birds received a generic identification (green or grey parrots), Tyther gave lengthier descriptions of unusual animals to get his readers' attention; in 1758, for instance, he presented "a long Tail Parroquet, its under Beak is black, and from it a fine black Streak on each Side [of] his Throat, the upper Beak is Red, and various beautiful Colours on the Top of his Neck, very fine in Feather, and talks when spoke to."[80] On another occasion he offered "a Beautiful and tame Mackaw from the Brasils, of the blue and yellow Sort"; it talked "as plain as any, and as much as most Parrots in England," but Tyther stressed that "'tis thought to be the finest feathered Bird in the Kingdom."[81] The animal was still for sale, it seems, in February 1758, when Tyther again advertised it, asking twelve guineas. In keeping with his usual sales pitch, he reminded buyers that all his parrots' "Goodness will be warranted."[82] He may have been responding to growing public distrust of fraudulent bird merchants.[83] Tyther thus embodied many of the characteristics of the new eighteenth-century consumer culture. He seems to have responded to customer demand, identifying the animals most likely to sell, and he also sought to feed that demand through advertising designed to stimulate desire while providing reassurance about quality control. Where others were marketing china or watches, however, Tyther was catering to London's demand for pets. That he clearly saw this business as compatible with the luxury trade in which he was already engaged reflects the fact that animals were important luxury products by the middle of the century. Canes, musical instruments, and pets all satisfied the desire of consumers for goods both ornamental and entertaining.

By the last third of the century, commercial menageries had arrived on the scene, combining elements of the pet shop with those of the modern zoo.[84] Unlike Tyther's establishment, their businesses were dedicated entirely to animals, and they charged admission to spectators. But unlike modern zoos, the menageries' stock included both unusual specimens and more mundane ones like dogs, and they encouraged clients to buy the animals on display if they had the desire and funds to do so. When Joshua Brookes first began advertising his menagerie, for instance, he presented a large collection of exotic birds.[85] But his ambitions were perhaps evident in his announcement that "the Nobility and Gentry may be supplied with any Quantity of Foreign or English Pheasants, or any other kind of Poultry; and proper Conveniencies for carrying them to any Part of the World."[86] By the 1780s, Brookes was filling individual orders, as when he provided reindeer from Lapland for the duke of Norfolk.[87] Wealthy visitors could thus combine the pleasures of consumerism with those of Enlightenment-influenced natural history.[88] In the same spirit, Lady Mary Coke went to an "exhibition of birds and beasts" in 1767 where her sister bought a pair of birds for three guineas. (Lady Mary considered buying an unspecified "small beast" but thought her dog would be unhappy with the new arrival.)[89] These menageries also served as important sources for naturalists in an era when living specimens of exotic animals were difficult to obtain; George Edwards, for instance, noted that he had seen a monkey similar to the one he called the "Middle-sized Black Monkey" exhibited "at a house where they shew wild beasts."[90] Brookes even allegedly made his own contribution to natural history; Thomas Pennant claimed that Brookes had successfully bred a wolf with a Pomeranian and that he himself had seen one of the puppies.[91]

If the menageries explicitly appealed to elite buyers and those with educated tastes, however, they were not exclusive in either the kinds of animals they offered or the clientele they sought. Bennett's warehouse at the Red Lion and Three Pigeons, located near Leicester Fields, was such an establishment, offering an array of exotic birds from Asia and America along with "Harlequins, Greyhounds, Newfoundland Dogs, small Dogs for the Lap, Spaniels for the Field, large Grey[h]ounds, large Mastiffs, Cenaries, Dogs, from Hungary." A note at the end of the advertisement added, "To prevent Trouble, those who do not buy to pay Six-pence each Person."[92] Spectators a year later were offered the chance by the same establishment to see, along with "curious foreign Sheep" and exotic birds, "the white Negro Girl, the only one in the World." The price for this experience was one shilling per person, "Quality what they please."[93] Such prices would have made the menageries an attainable outing, if not a regular one, even for laborers at a time when a shilling or two could purchase an ounce of tea, a pound of sugar, or a handkerchief.[94] Indeed, Bennett's distinction between the "Quality" and everyone else implies that he assumed that his business would attract more than just the very rich.

Menagerie owners were usually aggressive in seeking out animals for purchase and resale, and they operated on a much larger scale than vendors like Tyther. Thus "William James's Managery" in Holborn sold birds, dogs, squirrels, dormice, and monkeys, and simultaneously offered "the most Money given for all sorts of curious Birds, and all other Curiosities."[95] The owner of a similar business at the Parrot announced, "Any Person having a Bird called a Cockatoo, or any Foreign Birds to dispose of, may have a great Price, by applying as above."[96] Christopher Plumb has noted, "In the 1760s, a distinct geography of animal exhibitions and commerce emerged in London as animal merchants and menageries began to line the Strand, Piccadilly, and St James's."[97] But this area catered to the royal and aristocratic clients who would be most likely to buy expensive, exotic animals,[98] and it was not the only center for animal merchants. Lower-end businesses in other areas focused on pets accessible to those in the middling orders. Samuel Jackson Pratt, writing at the start of the nineteenth century, claimed that Middle Row, Holborn, had "long been . . . remarkable for . . . the bird and dog repositories of this all-accumulating metropolis." He described a shop that sounds like a grotesque parody of Noah's ark: "a wolf dog and a tame lamb, a dirty swan and a guinea pig, a parrot and a pigeon next neighbours to a goose, and a goldfinch, a linnet, and a canary bird beside a goat and a couple of rabbits. And to close the whole, not more congenially matched than the rest, a squirrel and a pair of doves."[99] These animals were hardly the making of an elite menagerie. Other shops specialized in specific kinds of animals. Although many canaries were bred in the Tyrol and imported into England, we see them offered for sale in Ludgate Hill by "Thomas Payne, Breeder, from Colchester in Essex."[100] Another canary specialist was Thomas Smith, near Exeter Change in the Strand; he offered "fine English-bred Canary Birds" from Ipswich.[101] "WARD's Turtle Warehouse" in Mark Lane near Tower Hill offered, not surprisingly, turtles ("just arrived from the Bahama Islands"), but perhaps less expected were the pineapple plants and parrots he was also selling. If the turtles were most probably intended for eating, the same cannot be said for the parrots.[102] In 1775, a seller at St. Chad's Wells was offering "Gold and Silver Fish" along with "Curious Machines, to carry them to any part of the Globe by Sea or Land."[103]

London thus accommodated an enormous variety of animal vendors catering to an equally varied clientele. Poorer people undoubtedly continued to rely on free animals from unwanted litters or birds and beasts sold by street peddlers. The middling sorts could gawk at exotic specimens in menageries while shopping at smaller, more specialized establishments or venues that combined animals with other products. And the wealthy could take advantage of the vast range of animals from all over the world now at their disposal. By the middle decades of the eighteenth century, animals had become familiar consumer goods for people at all social levels, one more option among the dizzying array of temptations to open one's purse.

If it is possible to ascertain how eighteenth-century pet owners acquired their animals, it is more difficult to establish just what they paid. Most direct information about the cost of pets comes from advertisements offering animals—particularly birds—for sale and from naturalists' references to prices. Prices almost always referred to exotic animals, however, and there is little evidence about the cost of more common and cheaper pets like dogs or even squirrels, although these animals were offered for sale alongside the rarer and more expensive beasts. Eleazar Albin mentioned in 1731 that macaws, the largest of the "Parrot Kind," usually cost ten guineas, and that "the Small Green Paroqueet from East India" could be purchased for two guineas a pair "at Mr. *Bland's*, at the *Tiger* on *Tower Hill*."[104] Beginning in the 1750s, many more exotic birds came on the market, but their prices seem to have remained fairly stable. An advertisement for a pair of "beautiful young Grey PARROTS" announced that, "to prevent Trouble, the Price of one is two Guineas and a half, and the other three Guineas and a half." The same shop offered "a very young Green Parrott from the Main" for four guineas.[105] Nonpareils (painted buntings from the American South) were offered for a guinea each by an animal seller in 1765.[106] Some of the most detailed prices were listed by the Noah's Ark in the same year: "SEVERAL young grey Parrots, at £1 11s. 6d. each; green ditto, £1 1s. [a guinea] each; Parroquets £1 11s. 6d. each; red Birds £1 1s. each; Nonpareils £1 1s. each; a pair of Aberdewats £2 12s. and 6d. Doves, white Mice, 5s. each."[107] In May 1758, a dealer at the St. Andrew's Cross in Charing Cross offered a "Parrot of the Mackaw Kind"; this bird, the reader was assured, was a bargain "at only four Guineas, though a very uncommon and scarce Bird."[108] In November of that year, Tyther offered a grey parrot, "which talks as well as any Bird in England," for the spectacular price of ten guineas.[109]

Extremely rare animals also got special notice, as when an animal seller presented "one of those very scarce and valuable Birds from the East-Indies called a Lewrey [i.e., lory]. Its Colours are most wonderfully fine, it talks very plain, is exceeding tame, and is one of the finest feathered Birds in the Kingdom." Such an impressive specimen was worth, in the eyes of the vendor at least, the equally impressive price of twenty-five guineas.[110] Years earlier, Eleazar Albin saw a bird of the same species (which he said was "the most beautiful of all the Parrot Kind that I have yet seen") for sale for twenty guineas, so it may not have been as far-fetched a demand as it seems.[111] These prices, even at the lower end of a pound or two guineas, placed such animals out of reach of many Londoners at a time when the laboring poor rented London lodgings for one to seven shillings per week; a female mantua maker around 1750 earned between 6s. and 10s. 6d. a week.[112] Yet, as Christopher Plumb has pointed out, exotic animals were kept not only by the aristocracy and gentry but also by the middling sort: "Clerks, merchants, inn-keepers, coffee house proprietors, physicians and apothecaries were also owners of exotic animals."[113] Some, like the owners of inns and coffeehouses, may well have seen the animals as investments that would make their premises more alluring to visitors, but it is hard to see why an apothecary would find it lucrative to own a mongoose or a toucan. Some animals were probably obtained as gifts or even perhaps in trade for other goods or services.

Canaries, not as desirable as parrots by the mid-eighteenth century, could be had for considerably less money; one seller advertised females—less valuable than males because they did not sing—for 2s. 6d. apiece.[114] In other cases, audiences unfamiliar with a bird might need some prompting, as when a seller offered half a dozen "young Carolina Birds just come over" at six shillings each and assured potential buyers that "they are a Bird that gives great Attention to the Pipe or Whistle, and have naturally a very Musical Note."[115] Bullfinches could be considerably more expensive; John Tyther asked two to five guineas in 1758 for "Piping Bullfinches, several of which Pipes at Command," although their training probably inflated the price.[116] Even within species, there might be significant distinctions; Thomas Pennant asserted that a variety of goldfinch known as a "*cheverel*" was particularly rare and thus "sells at a very high price."[117] He also provided more detailed information about prices: a chaffinch that was unusually gifted at singing once sold for five guineas to someone who planned to use it to train other birds; nightingales, he said, were usually a shilling each. According to the bird seller he used as a source, a nightingale that had been well trained during a lengthy period of ownership might sell for a maximum of a guinea.[118]

Although prices for nonavian animals are more difficult to identify, the apparent ubiquity of parrots for sale does not seem to have diminished their value in relation to other animals. Familiarity with other birds, such as earlier experience with keeping caged birds, might even have helped; even if one had never owned a parrot before, it was still a bird. And the potential entertainment benefits provided by its vocal skills probably added another incentive to buy. Other exotic animals, though rarer than parrots, might fetch lower prices; a 1755 advertisement asked two guineas (42s.) for a "Young green Parrot that talks well," while offering "a small Macock or Mongose, from Madrass" for a half guinea less (31s. 6d.).[119] The shop appeared to have difficulty unloading the mongoose, since several advertisements with more detailed descriptions followed, and the animal was still for sale in mid-September.[120] Another mongoose was on offer for a similar price (36s.) from the same shop a year later.[121] Such animals might have the lure of exclusivity, but their unfamiliarity may have made them less desirable.

In a competitive market, with ever-growing numbers of birds available, parrot vendors relied on marketing to attract customers. Most common were the claims that a bird was newly arrived in England (and thus presumably likely to be healthier and younger), and that unusual circumstances meant that buyers could get a special deal. For instance, several young green parrots "just arrived from the Spanish Main" in December 1755 were offered for prices ranging from one and a half to three guineas, which the seller promised were great bargains thanks to their not being "in a Dealer's Hands."[122] Another seller presented a parrot "just come from the Spanish Main" for a mere "Three Guineas, tho' far short of its Worth," because its intended owner had died.[123] In March 1759, another individual offered a "long Tail Parroquet"—"very young, talks plain, and is one of that Sort which are much beyond Parrots for talking"—for "only three Guineas," on the grounds that the current owner had "no Time to tutor it."[124]

The seller at the St. Andrew's Cross, Charing Cross, was particularly fond of this sort of approach. In November 1756 he presented a "Very young and tame grey Parrot . . . just brought over" for what the reader was assured was a bargain at two and a half guineas (though "well worth three Times the Money"), a discount made possible only because the current owner was about to leave England.[125] In July 1757, he offered a parrot "just come from the Spanish Main, which is where the best talking and singing Parrots come from," for a mere three guineas; "the Money is wanted, or no price would purchase him." But a few months later, what seems to be an identical parrot again appeared for sale, allegedly "just come from the Spanish Main, where the best Birds come from"; in this case, he explained the asking price of two and a half guineas on the grounds that "it was designed for a Present" but the owner now needed money. The claim about the "Spanish Main" origins and the money being wanted had clearly become part of his routine sales pitch. Again in the spring of 1758, the dealer offered exactly the same kind of bird in exactly the same terms: the parrot "was designed as a Present, but the Owner wanting Money, it may be had at Four Guineas, and no less, it being well worth Ten."[126] A month later, the tactic varied slightly, with "an East-India Parroquet" available for six guineas, "the Lady being dead who own'd them."[127] It is possible that the St. Andrew's Cross dealer specialized in selling freshly imported young parrots on behalf of people who happened to need money quickly. It is more likely, however, that he relied particularly heavily on sales tactics also used by others. There is no way of knowing how successful the approach was, although the fact that he continued to employ it for more than a year suggests that he believed it was working.

Advertisers never failed to mention whether a bird already knew words or tunes or was young enough to be taught them. Training clearly increased the value of birds; not only did ads mention parrots' ability to speak, but we also see, for instance, the Moorfields cane-shop owner John Tyther offering a "Bull-Finch that pipes, Britons rouze up your great Magnanimity, at Command," along with two starlings that could also speak.[128] Another bullfinch from the same shop was allegedly "taught last Year one of Corelli's Minuets; it also talks extremely plain."[129] Docility was also important, particularly for species known to be temperamental; thus a seller offered a young parrot for a mere two and a half guineas, with the additional promise that it was "so gentle that a Child may handle it."[130] Another shop offered a "Beautiful, large, young green Parrot, that talks very well, and has many of the Cries about the Streets: also, a very young grey Parrot, both quite stout and healthy Birds"; as a last enticement, the seller promised that "the green Bird has no indecent Words."[131]

Given the absence of direct evidence about the cost of more mundane animals, we must rely on indirect sources. A story for children, for instance, tells of a boy who stole a small greyhound pet from a pair of siblings, saying that she must be worth at least two guineas.[132] Newspaper advertisements for lost dogs show that animals were both loved enough to be sought out and worth paying to retrieve.[133] Advertising in a paper usually cost about three shillings; something between a half crown and a half guinea (2s. 6d.–10s. 6d.) seems to have been the going rate for the return of a lost or stolen dog. The costs involved thus prohibited the poor from placing such advertisements, but they were within the reach of the middling orders. Advertisements followed a simple format: a description of the dog, information about its owner, and the reward. A 1744 advertisement in the *St. James's Chronicle*, for instance, announced that a King Charles spaniel wearing "a Brass Collar lin'd with a Blue Velvet round his Neck, with this Inscription, *Elizabeth George, at the Right Honourable the Earl of Stanhope's*," had been lost "*from a Door in* Audley-street." A five-shilling reward was offered for the dog's safe return, "no Questions ask'd."[134] But a "Harlequin Dog" lost from Campden House, Kensington (wearing an engraved brass collar tied with a blue ribbon), was perceived by his owner to be worth a guinea's reward.[135] Not surprisingly, aristocrats' dogs seemed to evoke the larger rewards of a guinea or so.[136] Advertisements frequently included the notice that no greater reward would be offered in future, sometimes with claims that "the Dog can be of no Value to the Finder, being a Mungrel."[137] Others resorted to threats, as when one Mrs. Barnard of Leicester Fields advertised for her lost dog; she gave a detailed description of the "little brown Bitch" named Loide or Lowdy, then threatened prosecution of anyone who stole the dog or bought her from a dog dealer, and offered a reward (a guinea and a half) for anyone turning in the perpetrator.[138] Such evidence obviously does not relate directly to the cost of dogs, but it is unlikely that people would offer larger rewards for their dogs than they considered them to be worth. Unfortunately, it is impossible to distinguish between monetary and emotional value in these cases.

~   ~   ~

Unlike most possessions, pets functioned not only as goods but as consumers—of food, of course, but also of other goods and services. The costs in money and resources of food for pets were particularly upsetting to many commentators in an era when scarcity was still a frequent problem. Critics of impoverished pet owners suggested that the dogs of the poor shared the porringer of the children or simply poached game from nearby lands. In 1775, Charles Varlo argued that it cost £1 a year to maintain an ordinary dog, and that "gentlemen's hounds, greyhounds, pointers, and my lady's lap-dogs . . . cost a great deal more." Indeed, he estimated that a lady's lapdog consumed £4 11s. 3d. worth of food each year, in delicacies that included a pound of meat each day, along with bread and butter and tea.[139] Yet stories like Varlo's of lavish expenditure on dainties for favored pets were probably more the stuff of myth than fact, even among the elite; it is likely that most dogs, like their human owners, ate mostly bread, because they subsisted primarily on household scraps. The reliance on scraps for pet food was almost certainly common to both large country houses and those of the poor, although the abundance and quality of the food differed.[140] One elite pet owner, Lady Isabella Wentworth, even had to plead with her son (who held the purse strings) for permission to give her favorite dog a bit of meat for medicinal purposes.[141] Scraps for dogs and cats could be supplemented by offal sold by street peddlers in urban areas (fig. 3).[142]

But cats probably depended largely on their skills as mousers, and small animals like birds and squirrels could survive on relatively little. It is likely that the popularity of caged birds as pets was related not just to the song they provided but also to the fact that they were cheap to feed, house, and care for. In eighteenth-century Bristol, according to Carl Estabrook, "caged birds were on display in the houses of all sorts of people: a linen draper worth over £1,611 in 1729, a poor farrier worth only £12 8s 9d in 1731, surgeons, fishmongers, mariners, grocers, and artisans. One victualler owned seven live caged birds in 1762."[143] A shipwright's widow from Deptford around 1730 owned seven canaries, held in seven cages.[144] There is evidence, however, that more highly valued songbirds like canaries were fed special diets of specific kinds of seeds; certainly, such diets were recommended in natural histories and bird-care manuals, and bird sellers also offered birdseed. Specialized food might have distinguished the birds of the elite from those of the poor even more than species did, given the popularity of songbirds across the social spectrum.

If pet food had not yet become the household necessity that it is today, plenty of other goods and services intended specifically for pets were on offer. Just as the differentiation of domestic spaces was accompanied by the specialization of furniture and other consumer goods—like the dining room table or the tea set—so the differentiation of pets from other animals gave rise to occupations catering to their needs. For example, it is in this period that we see the first references to the "dog doctor." Smollett

Fig. 3   T. L. Busby, *Dogs Meat,* ca. 1800.
Etching, hand-colored, 14 × 9 cm. Courtesy of
the Lewis Walpole Library, Yale University,
800.00.00.67.

DOGS MEAT

refers to this profession in both *The Adventures of Sir Launcelot Greaves* (1762) and *Humphry Clinker* (1771), as does Frances Burney in *Cecilia* (1782).[145] Nor was the term a purely literary invention. Lady Mary Coke referred to someone seeking the advice of such an expert after a bite by a suspected mad dog, and she was upset to learn from her own "dog doctor" that nothing could be done to help her beloved pet Alphen in 1771.[146] For other kinds of pets, finding knowledgeable medical assi stance was proba- bly more difficult.[147] One children's story described a woman sending for help from a professional bird catcher when her parrot became ill, although it seems unlikely that his talent for snaring domestic songbirds would have been of much use.[148]

The specialist dog doctor probably first arose to meet the demand of owners of valuable working dogs—those used in hunting, for example. But it is clear that such doctors also catered to "useless" pets like Lady Mary's. A similar development can be traced in the spread of dog collars, for which the best evidence is the collection housed at Leeds Castle in Kent. The earliest medieval collars in the collection were designed for hunting dogs and were meant to protect the dogs from wolves, boars, and other wild animals. By the eighteenth century, however, the collection reflects the growing use of collars by urban dog owners seeking to ensure their pets' safe return, in the event that a dog ran away or was lost. Ordi- nances like those passed by the London authorities in 1760 during a panic over rabid dogs, which mandated the extermination of all street dogs, also encouraged owners to identify themselves.[149] A collar inscribed "Stop me not but let me jog for I am S. Oliver's Dog" is one such example (fig. 4).

Newspaper advertisements for lost dogs frequently noted that the ani- mal in question was wearing a collar engraved with the owner's name and address. Collars might also have provided a way to help catch dog thieves; one notice appealing for the return of a King Charles spaniel with a silver collar asked, "If the Collar is offered to be pawned or sold pray stop it."[150] Many collars were simple brass circles, with just the name and location of the owner.[151] Others were embellished; they were often lined with leather or fabric (presumably to make them more comfortable for the dog), and sometimes, as in the case of a lost lapdog from 1731, one might come "with Bells."[152] Silver collars were popular with those who could afford them; according to Katharine MacDonogh, the most basic silver collar cost about 10s.[153] It is unlikely that many collars reached the level of extravagance of the diamond-studded collar given to the fictional lapdog

Fig. 4 Brass dog collar inscribed "Stop me
not but let me jog for I am S. Oliver's Dog.
Bicknell," eighteenth century. Trustees of Leeds
Castle Foundation.

Pompey the Little in Francis Coventry's novel,[154] but some were quite
elaborate, as with an early eighteenth-century silver collar, lined with
leather and decorated with images of summer flowers (fig. 5). Another
collar in the Leeds Castle collection, inscribed "Miss Harriett Cross
Exeter 21st July 1783," which was the recipient's birthday, suggests that
Miss Cross may have received both animal and collar as gifts for the occasion. Collars, like human clothing, could be the sites of luxurious display,
sentimental attachment, or modest utility.

≈   ≈   ≈

Dog collars, although the most common accessories created for pets, were
hardly the only ones. Leashes were relatively rare (stories abound of dogs
running away while out with their owners), but related to collars were the
chains used to keep animals like monkeys and squirrels under control.
Judging from the visual evidence of the period, monkeys were generally

Fig. 5   Leather and silver dog collar, eighteenth
century. Trustees of Leeds Castle Foundation.

Fig. 6 / opposite   *Lady Fashion's Secretary's Office, or
Peticoat Recommendation the Best*, 1772. Mezzotint,
hand-colored, 35.1 × 25 cm. Courtesy of the
Lewis Walpole Library, Yale University,
772.00.00.15+.

kept on chains tied around their waists and attached to a ring on the
floor.[155] Chains had the advantage of allowing a fairly wide range of movement—and the sources agree that a major reason for the popularity of pet
monkeys came from their antic behavior—while addressing the fundamental problem that monkeys could not be fully domesticated. Satires on
fashionable pet keeping frequently referred to monkeys breaking free of
their chains or wreaking havoc when an unfortunate passerby came within
their grasp.[156] The speed of squirrels, rather than their danger, was probably the reason for keeping them on chains.[157] Parrots were also often portrayed chained to a freestanding wooden pole (fig. 6). Occasionally, we
get a glimpse of more outlandish accessories. In 1757, for instance,
William James offered for sale at his "Managery" not only a vast assortment of domestic and exotic animals but in particular "two Monkies both
tame, . . . with three different Suits of Cloaths, and a neat House."[158]

LADY FASHION's SECRETARY's OFFICE, or PETICOAT RECOMMENDATION the BEST.

Printed for Carington Bowles, Map & Print seller, N.º 69 in S.t Pauls Church Yard London. Published as the Act directs

Housing for pets was another important area of consumption. We often think of animal houses today primarily in terms of the outdoor dog-house, and the eighteenth century saw the construction of massive, elaborate dog kennels kept for the hunting dogs of the very wealthy. But indoor companion animals also had their own housing (fig. 7). Sarah Trimmer's cautionary tale against overindulgence in pets described a woman who kept, among many other animals, "a squirrel and a monkey, which had each a little house neatly ornamented."[159] The indoor dog bed also seems to have been familiar by the middle of the century; Lady Mary Coke complained that her boorish mother showed off her pug's bed to visitors in 1766.[160] Dog beds may even have been common among the lower classes. An image from the 1770s[161] of a cobbler's home/workshop, for example, shows a small dog reclining comfortably on a cushion—obviously intended specifically for that purpose—at the feet of its master (fig. 8).

Most birds required cages, which could be simple shapes made of wire or tin or elaborate confections of wood and gilded metal; they were usually accompanied by feeders and watering bottles, often made of glass. Birdcage makers were grouped with "turners" in one eighteenth-century guide to trades because so many cages included "some Turned-Work"; the very finest might be made of silver plate, and it is possible that even the Chippendale workshop produced birdcages.[162] Combinations of bird-cages and fishbowls, designed so that the bird appeared to be fluttering inside the water, seem to have been a fad in the late eighteenth century.[163] Cages in turn came with their own accessories. One vendor offered "Pul-lies, Lines, and Counterweights [probably for raising and lowering a cage from the ceiling], Brushes, and Scrapers, Glasses, and whatsoever belongs to these Birds, and Cages, to keep, and hang them up conveniently." He helpfully produced a pamphlet for his customers with detailed information about the care of both canaries and their cages.[164] Birdcage making could be a lucrative business; the trade guide noted that it was possible for a London journeyman in the field to earn twelve to eighteen shillings per week: "The Trade is not much over-stocked, and the Bird-Fanciers in and about *London* are so numerous a Tribe, that there is a pretty good Demand for their Goods."[165]

With the popularity of keeping songbirds came the development of the bird organ or "serinette" (from the French for canary, *serin*). The bird organ was a small barrel organ designed to help teach birds to sing; it was first developed in France in the seventeenth century but was most

Fig. 7 Charles Grignion, after John Collet,
January and May, 1771. Etching and engraving,
35.2 × 25.5 cm. Courtesy of the Lewis Walpole
Library, Yale University, 771.04.16.01+. Note
the squirrel house at bottom right.

C O B L E R 's H A L L .

Fig. 8   Cobler's Hall, ca. 1793. Mezzotint with
etching, 25.3 × 35.8 cm. Courtesy of the
Lewis Walpole Library, Yale University,
778.00.00.07.2+. Note the dog bed at left and
the birdcage hanging from the ceiling.

popular between about 1750 and 1850; Thomas Jefferson bought one in
Paris in 1785 for eighteen francs.[166] Bird organs were widely available in
Britain. Images from the eighteenth century frequently show them along
with caged birds; the best known of such images is probably Hogarth's
1742 group portrait *The Graham Children* (fig. 9), which includes a boy,
seemingly unaware of the cat that has clambered onto the back of his
chair, enthusiastically cranking away on a bird organ before an anxious
finch in a cage.[167]

Fig. 9 William Hogarth, *The Graham Children*,
1742. Oil on canvas, 160.5 × 181 cm. National
Gallery, London. © National Gallery, London /
Art Resource, New York.

Animal shops frequently offered bird organs along with the birds
themselves; one shop even advertised a "Parrot Organ . . . that taught a
Parrot to sing."[168] Smaller birds might be taught with a flute or a "bird
flageolet." Sheet music for teaching birds specific tunes was also available.[169] Other accessories for pet birds included tiny ivory buckets on

pulley systems, with which they could be trained to draw up water. Buffon provided a detailed description of such accessories for goldfinches: "they can be instructed without much trouble . . . to draw up small cups containing their food and drink; but for this last purpose they must be *clothed*. This clothing consists of a small belt of soft leather two lines broad, with four holes through which the feet and wings are passed, and the ends joining under the belly, are held by a ring which supports the chain of the cup."[170] Such products were clearly designed to increase the entertainment value of pet birds for their owners, although (as we will see in the next chapter) they were not without their critics. They were part of a process at work throughout the century, in which one kind of consumer good—in this case, birds—spawned many others intended to take advantage of its popularity. Consumer desires could be satisfied while new desires were created; consumption fostered further consumption.

~ ~ ~

Such specialized accessories as silver-plated birdcages or suits for monkeys were undoubtedly confined to wealthy pet owners. But we should not assume that pet keeping itself was similarly restricted. If parrots and monkeys were out of the reach of most people, songbirds and mongrel dogs would have been accessible to all but the destitute. Moreover, as we will see, all kinds of animal ownership began to be framed increasingly in terms of pet keeping, so that even the blind beggar's guide dog came to be seen as a loving friend and companion, not merely a necessary worker. Such changing attitudes may not have been shared by the beggars themselves, but they do reflect a society in which pet keeping was becoming an important lens through which people viewed human-animal relationships. The emergence of vendors catering to the demands of consumers who sought larger numbers and a wider variety of pets reflected the spread of pet keeping throughout the society; after all, once canaries became common and cheap, rarer birds needed to take their place for those who sought to distinguish themselves from the hoi polloi of animal owners. These changes did not come without controversy. Pet ownership was deeply mistrusted in the early eighteenth century, and it took decades before it ceased to be seen as morally suspect. At the same time, however, the pervasiveness of pets across all social strata meant that they could not be ignored. Their novelty ensured that they were inevitably associated with the enormous social transformations that also made them widely available. Eighteenth-century social commentators turned increasingly to pets when debating the great issues of the day—as metaphors, as evidence in scientific arguments, as symptoms of moral decay—because they were becoming ubiquitous.

2 ∾ DOMESTICATING THE EXOTIC

In September 1738, the *Gentleman's Magazine* announced the arrival of a female chimpanzee that would become one of the most famous of the many exotic animals displayed in Britain in the eighteenth century.

> A strange Creature taken in a Wood in *Guinea*, is brought to Town; 'tis a Female, about four Foot high, shaped in every Part like a Woman, except its Head which nearly resembles that of an Ape! She walks upright naturally, sits down to her Food, which is chiefly Greens, and feeds herself with her Hands as a human Creature. She is very fond of a Boy, and observed to be always sorrowful at his Absence, is clothed with a thin silk Vestment, and shews a great Discontent at the opening her Gown to discover her Sex.[1]

The magazine's brief announcement already contains the ingredients of much of the fascination that this chimp held for those who saw her: her physical resemblance to humans and her humanlike emotions.[2] "Madame Chimpanzee" (fig. 10) was enormously popular, and she had a significant impact on the field of natural history thanks to her status as one of the only humanoid apes successfully brought to Europe alive.

The text accompanying the illustration notes that she "walks erect, drinks Tea, eats her food & sleeps in a humane way" and has "a Capacity of understanding & great Affability."

Her similarity to humans was simultaneously intriguing and disturbing. On one level, her very presence in England demonstrated European world power, and her submission to a mere "Boy" reassuringly affirmed humans' ability to dominate all of nature. But at the same time, the ape inevitably raised questions about the idea of human uniqueness. If this creature seemed so civilized, then what, exactly, was distinctive about humanity? The contradictory ideas and emotions she inspired typified the many ways in which contact with non-European animals and cultures influenced eighteenth-century thinking not only about animals but about relationships among humans.

Exotic animals had long been status symbols and had been used, along with spices, plate, and expensive fabrics, as lavish gifts among the elite. Samuel Pepys, for instance, received canaries—then a rare and exciting species—as a gift in 1661.[3] He also recorded gifts of parrots, and in 1664 he was impressed by the sight of a mynah bird brought to England from the East Indies.[4] But by the eighteenth century, many formerly exotic and expensive pets, like Pepys's canaries, were becoming much more common. This transformation was accelerated by the almost constant warfare of the period, with its concomitant increase in international contact of all kinds. One effect of this expansion was to make available a much wider variety of exotic pets, like parrots and monkeys—an immediate material demonstration of Britain's power. Hence, for the natural philosopher Ebenezer Sibly, exotic animals were proof of the glorious extent of a modern imperialism that put the Roman Empire to shame: "So great is [parrots'] variety, that nothing seems more remarkable, than that only one species of them was known to the ancients, at a period when they boasted of being masters of the whole world. Of more than an hundred species now known, scarcely one naturally breeds in the countries that acknowledged the Roman power; a striking proof how ill founded the pretensions of that people were to universal domination."[5] What Rome had only dreamed of, it seemed, Britain had achieved.

Yet, like imperialism itself, the trade in exotic pets was also inextricably bound up with slavery. At the most basic level, traffic in humans, along with other international trade, enabled Europeans to come into contact with many exotic species and bring them back home. At times this could lead to confusion, as George Edwards noted in his description of the "Little Red-headed Parrakeet, or Guiney Sparrow." He believed that it came from Africa, although others claimed it was South American, a dispute he saw as a direct result of the slave trade: "The reason of this variety of accounts is, that this bird is generally brought to us by ships whose last departure was from America; for they who trade to Guiney rarely return directly from thence to Europe; but, in pursuance of their abominable and unnatural traffick in the human species, sail with shiploads of Negroes to the American colonies, where they sell the unhappy wretches, as civilized people do brute beasts; after which they return to Europe with their ill-acquired gains."[6] Edwards obviously abhorred the slave trade, but slavery and pet keeping also overlapped in the fact that, as Yi-Fu Tuan and others have pointed out, slaves could function as one sort of exotic pet. They were displayed in cosmopolitan households along with monkeys and parrots, sometimes allegedly even wearing collars manufactured by the same people who made dog collars.[7] Owners of both pets and slaves bestowed names upon them, often mock-heroic ones such as Pompey or Caesar. In these ways, exotic animals and people both functioned as living demonstrations of British imperial power and wealth. Parrots, monkeys, and human slaves joined tea, porcelain, and "japanned" furniture as fashion statements.

But increasing contact with previously unknown people and species, especially those from Asia and Africa, also had effects that the British found much more unsettling. This contact increased awareness of the massive diversity of species in existence. If Sibly could reflect with satisfaction on Britons' superior knowledge to that of the ancient Romans, many others found the multitude of living things a daunting challenge to natural history's goal of classifying and ordering the natural world. The discovery of the humanoid apes (the chimpanzee and the orangutan)[8] posed particular challenges to the assumptions that for centuries had informed beliefs about "man's" relationship to animals, threatening to unseat humans from their exalted position at the top of the great chain of being. In response, some naturalists chose to accept the similarities between apes and "savage" humans while drawing a clear line between civilized Europeans and such "savages." But most simply insisted all the more forcefully on the special characteristics shared by all humans, characteristics ostensibly unattainable by even the most human-looking apes.

This universalizing language held enormous implications for the debates about the morality of human slavery at a time when the slave trade was an increasingly vexing problem. The trade seemed central to British political and economic power, yet it conflicted with the growing emphasis on liberty as a defining value of British society. If characteristics shared by all people (but not by animals), such as reason, were the most important attributes of humanity, then it might become much more difficult to justify enslaving one group of people simply because of their skin color or place of origin. The British tried to work through these questions, in part, by considering animals. Naturalists explained the relationship between humans and domestic animals as that of master and slave, and slavery was not simply a metaphor. Because it was meant literally but applied to an area that seemed much less problematic than human slavery, animal slavery became an ideal testing ground for ideas about the morality of all forms of enslavement. Advocates of the nascent humane movement thus linked abolition to their goal of improving the treatment of animals, a move that unintentionally revealed the limits of such thinking regarding both humans and animals.

Even more significant than the relatively small humane movement was the way in which debates about animal slavery played out in thinking about pets. Animal slavery seemed to be a necessary precondition for human survival, but this justification assumed that the animals in question served humans as workers or food. Pets, by contrast, existed merely for their owners' amusement or companionship, and thus could potentially embody the most egregious form of human tyranny. Two very different case studies reveal the ways in which eighteenth-century thinkers wrestled with the morality of pet keeping as slavery. François Le Vaillant, a naturalist and explorer of South Africa, kept a pet baboon that led him to consider whether any living creature could be happy without liberty, even as he offered a series of parallels between his baboon and the native Africans he encountered. His memoir constructed a complex web of associations among civilization, race, and friendship. Closer to home, caged songbirds presented a more direct challenge to the morality of pet keeping; with their obvious desire for liberty, they forced writers to question whether there was ever sufficient justification for imprisoning another living being. In both cases, the solution seemed to lie in the possibility that slavery might be beneficial under a benevolent master. Discussions of pet slavery thus ended with the same kinds of unhappy compromises that marked discussions of human slavery; rather than endorse abolition, many people groped their way toward a solution that would permit the practice while ameliorating its worst abuses.

~   ~   ~

Europeans had long been fascinated by the similarities between humans and monkeys, and the supposed tendency of such animals to "ape" human actions added to that fascination.[9] Widely held beliefs about ape behavior, some of them dating back to medieval or ancient times, not only emphasized the physical resemblance between apes and humans but also suggested even more significant parallels in gender roles and culture. The question of the boundary between humans and apes became especially pressing in the eighteenth century. The rise of natural history, with its focus on systematizing knowledge about nature, led to debates about how to organize and classify the natural world. At the same time, imperialism and global exploration made the British increasingly aware of the dazzling diversity of life around the world—an awareness that could make the task of classification seem impossible.[10] Naturalists became depressingly certain that such attempts were inevitably arbitrary and partial. The discovery of the humanoid apes only added to the confusion and made the issue of defining human uniqueness all the more pressing. Linnaeus's decision to group together as primates humans and apes, along with bats and lemurs, brought the issue to a head for many people because it opened the possibility that apes might indeed be raised to the level of humans—or, more disturbingly, that humans might be debased to the level of monkeys.[11]

Many naturalists were particularly interested in the question of the extent to which such anatomical resemblances might also imply similarities of intellectual, moral, or emotional capacity. Oliver Goldsmith provided multiple examples of reports that humanoid apes engaged in behavior like that of human beings—sharing human notions of status, using polite gestures, and performing tasks—although he did not accept the idea that this behavior implied any fundamental equality.[12] Others went further. Famously, Lord Monboddo asserted that the orangutan was in fact a kind of human; for instance, he said, it could use sticks as weapons (which showed the ability to engage in complex reasoning), it built huts, it could be tamed, and, most important for Monboddo, it had "what, I think, [is] essential to the human kind, a sense of honour." All of this behavior would be possible only in a true human, he claimed.[13] As Dror Wahrman points out, however, Monboddo placed orangutans in the category of humans "in order to *preserve* the clarity of the human/animal distinction."[14] Monboddo's solution to the problem of an ape that appeared to blur the boundary between humans and animals was to move this particular animal into the category of the human. He was widely mocked for his beliefs, but for many people the question of how to identify the difference between such apes and humans was a real one. If Linnaeus presented one option—to accept that humans and apes were fundamentally similar—Monboddo offered another answer that maintained an absolute boundary between species. These two views represent the two dominant models used by writers who addressed the problem of the human-animal boundary.

The most common response to the potential for apes to blur the boundaries between humans and animals was to reject the idea entirely and to insist ever more strongly on human uniqueness.[15] If Linnaeus's decision to classify humans and apes together was influential, it was certainly not uncontested. Thus Thomas Pennant, in his own natural history, rejected Linnaeus's taxonomy "because my vanity will not suffer me to rank mankind with *Apes, Monkies, Maucaucos* and *Bats*, the companions LINNÆUS has allotted us."[16] His *Synopsis of Quadrupeds* included a section on "animals approaching the human form," such as apes. But he carefully added a footnote clarifying that this description should "be taken in a limited sense . . . resulting from the structure of their parts only, not from any superior sagacity to that of most others of the brute creation."[17] We can see in these comments the way that many responses to the potential mingling of apes and humans operated. Pennant freely admitted that his initial refusal to accept Linnaeus's ideas resulted from his own "vanity"; his first reaction was that humans were self-evidently better than monkeys or bats. But in dealing with the specific issues raised when trying to impose an orderly classification system on the apparent chaos of the natural world, Pennant insisted on real differences between humans and apes even as he recognized their anatomical similarities. And his clarification that such similarities did not necessarily imply apes' "superior sagacity" to other animals, let alone their equality with humans, was echoed by many of the naturalists of the eighteenth century.

Most significant in the classification wars opposing Linnaeus were Buffon and his close follower Goldsmith. Buffon met the apparently disturbing similarities between men and animals head on, insisting that what might appear to be a permeable boundary was in fact absolute and indestructible. He noted that the "orang-outang" greatly resembled a human in its anatomy, its attraction to human women, its use of weapons, and its tendency to walk upright: "This orang-outang or pongo is only a brute, but a brute of a kind so singular, that man cannot behold it without contemplating himself." Yet, he immediately continued, neither could man behold the ape "without being thoroughly convinced that his body is not the most essential part of his nature."[18] Further on, he clarified and expanded his reasoning, insisting that it was man's "divine spirit" that differentiated him from all other animals; had any other animal, even the "meanest," had such a spirit, it "would soon have become the rival of man." But humans were unique, no matter how great the similarities between human and ape anatomy: "Whatever resemblance, therefore, takes place between the Hottentot and the ape, the interval which separates them is immense; because the former is endowed with the faculties of thought and of speech."[19]

What mattered to Buffon were the characteristics that all humans had in common; God had granted these characteristics only to humans, and any other differences implicitly paled into insignificance, just as the apparent similarities to apes did. His comments on the ape identified three crucial, interrelated human characteristics: a "divine spirit," reason, and speech. In his later work on birds, he again developed these ideas when addressing parrots' ability to mimic human speech. For Buffon, the fact that apes, which so strongly resemble humans in other respects, do not have speech was proof of God's goodness: "had the voice of the Parrot been bestowed on the ape; the human race would have been struck dumb with astonishment, and the philosopher could hardly have been able to demonstrate that the ape was still a brute." Thus we should be grateful that parrots can imitate our speech but not our behavior, while apes can imitate behavior but not speech. Although nature had given apes "the same members and organs, with man, she has reserved for him alone the power of improving them; that noble mark of our pre-eminence, which constitutes our empire over the animated world."[20] For Buffon, then, it was not the act of speaking per se that made humans unique and distinguished them from apes: it was that the speech revealed reason, and thus that humans alone could learn and teach others. Only humans could "improve" as a species. Reason was God's gift to humans, and it in turn revealed humans' unique possession of a "divine spirit."

Like Buffon, Oliver Goldsmith was committed to an ineradicable distinction between humans and animals. He noted that the anatomy of members of "the monkey class" was so similar to that of humans that it "may well mortify the pride of such as make their persons alone the principal object of their admiration." But his remark also indicates the limit to the likeness: it was in their "persons alone." He thus transformed a potential threat to human pride in humans' superiority as a *species* into a condemnation of *individual* vanity. That the "Ouran Outang" was so close to humans "in conformation" was surprising, he confessed, but the similarities meant little: "The tongue, and all the organs of the voice, were the same, and yet the animal was dumb; the brain was formed in the same manner with that of man, and yet the creature wanted reason: an evident proof (as Mr. Buffon finely observes) that no disposition of matter will give mind; and that the body, how nicely soever it is formed, is formed in vain, when there is not infused a soul to direct its operations." Goldsmith's most detailed engagement with the problem of anatomical similarity came in his discussion of monkey hands. He admitted their great likeness to human hands, even suggesting that their greater delicacy might seem to imply greater dexterity than humans could achieve. Yet they were unable to master more than the most basic tasks, like picking fruit or wielding a stick as a weapon. The crucial difference, he said, was reason, of which man was the sole possessor. Reason could overcome any physical handicap—even hooved animals or those with paws would dominate the world if they possessed reason, but without it, monkeys' graceful hands were "almost useless."[21]

In his insistence on human uniqueness, Goldsmith even argued that the apparent similarities between humans and apes were, paradoxically, the best evidence of the huge gulf between humans and animals: "From this description of the Ouran Outang, we perceive at what a distance the first animal of the brute creation is placed from the very lowest of the human species. Even in countries peopled with savages, this creature is considered as a beast; and in those very places where we might suppose the smallest differences between them and mankind, the inhabitants hold it in the greatest contempt and detestation." While all the other links in the great chain of being depended on such tiny differences that it was difficult to tell where one species ended and another began, he claimed, it was perfectly obvious that the boundary between man and ape was absolute. "It is in vain that the Ouran Outang resembles man in form, or imitates many of his actions; he still continues a wretched, helpless creature, pent up in the most gloomy part of the forest, and, with regard to the provision for his own happiness, inferior even to the elephant or the beaver in sagacity."[22]

Goldsmith thus not only insisted upon the orangutan's inferiority to humans but argued that the ape ranked below other animals, such as the elephant or beaver, in "sagacity." This focus on "sagacity" created a ranking system that distanced humanoid apes from humans, with several other species occupying coveted spaces closer to people in the great chain of being. Many others followed Goldsmith's assertion that monkeys' apparent resemblance to humans was an illusion, and that other species were far superior to simians. Thus Richard Brookes insisted that "Monkeys, that so nearly resemble man in figure, yet if compar'd even to some quadrupeds of the lower orders, will be found less cunning, and endowed with a smaller share of useful instinct, than they. The habitation of the Beaver is a much more convenient place than any the monkey has been found to build, so that if they approach us in form, there are other creatures that approach us more nearly in sagacity."[23] Charles Taylor argued that apes that had been recorded as walking upright had been trained to do so against their natural inclination. Not only did this mislead European observers, he said, but it was cruel to the "Ouran Outang": "thus educated, an ape, or a quadruped, may be an admirable object for human curiosity, but little advanced in regard to its own felicity; its conveniencies for its manner of life are neither improved nor augmented: all its acquisitions are useless to itself, and calculated to cause wonder in spectators, not to rank their possessor a single step higher on the scale of being."[24] In his popular children's book *Keeper's Travels in Search of His Master*, Edward Augustus Kendall inserted a reflection on the relative merits of primates and dogs in which dogs easily came out on top. A wise magistrate announces that "the understanding of dogs . . . surpasses that of all other animals, except man and the elephant." When asked whether apes and monkeys are not also "very sensible," he replies, "They are reckoned among the most stupid of quadrupeds . . . the appearance of understanding in them, is entirely in consequence of the resemblance which their form bears to that of man: but this similarity is, in fact, a convincing proof of their total want of capacity." If simians were really intelligent, then they would not be outdone by the dog, elephant, and horse. Ultimately, in this circular argument, the superiority of dogs was a result of their close relationship with humans, which created "their sensibility. This makes them susceptible of affection, and capable of attachment. Nature has given them this disposition, which is improved by a constant society with man."[25]

All of these assessments ultimately depended on the assumption that the best animal was that which was most useful to mankind. The sagacity of an animal was demonstrated through its ability to serve humans, and therefore apes had to be inferior to more helpful animals. Ebenezer Sibly made the connection explicit when he remarked that orangutans were closest to humans in anatomy but that dogs, horses, elephants, and camels were "to be preferred" because their "sagacity and intelligence bespeak an intellect, which by culture and education might be made subservient to the domestic conveniences of man." Were it possible, as he thought it might be, to train an orangutan as carefully as those animals had been trained, then perhaps the ape might become "equally prompt for domestic purposes."[26] In the vision of human-animal relations espoused by Goldsmith and his followers, domestication became a moral yardstick.

In making his case about the inferiority of apes even to animals less similar to humans, however, Goldsmith also glossed over the differences between "civilized" and "savage" humans, insisting that even the "lowest" humans recognized their superiority to the ape. This move was common among those who sought to emphasize God's special care for humanity, even though they would have recoiled at the idea of seeing other cultures as equal in value or achievement to their own. Yet the rhetoric of human uniqueness necessarily implied recognition of the capacity for reason, speech, and learning among *all* humans, and it required that these similarities outweigh any cultural or racial differences. Thus Johann Lavater, whose famous work on physiognomy was hardly a monument to racial equality, nevertheless took pains to emphasize the differences between all human and all monkey skulls despite their superficial resemblance: "exact observation, and comparison of the sculls . . . will make the great difference conspicuous; and render the eternal unattainableness of the monkey to man more than probable." He went on to enumerate the differences in formation of foreheads, eyebrows, and other facial features. In his eagerness to deny the possibility that monkeys could ever attain humanity, he discounted the differences between different races of humans: "a newborn child, of the most savage nation, has all the characteristics of man. Let it be compared to a new-born orang outang, and, in the first, will certainly be discovered a much greater possibility of becoming an angel, than, in the second, of becoming a man."[27]

A particularly detailed attempt to work through the implications of these ideas, with direct (albeit unattributed) reference to the views of Buffon and Goldsmith, appeared in a dialogue between a boy and his father in the popular children's book *Evenings at Home*. The father begins by explaining that humans are "quadrupeds" and that Linnaeus put them in the same category with "apes, macocos, and bats." But, he reassures his son, "Man is an animal possessed of *reason*, and the only one. This, therefore, is enough to define him." Although it is possible to argue that some animals, such as dogs, have a "little" reason, "the superiority of the human faculties is so great, that man is in many points absolutely distinguished from brutes." In particular, humans have speech (and writing)—which in turn makes it possible to improve themselves over generations—as well as the ability to plan for the future and make tools. The child, not entirely convinced, worries about the boundaries between apes and people. He asks about "wild men bred in the woods that could do none of these things" and is told that these men are exceptions because they were not brought up in society, where humans are naturally meant to be. Then the child asks about the "Hottentot," who seems to be "little above the brutes." Again, he is reassured:

> The difference, indeed, is great, but we agree in the most essential characters of *man*, and perhaps the advantage is not all on our side. The Hottentot cultivates the earth, and rears cattle. He not only herds with his fellows, but he has instituted some sort of government for the protection of the weak against the strong. He has a notion of right and wrong, and is sensible of the necessity of controuling present appetites and passions for the sake of a future good. He has therefore *morals*. He is possessed of weapons, tools, cloathing, and furniture, of his own making. In agility of body, and the knowledge of various circumstances relative to the nature of animals, he surpasses us. His inferiority lies in those things in which many of the lowest class among us are almost equally inferior to the instructed.

The work does go on to argue that some populations remain in a state of ignorance or savagery, never employing their natural curiosity—a gift supposedly in greatest supply among Europeans ("in these countries man may be said to be *most man*").[28] But the general effect of the dialogue is to insist on the common humanity of all races in contradistinction to the radical difference between humans and beasts.

This perception of the relationship between humans and other animals, established by Buffon and Goldsmith, dominated eighteenth-century discussions of apes. Their works were reprinted, excerpted, and blatantly plagiarized in other natural histories as well as in anthologies for general audiences and even in children's literature. Threatened with a potential end to the long-standing view of humans' unique superiority, these writers responded with an even greater insistence on humanity's special status. This move created problems of its own, however. The rhetoric insisted on the common characteristics of *all* humans, from the greatest minds of Europe to the "Hottentot." In so doing, it left open the question of how to reconcile this basic similarity with the subordination of other races, particularly through the institution of slavery. Conversely, growing criticism of the institution of slavery also influenced the development of a movement for the humane treatment of animals, in ways that were equally problematic.

≈   ≈   ≈

One reason for the popularity of the belief in an enormous gulf between humans and apes, supposedly sustained by God's unique gift of reason, was that it complemented the existing Christian tradition that God created animals for human use.[29] By emphasizing the vast distance between humans and other animals, it was easy to imagine that humans in fact had godlike powers over the animal world. For many naturalists, domestication was the most vivid demonstration of such command. Humanity's power over animal life and death, and the ability to transform animal physiology for human convenience, seemed to many people to prove that animals were slaves to human authority. Again, the terminology of slavery was meant literally. But this language also inevitably reflected contemporary debates about the practice of human slavery. Writing about human dominion over animals raised uncomfortable questions about the extent and possible abuse of such enormous power.[30]

The vocabulary of animal slavery affected even the basic categories used to organize nonhuman species. Like other naturalists, Oliver Goldsmith constructed a fundamental distinction in "quadrupedes" between "the Domestic and the Savage," and the language he used to define those two categories was telling: "by Domestic I mean, such as man has taken into friendship, or reduced to obedience; by the Savage, those who still preserve their natural independence and ferocity."[31] For Goldsmith, "friendship" and "obedience" were two sides of the same coin, as were "independence" and "ferocity." The tension implicit in this language between the positive values of "friendship," on the one hand, and "independence," on the other, underlay many eighteenth-century discussions of domesticated animals.

Naturalists agreed that human survival depended upon people's ability to bring animals under control, and that this endeavor had been so successful as to render "man's" impact on the animal world almost incalculable. "The savage animal preserves at once his liberty and instinct," Goldsmith asserted, "but man seems to have changed the very nature of domestic animals by cultivation and care. A domestic animal is a slave, which has few other desires, but those which man is willing to grant it."[32] For Goldsmith, domestication was an assertion of raw power, placing "nature . . . under a kind of restraint." This power extended to human influence over animals' size, color, hair texture, and even the floppiness of their ears. The result, he said, was "a new race of artificial monsters," created "rather to answer the purposes of human pleasure, than their own convenience. In short, their very appetites may be changed; and those that feed only upon grass, may be rendered carnivorous."[33] Goldsmith's unease is palpable here. If humans benefited from domestication, they did so by creating "monsters." Domestication was coercion; enslavement altered nature's intent.

Here as elsewhere, Goldsmith drew heavily on the work of Buffon. Buffon argued that the domestic animals of the temperate climes (which he identified as the most civilized parts of the world) revealed "the most evident marks of the antiquity of their slavery."[34] In his "Essay on the Degeneration of Animals," Buffon explained that "the temperature of the climate, the quality of the food, and the evils produced by slavery, are the three causes of the changes and degeneration of animals." "We will be astonished," he added, "at the degree to which tyranny can degrade and disfigure Nature; we will perceive the marks of slavery, and the prints of her chains; and we will find, that these wounds are deeper and more incurable, in proportion to their antiquity."[35] Eighteenth-century naturalists thus recognized both human power over animals and the potentially negative implications of such power, visible in Buffon's language of "tyranny," "chains," and "wounds."

Even in cases where animal enslavement might seem to be most justifiable, discomfort with the practice could still surface. It was widely accepted, for instance, that all felines, from lions to the smallest house cat, were treacherous, cruel, and cunning. Buffon referred to cats as "the genus of cruel and rapacious animals" and noted that "they are all destructive, ferocious, and untameable." They thus resisted domestication and, most naturalists agreed, could never truly be servants or friends to humans. Even the house cat, "which is the least and smallest species, though reduced to slavery, is neither less perfidious, nor more obedient."[36] But was resistance to slavery really wrong? The anonymous *Beauties of Natural History* echoed Buffon in referring to felines as "creatures full as cruel, though not quite so cunning as those of the human kind." "Even such of them as we find means to tame and let loose on the rest," it went on, "sometimes recall on a sudden their original and hereditary antipathies, and die revenging their slavery."[37] Obviously, this was an unflattering picture of cats (and in this context the author was referring primarily to large animals such as lions and tigers rather than to house cats), but the deliberate comparison between human and feline cruelty, as well as the ennobling language of "revenging their slavery," destabilizes the easy superiority of humans. The *Universal Spectator* went further and argued that humans' ability to domesticate some animals was no sign of superiority of species, because "it is no more than what we do by one another; nay, in this they act more *generously* than we, for one *Lion* never makes another *Lion* become his *Slave*, and do his *Drudgery*."[38] Foucher d'Obsonville commented on the tiger in a way that exhibited similar tensions: "the Tiger, when caught young, may be familiarized to a certain degree, but his character cannot be subdued, even by chains. The Dog, born fortunately for slavery, creeps to kiss the hand that has punished him unjustly; but the Lion and Tiger tremble with indignation at ill-treatment. If their courage was of a more generous nature, we should say, perhaps, their pride was a certain indication of the nobleness of their race."[39] His attempt to distinguish between the behavior of the tiger and the pride that indicated true "nobleness" demonstrates the difficulty of trying to apply human morality to animals. He is left to damn with faint praise the fawning dog, "fortunately" destined to be a slave. Animals were useful to humans for the very reasons that made them despicable, and commentators struggled to reconcile the desire to evaluate the relative nobility of animals with the need to subjugate them.

Some writers went even further in considering domestication as slavery, insisting on its corrupting rather than beneficial effects and drawing parallels between its corruption and the dangers of civilization itself. The domesticated animal was the quintessential representative of human culture, and naturalists agreed that the more civilized a culture, the more extreme the effects of domestication. Such thinking led François Le Vaillant to offer a spirited defense of wildness over domestication: "The domestic state is a state of servitude, in which the individual, and even the species, more or less degenerates. Its natural instinct being thus altered, the animal is purposely heated by a particular kind of food: it is separated from the females and males of its own species, and is forced to produce monsters, which are only a deviation from nature. . . . In a savage state the individual, perfectly free, invariably follows these [natural] laws, copulates with those of its own species, and never with those of another." Therefore, he concluded, "the state of servitude in which a domestic animal lives, the food to which it is confined, and the education given it, alter and modify its nature. By living with us it appears, so to speak, to become corrupted and to assume our vices. . . . I have been informed that, at the house of an upholsterer in the street Croix-des-Petits-Champs at Paris, a she-cat and a dog produced young ones, which lived. Had these animals been reared in a forest, sooner than copulate together, they would have devoured each other."[40] Le Vaillant thus took to its logical conclusion Buffon's and Goldsmith's idea of domestication as tyranny and domestic animals as degradations from nature. Here, the monsters become literal, obscene hybrids of species that interact only because they have been stripped of their liberty.

It was easy for such ideas to suggest a condemnation of civilization itself. John Gregory, in his *Comparative View of the State and Faculties of Man, with Those of the Animal World*, compared humans unfavorably to animals on the grounds that animals, unlike humans, always lived pleasant, long lives and were "strangers to pain and sickness." But he emphasized that he referred to *wild* animals only: "Those that are tame and under our direction partake of all our miseries."[41] For Gregory, differentiation from the natural world brought with it both benefits and problems, which he thought were visible when considering other races. Thus he suggested that "the advantages, which the Brute Animals have over us, are possessed by those of our own Species, who are just above them, guided in a manner entirely by Instinct, equally strangers to the noble attainments their Natures are capable of, and to the many miseries attendant on their more enlightned [*sic*] Brethren of mankind."[42] Gregory's erstwhile student at Edinburgh, William Smellie, also emphasized the advantages of a more "natural" life: "Man in society, like domestic animals, by luxury, by artificial modes of living, by unnatural and vicious habits, debilitate their bodies, and transmit to their progeny the seeds of weakness and disease"—problems avoided by "savages" and the lower classes of civilized countries.[43] Thus not only were infants and savages more like animals than civilized adults were, but Smellie saw distinct advantages to such a life.

Ideas like these took the vaunted superiority of humanity and transformed it from a benefit into a curse. Domesticating animals enslaved them, leading to unnatural and obscene monsters; civilization itself, the human analogue to domestication, disfigured and debilitated beings ostensibly created in God's own image. One source for these views was the idea of the "noble savage," who allegedly represented humanity in its natural, uncorrupted state. But in such comments we also see the principle underlying many attacks on slavery, both human and animal—the belief that slavery corrupted slave and master alike. Decadence and domestication might ultimately be the same thing. This is not to say that most critics of civilization believed in racial equality or opposed the slave trade, but to recognize that slavery, domestication, and civilization all raised similar troubling questions. And animals, which seemed to be most thoroughly enslaved in the most civilized cultures, stood at the nexus of these anxieties.

Most eighteenth-century writers, however, stopped short of questioning the value of civilization. Instead, they encouraged their readers to use wisely the enormous power granted to their species. This position had a place in the Christian tradition, one that emphasized "man" as steward over God's creation, with a responsibility not to abuse his delegated authority. One response to the problem of animal slavery was thus to think of it in different terms; to see such power not in terms of the violent tyranny of a slave master but as a paternalistic responsibility to be exercised wisely. In this view, if humans were godlike in relation to animals, then they must exercise the wisdom and mercy of God as well. Georg Christian Raff, for instance, offered an image of human dominion that was at once sweeping and fraught with responsibility. God "seems to have surrendered up nature to our pleasure; so that we seem to be the sovereigns of it. . . . You see how we have tamed and reduced to slavery, several species of animals which we chain down to our service, or slaughter for our sustenance. . . . Is not this to be *king*? But this empire is not that of a sluggard, who[,] reclined on a sopha, thinks it sufficient to will and to command; it is the empire of vigour, of address, of wisdom, of industry, of persevering indefatigable labour. All this is necessary, not to be a beast."[44] Thus human power was absolute, but, like absolute rule, it also entailed enormous responsibility and effort. The tyrant who extracted benefits without working in return was no better than a beast; being fully human implied wisdom, discretion, and a prudent exercise of power. William Fordyce Mavor similarly argued that the strong resemblance between humans and quadrupeds "ought to teach us mildness and humanity to [animals] and at least to abstain from wanton cruelty to those that are either useless or noxious to us."[45]

Raff's and Mavor's comments appeared in books intended for children, and children's literature, with its goal of creating moral citizens, was particularly concerned to instill in readers respect for the careful exercise of power.[46] Sarah Trimmer's *Fabulous Histories*, for instance, includes a conversation among a group of adults in which they question whether it is possible for animals to have real intellects. Her wise heroine, Mrs. Benson, concludes the conversation by saying that she simply accepts that the extent of animal intellect is something God has chosen to keep from human knowledge. But, she insists, it is still clear how animals should be treated: "That they are in the power of man, and subservient to his use and pleasure, gives them a sufficient claim to our compassion and kindness, and whilst I am partly fed and clothed at the expence of the animal creation, I could not bring myself to inflict wanton cruelties upon them. On the other hand, as Providence has placed them so much beneath us in the scale of beings, I should think it equally wrong to elevate them from their proper rank, and suffer them to occupy that share of attention and love, which is due to our own species only."[47] A dialogue in Aikin and Barbauld's *Evenings at Home* about the purpose of flies also reflects both an assumption of human superiority and a sense of its limits. When the child Sophia complains about flies and wonders how they could possibly contribute to human use, her father tells her that animals do not exist solely for human use; instead, God has made them "to be happy. It is a manifest purpose of the Creator to give being to as much life as possible, for life is enjoyment to all creatures in health and in possession of their faculties." At the same time, however, humans "have a right to make a reasonable use of all animals for our advantage, and also to free ourselves from such as are hurtful to us. So far our superiority over them may fairly extend. But we should never abuse them for our mere amusement, nor take away their lives wantonly."[48] If the idea of human dominion raised the specter of tyranny and slavery, works like these offered a much more palatable alternative. Humans could retain their authority and continue to treat animals as resources, but with due restraint such power would be a force for good rather than evil. Both animals and humans would embrace their roles in God's creation, and both would fulfill God's intention that they find happiness.

~ ~ ~

In the last decades of the eighteenth century, a new strand of humanitarianism emerged, focused not on the responsibility that came with God's gift of reason but on the experiences and feelings shared by both humans and animals. Some theorists of natural law began to suggest that natural rights should apply to animals as well as to humans.[49] In the arts, the concept of sensibility, with its emphasis on heightened emotion and compassion for the suffering of others, could easily be relevant to animals as well as to humans.[50] At the same time, humanitarian movements aimed at ameliorating the suffering of people, including the poor and slaves, became a significant force in British society and a source of pride for many Britons.[51] We can see the convergence of these strands of thought in Jeremy Bentham's famous footnote comparing the grounds for opposition to slavery and to animal abuse. The capacity for reason, he said, was irrelevant: "the question is not, Can they reason? nor, Can they talk? but, Can they suffer?"[52]

Those who promoted such ideas equated the end of animal abuse with other kinds of social progress.[53] Thomas Young, for instance, created a deliberate parallel between his agenda and other reform movements when he remarked that he hoped for a positive reception for his 1798 *Essay on Humanity to Animals*: "the exertions which have been made to diminish the sufferings of the prisoner, and to better the condition of the poor; the flourishing state of charitable institutions; the interest excited in the nation by the struggles for the abolition of the slave-trade; the growing detestation of religious persecution—all these, and other circumstances" gave him hope that this was a good time to raise the issue of the treatment of animals.[54] Nor were such comparisons confined to a general appeal to humanitarian ideals of progress. The most sustained works advocating humane treatment were produced in the last quarter of the eighteenth century, which was also, not coincidentally, the period when the abolitionist movement became a major social force.[55] Advocates for improving the treatment of animals intentionally drew parallels between human and animal slavery, using the comparisons to appeal to readers' sense of justice and mercy. Like the abolitionists, they drew on the concept of sympathy, the idea that moral behavior entailed an ability to imagine oneself in the position of another.[56] But where the famous abolitionist motto asked, "am I not a man and a brother?," the new movement hoped to make readers recognize *animals* as fellow sufferers. Thus Samuel Jackson Pratt condemned overweening human pride that reveled in tyrannical power: "Thou Animal sublime, we human call, / Who deem'st these attributes but Instinct's sway, / Thyself sole reasoning Tyrant of the ball, / The rest thy slaves, to tremble and obey."[57] And, like those who appealed to the common humanity of blacks and whites, John Oswald insisted on the kinship between humans and other living beings: "sovereign despot of the world, lord of the life and death of every creature,—man, with the slaves of his tyranny, disclaims the ties of kindred." Unwilling to accept that animals might feel and reason like humans, people trained their minds, he said, to accept "remorseless tyranny" and the "foul oppression" of weaker species.[58] Oswald's insistence on the extent of human-animal kinship was more radical than most of his contemporaries were willing to accept, but he was drawing on a widespread belief that feelings could cross the species boundary.

Of course, such arguments also opened the way for critics to complain about humanitarians who wept over bullbaiting or the death of a fly while ignoring the suffering of their fellow humans. But the vocabulary of animal slavery raised further problems for animal rights advocates. If parallels with the injustices of human slavery could prove useful by appealing powerfully to emotion, few were willing to follow the comparison to its most obvious conclusion. Consider Humphry Primatt, who was particularly explicit in his depiction of the power relations at work between humans and beasts. Primatt remarked that it was lucky for humans that domestic animals lacked reason, for if they were capable of reasoning, their awareness of their own "subordinate and servile Condition" would make them unhappy and perhaps less easy to manage. Speech combined with reason would be worse yet: "by their constant intercourse with men they would soon discover our natural weakness, and their own stature and strength; and the sense of their hard slavery, and of the injurious treatment they meet with from us, would probably awaken their resentment to a general insurrection, if not to the total throwing off the human Yoke."[59] Despite this acknowledgment of the evils of animal slavery, however, when Primatt made the connection between human and animal slavery explicit, he changed the terms of the comparison. The white man had "no right, by virtue of his *colour*, to enslave and tyrannize over a *black* man," he said; and by the same principle, "a man can have no natural right to abuse and torment a beast, merely because a beast has not the *mental* powers of a man."[60] Primatt shifted the problem from enslavement itself (color is no reason to enslave a black man) to abuse of the enslaved (superior reason is no excuse for abusing animals). Advocates of humane treatment of animals were thus forced into a corner by the conflict articulated so clearly by Buffon; if humans were to survive, they would have to rely on their domination over the animal world. Kind treatment of animals could not lead to equality for animals.[61]

Other anticruelty writers faced the same dilemma, and their arguments reflected varying degrees of willingness to confront it. John Lawrence, for instance, announced that "the God of Nature has placed the whole animal creation in a state of slavery to the human race" because of beasts' inherent inferiority. Yet he insisted on the "natural and unalienable rights" of animals.[62] His condemnation of human tyranny and animal slavery notwithstanding, Samuel Jackson Pratt also accepted these conditions as inevitable; his views led him not to animal liberation but to faith in an afterlife for nonhuman creatures: "I dare ask, whether a servant and a slave, faithful in both characters without one criminal tendency, nay, adorned with many qualities of which man himself is proud, and yet enduring the sufferings of the most guilty, is left without claim and without appeal? shall he be condemned to ceaseless stripes—to hard fare, harder usage; and to go mourning all his life long, and then die hopeless at last?" To think so "would be blasphemy."[63] Pratt did advocate more humane treatment of animals, but he found greater hope in the immortality of the animal soul. The works of men like Primatt, Lawrence, and Pratt, which consciously referred to the abolitionist movement, thus also embodied some of the same conflicts visible in eighteenth-century critiques of slavery. Just as the animal rights writers stopped short of advocating an end to animal slavery, unable to envision a world in which that would be a viable option, many critics of slavery stopped short of advocating its total abolition throughout the British Empire. Instead, like Primatt, they sought the amelioration of slave conditions (or the abolition of the slave trade, often seen as especially abusive). And, like Lawrence and Pratt, many of them turned to God's will for both an explanation of slavery and, through Christian conversion and eternal salvation, the best hope for a better future for slaves.[64]

Discussion of animal slaves could also raise difficulties absent from considerations of human slavery. Human slavery was seen above all in terms of work, and the debates about slavery related to the question of whether the economic benefits of slave labor could ever outweigh the injustice of treating another human as property. Those who accepted nonhuman slavery but who advocated better treatment of animals found their way to this position because, like Buffon, they saw such slavery as essential to human survival. Humans needed to enslave animals for their labor and their meat. But what about animals that provided neither? In other words, what about pets?[65] If domestication was the analogue of civilization, then pets were the ultimate expression of both, and they seemed to offer the most extreme example of animal slavery—they were creatures domesticated for no other purpose than the amusement of their masters.

≈   ≈   ≈

Most animal rights advocates did not deal directly with pets; the humane movement tended to focus on abuse of animals by lower-class people, either laborers abusing their work animals or poor people engaging in popular recreations such as bullbaiting or throwing at cocks (a bias not lost on their opponents).[66] Thomas Young was one of the rare exceptions. He began by presenting pet keeping as an apparently clear-cut case of abuse: "What right have we to tame such animals as birds, squirrels, and hares, and to cage and confine some of them . . . and all this merely for the sake of amusement?" But he qualified this judgment.

> It may however be justly alledged in excuse of the practice, that so far from proceeding from any barbarous motive, it generally originates in a fondness for the animals; and that by proper management it might be converted into a source of gentleness and humanity. . . . It also makes an essential difference in the cruelty, of what kind the animals are, and by what means they come into our hands. The more enemies an animal would be exposed to in a state of nature, the less cruel it evidently is to take it out of that state.[67]

For Young, then, the enslavement of pets could be justified for two reasons, one based on benefits to humans and the other on benefits to animals. First, the practice could, counterintuitively, have a beneficial moral effect on the human pet owner: whereas abuse resulted from evil intent, the positive intentions of the pet owner might actually encourage benevolence toward other animals. Second, pet keeping could be seen as a form of protection for vulnerable animals.

Young's vacillation on the question of pet slavery and his two major justifications for keeping pets were reflected in many of the discussions of pets as slaves in the eighteenth century. Eighteenth-century writers were well aware of the parallels between pets and human slaves.[68] A 1710 issue of the *Tatler*, for instance, included a letter from "a Black-moor Boy" named Pompey, who complained that his mistress loved her parrot as much as she did him, and that she had given her "Shock-Dog . . . a Collar that cost almost as much as mine."[69] Another author constructed an extended joke based on a lover's gifts to his mistress of a pet monkey and "a Black," remarking that the slave respected the monkey because it had the greater "Understanding."[70] Examples like these show that contemporaries understood that slaves and pets could perform similar roles, partly because both were associated with femininity, fashion, and consumerism, as we will see in chapter 3. But eighteenth-century writing on pets and slavery went beyond such parallels to consider the potential moral problems caused by keeping pets. Distant as pets may seem from the questions raised by humanoid apes, they nevertheless posed similar problems over the rights and wrongs of human dominion. If all humans were infinitely superior to all animals, was there any limit to their authority? Was there any form of exploitation that went too far? Physical abuse of animals was one obvious area that seemed to transform dominion into tyranny, but pet keeping could be equally troublesome for those who believed that animal slavery might be justified on the grounds of utility.

It is of course probable that many people happily kept pets without considering animal slavery at all; one of the distinguishing characteristics of the pet is precisely its role as simultaneously family member and property, living being and thing, and pet owners often live with this contradiction without giving it much thought. But one eighteenth-century naturalist does provide us with evidence of a man facing the conflicts embodied by the pet. Not coincidentally, the animal was a monkey, the creature that so often spurred humans to consider their relationship to the animal world, and his owner kept him in Africa, the continent at the center of the debate about slavery.

When François Le Vaillant explored South Africa in the 1780s, he took with him an enormous entourage of servants, hunters, guides, translators, dogs, oxen, food, clothes, and other equipment, along with specially designed cases for holding the natural specimens he collected. But he also took along one additional traveling companion: a chacma baboon named Kees.[71] Le Vaillant was French, but his memoirs of his expeditions were enormously popular across Europe; they were quickly translated into seven languages and became a standard reference for both naturalists and popular writers.[72] His stories about Kees, scattered throughout his travel memoirs, were of particular interest to Britons when the memoirs were published in English in the 1790s.[73] Through these stories, we witness Le Vaillant self-consciously constructing his own identity within a framework of Rousseauian ideals of masculine independence from the stultifying constraints of European society.[74] Paradoxically, the pet—which might seem the most extreme example of civilization and domestication—becomes in this portrayal the crucial symbol of Le Vaillant's liberty. But this construction relies upon a complicated relationship between man and animal, combining characteristics of friendship, service, and slavery. The instability of Kees's role in the narrative reveals the unresolved tensions in Le Vaillant's attitudes toward race and imperial power.

Le Vaillant does not specify in his memoirs how he acquired Kees, introducing him only as "an animal which rendered me . . . essential service, whose diverting presence has suspended, nay, even dissipated a number of disagreeable and painful reflections; and whose provident instinct seemed to outstrip the efforts of my reason" (*Travels*, 1:140). This introduction embodies the multiple views of Kees that Le Vaillant presents, as entertainer, assistant, and reminder of the limits of human ability. Initially, Le Vaillant emphasizes Kees's role as invaluable servant. Whenever he encountered fruits or roots that he and his human servants did not recognize, he says, he offered them to Kees to try. Those that Kees rejected they assumed were poisonous or at least unsavory (1:141).[75] He also relied on Kees as a sentry, noting that the baboon alerted the camp with his cries and gestures even before the dogs noticed any danger; in fact, Le Vaillant came to fear that the dogs had become so reliant on Kees that they would be of no use to him if Kees died (1:143–44). In Le Vaillant's telling, then, Kees was essential to his safety.

Yet the explorer also makes clear from the beginning his strong emotional attachment to the baboon, and the pleasure he obtained from the animal's company; if Kees was a useful servant, it is obvious that Le Vaillant valued him much more for the amusement he provided. Although Kees and Le Vaillant lived in camps rather than sharing a traditional domestic space, the baboon still enjoyed much of the same special treatment given to other pets. He shared Le Vaillant's food, including milk and brandy, a privilege reserved for Kees alone among the many animals in Le Vaillant's entourage. The two ate their meals side by side: "indeed, I had spoiled him, never eating or drinking any thing but he came in for his share; and if I seemed inclined to forget him, he ever took care to remind me, either by munching, or giving me a touch with his paw" (1:272). After devoting several pages to the monkey's behavior, Le Vaillant concludes with a half apology for the extensive description but insists on the emotional value he found in Kees: "I have hung on these details with pleasure. If they do not tend to the instruction of mankind, they are interesting to a soul like mine, delighted with the most simple objects; recollecting with pleasure my innocent pastimes, my days of peace, and only moments of my life in which I was sensible of the whole value of my existence" (1:148–49).[76] The comment also reflects Le Vaillant's consistent self-presentation as a man much more at home in "savage" Africa, far from other Europeans, than in "civilized" Europe or the Dutch colony on the Cape of Good Hope. His friendship with the baboon thus also serves as an implicit reprimand to the hypocrisy and bad behavior of Europeans, and he frequently attacks the practices of the colonial farmers. Throughout his memoirs, he returns to the idea of the baboon as a simple soul that is more loyal and trustworthy than many humans.

Le Vaillant believed that his affection for the baboon was reciprocated. When he was at the Cape, staying with Willem Boers (a friend and an official with the Dutch East India Company), Kees was there as well: "There could be no festivity unless he was of the party. Boers and myself were accustomed to visit him every day after dinner, and to take with us some of our dessert. Naturally gentle and caressing, he was free from the faults of his species, and had rather imbibed those of his master. He seemed also to have acquired some virtues, for he was sensible to kindness and civilities, and always eager to repay them" (New Travels, 1:16). Kees apparently hated only one human, a man who had pretended in jest to strike Le Vaillant in Kees's presence. From that moment on, Kees felt a "profound hatred" for the man, and attacked him whenever he came near (New Travels, 1:17). Kees's one act of violence, then, became the ultimate demonstration of loyalty to his friend. Hence also Kees's indication of desire to come on a hunting trip: "what gambols! what expressions of joy! would he manifest on seeing me prepare to depart: he would leap upon and caress me, seeming by his looks and actions to entreat me to hasten my departure, and express his gratitude for admitting him to be of my party" (*Travels*, 1:141).

Le Vaillant's attribution of human feelings of affection and hatred to Kees are part of his ongoing anthropomorphism; Le Vaillant evaluated Kees's morals as if they were human morals, and read into his behavior evidence of Kees's thoughts and feelings. One evening, sharing his brandy with Kees as usual, Le Vaillant played a trick on the baboon and lit the brandy on fire just as Kees was about to drink it, terrifying the animal. Although Le Vaillant tried to calm him down, he says, Kees was "too angry to be easily pacified, [so] he left us and went to his bed" (*Travels*, 1:273). Le Vaillant often remarks that Kees was a terrible glutton and a thief; left alone, he would steal food and then run away to avoid punishment, "though he used constantly to return about tea time, with an air of innocence" (*Travels*, 1:329). Both Le Vaillant and his African followers tried but failed to "reform him" (*Travels*, 1:148). A particularly telling example appears in Le Vaillant's lengthy explanation of his ongoing battle with Kees over who would get the eggs laid by their only hen. One day, discovering nothing but empty shells, he concluded that Kees had been stealing the eggs and decided to watch carefully the next day. Kees initially ran toward the hen when her cries alerted him that she had laid an egg; then, "stopped unexpectedly by my presence, he affected a careless attitude, balanced himself awhile on his hind-legs, and, winking his eyes with a silly air, walked backward and forward several times before me; in short, he employed all his cunning to take off my attention, and deceive me respecting his design. These hypocritical manœuvres confirmed me in my suspicions" (*New Travels*, 2:52).

Le Vaillant thus presents Kees as an animal who shared his moral sense and was aware that stealing is wrong, even to the point of attempting to conceal his misdeeds. Le Vaillant also believed that Kees was aware of his own superiority over other animals, particularly the dogs, which he would hit if they came near his food. Most notably, if Kees became tired while trekking with Le Vaillant, he would climb onto the back of one of the dogs, which would then carry him for hours: "He had acquired over the rest of my pack an ascendency, which was, doubtless, owing to the superiority of his instinct; for with animals as among men, it is frequently observable, that address subdues strength" (*Travels*, 1:146). Le Vaillant was thus comfortable assuming broad similarities between human and baboon, a comfort also notable in his reliance on Kees as a taster. "Animals of the monkey kind," he says in this context, "seem distinguished from others by their similarity to the human species" (*Travels*, 1:141).

Indeed, Le Vaillant comes close to suggesting that Kees was more human than animal. Kees recognized and feared other chacma baboons, perhaps, Le Vaillant thought, out of fear that they would force him to rejoin them; upon seeing a member of his own species, "he ran with the utmost precipitation, and trembling with fear, seemed to implore our protection" (*Travels*, 1:147). At the same time that Le Vaillant ascribes human emotions and loyalty to Kees, however, he also emphasizes that Kees was a wild baboon. He explicitly differentiates their relationship from the feminized pet keeping of Europe when he writes about watching a troop of chacma baboons. Their raucous behavior was extremely entertaining, he says, but "an idea of these monkeys should not be formed from those who languish out a wearisome life of slavery in Europe; perishing by the kindness of the ladies, or poisoned by their ill-bestowed dainties. The heaviness of our atmosphere deadens their natural gaiety, and they frequently play anticks more from a dread of punishment, than from real humour" (*Travels*, 1:384). Here we see the conflict inherent in Le Vaillant's presentation of Kees. Kees is clearly different from the other baboons, yet Le Vaillant also implicitly includes him in the distinction between animals in the wild and those experiencing "a wearisome life of slavery in Europe." This emphasis on Kees's liberty is part of a repeated distinction that Le Vaillant makes between domesticated and "savage" animals. He even admits that, given sufficient opportunity, Kees might have run away:

> It is not with the ape as with other domestic animals, whom instinct attaches to the soil where they have been brought up, and who always return to it; whether, like the dog, they have a greater fondness for the master than the house; or, like the cat, more attachment to the house than the master. The ape, on the contrary, indocile and refractory, incapable of lasting remembrance either of the one or of the other, retains a propensity to independence, which the mildest

education, or the tenderest treatment cannot correct. (*New Travels*, 1:18–19)

Kees is thus both a pet and a wild animal, for Le Vaillant, and part of his appeal lies in the difference between this baboon and the pets languishing in the salons of European ladies. Just as Le Vaillant portrays Kees as a welcome contrast to the duplicity and hypocrisy of Europeans, so he emphasizes Kees's freedom from the domestic "slavery" of being a European pet.

Although Le Vaillant stresses the independence of Kees's nature, and the freedom with which the two share meals, he also makes it clear that their relationship is unequal, and that he is the dominant partner. He frequently seems to amuse himself at Kees's expense with tricks that seem downright cruel, such as setting Kees's brandy on fire. On another occasion, after killing a large poisonous snake that he knew Kees feared, Le Vaillant tied the corpse to Kees's tail, apparently much amused by the "leaps and anticks [by which] poor *Kees* expressed his fright and impatience" (*Travels*, 2:313–14). Kees's role as servant thus appears not only in the useful services he renders, such as testing food or locating water, but also in the treatment to which he must submit. Le Vaillant frequently refers to beating Kees for perceived infractions. For instance, Kees was gifted at discovering a type of root that both he and the author enjoyed, and he would wolf them down in order to avoid sharing them with Le Vaillant. If he could not eat them quickly enough, he would try hiding them; "on these occasions I usually favoured him with a good box on the ear, which never failed to make him give up the residue, when he was obliged to content himself with the part I chose to allot him." But, Le Vaillant continues, "*Kees* never entertained any animosity, though I sometimes gave him occasion, by keeping the whole, to reflect on that greedy selfishness of which he had set the example" (*Travels*, 1:144).

Le Vaillant thus presents himself unquestionably as the master in this relationship, while Kees is the subordinate who is unable to keep from sinning but who never holds a grudge when punished. Later in the same passage, referring to Kees's ability to open up baskets of provisions and steal their contents, Le Vaillant writes, "I sometimes beat him myself for his mischievous tricks." Yet he acknowledges that beating Kees does nothing to reform him, attributing his intransigence to his incurably "perverse disposition." This reflection leads Le Vaillant to an extended discussion of animal character:

> An ape is in reality an intractable animal. It is true he possesses such powers of instinct, that he can often render important services; as mine did to me on more than one occasion. But if he has invention, and becomes useful, it is always for himself and not for you that he labours. Certainly no animal upon earth is so dexterous, or perhaps so artful. Yet if you attempt to employ him in any exercise or any work which is not voluntary, you will find him dull and awkward. It is only by dint of hunger and blows that you can discipline him to certain tricks: and of some faults that are natural to him it is impossible to correct him. He is lascivious, gluttonous, thievish, revengeful, and passionate; and if he has not the vice of lying, the savages say it is because he does not choose to talk. (*Travels*, 1:148)

Just as Le Vaillant shifts between presenting Kees as pet and wild animal, here the baboon plays the role of both highly anthropomorphized servant—repeating tropes found in theatrical comedy—and typical monkey, whose behavior is explicable in terms of species characteristics. In both cases, Le Vaillant remains the dominant figure. He alone has the power to reward and to punish, an authority he sees as his right by virtue of his natural superiority. The great chain of being and the hierarchy of master and servant unite here.

Le Vaillant's position becomes most visible when he discusses his ultimate expression of power: his ability to keep Kees in chains. In the egg-theft incident, for example, he says that the only way to keep Kees from stealing would be to chain him up all morning (*Travels*, 2:53–54). On another occasion, after Kees has run away and been recaptured only with great difficulty, he writes, "I had a great mind to tie him up, but that would have deprived me of the amusement his tricks afforded, I therefore pardoned him" (*Travels*, 1:330). Although Le Vaillant is concerned to emphasize Kees's freedom, and contrasts life in Africa with the miserable "slavery" of monkeys in Europe, exercising his power remains an option. His equation of power with the ability to chain and enslave is seen most clearly when he does confine Kees in a cage during their stay with Willem Boers. Le Vaillant explains that he was motivated only by affection for the animal and by fear that Kees, whose "fame had gained him such numerous friends," would be stolen by sailors, by the Dutch residents of the Cape, "or even by the slaves who would have roasted and eaten him." Yet Kees suffered greatly in confinement, Le Vaillant admits, although he was caged in "a very handsome kennel." Such melancholy was inevitable, Le Vaillant says, in a remarkable reflection that moves from the specificity of Kees's situation to broader issues of rights and back again. "Is there any enjoyment without liberty? My ape, besides, possessed a degree of moral perception, which rendered his situation more painful than it would have been to a vulgar ape. The moment he saw me, he flew the whole length of his chain to meet me; and it was me in particular that he seemed to upbraid with ingratitude for his captivity. . . . I hardened myself against his importunities, for I loved him too well to give him an imprudent testimony of my affection."

But Le Vaillant also admits that Kees might have escaped of his own accord, lured by "a sentiment still stronger than friendship"—lust for a female baboon.

> Kees had still his virginity, and had never known pleasure. The slightest spark would have set him on fire; an instant was sufficient to convert him into a libertine; and if, with all the indiscretion and vivacity of youth, he had once lusted after a female, his master would soon have been forgotten; he would have followed her into the depth of the woods, and would never more have returned. Extremely fond of Kees, and unable to prevail on myself to lose him, I used my power as a despot, and chained him up that I might dispose of him as I liked. (*New Travels*, 1:17–19)

This passage, though intended to be humorous, is also laced with politics, power, and gender. Kees had greater "moral perception" than "a vulgar ape" and thus suffered more in confinement. Yet the slightest exposure to the allure of the female sex would have undone all the bonds between man and baboon. Le Vaillant's affection for Kees made him use his "power as a despot" and keep the baboon for his own pleasure, but he implies that this decision was also for Kees's own good. Left to his own devices, he would revert to a mere animal, enslaved by lust, and thus his enslavement to Le Vaillant becomes, paradoxically, beneficial. Moreover, Le Vaillant remarks, once they set out on another expedition together, Kees became both happier and a better companion: while chained, he "had apparently lost his gaiety, but . . . from the moment he regained his liberty gave himself up to sports and anticks that were extremely diverting" (*New Travels*, 1:173). Even here, though, Le Vaillant emphasizes the entertainment he gained from the animal's "liberty"—a liberty, of course, over which Le Vaillant had complete control.

Le Vaillant's complex and internally contradictory depiction of Kees—as friend, servant, and slave—leads to a final reflection on how their relationship reveals broader assumptions about race and servitude. As noted above, Le Vaillant traveled with a large entourage of "Hottentots," and he devoted much of his memoirs to describing them and the many different groups of Africans he encountered on his expeditions.[77] Some scholars see him as a progenitor of modern anthropology, particularly because of his unusually sympathetic portrayals of native Africans and his willingness to condemn Dutch colonialism.[78] Indeed, he self-consciously contrasts his opinions with common European views of Africans, emphasizing the areas in which Hottentot behavior and culture had been misrepresented. But his portrayal of Kees, when juxtaposed with his discussions of human Africans, highlights the ways in which his ideas about animals and racial difference interacted with and influenced each other, adding complexity to both.

Le Vaillant's initial presentation of Kees as a valuable servant establishes the connection from the outset, implicitly putting Kees in the same category as the human members of his entourage. Moreover, Le Vaillant's relationship with "his" Hottentots reflects some of the same ambiguities that mark his relationship with Kees, who was both free and Le Vaillant's property. His human traveling companions were not slaves; Le Vaillant discusses paying his men with tobacco and brandy, and there are many occasions in his memoirs when various members of his group leave or threaten to leave the expedition, exercising their freedom to depart at will.[79] Moreover, he is effusive in his praise of one Hottentot in particular, Klaas, for his bravery, loyalty, and good sense (*Travels*, 1:249–53). Yet Klaas is always commended for his behavior toward Le Vaillant and contrasted with other Hottentots, just as Kees is distinguished from other baboons. One episode in particular highlights the peculiarity of the parallel Klaas/Kees portrayal. Le Vaillant is visiting Willem Boers, and he is pleased when Klaas arrives unexpectedly one evening, bearing gifts of exotic bird and insect specimens that he has prepared himself. Le Vaillant is clearly touched by this demonstration of affection and skill, which

reveals Klaas's awareness of the Frenchman's interests as well as a talent
for preservation. But Le Vaillant makes a telling shift from human to animal: "This unexpected visit on the part of Klaas brought to my recollec-
tion another companion of my travels; a good friend, a faithful servant,
extremely cunning, fruitful in expedients in times of emergency, and by
whom I had more than once been extricated from embarrassments"
(*New Travels*, 1:15–16). This "friend" and "servant" is, of course, Kees, and
Le Vaillant's easy shift from his friendship with Klaas to that with the
baboon reflects the way in which they were connected in his mind
through a network of utility and companionship. Discussions of Kees
frequently lead to discussions of the Hottentots in Le Vaillant's memoirs, partly because he sees them as sharing advantages and disadvan-
tages. His remark about the ill effects of "slavery" on European monkeys
echoes his many references to the depredations wrought on Hottentot
culture by the Dutch colonists.[80] In both cases, he sees humans and animals as innocent victims of a European culture that exploits and destroys
unthinkingly.

But he also presents both as suffering from many of the same vices.
Kees and the Hottentots allegedly shared an immoderate pleasure in
drinking brandy; Le Vaillant complains about the Hottentots' habitual
drunkenness (he blames the Dutch for introducing them to the habit),
and he describes Kees literally inhaling brandy in his enthusiasm for it
(*Travels*, 1:274). Le Vaillant also refers to his concern about theft on the
part of both Hottentots and baboon. In one case, for instance, he chose
to "pardon" Kees for stealing his dinner, reasoning that "perhaps he had
before been punished when he did not deserve it, for his character of
thievery made me ready enough to believe what was said to his disadvan-
tage; possibly I might be wrong in this, as it was far from unlikely that my
Hottentots had sometimes committed what poor Kees bore the blame
of" (*Travels*, 1:330). Le Vaillant's reflection on the baboon's faults—as an
animal who works only for himself, who will do only what he chooses to
do, and who refrains from lying only because "the savages say . . . he does
not choose to talk"—takes on a new meaning in this context, implicitly
linking the baboon to the "savages" themselves.[81]

Another telling incident involves Kees's discovering a badly needed
source of fresh water while on an expedition. Le Vaillant uses the occasion to reflect on the relationship between instinct and civilization: "I
shall more than once have occasion to mention circumstances in which

the instinct of animals has been particularly serviceable, having extricated me from several dilemmas. I do not doubt but man has received from his Creator the same advantages, which insensible depravity has made him loose [*sic*]; for the greater distance the savage is from us, the nearer he approaches to a state of nature" (*Travels*, 2:311). For Le Vaillant, then, civilization involved the loss of important talents, but the lesson he learned also implies a tight link between the "savage"—in this case the Hottentot—and the nonhuman primate. In this view, the talents of the Hottentots are akin to those of the baboon, and Le Vaillant's friendship with Klaas becomes an even clearer mirror of his friendship with Kees. In both cases, the relationship is one of superior and inferior, even if Le Vaillant was unusual in his recognition of the abilities of both man and beast. His comment that Kees had acquired both the faults and the virtues of "his master" (*New Travels*, 1:16) echoes his presentation of Klaas as unique; Klaas's extreme loyalty to Le Vaillant becomes a sign of his superiority over other Hottentots. Klaas alone is brave and sensible, while Le Vaillant depicts the other Hottentots as generally innocent but also cowardly and prone to gluttony and theft. Like Kees, Klaas has imbibed some of the virtues of his master. If Kees is both pet and servant, Klaas becomes both servant and pet. The anthropomorphism that leads Le Vaillant to ascribe human vices and virtues to Kees finds its counterpart in a theriomorphism that defines Klaas and the other Hottentots as more animalistic than Europeans, for better and for worse.

Le Vaillant's portrayal of Kees is worth unpacking in detail because it reflects many of the complexities in eighteenth-century thinking about pets, race, and the boundaries between humans and animals. Le Vaillant was deeply engaged with contemporary debates about race and natural history, frequently referring to what he saw as errors in Buffon and in the works of other travel writers; he was also a serious naturalist who had published a major work on ornithology and who planned to produce another on quadrupeds.[82] At the same time, his stories about Kees were amusing, and thus he mixed scholarship with pleasure in a way that appealed to a wide audience in Europe. Le Vaillant was unusual in publishing such extensive meditations on one exotic pet, but many others also struggled with the questions implicitly raised by his portrayal of the baboon. Kees was both friend and servant; he was wild and domesticated; he was at liberty but could be beaten and chained; he had unique talents but also vices that were ostensibly inherent in his animal character. All of these contradictions were also present in contemporary portrayals of non-Europeans and were reflected in debates about the pros and cons of civilization and the morality of human slavery. Just as Kees led Le Vaillant to ask whether there could be "any enjoyment without liberty," so too did thinking about animals, particularly pets, influence debates about relationships of power among human beings.

~ ~ ~

It may seem obvious that Le Vaillant's relationship with Kees would be particularly fraught, given apes' and monkeys' physical resemblance to humans and the significant role of Africa in European thinking about race and civilization. Yet the questions Kees raised about the relationship between friendship and freedom—whether domination could ever be compatible with true kindness and affection—also emerged in thinking about animals much closer to home. One of the most ubiquitous eighteenth-century pets, the songbird, inspired similar debate about these issues. As we saw in chapter 1, songbirds were easily obtained, inexpensive (or free if captured in the wild), and particularly appealing in an era before recorded music. Visual evidence suggests that even the very poorest households frequently kept birds; their cages took up little room and they could be fed crumbs left over from family meals.

Because birds needed to be caged, however, their natural love of liberty was particularly visible, and the problem of imprisonment was especially obvious. The metaphor of the cage as a prison dominated depictions of pet birds; the question, then, was whether a bird might grow to enjoy its own imprisonment. Naturalists agreed that birds, along with other animals, were radically transformed under human control, and that this control could have negative effects. Like many others, Oliver Goldsmith was enthusiastic in his praise of wild birds as models of domestic bliss, thanks to their apparent monogamy, their careful attention to their young, and the songs that seemed to indicate the pleasure they took in their family life.[83] He believed that all of these glories were lost when birds were removed from the wild. For instance, he insisted that "we must not take our idea of the conjugal fidelity of birds from observing the poultry in our yards, whose freedom is abridged, and whose manners are totally corrupted by slavery. We must look for it in our fields and our forests, where nature continues in unadulterated simplicity."[84] As he did when discussing other animals, Goldsmith insisted on the corrupting effects of avian slavery. Le Vaillant himself expressed a similar view, less poetically, when he compared the behavior of the single rooster and hen accompanying him on his travels with that of domesticated poultry. The male defended the chicks when they were attacked by dogs, something, he said, that cocks in "poultry yards" containing multiple males and hens would never do. He theorized that the cock's knowledge that the chicks were his own gave him an "attachment" to the hen and chicks that would be missing in the typical barnyard (*New Travels*, 3:291–92). The slavery of domestication, in this view, destroyed avian monogamy and, along with it, a sense of moral responsibility to the family.

If raising poultry for human consumption had a moral cost, caging songbirds was even more problematic, since their usefulness to humans was limited to the pleasures of entertainment. Not surprisingly, Goldsmith criticized the practice: "the music of every bird in captivity produces no very pleasing sensation; it is but the mirth of a little animal insensible of its unfortunate situation."[85] William Fordyce Mavor agreed that no feeling person could take pleasure in an entertainment dependent upon such suffering: "the music of any bird in captivity must necessarily generate somewhat of a disagreeable sensation in the breast of humanity. . . . Imprisonment and slavery, as they lessen the joys, so they detract from the powers of pleasing, in every thing that has life."[86] But people continued to respond to nature's beauty by trying to turn it into property. According to Buffon's *Natural History of Birds*, for example, the linnet had a lovely red color and beautiful song in its natural state. Yet, "endowed with such talent, it could not long preserve its freedom; and still less, when nursed in the bosom of slavery, could it retain unsullied the beauties of its original purity." In captivity, linnets' color faded, and "the free and varied modulations which spring and love inspire" were replaced with "the strained notes of a harsh music, which they repeat but imperfectly, and which has neither the beauties of art nor the charms of nature."[87] Georg Christian Raff agreed, arguing that one should go into nature to hear the nightingale sing, rather than cage it; "you will perceive what a difference between the sad warble of these captives, and the sublime strains of the natives of the woods! Nature constantly baulks the rich when they would purchase her for money."[88] At best, the song of a caged bird revealed its "insensibility"; at worst, it was a "sad warble" mourning lost liberty.

Caging birds might also have appeared to be a particularly egregious example of animal slavery because of the way they were treated. "Stopping" songbirds—confining them for a month in extremely small, hot quarters to induce premature molting—was believed to create louder, better singers, and many owners and sellers employed the method even as others condemned the practice.[89] Some people also blinded their birds in the belief that it would improve their singing.[90] But even less overtly cruel and painful practices might reduce birds to slaves. It was common to train songbirds to use a pulley system to haul up water to their cage "in a little Ivory Bucket made for that Purpose."[91] Raff disapproved of such amusements, complaining that the goldfinch was sometimes "made a galley-slave of, so as to be compelled to draw up its water in a little bucket, and carry its hemp seed along a bridge." "There might be some excuse for this slavery," he suggested, if, like horses and oxen, their labor benefited humans, "but for no end, but merely from caprice, to torment these poor birds, born to liberty and pleasure, . . . this is too much! some people must take great delight in exercising that authority over others which is exercised over them; and, in that case, they deserve a heavier yoke than that which has been imposed on them."[92] For Raff, this was abuse of power for its own sake, with unhappy humans taking out their resentment on weaker animals—not merely amusement but sadism.

Another particularly vivid criticism of the torments faced by pet birds appears in a story by Edward Kendall, told from the point of view of a sparrow. Captured in the wild and sold to a boy, the sparrow describes the horrors of the imprisonment he must face: first his wings were to be clipped, then "I was to have a chain upon my leg—beside these, it was debated, whether it would not be practicable to teach me the fine art of drawing a bucket, and getting my food out of a box."[93] Fortunately for the bird, a sympathetic girl frees him before these plans are implemented, but the parallels between the life laid out for him and that of a workhouse prisoner or slave would have been obvious to Kendall's readers.

Children's stories like Kendall's, with their explicitly moralizing agendas, were among the most critical of caging birds, and they freely employed the metaphors of imprisonment and slavery. One tale condemned a boy who goes from destroying birds' nests to saving one, merely in order to "enjoy the cruel pleasure of confining in a cage the poor birds, who had the same natural right to liberty with himself." When a cat finds and eats the birds, the boy is enraged, although the narrator observes that the cat was simply following its instinct, while the boy had ruined the lives of many birds without any such excuse.[94] In another story, a child captures a swallow, only to have his mother insist that he let it go: "confinement of any kind is against its nature. . . . Be generous, then, my boy, and restore it to liberty."[95] Cautionary tales against stealing nests or chicks frequently drew on the vision of avian domestic bliss in works like Goldsmith's to paint devastating pictures of parents returning to find their "infants" stolen; the destruction of families was also one of the key motifs in abolitionist literature, so a political dimension was always present in such narratives.[96] In one story, a mother tells her horrified son that his entire family is about to be arrested and imprisoned, before explaining that she was only pointing out to him how the linnet he proposed to keep in a cage would feel. She warns him to "forget not that birds, as well as every other creature, were created to enjoy their liberty."[97] Anna Laetitia Barbauld's "Epitaph on a Green-Finch" takes these ideas to their logical conclusion, in verse redolent of the terrors of African enslavement. It tells the story of Richard Acanthis, who was stolen from his parents by "a two-legged monster without feathers." Although he loved freedom, he was kept in a prison where he lamented his fate by singing. At last, "His indignant spirit broke the prison / His body could not." The poem leaves the reader with the hope that Richard now lives again in "some humble Elysium, / Beyond the reach of man, / The tyrant of this / Lower world."[98]

Works such as these reacted against an instrumental view of the animal world as created for human use and enjoyment, emphasizing instead the feelings of nonhuman beings. Like the humane advocates, these children's authors drew on the theory of sympathy. Just as sympathy with other humans was seen as fostering moral character, so these writers hoped to encourage the moral development of children through sympathy with the nonhuman world. The parallels between human and animal slavery were not mere metaphors. Tyranny and slavery might not be exclusive to the world of adult humans, and that fact created the opportunity to train children to reject such behavior in all its forms. This is not to say that these writers were all abolitionists, or even that they consciously considered the implications when they condemned animal slavery. It is, however, important to recognize that the language of slavery presented the treatment of animals in especially powerful moral terms.

But not everyone agreed that imprisoning birds was wrong. While some saw the song of a captive bird as the plaintive note of a prisoner mourning his loss of freedom, others saw birdsong as evidence that the caged animal was content. Despite his remarks about the ill effects of "slavery" on linnets, Buffon himself suggested that some birds would thrive in captivity. He noted that the bullfinch, for instance, was "susceptible of personal attachment, which is strong and durable. Some have been known, after escaping from the volery and living a whole year in the woods, to recognize the voice of the mistress, and return, to forsake her no more. Others have died of melancholy, on being removed from the first object of their attachment."[99] Nor was strong "personal attachment" essential for a bird to be happy in captivity, according to some naturalists. Goldfinches, Eleazar Albin assured his readers, were "of a mild and gentle Nature," and after being captured would soon become "in love with their Imprisonment."[100] Samuel Ward agreed that goldfinches were "soon reconciled to their imprisonment in a cage; and after they have remained there a considerable time, they become so fond of it, that if the door of the cage is opened they will not fly away, but usually fly to the cage for shelter if any thing should terrify them."[101] Similarly, Thomas Pennant reported that the redpoll was "as chearful five minutes after it is caught as a *French* prisoner is said to be after the same short captivity."[102] Some birds, in other words, seemed to be born for imprisonment.

Pennant's joke about the resemblance between redpolls and French prisoners points to another distinction common to British discussions of pet birds. For many writers, there was an essential difference between British birds, which both deserved and required liberty, and foreign birds, particularly canaries. By the mid-eighteenth century, most canaries were actually bred in Germany, but they were still seen as exotic tropical birds from the warm climes of the Canary Islands.[103] Compare Edward Kendall's eponymous canary bird to the miserably imprisoned (English) sparrow in his earlier tale. The canary escapes from his cage but soon longs for his mistress and the joys of "domestic life" with her; fortunately, he is taken in by another woman, who turns out to be a friend of his owner.[104] Sarah Trimmer warned her young readers against stealing nests or taking English birds from the wild, but she found a captive canary perfectly acceptable: "He never knew what Liberty was, and therefore does not want it; nay, if you should turn him loose, he would starve and die."[105] Another of Trimmer's tales began with the usual admonitions against caging birds (in this case redbreasts): "Should you like to be always shut in a little room," a mother asks her son, "and think it sufficient if you were supplied with victuals and drink? . . . Though these animals are inferior to you, there is no doubt but they are capable of enjoyments similar to these; and it must be a dreadful life for a poor bird to be shut up in a cage." But the mother also insists that canaries are a "very different" case. "By keeping them in a cage, I do them a kindness. I consider them as little foreigners who claim my hospitality." They would die outside in England's cold climate; "and there is another particular which would greatly distress them were they to be turned loose, which is, the ridicule and contempt they would be exposed to from other birds."[106] Another work for children created a fictional dialogue between a caged canary and a wild linnet; when the linnet criticizes the canary for foolishly singing in celebration of his imprisonment, the canary replies that he does "feel the loss of liberty" but that he is grateful to have escaped the "hardship, famine, and danger" that the linnet faces. "Allow me then, without reproach, to express my thankfulness to God in songs of praise; to bear my lot with chearful resignation."[107]

Caged songbirds did not serve any useful purpose, and the language of the cage as prison was ubiquitous. If domesticated poultry were so deeply corrupted by their slavery to humans that they lost the sexual morality of their natural state, as Goldsmith suggested, at least such slavery benefited humans directly by producing food. It was much more difficult to explain or justify the enslavement of songbirds, whose only purpose was to provide pleasure for their captors. Many commentators thus condemned the practice. But for others, the "imprisonment" of birds—at least "foreign" birds—could be rationalized and the cage transformed into a refuge. Such views drew two major distinctions between justifiable and unjustifiable imprisonment. First, British birds needed and deserved liberty, while "foreign" canaries were born for captivity, and would in fact die if left to their own devices. Imprisonment was good for them. Second, humans had a moral responsibility to helpless birds. In this reading, the cage ceased to be a prison and instead became a sanctuary, protecting its inhabitant from the dangerous world outside. Both of these arguments sought to mitigate the evils of animal slavery by transforming the relationship to one of benevolent paternalism.

≈   ≈   ≈

Chimpanzees and canaries might seem to have little in common, but both inspired soul-searching about the relationship between humans and animals. The discovery of the anthropoid apes threatened to overturn long-standing assumptions about humanity's distinct place in the natural world. In response to this threat, most writers responded by doubling down on humanity's special status. What made humans unique was reason, they argued. By stressing that dogs or elephants had more "sagacity" than apes, and by using the possibility of domestication as their evidence, these writers hoped to answer the threat to human superiority. Yet insisting on human uniqueness came with its own hazards. With its focus on universal human reason, this view raised questions about the justice of one race of humans dominating another at precisely the moment when Britain was benefiting most from imperial conquest and the slave trade. Moreover, domestication itself was widely viewed as animal slavery. Recognizing human domination over animals and human reliance on that domination, writers employed the concept of slavery because it encapsulated the notions of power, property, and economic benefit that they saw as inherent in human-animal relations. In considering both humans and animals, Britons were thus forced to weigh the values of universal human reason and liberty against the political and economic benefits of slavery. Abolitionism was one response to this dilemma in the human realm, and abolitionism itself helped spur the creation of the humane movement. But applying abolitionist concepts to the animal world raised new difficulties. Slavery was evil, harming both slave and master, but it was also seemingly indispensable.

Faced with this dilemma, eighteenth-century commentators developed a variety of theories to justify or improve the condition of animals (just as the problem of human slavery fostered a variety of responses). They urged readers to remember that with great power came great responsibility, and that dominion over the animal world did not justify tyranny. But, as frequently happened with discussions of human slavery, debates about animal slavery could not allow compassion to lead to total abolition; human survival depended on the slavery of domestication. In this context, pet keeping was especially problematic, for it could be seen as the least justifiable form of animal slavery. In Le Vaillant's stories of his baboon, Kees, and in the very different situation of caged songbirds, we can see individuals working through the conflicts between the values of liberty and the pleasures of owning an animal. The argument that loss of liberty was ultimately beneficial to animals, like the argument that human slavery benefited slaves by exposing them to Christianity and civilization, represents one major response to this problem. Yet this argument had extremely limited application. Perhaps it could be used to justify caging a canary, but it could not apply even to all birds, much less to other animals, like dogs. The idea of the servile, fawning, and useless lapdog—the antithesis of the useful working dog—dominated much of the discourse around pet keeping, drawing not on the metaphor of happy imprisonment but on the corrupting effects of both civilization and slavery. It is to this discourse that we now turn.

3 ～ FASHIONING THE PET

In 1786, James Wicksteed published a print entitled *Animated Nature, or Lady en Famille* (fig. 11). The print shows a young woman dressed in an exaggerated version of the high fashion of the day: a large hat with ostrich plumes, an enormous muff, and a "cork rump" artificially extending her rear. Were this the only content, the image would be unremarkable; satires on fashionable dress were especially common in the 1770s and 1780s. But this woman is not only wearing fashionable clothes; she is also literally wearing her pets. A lapdog sits on the muff, gazing with interest at a kitten sleeping on the woman's shoulder. Meanwhile, a monkey pops out of the muff, lunging at a squirrel perched on top of the cork rump as the squirrel draws back in alarm. The woman herself seems oblivious to the furious activity around her, effectively treating the pets as accessories similar to the hat and muff. The print thus visually links the animals to the extremes of fashion represented in her outfit. At the same time, the title gestures ironically to images of women out promenading with their families—here replaced by a different sort of "family"—so it also insists on the fact that the animals are living beings (as does their extremely "animated" behavior). The woman's apparent inability to distinguish between pets and husband or children becomes another element of the critique, drawing on common perceptions that fashionable women neglected their spouses and household responsibilities to pursue the whirl of the beau monde. The chaotic collection of animals represents both the familial disorder allegedly inevitable when women pursue fashion, and fashion itself.

Wicksteed's print points to the complex network of associations produced by the potent combination of fashion and pet keeping. On one level, as his image suggests, pets were fashionable consumer goods. Trends in pet keeping rose and fell over the course of the eighteenth century, just like fashions in clothing. Some of these trends are well known: the court of William and Mary brought the pug from the Netherlands into England, where it was briefly in vogue before losing its cachet. In other cases, animals that had been confined to a wealthy few were now accessible to new owners, as in the case of canaries and parrots, as well as monkeys and other small primates. The new pet shops, discussed in chapter I, made exotic species from around the world, particularly a huge variety of birds, easier to obtain. Deliberate breeding for sale could trigger changes in fashion: the massive growth in the availability of European-bred canaries transformed a rare and prestigious bird into the fairly common pet that it is today, its place as exotic status symbol filled by rarer, larger, and more colorful birds from Africa, Asia, and the Americas. Squirrels are another example of a pet that became extremely popular in the eighteenth century, although they were obviously not exotic imports; instead, their appeal lay in the growing popularity of pet keeping and their attractive characteristics as small, clever, and fairly clean animals. Like other consumer goods, then, pets reflected the changing tastes of British consumers.

The eighteenth century is now widely recognized as the period in which fashion in the modern sense emerged—when styles began to change rapidly and arbitrarily.[1] Many of the factors that made fashion possible, such as growing disposable incomes and the concomitant expansion of available consumer goods, also made possible the expansion of the number and variety of pets. Both pets and fashion raised concerns among critics anxiously surveying what they perceived as growing signs of luxury

Fig. 11 *Animated Nature, or Lady en Famille*, 1786.
Etching, hand-colored, 27.7 × 17.8 cm.
Courtesy of the Lewis Walpole Library, Yale
University, 786.02.20.02.

ANIMATED NATURE

OR LADY EN FAMILLE

Febru...1795 by J Wakstid No 20 Henrietta St ...London

and decadence in their society. In many ways, pets embodied the worst excesses of fashionable consumption, thanks to the fact that in addition to their status as fashionable goods, they were also literally consumers, draining resources that many people believed could be better used to alleviate human poverty. Anxieties about pets were bound up with eighteenth-century concerns about the effects of luxury on British society, and with a cultural memory that identified the decadence of the Roman Empire with its inevitable decline. For some critics, such decadence was even a sign that Britain would soon follow in Rome's footsteps, its wealth and power merely the precursors to a fall.[2]

Many eighteenth-century observers thus noticed the growing presence of pets in their society and were horrified by what they considered a perversion of humans' relationship to the natural world. Traditional attitudes toward animals were rooted in a Christian tradition that saw animals as created for human use. When Adam named the animals, the thinking went, the naming was a process of establishing dominion over them, and many people preserved this belief in the fundamental meaning of the human-animal relationship. Indeed, a central question for naturalists was what purpose some animals, such as large predators, could serve; if an animal preyed upon humans, or, like many insects, seemed simply to be annoying, then why did such a creature exist? Some searched for answers in the great chain of being: insect pests might exist in order to provide food for higher-order animals that were useful to people. Alternatively, it could be argued that the dazzling variety of animals was meant to instill wonder at God's creativity and the beauty of the natural world. Whatever the reasons for the existence of individual species, however, this tradition took a utilitarian view of the animal kingdom. But its proponents did not necessarily condone abuse or wanton destruction. If God had created animals for human uses, then it was up to humans to be benevolent stewards, caring for God's creation and not abusing the power he had bestowed upon them.[3] From this perspective, pets were problematic, because they seemed to be animals that not only lacked a clear purpose but were being misused by humans. Thus, as a moralizing tale for children put it, a deep affection for pets "is more than ridiculous . . . ; it is really sinful."[4] These views fit well with anxieties about fashion; after all, the problem with fashion was that it transformed the utilitarian matter of clothing and household furnishings into an exercise in useless self-indulgence. Under such circumstances, pets became powerful vehicles for social satire, representing wasteful luxury as well as a deeper perversion of God's will.

Such views of pets are particularly visible in discussions about that most useful animal, the first to be domesticated by humans: the dog. By 1700 there was already an established tradition of classifying dogs according to their uses for humans. John Caius, for instance, in his sixteenth-century taxonomy of dogs, defined different breeds according to the tasks they performed. Thus his basic categories were "a gentle kind serving the game, a homely kind apt for sundry necessary uses, or a currish kind, meete for many toies."[5] Edward Topsell, writing in the early seventeenth century, struggled to find a reason for the existence of lapdogs, since he assumed that all dogs must serve some human purpose. He speculated that the "Spaniel gentle" must have been designed to comfort people with stomach problems: "we find that these litle dogs are good to asswage the sicknes of the stomack, being oftentimes thereunto applied as a plaster preservative, or borne in the bosom of the diseased and weake person; which effect is performed by their moderate heat."[6]

Later naturalists continued the tradition of identifying breeds with specific purposes. Dogs in general were often described (along with horses) as the noblest of species, thanks to their loyalty, bravery, and utility; Buffon's encomium on the dog as "the most intelligent of all known quadrupedes, and the acknowledged friend of mankind" was quoted by Oliver Goldsmith and virtually all of his followers. "The dog," Buffon continued, "independant [sic] of the beauty of his form, his vivacity, force, and swiftness, is possessed of all those internal qualifications that can conciliate the affections of man."[7] But Goldsmith noted that the number of dog breeds in England seemed to be constantly and rapidly increasing. For him, the explanation for these changes lay in British wealth and trade: "this must happen in a country so open by commerce to all others, and where wealth is apt to produce capricious predilection. Here the ugliest and the most useless of their kinds will be entertained merely for their singularity; and, being imported only to be looked at, they will lose even that small degree of sagacity which they possessed in their natural climates. From this importation of foreign useless dogs, our own native breed is, I am informed, greatly degenerated."[8] The language here is significant. Goldsmith tied the multiplication of breeds directly to the "degeneration" of "native" dogs. Moreover, the idea that wealth generates "capricious predilection," the disapproving commentary on "singularity" for its own sake, and concerns about the ill effects of foreign imports all echo contemporary complaints against fashion in clothing and other forms of consumption. And because women were seen as the primary generators and consumers of fashion, the criticism contains gendered implications.

In his own classification of dogs, Goldsmith summarized Caius's divisions and then added a few more, as well as "a variety of lap-dogs, which, as they are perfectly useless, may be considered as unworthy of a name." Goldsmith did not hide his disdain for such "useless" dogs; the "harlequin," for instance, "is not much unlike the small Dane, being a useless animal, somewhat between an Italian grey-hound and a Dutch mastiff." Summing up the category of lapdogs, he said merely that there are "various kinds and sizes . . . but the more aukward and extraordinary they are, the more they are prized."[9] Naturalists like Goldsmith could dismiss "useless" dogs in part because such creatures simply did not fit their conceptions of what dogs were. Dogs were valuable and interesting because of their special role as assistants to humans, so a dog that did not work was in some sense not a real dog at all. Thus Samuel Johnson, in his dictionary, defined "dog" as "a domestic animal remarkably various in his species. . . . The larger sort are used as a guard; the less for sports."[10] Although Johnson famously kept pet cats, which he loved very much, his definition of "dog" did not allow for nonworking, useless animals.

We can thus begin to see how anxieties about pet keeping overlapped with those regarding fashionable dress. Both practices represented useless self-indulgence, and both were examples of an unnatural perversion of something originally good for society. Both pets and fashion were strongly associated with women, who were, like their pets, frequently portrayed as useless consumers. Like indulgence in fashionable clothing, pet keeping also revealed hopelessly misguided priorities, as pet owners lavished resources and affection on animals rather than on the human beings who were the rightful objects of human love. But if commentators attacked both pets and fashion for being useless, pets were also problematic, paradoxically, because they served *too* many functions. Pets were both family members and property, embodying a confusion of categories that resonated with many contemporary concerns about the effects of fashion on British society. Worst of all was the way in which pets seemed to violate the very notion of a distinction between human and animal. Coddled and cuddled in the arms of their mistresses, pets usurped the role of human lovers and children. As they blurred the boundary between human and animal, pets implied a dangerous permeability in other ostensibly clear borders of gender and social status. At the same time, pets were particularly convenient for satirists because they made it possible to reduce the anxieties surrounding gender and fashion to a manageable, even laughable, size. If a lapdog represented the greatest danger to British society, perhaps civilization was not at such risk after all.

This chapter explores the ways in which writers and artists dealt with the network of ideas around fashion, gender, status, and pet keeping. It focuses on three major themes: the modish woman, who was naturally attracted to fashion even as fashion itself was fundamentally unnatural; the old maid, herself a perversion of the already corrupt excesses of fashionable femininity; and fashionable men, who violated gender norms simply by virtue of taking an interest in things defined as inherently feminine. Finally, Francis Coventry's popular "it-narrative," *The History of Pompey the Little*, brings together in a single text all of the interests and anxieties discussed in this chapter. The result is a satire that is both complex and radically unstable.

≈   ≈   ≈

Women's fascination with both fashion and pet keeping was widely described in the eighteenth century as innate and as visible from a very early age. Girls' attraction to pets was naturalized in both words and images. As children's literature developed into a popular genre, it became commonplace to talk about boys' natural tendency to torture animals—for instance, by stealing birds' nests or by pulling the wings off flies—while girls were portrayed as trying to rescue the unhappy victims of such crimes. Their affection for animals often took the form of a desire to keep pets, just as adult women were predominantly presented as pet owners. But if girls' love of pets was naturalized, it was also problematic. Girls' tendencies to smother their pets with affection was frequently noted. A first-person narrative by a cat, for instance, remarked that her owner was a good girl but that she failed to observe the difference between their species:

> One time she took it into her head that I should catch cold if I went out of the house without something being put on me to keep me warm; so she made me a cloak with a hood to it, and little bags for my ears. This I was to be wrapped up in every time I stirred; and though I am well convinced she did not mean to hurt me, yet she

very frequently did, as she pulled my ears to put them into their hoods, as she called them; besides, she tied the cloak much tighter round my throat and body than was agreeable. Then she made a spencer for me; and my fore paws were to be crammed into little sleeves every time she chose I should wear it, which was also a very uneasy job. At last my patience was so tired out by these trouble-some dresses, that I kicked and scratched every time she attempted to put them on; this she thought necessary to punish; and, making a little rod, she whipped me heartily.[11]

The girl's mother intervenes, reprimanding her for "teizing" the cat "by dressing her up so foolishly, and contrary to nature."[12] The critiques involved in such scenes relied on a belief that girls' natural love for animals might all too easily be distorted by a failure to distinguish between animals and humans. In the case of the child and her cat, the girl's natural affection for her pet becomes something "contrary to nature." Nor is it coincidental that the incident revolves around an attempt to dress the cat in human clothes. The girl begins with a concern that the cat might "catch cold," but she moves from there to putting the animal in a spencer, a fashionable gar-ment that she does not justify on utilitarian grounds. Of course, from the cat's point of view, all clothes are superfluous, but it is notable that the child's interest in caring for her pet is rapidly transformed into an interest in clothes for their own sake. The girl's affection for her cat is perverted first into a misguided attempt to care for it and then into behavior that is unrelated to the pet's well-being, as she moves further away from an awareness of the distinction between human and animal.

The causal chain developed in this anecdote, from love of pets, to love of fashion, to the transgression of boundaries, is at the root of many rep-resentations of adult women, where the potent triad of pets, fashion, and female sexuality formed the basis of a great deal of anxiety. Yet an unset-tling painting by Joseph Wright of Derby, *Dressing the Kitten* (ca. 1768–70), reveals how even images of childhood might participate in such concerns in a much more overt way than in the children's story (fig. 12).

Fig. 12 Joseph Wright of Derby, *Dressing the Kitten*, ca. 1768–70. Oil on canvas, 90.8 × 72.4 cm. Kenwood House, London. © English Heritage.

The painting works simultaneously as a sentimental fancy picture and as a more disturbing commentary on femininity, fashion, and pet keeping.[13] At first glance, it appears to be simply a charming depiction of two girls at play.[14] They hold an obviously distressed kitten on its hind legs, imitating a human stance, as they dress it up in a doll's clothes. Their neglected doll lies to the side, both presenting the source of their inspiration and creating a visual parallel with the girls themselves. They wear costumes rather than ordinary clothes,[15] and along with the proximity of the doll, the painting implies that they, too, are primarily ornamental playthings. The presence of the kitten alludes to the supposed closeness between women and nature while at the same time drawing attention to the artificiality of fashion.

But the image goes much further. The doll, lying prone with its skirts lifted, and the intimate nighttime setting add an element of precocious sexuality that bespeaks male anxiety about feminine fashion. Moreover, by placing a living pet in the picture, Wright draws the viewer's attention to the girls' exercise of power. With the phallic tail pointing between its legs, the kitten is gendered male, and the act of dressing it up becomes a transgression not only of species but of gender boundaries. As both the kitten and the girl on the left look directly at the viewer, the human and animal are equated, while the child's gaze violates the decorum expected of girls, who were trained to look demurely down and away. The image thus implies that this behavior reduces girls to animals. A second visual parallel between human and animal emerges in the bonnet they have put on the kitten, which is echoed in the feathers in their own hair, each illuminated in the light of the candle. By showing the discomfort of the kitten, Wright draws attention to how unnatural the girls' behavior is; but through the series of visual echoes between the humans and the animal, he also suggests that women's connection to fashion is natural, even as fashion itself is fundamentally unnatural and potentially dangerous. The painting implies the erotic potential of feminine engagement with both pets and fashion, a potential made explicit in images of adult women.[16]

Young girls were often portrayed with kittens, an association between felines and femininity that, as we will see, was adopted and transformed in images of old maids. Yet the quintessential animal involved in critiques of feminine fashion was the lapdog; Jodi Wyett notes that by defining a lapdog as "a little dog, fondled by ladies in the lap," Samuel Johnson made female ownership an essential characteristic of the dog.[17] There was, of course, a long tradition of using lapdogs and other pets to satirize women, but lapdogs were particularly useful for eighteenth-century satirists' purposes because so many of their characteristics mirrored contemporary criticisms of fashionable dress. Like fashionable dress, for instance, lapdogs were seen as continental imports. Many owners also clipped their dogs' hair into fashionable French styles, and the French "dog barber" was himself satirized.[18] Simply by being so small, lapdogs embodied the worst characteristic of pets: they were utterly useless as working dogs. Just as fashionable dress, often perceived as uncomfortable and impractical, seemed to defeat the very purpose of clothing, lapdogs seemed to undermine the original rationale for keeping a dog. In satires, the defining characteristics of lapdogs—their ridiculous size and bizarre hairstyles—served to point up the distortions and impracticality of women's fashionable dress The dogs thus served as stand-ins for their mistresses even as they were themselves presented as fashionable accessories, a slippage made possible because of their position on the border between the human and nonhuman world, and between living creatures and property.

Fashionable dress was the site of enormous social anxiety in the eighteenth century. The very idea of rapid and arbitrary change in apparel was a new phenomenon, one that seemed to embody the worst elements of consumer excess. It was by definition irrational, and it encouraged wasteful expense because fashionable women abandoned clothes that were still perfectly wearable. Moreover, because women frequently gave their relatively new castoffs to servants, moralists fretted that it was becoming impossible to distinguish the lady from her maid. The garments themselves, with large hoops or padding, embroidery, and other decoration, seemed to require an excess of material. And because many fashions originated in France, a country with which Britain was at war for much of the century, fashionable dress represented a slavish obedience to foreign despotism at a time when national pride was most needed. Women's insistence on following fashion despite all of these obvious problems seemed to demonstrate an unnatural abandonment of domestic duty, in every sense of the word.[19]

It was therefore no coincidence that the fashions that seemed most extravagant in their size and the way they distorted the figure came in for the most criticism in caricatures.[20] Very large headdresses that formed an inverted pyramid were one French import worthy of notice.[21] In *Lady All-Top* (1776), for instance, a woman is portrayed wearing an enormous headdress that doubles her height (fig. 13). Her prominent beauty patches and extremely low décolletage add to the effect of a woman distorting her natural looks and drawing attention to her own artificiality. Tucked under her right arm is a tiny lapdog, its diminutive size emphasizing the ridiculously unnatural proportions of the woman's attire. At the same time, the dog functions as a fashionable accessory.

But headdresses were not the only targets of satire. Along with an enormous head came an extremely small waist, achieved by tightly lacing the stays.[22] In *Tight Lacing, or Fashion Before Ease*, a young woman in obvious pain clings to a bedpost as her husband, a maidservant, and a black boy in a turban line up to pull; the man clutches the laces of her stays, the maid pulls on his waist, and the boy on the maid's.[23] A lapdog with a bow collar sits on the bed, yapping at the proceedings; along with the elements of chinoiserie (a Chinese vase, a parasol) and the other ornate decorations, the dog functions as one more example of the woman's commitment to useless fashion. In the right foreground, a monkey sits pointing at an open book on the floor, whose pages read "Fashions / Victim a Satire." The print presents the woman as a literal slave to fashion, an idea highlighted by the presence of the exotic monkey and the black servant, both of whom would have suggested ongoing debates about slavery and debasement.[24]

The towering headdresses combined women's own hair with artificial additions, and tight lacing used mechanical means to restructure the body. Padding, another element of the fashionable wardrobe, also seemed to turn women into caricatures of their natural shapes. The false rump made of cork or other padding was a particularly obvious target, since it not only altered the body but did so in a way that seemed blatantly sexual.[25] Many prints satirized these rumps by portraying them as convenient seats for pets. *The Cork Rump or Chloe's Cushion*, for instance, presents a rather surprised-looking lapdog perched on such a rump (fig. 14). Its ridiculous appearance, with its frizzled hair and large bow, plays up the foolishness of the young woman's entire outfit.[26]

Another print, ostensibly responding to such satires, insists that the cork rump is "the Support of Life"; it shows a woman, buoyed up by her rump, floating serenely next to a capsized boat as others drown around her.[27] In her lap sits a tiny dog, its diminutive size especially noticeable in contrast to her towering headdress. A later pair of prints, *The Bum Shop* and *The Supplemental Magazine*, portrays women in shops that sell, respec-

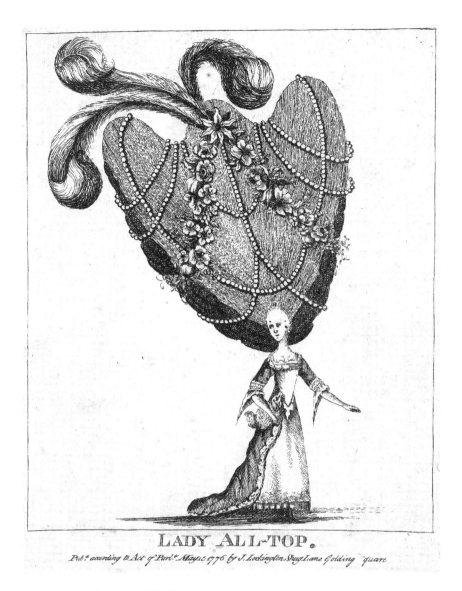

LADY ALL-TOP.

Pub.d according to Act of Parl.t May 15 1776 by J. Lockington Snug Lane Golding Square

Fig. 13 Lady All-Top. 1776. Etching, 194 × 155
mm. Courtesy of the Lewis Walpole Library,
Yale University, 776.05.15.01.

tively, false rumps and pads to enhance the bosom. In each image, a small
dog is prominent in the foreground, shaved so that its bottom half is
naked while its forequarters are covered in luxuriant hair.[28] In *The Bum
Shop*, the shaved bottom half and luxuriant top half of the dog, which

Fig. 14   *The Cork Rump or Chloe's Cushion*, 1776.
Etching and aquatint, 162 × 122 mm. Courtesy
of the Lewis Walpole Library, Yale University,
776.11.19.01.

stands on its hind legs, create an inverted image of the outlandish shapes
on the women, with their projecting bottoms. The parody is even more
straightforward in *The Supplemental Magazine*, in which the dog's hair
creates a false "bosom" to match those of the ladies in the shop (fig. 15).

A *Nest for Puppies, or the Fashionable Bosom* (1786) takes these themes to
their logical conclusion by showing a woman with a litter of tiny dogs
tucked into her well-padded front.[29] In all of these images, of course, the
dogs are employed to satirize female dress, parodying the women or highlighting the inanity of their fashion choices. But they are also pets, and

THE SUPPLEMENTAL MAGAZINE.

Fig. 15 *The Supplemental Magazine,* 1786. Etching
and engraving with stipple, hand-colored, 27.8
× 43.3 cm. Courtesy of the Lewis Walpole
Library, Yale University, 786.01.01.05+.

thus another example of the fashionable consumer items they are mirroring. Just as outlandish headdresses, inordinately tight stays, and padded
bosoms or bottoms were frequently portrayed together as part of a single
image of "fashion," so were lapdogs presented as an element of the fashionable wardrobe. Women's treatment of animals as accessories functioned as one more piece of evidence in the general condemnation of
fashion's unnatural effects.

False bosoms and rumps also exercised a particular fascination because
they so blatantly drew attention to female sexuality. If women were deliberately drawing men's eyes toward unnaturally large breasts and buttocks,
then this might be proof that fashionable women were whores in their
hearts, if not in practice. And an image like *A Nest for Puppies* suggests how
pets, especially lapdogs, might feed anxieties about female sexuality in

other ways. Fashionable dress revealed women's poor judgment and sexual incontinence; it was easy to read their relationships with their pets as another dangerous form of "immoderate love."[30] One corollary to the association between women and pets was the accusation that female pet owners lavished affection on their animals rather than devoting themselves to men, the more suitable objects of their attraction. At one extreme, critics presented animals as sexual surrogates; Thomas O'Brien MacMahon's screed against lapdogs is a particularly vivid (and vicious) example:

> The Virginal Mistress of our animal is a Maiden, not so much through choice as *compulsion*. She *longs* for the *most intimate familiarities*, with those of the other sex; but, to gratify her pride, vanity, or through some other selfish, though, *as yet*, more powerful consideration, she will not, at present, admit them. However, as she *really* loves the amorous intercourse, and that *vehemently*, she is desirous of indulging a representation, however faint, of dalliances, which so constantly occupy her thoughts, and which it is not yet her convenience to enjoy in reality.
>
> The caresses then she lavishes on her dog, be it male or female, frequently bring to her mind, and entertain there, thoughts of the *embraces of men*, which her polluted imagination is for ever painting in colours the most *rapturously engaging*. Hence the delight she takes in incessantly giving to, and receiving from, a beast, embraces which would certainly be extremely disgusting to her, did she not *connect* them in her *imagination* with ideas of the *lustful pleasures*, that have engrossed so many of her faculties.[31]

For MacMahon, lapdogs were the conduit for the expression of women's most animalistic desires. His comment that women used both male and female dogs as sexual substitutes points to the extreme anxiety underlying his complaint: young, unmarried women, he feared, not only violated the decorum expected of virgins but became voracious sexual predators, willing to defy the bounds of species as well as gender.

MacMahon's was a particularly explicit critique, but the ideas he presented were implicit in many depictions of women's relationships with their animals. If God intended animals for human use, then this was one of the most egregious cases of misuse. Thus Jonas Hanway, explaining his disapproval of a young woman who wept at the loss of her pet monkey, noted a crucial difference between the treatment of working animals and of pets: "a man of taste and sentiment may look on a country girl milking a cow, with great complacency: his pleasure may be proportioned to her figure, and beauty, because she is acting in character, and performing a useful office. But the same person will be SHOCK'D to see a lady ravishing a dog with her caresses; and the more distinguished she is for her personal charms, the more shocking she will appear."[32] Hanway thus links feminine attractiveness to the proper relationship with animals; "ravishing" a dog, with its suggestion of bestiality and rape, is a disturbing transgression of both gender and species boundaries. No man could be attracted to a woman who failed to observe those boundaries.

MacMahon and Hanway were deadly serious in their condemnations of feminine pet love, but their concerns found expression in a wide variety of venues. These ideas made possible the many satirical stories and poems about women who loved their animals more than they loved men; their alleged tendency to lavish affection on inappropriate objects served as a demonstration of their frivolity and general inability to understand what really mattered in life.[33] One particularly common trope was listing the objects of women's affections, yoking together man and beast, living thing and inanimate object, to represent the instability of feminine affection. Alexander Pope's mock epic *The Rape of the Lock* is a particularly famous example, juxtaposing dead husbands and dead lapdogs ("Not louder Shrieks to pitying Heav'n are cast, / When Husbands or when Lap-dogs breathe their last"; "Sooner let Earth, Air, Sea, to Chaos fall, / Men, Monkies, Lap-dogs, Parrots, perish all!").[34] But Pope's deployment of the lapdog in this way is just one among many similar examples. In a letter from "Peter Puzzle" to the *Guardian* in 1713, Peter describes a dream in which he witnesses a woman's love transfer rapidly from object to object, including fans, cards, a puppet show, and shoes: "These were driven off at last by a Lap-dog, who was succeeded by a *Guiney* Pig, a Squirril and a Monky. I my self, to my no small Joy, brought up the Rear of these worthy Favourites."[35] In the stage play *The Coquet* (1718), a fashionable woman presents a similar train of affection: "I was passionately in Love with my Parrot, now I begin to grow tir'd of that, I'd give any thing in the World for a Monkey; and if that should be so unfortunate as to grow out of Favour, as who can answer for one's Heart, perhaps, the next thing I should take a Fancy to, may be either a Lap-Dog, or a Husband, or a piece of China."[36] Mary Jones alluded directly to Pope in her 1755 "Elegy on a Favourite Dog, Suppos'd to Be Poison'd": "Now die, O Tabby! all ye fav'rites fall! / Dogs, parrots, squirrels, monkeys, beaus and all."[37] These dizzying lists reveal the fickleness of female affection, which might seize upon any object in a worrisome failure to distinguish kind from kind. China, puppet shows, pets, husbands—in these portrayals, women see them all as equally deserving of love. In such a world, the characteristic position of pets on the border between human and animal makes them particularly dangerous, precisely because women might so easily slip from human love to dog love. At the same time, however, by emphasizing the extremes of feminine affection, the satires move the anxiety into an area where it seems more humorous than threatening: it is one thing if a woman were to fall in love with the wrong man, but a woman who might fall in love with her lapdog becomes simply ludicrous.

Because it was a common trope to suggest that women foolishly loved their pets rather than seeking out sensible men, it was a short step in visual satires to use pets as stand-ins for the humans being satirized. Such images could both imply women's inane affection for animals and also demonstrate the kind of man who might attract such women. In *The Canonical Beau, or Mars in the Dumps*, a handsome young curate sits on a sofa, adoring women crowded around him as he sips tea and nibbles on a biscuit (fig. 16). Directly in front of him, a pug sits up and begs. At the far end of the sofa sits a disgruntled man with a wooden leg, presumably a disabled soldier; a much larger dog rests its head on his lap and looks up at him. Here the two dogs mirror the scene playing out as the women ignore the more deserving, and more manly, soldier, just as the small and useless pug contrasts with the much larger working dog.

A later print, *The Polite Alderman, Advancing to Future Happiness*, shows an obese man asking an equally fat woman to dance with him at the Lord Mayor's Ball.[38] She wears a hat that resembles an inverted colander and holds an enormous muff; out of the muff peeks a tiny lapdog, emphasizing her commitment to fashion while highlighting the awkwardness of both woman and outfit. Her pleased, even smug smile is echoed in an almost identical facial expression on the dog. The alderman is also accompanied by a dog, whose stout body mirrors his master's proportions and whose panting suggests that the alderman will not be a figure of grace on the dance floor. The pets in these images are, by virtue of their status as pets, the objects of feminine affection; at the same time, they enact the

Fig. 16 John Goldar, after John Collet, *The Canonical Beau, or Mars in the Dumps,* 1768. Etching and engraving, 33.1 × 37.3 cm. Courtesy of the Lewis Walpole Library, Yale University, 768.10.25.01+.

human relationships in the scenes. In these prints, then, not only are the pets both human and animal, but so are their mistresses. If the dogs cross the boundary into human territory, these women also get reduced to the status of animals.[39] The men they find attractive are exactly the men they deserve.

The satirical prints thus demonstrate the variety of ways in which artists engaged with the connections between femininity, pets, fashion, and sexuality. A more formal portrait reveals how one image might explore these intersections in all their complexity. Joshua Reynolds's 1771 painting *Mrs. Abington as Miss Prue* (fig. 17) shows the actress Frances Abington in the character of Miss Prue from William Congreve's comedy *Love for Love*; Mrs. Abington had played the character with great success in the 1769–70 season.[40] In the play, Miss Prue is a naïve girl whose father summons her from the country to London, where she is nearly seduced by a foolish rake named Tattle. Tattle teaches her to say no when she means yes, as he assures her all fashionable women do, and she is rescued from ruin only by the timely appearance of her nurse. Having come so close, however, she is now insatiable, demanding of her father that he find her a man to marry. When her horrified father threatens to beat her, she insists again on a husband, "and if you won't get me one, I'll get one for my self: I'll marry our *Robbin*, the Butler."[41] She is thus willing to violate not only gender roles but class boundaries as well, in the service of her newly awakened animal appetites. Miss Prue appears in only a few scenes in the play, but Mrs. Abington's portrayal obviously made a mark.

In the portrait, Mrs. Abington leans against the back of a chair, looking directly at the viewer. She holds her thumb to her parted lips in what Martin Postle calls "a gesture which is at once vulgar and sexually charged."[42] Her direct stare and gesture suggest both the character's coarseness and her sexual desire, characteristics that would be reinforced through the audience's awareness of Mrs. Abington's reputation as a courtesan and a social climber. Her dress, with its pink silk and elaborate ruffles, would also remind viewers of Mrs. Abington's enormous influence on eighteenth-century fashions[43] as well as the character's desire to be seen as fashionable.

Seated on the chair with her, looking through its back, is a shock dog, the kind most associated with frivolously fashionable ladies (as with Belinda's Shock in *The Rape of the Lock*). The scene is not taken directly from the script, nor does the play mention Miss Prue's having a dog. Crucially, however, the dog in the painting echoes and reinforces all the connotations in the presentation of Mrs. Abington herself. Because the lapdog is the quintessentially fashionable pet, on one level it functions as another fashionable accessory, like the Chippendale chair, the lace, and Abington's bracelets and earrings.[44] On another level, by having the dog echo the sitter's pose—sharing the seat and looking directly at the viewer—Reynolds invites comparisons between the two, suggesting both empty-headedness and animal instinct. The dog reminds the viewer of Miss Prue's (and Mrs. Abington's) animalistic desires, the dominance of sensuality over reason. The dog thus functions as a commentary on the

Fig. 17   Joshua Reynolds, *Mrs. Abington as Miss*
Prue in "Love for Love" by William Congreve, 1771.
Oil on canvas, 76.8 × 63.8 cm. Yale Center for
British Art, Paul Mellon Collection.

character of Miss Prue and on Mrs. Abington's character as well; both demonstrate the feminine weakness of an obsession with fashion, and the supposedly immoral effects of such an obsession on women. Miss Prue's fate, in which her desire to be fashionable leads to her seduction, is a particularly blatant demonstration of the ways in which fashion ostensibly made women vulnerable to a loss of reputation; here, the image visually emphasizes the connections between fashion and lost reputation.

Yet, as Joseph Musser has noted, Reynolds's portrait is also an affectionate one, and Mrs. Abington was one of his favorite subjects as well as a friend.[45] Although on one level the painting can be read as a satirical commentary on the relationships among women, sex, and fashion, with the dog embodying and reinforcing those connections, the painting is more than that. The presence of the dog, linking the female sitter to the natural world, also naturalizes those other connections, suggesting that women are inherently drawn to both fashion and men; they literally cannot help themselves. The dog is a fluffy, pretty thing, like its mistress: to criticize Mrs. Abington for her behavior would be as ridiculous as criticizing a dog for behaving like a dog. In this way, the portrait combines innocence with suggestiveness, a combination that helps to explain its appeal.

~   ~   ~

If Reynolds's portrait can be seen at least in part as a celebration of feminine fashion and sexuality, *A New Fashion'd Head Dress for Young Misses of Three Score and Ten* is a grotesque parody of that kind of celebration (fig. 18). In this print from 1777, an aged hag sits in front of her dressing room toilette, wearing heavy pearl earrings that draw attention to her deeply wrinkled face, almost bald head, and hooked nose. She admires herself in the mirror as two grinning male servants hoist an enormous headdress, outfitted with a huge nosegay and six ostrich plumes, onto her head. The delicate lace and elaborate ornamentation of her dress contrast with the heavily veined hand she uses to caress the spaniel she holds in her lap. Literalizing the sexual connotations associated with women and their lapdogs, the spaniel paws at her bosom, licking her neck in a lampoon of masculine lasciviousness. What could be lightheartedly erotic in depictions of young women here becomes a revolting display of the basest animal desire.

A New Fashion'd Head Dress reveals how ideas about pets and female sexuality were employed to present old maids as unnatural perversions of

A New fashion'd HEAD-DRESS for Young Misses of Three score and Ten.

Printed for JOHN BOWLES, N°13 in Cornhill

Fig. 18 Philip Dawe, *A New Fashion'd Head Dress for Young Misses of Three Score and Ten,* 1777. Mezzotint, 354 × 252 mm. Courtesy of the Lewis Walpole Library, Yale University, 777.05.08.01+.

true femininity. Since pets were associated with female sexual desire, they were useful symbols in attacks on old maids, who were universally blamed for their failure to marry. Thus the love of pets, which in younger women could be presented as problematic but natural, became in old maids a demonstration of their failure to achieve full womanhood, and depictions of old maids and their pets moved much closer to explicit suggestions of bestiality. A 1710 issue of the *Tatler*, for instance, remarked that members of the "Fair Sex . . . are by Nature very much formed for Affection and Dalliance," and "that when by too obstinate a Cruelty, or any other means, they have disappointed themselves of the proper Objects of Love, as Husbands, or Children, such Virgins have exactly at such a Year grown fond of Lap-dogs, Parrots, or other Animals."[46] The problem, implies the *Tatler*, is not with pet keeping in itself but with old maids' failure to observe the proper boundaries of the human-animal relationship, a result of the fact that they "have disappointed themselves" of love and happiness. Their loneliness is a result of their own failure of self-discipline.

The connection between women's love of pets and their misplaced sexual desires also appeared in the many images satirizing the courtship of old maids. In *The Happy Consultation, or Modern Match*, a father is arranging a match between his son and an elderly spinster, Miss Biddy Lackit (fig. 19). Playing upon the traditional disapproval of highly disparate ages in marriages and drawing on contemporary anxieties about mercenary matches, the image heightens the satire by surrounding Biddy with pets, including a cockatoo, a monkey, a spaniel, and a squirrel (kept inside a tiny house). Biddy, whose age is only heightened by the frills and flounces of her dress, is implied to have kept pets as a substitute for men. The print thus visually presents the argument of the *Tatler* that pets stand in for "proper Objects of Love." The artist also implies parallels between the bridegroom and the simian, as the monkey sticks its leg through Biddy's muff in a none too subtle visual innuendo.

In a later print, *The Elopement!*, a middle-aged, extremely homely woman sneaks out of her house with a soldier.[47] She carries a parakeet and a lapdog and holds a chain to which is attached a monkey, walking behind her. Her maid carries a cage containing two cats. Once again, the monkey serves as ironic commentary on the scene, for it, too, wears a military uniform. If the monkey is a visual metaphor, however, it is also a pet, and the animals also place the woman firmly in the realm of desperate old maids who have relied on animals as sexual surrogates. Not knowing how to direct her affections properly, the woman is allowing herself to be led into this match by the ridiculous-looking soldier. Poor judgment is on display again in *The Disagreeable Intrusion, or Irish Fortune Hunter Detected*.[48] In this print, an ugly but fashionably dressed old woman reacts in horror as bailiffs rush in to arrest her suitor in the middle of his marriage proposal. Rather than feel grateful for her narrow escape from the swindler, she

Fig. 19   James Roberts, *The Happy Consultation,
or Modern Match*, 1769. Etching and engraving,
250 × 354 mm. The British Museum.

attempts to sic her tiny lapdog on her rescuers, displaying her inability to
judge the character of both men and beasts: she is equally unable to recognize an unworthy lover and a useless dog.

All of these images rely for their impact on the relationship between
pet keeping and the old maid's more fundamental failure in judgment.
The sexual overtones associated with pets and women are only heightened in scenes revealing the pathetic men on whom they pin their hopes;
men, monkeys, and lapdogs are all, as Pope suggested, potentially inter-
changeable. But whereas Pope was referring to the fanciful and fickle
desires of a young woman, the satires become even more bitter when
directed at old maids. Here, there is no hope for redemption, no prospect

of reform and true love: these women have irrevocably doomed them-selves to a life of isolation with only the poorest facsimile of real affection in their lives.

Pets thus implied the old maid's failure of discipline as well: failure to discipline her household, and failure to discipline her own affections. These shortcomings, in turn, reflected her ultimate failure: the failure to achieve full womanhood by fulfilling her natural destiny as wife and mother. These ideas help explain the dominance of the cat in the iconog-raphy of the old maid, in contrast to the presence of lapdogs in depictions of youthful femininity. Cats had, of course, long been associated with women; where dogs were gendered male, cats were usually gendered female, whatever their actual sex.[49] The *Spectator* drew on Simonides to compare women and cats (as well as other animals), and in *Pompey the Lit-tle*, Francis Coventry recalled the comparison, noting that "it holds exactly between ancient Cats and ancient Maids; which I suppose is the Reason why Ladies of that Character are never without a grave Mouser in their Houses, and generally at their Elbows."[50] Whereas lapdogs were associ-ated with fashion and frivolous luxury, cats carried opposing connota-tions—cats were the pets of poverty rather than of luxury.[51] Moreover, while (working) dogs were applauded for their noble qualities of service, sagacity, and loyalty, cats were almost universally decried as treacherous, vicious, and self-interested.[52] These qualities were easily transferred to their elderly mistresses, neatly fitting in with stereotypes of women's ten-dency toward backbiting gossip, and applying particularly well to women who lived without the companionship of men. The associations of kittens with young girls added another element to the stereotype; if kittens were appropriate pets for young girls, then adult women with adult cats revealed a failure to accept the realities of growing up. All the problems associated with pet-keeping women in general—the misplaced affection, the waste of resources on useless animals—could apply to old maids and their cats, but without even the excuse (increasingly powerful over the course of the century) that women were receiving real affection from their animals in return. Cats became not merely the quintessential pets of old maids but metonyms for old maids themselves, even as cats increas-ingly appeared in other kinds of images as indicators of domestic content-ment and coziness.[53]

We can see the metonymic association of cats and old maids in the 1789 print *Old Maids at a Cat's Funeral* (fig. 20).[54] Eleven old women form a proces-

Fig. 20 John Pettit, *Old Maids at a Cat's Funeral*, 1789. Etching with stipple, hand-colored, 29 × 60.5 cm. Courtesy of the Lewis Walpole Library, Yale University, 789.04.10.01.

sion, the two at the front holding a small coffin with a cat's face pictured on it; behind them walks Grimalkin's distraught mistress, clutching a handkerchief. Each of the other women in the train holds her own cat, adorned with a large black ribbon. The caption notes the absence of lovers, parents, and friends of these women, who save all their kisses for "Happy Grimalkin!" The mock elegiac tone here both emphasizes the women's loneliness and employs sexual innuendo to question their virginal status by implying that they are too much in love with their animals. Similarly, other prints satirize old maids' relationships with their cats by suggesting that the pet of an elderly mistress would join her in fending off unwanted suitors.[55]

But not all such satires relied on sexual innuendo; many simply employed cats to suggest the meager resources, poor taste, and restricted social life of old maids. So strong did the association become that referring to gossipy old women as "cats" became a common idiom; Hester Lynch Piozzi, for example, discussing her life as a widow in Bath, visiting, drinking tea, and playing cards, referred to herself as "a Bath cat."[56] *The Old Maids Occasional Concert* presents a group of elderly women crowded around a stage, hands clasped in pleasure, as they listen to a concert performed by cats.[57] The satire thus takes aim at both their love of cats and their lack of musical taste, a theme that emerges in many satirical prints in which animals howl or bark along with old women attempting to make music.[58] The stereotype of the old maid thus combined the personality problems implied by "cattiness" with the role real cats played in society as cheap and disposable objects of ridicule or torment. These ideas come together in Thomas Rowlandson's iconographic image of an old maid, *Virginia* (fig. 21). It shows a warty, wrinkled, and extremely ugly old woman's head, with a distinct five o'clock shadow and strongly masculine features. From her right ear hangs a large earring with several items attached: a paper labeled "cure for cholic," a bag labeled "Cats Meat," a heavy padlock, a sheet labeled "Anonymous Letters," a watch on a chain, and a pincushion. By the left side of her face sits a large parrot, which appears to be speaking into her ear; its crest deliberately mirrors the woman's frilly cap, and its face is very similar to her own, thus drawing attention to the association of women with pet parrots as well as empty gossip. Below the parrot dangle a box labeled "snuff," another box of "corn plasters," and a heavy bag labeled "Winnings at Quadrille." Beneath the woman's head, two cats sit on a large volume labeled "Scan[dal]. Mag," with a bowl of milk or cream before them. The cats become the woman's mascots, both her defining possessions and the representation of her false priorities.[59]

The visual and literary identification of old maids with cats is in some ways ironic, given that the most famous pet cats of the century, both real and fictional—Isaac Bickerstaff's cat, Samuel Johnson's Hodge, Christopher Smart's Jeoffry—belonged to men. But the identification became a powerful one because of the ways in which negative connotations of pets, cats, and old women fed into one another. For men, cats could simply represent companionship, even if others did not always fully approve.[60] But cats and women made for a dangerous, even a potentially deadly, combination, as in a particularly gruesome story from *Tommy Trimmer's Historical Account, of Beasts, Reptiles, Fishes, Birds*. A natural history book for children, it remarked that a cat could be "a useful domestick in a family, . . . when kept in [its] proper place," but warned against too much affection. For an example of what to avoid, the book presented "a maiden lady at the west end of the town" who made the mistake of sharing her meals with her pet cat. She "always gave it the first piece she cut; but one day she accidentily put the first piece she cut into her own plate; the offended animal immediately flew upon her, and before any person could come to her assistance, both her eyes were torn out, and her face a shocking spec-

Fig. 21 Thomas Rowlandson, *Virginia*, 1800. Etching, hand-colored. Courtesy of the Lewis Walpole Library, Yale University, 800.08.15.03+.

VIRGINIA

tacle, and they were obliged to kill the cat, before they could get it from off her throat, and she expired in the most excruciating pain; thus died a lady, who if she had kept the cat in its proper place, [it] might have been of service, and she preserved her life for many years."[61] The idea of the cat as "domestick," useful "in its proper place," highlights the transgression the woman has committed here. By pampering her pet rather than treating it as a mere servant, she encourages the cat's rebellion. And like all rebellions, this one is vicious and bloody. In "Tommy Trimmer's" story, then, we see a warning not just against the dangers of keeping cats as pets but against the foolhardiness of old maids, who can manage neither their affections nor their "domesticks."

~ ~ ~

Women young and old were the subjects of enormous anxiety focused on the nexus of fashion, sexuality, and pet keeping. Yet men were not immune to criticism, and an examination of satirical attacks on men reveals another element of the potent mix. Men became vulnerable to satire when they violated gender norms. Thus dancing masters—who taught the supposedly useless and fashionable skills of posture and dance—were targeted, as were fops and "macaronis"—terms for men who were obsessed with fashion and who were too comfortable in female society.[62] As in the satires on women, pets in satires aimed at men functioned in part as fashionable accessories, locating the subject in the world of fashionable consumption and wasteful extravagance. Because fashion was defined as an inherently feminine pursuit, any man who engaged with that world was by definition not fully masculine. Pets blurred the boundaries between humans and animals; men with an interest in fashion blurred the boundaries between the sexes. In the process, they were dehumanized, made literally less manly.

The dancing master was among the male figures most vulnerable to attack on these grounds. He was problematic because he represented the fluidity of boundaries—of social status and gender—that were supposed to be rigid. Of much lower social rank than most of his students, he nonetheless entered their homes and provided instruction that was essential if they were to demonstrate their status successfully. Ironically, then, he made it possible for the elite to exercise their birthright by teaching them skills that were supposed to come naturally. He was also a man whose career involved training young women in the skills that would enable them to attract other men. In short, he spent too much time in the company of women, his career was focused on an ostensibly trivial pastime, and he crossed class boundaries. As the century progressed and the elements of elite breeding, such as dancing instruction, became more accessible to their social inferiors, this problem only deepened.[63]

Satires of dancing masters focused especially on the attempt to use dancing lessons to improve one's social standing. In these cases, the dancing master was not only a man who crossed lines of social status but the means by which others attempted to do the same. These satires thus sought to reinforce the social hierarchy by demonstrating the futility of attempts to challenge its bounds. In *Grown Ladies Taught to Dance*, for instance, a fat and homely woman faces a scrawny instructor as he tries to

Fig. 22 P. Crotchet, after Daniel Dodd,
Grown Ladies Taught to Dance, 1768. Etching and
engraving, 32 × 25 cm. Courtesy of the Lewis
Walpole Library, Yale University,
768.01.01.04+.

teach her the proper steps (fig. 22). Behind her, a lapdog dances on its
hind legs, drawing on the network of associations between women, lapdogs, and fashion while highlighting the futility of her endeavor. In the
foreground, a monkey plays with a fan. Facing in the same direction as the
dancing master, its posture echoing his, the monkey both mocks the

attempt to teach the rituals of politeness and calls into question the manliness of the instructor. Woman, lapdog, dancing master, and monkey all come together in a mutually reinforcing web of signification.[64]

Similarly, in *Boarding School Education, or The Frenchified Young Lady*, the mincing dance instructor is on the right, his legs and arms at exaggerated angles and his bouffant wig highlighted (fig. 23). The enormous headdresses of the two ladies draw further attention to his wig, which parallels theirs in shape. At bottom left, a monkey instructs a lapdog in the same steps, their legs at angles similar to the dancing master's. The monkey also carries a toy sword and stick in imitation of the master's baton (the dog carries a glove in its mouth, furthering the identification between lapdog and mistress). Thus, though the caption presents the satire as aimed at "the Frenchified young lady," the greater target is the instructor himself. The animals represent one more fashionable element, while they also remind the viewer of the ridiculousness of the situation.

A *New Academy for Accomplishments* takes these ideas to their logical conclusion (fig. 24). Here, the dancing master returns, but the fashionable young woman in the scene is an approving observer, not a student; the "pupils" are two dancing lapdogs, while a cockatoo seems to sing along. This print contains all of the satirical elements discussed above, demonstrating the ways in which those elements played off and reinforced one another. Once again, the dancing master is feminized and his profession shown to be a useless "accomplishment." Even an animal could be taught these skills, the picture implies, while also suggesting that the dance instructor is incapable of doing his job well—the print alludes to the gracelessness of the proverbial dancing dog. At the same time, the print attacks female accomplishments, feminine love of pets, and the lavish expenditure associated with those pets. The animals themselves become visual metaphors for the young woman, while also still carrying the weight of the satire against pet keeping itself. Yet because the dancing master is presented as entirely invested in this performance, he is as much the butt of the joke as the women and animals. Animal performers were popular entertainments in the eighteenth century; here, the image implies, we find ourselves in a topsy-turvy world in which men perform for the pleasure of animals (and, of course, women). Subject to the approving gaze of the young woman with her lorgnette, the dancing master becomes another fashionable pet, his potential for breaching the bounds of gender and sta-

BOARDING SCHOOL EDUCATION, OR THE FRENCHIFIED YOUNG LADY.

Fig. 23   Boarding School Education, or The Frenchified
Young Lady, 1771. Etching, hand-colored, 24.6 ×
35 cm. Courtesy of the Lewis Walpole Library,
Yale University, 771.10.19.01.2+.

tus safely contained and subject to the ridicule of the implicitly superior
viewer.

   The exaggerated outfits and poses of the dancing masters in these
images lead to an even more popular satirical target. Because fashionable
dress was perceived as a feminine concern, fops and macaronis, with their
interest in outlandishly fashionable clothes, were seen as engaging in a
dangerous incursion into feminine territory. Pets in these images both
highlighted the general satire—because of the association between
women and pet keeping—and reflected on the human activities played
out in the scenes. Just as women's fashions of the 1770s and 1780s made
particularly attractive targets for satirists, the rise of the macaroni at the

A NEW ACADEMY FOR ACCOMPLISHMENTS

Fig. 24 *A New Academy for Accomplishments*, 1778.
Etching, 351 × 235 mm. The British Museum. ©
The Trustees of the British Museum. All rights
reserved.

same time coincided with the flourishing of visual satire in the period.[65] Satires against macaronis are so common that they form their own sub-genre. Many rely on parallels between macaronis and animals,[66] but depictions of pets and macaronis deepen the connections among animals, fashion, and gender. In *The Macarony Dressing Room*, for instance, various men are shown preening themselves, while one causes chaos by thrusting his sword into the door just as a servant enters with a tray of drinks (fig. 25).[67] The print incorporates many of the tropes associated with satires of fashionable society—the presence of the black servant or slave, the exaggerated postures, the elaborate dress. But, oblivious to the antics in the rest of the room, a solitary macaroni on the right engages in rapt contemplation of a cockatoo, who stares back at him. On one level, the cockatoo is a fashionable pet, linked, like the black page, to the consumption of exotic goods. But the artist has deliberately constructed a much stronger visual association between macaroni and bird. The man's wig is teased up into a high crest, identical to the crest on the cockatoo. His pose mirrors the arched back of the cockatoo, while the flare of his jacket mimics the flaring tail feathers of the bird. The man's nose is also shaped like the cockatoo's beak, with the same dark shading. Here, the bird takes the place of the mirror in which many satires showed the fashion-obsessed admiring themselves, but the affectionate way in which the man strokes the cockatoo also identifies the bird as a pet. The man's inability to see the resemblance, while nevertheless clearly taking pleasure in the connection, creates the satire in the image. The bird is, for the macaroni holding him, both animal and human, and the print suggests that the man has himself crossed the border between human and bird. The macaroni becomes as empty-headed as the bird, and his elaborate outfit is as pointless as the bird's plumage.

When dogs were employed in satires of fashionable men, they highlighted the collapse of masculine identity through deliberate reference to the identification of lapdogs with women. For example, a print from 1786 entitled *Which Is the Man* targets both male and female fashion by suggesting that the two sexes have lost their distinction (fig. 26). Two slim individuals sit facing each other on a park bench, each with a broad-brimmed hat, elaborate lace collar and cuffs, and a long cane. The figure on the left is accompanied by a large dog, while the one on the right holds a lapdog. The joke is that the person on the left is a woman, her left leg crossed in a

THE MACARONY DRESSING ROOM

Fig. 25 Charles White, after Captain Minshull,
The Macarony Dressing Room, 1772. Etching and
engraving, 25 × 35 cm. Courtesy of the Lewis
Walpole Library, Yale University,
772.II.09.01+.

decidedly unfeminine pose, while on the right a man sits with his legs
tucked daintily under the bench.[68]

Although the print mocks the masculine attire fashionable for women,
the question in the title indicates the greater point of the satire: the problem is less that the woman looks masculine than that it is impossible to
identify the man as a true man. The lapdog he holds becomes the ultimate
indicator of his effeminacy, even more than his delicate pose or flowing
lace. In the satirical print *Jimmy Lincum Feadle,* a little dog wears a ruff collar that echoes the elaborate neckwear of the fashionable man at the center of the portrait. Lest the viewer miss the point, the caption adds a
poem about how "Jove" once transformed "a tribe of worthless men" into
"monkies." Beasts recoiled from this new creation, "but Woman lik'd the

WHICH IS THE MAN

Fig. 26   Which Is the Man, 1786. Etching and
engraving, 23 × 26.5 cm. Courtesy of the
Lewis Walpole Library, Yale University,
786.05.30.06.

motley breed / And Call'd this thing a Beau."[69] Portrayed with the most
feminine of pets, the "beau" has abandoned the qualities of good sense
and sober dress that were supposed to define a man, yet, as the caption
notes, women are still attracted to this monkey man.[70] The notion of the
"motley breed" ties together the ideas about gender, fashion, and pet
keeping at work in these images: pet owners treated their animals like
family, in a way that violated the hierarchies of species and seemed to

open the possibility of other kinds of transmutations. If animals could become like people, then people could become like animals, men and women could become indistinguishable, and women could fall in love indiscriminately with monkeys or beaus. At the heart of the anxiety here is a dangerous transgression of the boundaries that maintained social propriety and of the hierarchies of status and gender as well as species.

The reference in *Jimmy Lincum Feadle* to turning men into monkeys highlights an especially common trope in satires targeting failures of masculinity. Like satires against women and lapdogs, there was a long tradition prior to the eighteenth century that employed monkeys to criticize humans.[71] This tradition relied on the similarity of anatomical characteristics as well as the notion of "aping" one's social superiors. But whereas the quintessentially feminine pet was the lapdog, with whom the fashionable mistress had a dangerously intimate relationship, the pet most employed in satires of men was the monkey. Although monkeys resemble women as much as they do men, in eighteenth-century satires they were overwhelmingly associated with men. Like dogs, monkeys were consistently gendered as male, perhaps because their character traits— exuberant physical activity, including unselfconscious sexual display— seemed masculine. The monkey, with its strong resemblance to humans, served as a mirror in which the inanity of fashionable men was reflected. The monkey in the satires, "aping" the dress and manners of men, implied that the men themselves were no more than monkeys. Moreover, the habit of some monkey owners of dressing up their pets in human clothes made this animal a particularly obvious source for those looking to mock masculine dress.[72]

A common characteristic of satires involving monkeys, unlike those with other pets, is the willingness to present a scene in which the pet is both participant and (nonverbal) commentator. The monkey is thus a stand-in for the audience, helping to shape the response to the satire even as he mirrors the dress and behavior of the fashionable men being satirized. A 1733 letter from "Pug," a pet monkey, to the *Gentleman's Magazine* complained, "I Live in a Family, where the eldest Son is a most notorious FLAP; to shew him his Folly, my Master has converted ME into *one*; I mean, as to Dress, for he cannot curtail my Understanding to the pitch of a FLAP's."[73] The monkey as mirror was even more useful in visual satires, in which the point could be made without words. In *The Macarony Brothers*, a tough-looking sailor turns away in disgust from a fashionably dressed young man (fig. 27). The sailor's pet monkey, perched on his shoulder, points at the young man, drawing attention to the fact that the monkey's jacket, hat, and cuffs are identical to those of the discomfited macaroni. The monkey's joyful recognition of the resemblance—its grin and gesture acknowledging a "brother"—ensures that the implications are clear. A man who obeyed the vagaries of fashion, which were by definition irrational, demonstrated that he lacked the reason that was supposed to distinguish man from beast. A man without reason was simply a monkey in human clothes.

The Footman, from Woodward and Rowlandson's series Country Characters, makes these ideas even more explicit. Gazing at a London footman as he preens in the mirror, two servants express their horror at the peculiar creature. "Nan," exclaims the man to the woman, "did'st ever see such a conceited Monkey! old Jack the Baboon is a fool to um!!" Sure enough, standing with them is an ape, looking eagerly toward the footman and holding a stick to his nose in the same manner in which the footman holds his nosegay.[74] The image literalizes the phrase "conceited monkey," making man identical to monkey.

Like lapdogs, monkeys also formed part of a potent triad involving pets, fashion, and sexuality. Rather than rely on the suggestive intimacy between women and lapdogs, however, satirists used monkeys to suggest the failure of men to achieve full male adulthood, with its implications of self-sufficiency, self-control, and reason.[75] A print from the early 1770s shows "a well-known macaroni" wooing Poll Kennedy, a courtesan.[76] Kennedy sits with her legs spread apart while the macaroni kneels before her; a monkey perches on the back of the settee, wearing a wig in the same style as the man's and smirking at him through a glass. The monkey's face, with its strongly human features, emphasizes the slippage between simian and man. In The Discovery, one of a series of three prints from 1774 depicting illicit liaisons in a household, an obese woman sits on the edge of a bed, clasping the hand of a young man as a maidservant appears in the doorway with the woman's enraged husband.[77] A lapdog scratches itself at the woman's feet, forming the left-hand base of the visual triangle in the scene; the right-hand base, parallel to the dog, is a grinning monkey holding out An Essay on Man. As with the prints against sartorial fashions, the image here implies that this is no proper man but a mere ape, his idiotic smile supporting the monkey's case. Deceitful Kisses, or The Pretty Plunderers (1781) is even stronger in its critique of man as prey to voracious

THE MACARONY BROTHERS.

London,Printed for Robt. Sayer,No.53 Fleet Street,&J. Smith,No.35, Cheapside, as the Act directs,25 July,1772.

Fig. 27   James Caldwall, after Michel Vincent
Brandoin, *The Macarony Brothers*, 1772. Etching
and stipple engraving with engraving, 19.8 ×
13.9 cm. Courtesy of the Lewis Walpole
Library, Yale University, 772.07.25.01.1.

women.[78] A man in a brothel grins as he is embraced by three prostitutes, unaware that they are stealing his wallet, watch, and even a ring off his finger. A monkey sits on top of a wardrobe on the far right, looking knowingly out at the viewer as he holds a sheet inscribed *Who's the Dupe*, the title of a popular play as well as a reference to the male character in the print. Once again, the beast is more aware of the situation than the man, highlighting the failure of masculine sexual dominance.

It was a short step from this sort of image to the claim that one might mistake a fashionable woman's husband for a monkey, or vice versa. A dream recounted in the *Spectator*, for instance, parodied an ancient tale in which women rescued their husbands by carrying the men from a besieged town on their backs. The dreamer observed women carrying off their china, playing cards, and a lapdog; at one point he thought he saw a husband's "little withered Face" but then realized that the woman in question was simply saving her pet monkey.[79] A 1785 issue of the *Lounger* reversed the joke, describing a man whose life is made miserable by his wife's many pets and who suffers the final indignity of being mistaken for her pet monkey when he is crammed into a corner of their carriage along with her luggage and lapdog.[80] In such cases, men are made the toys of fashionable women, their sexual potency transferred to the pet monkey while they themselves become the butt of the joke—the entertainment that the monkey is supposed to provide.[81] When the animal recognizes its own kind in the man, human superiority vanishes, replaced by a leveling of man and beast. The entrance of the monkey into the home risks the possibility of substituting monkey for man, or at least rendering the differences negligible. With some men, these satires suggest, only the absence of a comparison maintains the fiction of a difference between human and animal.

≈   ≈   ≈

A detailed reading of Francis Coventry's *History of Pompey the Little*, the most extensive engagement with pet keeping, gender, and fashion published in the eighteenth century, unites all of the ideas discussed in this chapter in a single text.[82] *Pompey* (first published in 1751, with a substantially revised third edition appearing in 1752) is an early example of a popular genre of the eighteenth century: the it-narrative, in which a story follows the progress of an object or animal through a series of events, often in order to construct a satirical commentary on social norms and practices.[83] Pompey, the "hero" of Coventry's tale, is a Bolognese lapdog, and the narrative follows him through a series of owners and situations in both high and low society. Many of the themes present in other satires of fashion and pets return in *Pompey*, including the associations among pets, femininity, and sexuality. But *Pompey* also embodies other anxieties around gender and fashion, for the canine hero occupies a liminal space similar to that of the dancing master and the fop. Anatomically male but decidedly not masculine, and shifting easily from one social status to another, Pompey represents the dangerous fluidity of fashion, but the satire also seeks to contain and minimize the danger by embodying it in the figure of a tiny nonhuman animal.

One crucial effect of making a dog the center of the narrative is that it destabilizes the satire; the enormous network of associations and allusions related to dogs in general and lapdogs in particular means that there is no single satirical target. Even the role of Pompey himself changes: at times, he is simply a means of taking the reader into specific social situations, while at others, Pompey's identity as a dog becomes central to the narrative, and pet keeping itself becomes the target of the satire. This instability is indicated at the very beginning of the tale, when the narrator defends the importance of his subject. Coventry begins with language familiar from many natural histories, in which the admirable qualities of dogs are discussed: "And can we, without the basest Ingratitude, think ill of an Animal, that has ever honoured Mankind with his Company and Friendship, from the Beginning of the World to the present Moment? While all other Creatures are in a State of Enmity with us, some flying into Woods and Wildernesses to escape our Tyranny, and others requiring to be restrained with Bridles and Fences in close Confinement; Dogs alone enter into voluntary Friendship with us, and of their own accord make their Residence among us." Dogs are useful as guards, companions, and hunters, the narrator continues, but then his tone abruptly shifts. "I have heard of a Dog's making a Syllogism; which cannot fail to endear him to our two famous Universities, where his Brother-Logicians are so honoured and distinguished for their Skill in that *useful* Science," he announces, adding, finally, that "it may be thought too ludicrous, perhaps, to mention the Capacity they have often discovered, for playing at Cards, Fiddling, Dancing, and other polite Accomplishments."[84] From a beginning that could be read as entirely sincere, Coventry moves to mockery of academicians before finally turning to the areas in which dogs have indeed been trained to entertain humans. What should we make of this commentary? Is Coventry praising dogs and mocking only humans here, or is he mocking both? As noted above, there was a long-standing practice of contrasting the virtues of the loyal dog with the moral failings of humans, but Coventry's work does not fit easily into that tradition, partly because the text is anchored so firmly in the activities of real dogs and not just those used as metaphors. The slippage here between satirizing pets and satirizing people reemerges throughout the narrative.

As was common in it-narratives, many of Pompey's adventures involve sexual encounters. Pompey himself is the product of an illicit union; an Italian nobleman "had an Intrigue with a celebrated Courtesan," and the nobleman's dog "commenced an Affair of Gallantry with a Favourite little Bitch," the result of which was Pompey (10). He is given to his third owner, Lady Tempest, in return for her sexual favors (45–46). Later on, he comes into the possession of a young lady; though the text describes her as a paragon of virtue, Pompey clearly serves as a sexual substitute for the girl, whose desire has been aroused by her love for a suitor: "When she awoke in a Morning, she would embrace him with an Ardour superior to his Deserts, and which the happiest Lover might have envied: Our Hero's Vanity, perhaps, made him fancy himself the genuine Object of these Caresses, but, in Reality, he was only the Representative of a much nobler Object" (164). Pompey is banished from this abode when he awakens his mistress from a dream about her lover. The revised edition of the book adds other adventures, including a scene in which Pompey is provided as a stud to a bitch named Veny: "Mrs. *Racket* had two daughters, who had greatly improved their natural relish for pleasure in the warm climate of a town education, and were extremely solicitous to inform themselves of all the mysteries of love. These young ladies no sooner heard of *Pompey*'s arrival, than they went down stairs into the parlour, and undertook themselves to introduce him to miss [*sic*] *Veny*: for love so much engrossed their thoughts, that they could not suffer a lap-dog in the house to have an amour without their privity." The ladies are caught by a visitor, who soon understands the source of their "uncommon joy and rapture."[85]

What is the purpose of the dog in these instances? First, Pompey serves as a sexual surrogate, as when Lady Tempest negotiates with Hillario, Pompey's previous owner, over visitation rights (to Pompey and, by implication, to Lady Tempest).[86] Young women in the story both project their sexual fantasies onto the dog and, in the later edition, use him for their own sexual education. The background provided about Pompey's birth suggests this deep-rooted association with sexuality. All of these scenes also incorporate another familiar satirical target—the fashionable, sexually insatiable woman. At the same time, however, the scenes are intended to be funny because of the implied impossibility of actual bestiality; it is Pompey's innocence, paradoxically, that makes the satire work. The real objects of women's affections are, or should be, men; Pompey serves either as a cover for the "real" liaison (as with Lady Tempest and Hillario) or as a rehearsal for the "real" thing. The joke is that women are seeking sexual satisfaction where they cannot possibly find it; men are the proper objects of such desires, but women consistently miss the mark.

Pompey functions in this way because, although he is male, he is neither fully masculine nor fully feminine. The narration persistently comments on his popularity among the female sex, but in this way he is like a fop or beau, problematic less because he threatens to seduce women than because he encourages their attraction to something other than the masculine ideal. A male who was too comfortable in female society was a problem. Thus even though Pompey is presented as a (male) sexual substitute for women, he is also consistently feminized. Lady Tempest, for instance, teaches him to play cards, at which he is so adept "that in less than three Months he was able to sit down with her Ladyship to Piquet, whenever Sickness or the Vapours confined her to her Chamber" (54). Later, his ability "to behave himself with Complaisance and Good-manners" leads to another adoption, as he pays court to a pair of ladies visiting the inn where he is living, and his hopes of returning "to the Beau-monde" are gratified (137–38). But perhaps the best example of this feminization, and its link to fashion, comes during Pompey's stay with a milliner. In the first edition, Coventry has the milliner make Pompey "a laced Ruff, made in the newest Fashion, worn by Women of Quality," who all admire and pet him when they visit the shop (183). In the revised third edition, the comparison goes even further; the milliner makes a new "cambrick ruff" for Pompey, and it is this ruff that becomes the inspiration for "the modern fashion of ladies wearing ruffs around their necks."[87]

In both fashion and sexuality, Pompey's gender is fluid, and this fluidity makes for much of the humor in the book. Moreover, the fluidity itself depends upon another form of boundary crossing: the ambiguity in Pompey's status vis-à-vis the animal-human boundary. Many of the jokes focus on women's use of the dog as a substitute for a man, either as double entendre, as in the case of Lady Tempest, or through their misplaced affection for the dog. Pompey also functions as a beau, that man who is too comfortable with women, too content to waste time in useless activities like playing cards, and too fascinated by the whims of fashion. These ideas spill over into the other ongoing analogy in the book, Pompey's role as courtier. The narrator consistently refers to the dog as fawning like a courtier, drawing on long-standing analogies—such as, famously, in Alexander Pope's collar for George II's dog: "I am his Highness' Dog at *Kew*; Pray tell me Sir, whose Dog are you?" As with Pope's joke, Pompey's collar represents the courtier, but Coventry also emphasizes the connection to fashion and consumerism.[88] Pompey wins his collar early in life, when Hillario, the lover of Pompey's original courtesan owner, presents him "with a Collar studded with Diamonds." Pompey is so pleased by the gift that from then on "he would eat Biscuit from *Hillario*'s Hands with twice the Pleasure, with which he received it from any other Person's" (15). Later, the narrator remarks that Pompey has become a social snob, unwilling to consort with dogs of a lower class and "extremely proud to shew *his Collar at Court*; in which again he resembled certain other Dogs, who are equally vain of their Finery, and happy to be distinguished in their *respective Orders*" (52–53). This is, of course, a reference to courtiers, and particularly to the distinguishing collars worn by members of such chivalric orders as the Order of the Garter. Finally, in the summary of Pompey's character at the end of the book, the courtier analogy is extended and completed: "he was a Dog of the *most courtly Manners*, ready to fetch and carry, at the Command of all his Masters, without ever considering the Service he was employed in, or the Person from whom he received his Directions: He would fawn likewise with the greatest Humility, on People who treated him with Contempt, and was always particularly officious in his Zeal, whenever he expected a new Collar, or stood

Candidate for a Ribbon with other Dogs, who made up the Retinue of the Family" (269–70). Pompey's beauty, superficiality, and fawning manners are what make him so popular and successful in life. Again, the language is heavily feminized, with its references to ribbons and collars, and the associations among fashion, effeminacy, and the court all echo and reinforce one another.

Pompey embodies the slippages among gender, status, and species that made pets both objects of cultural anxiety and useful tools for satirists. Pompey's ability to move easily from one owner to another, among all social classes, demonstrates his disturbingly malleable identity, as do his comfort at court and his appeal to women. Like the macaroni and the dancing master, he embodies the fluidity of fashion and the many ways in which people from radically different social strata could and frequently did cross paths. If, in the other works discussed in this chapter, we see humans reducing themselves to the level of animals, Pompey accomplishes the transition from animal to human. But it is not an ennobling or edifying experience.

Francis Coventry's innovative narrative, the first extended work of English fiction centered on a pet dog, follows its pint-size hero from Italy to England, from St. James's Park to country inns, from garrets to taverns. Pompey circulates like the coins or clothes of other it-narratives, his easy transition from one setting to another providing a glimpse into a wide array of social situations. Yet he is unlike those goods because he is also a living animal, and thus we observe not only the behavior and words of the people around him but also his own responses to the situations in which he finds himself. The narrative depends upon the quintessential characteristic of the pet: Pompey is both object, to be exchanged for goods and services, and active, feeling subject, responsible for many of his own experiences. Coventry frequently reminds the reader of parallels between the lapdog and the humans who buy him, trade him, love him, and lose him. And it is because of these parallels that Pompey becomes such a powerful representation of the permeability of the social boundaries that were so important in eighteenth-century Britain. He is a male who sets the fashion in women's wear, a bastard product of an illicit Italian liaison who triumphs in elite society, a dog who becomes a courtier. His is the story of a world without clear limits of any sort. Coventry's narrative presents both the boundless opportunities and the disorienting chaos of a world ruled by fashion, in which anything is possible. It thus reflects all the anxieties that we have seen in the other works discussed here, with their fears about the potential instability of gender, class, and even species. But, like those other works, *Pompey the Little* ultimately seeks to contain the threat of such instability by suggesting that it is no greater than that posed by a tiny, yapping lapdog.

4 ～ A PRIVILEGE OR A RIGHT?

In *Liberal Opinions, Upon Animals, Man, and Providence*, his collection of sentimental fiction and poetry, Samuel Jackson Pratt included a half-serious greeting to a newly acquired lapdog. The note draws on many of the associations between lapdogs and femininity, as Pratt both welcomes and cautions the animal about its new station in life. But it also moves beyond those associations to engage with concerns about the effects of comfort and "luxury":

> Welcome—thrice welcome to the downy carpet—the velvet cushion—and the gay apartment. Delicate—endearing, and envied are now the perquisites of thy distinguished station—The gentle pat, the fond embrace, the tender stroke—the tortoise comb, and the most exquisite viands. Long may the hand that cherishes, protects, and feeds thee, continue its indulgence—As long may'st thou deserve it. Be grateful, and be happy.—But, ah! beware of the common vice of prosperity—beware of luxury. Lap-dogs, lords, and ladies, have been equally the victims of voluptuousness. The plenitude of unexercised ease hath been often fatal; and the bills of mortality are swelled with the luxurious, rather than with the indigent. Consider, dear creature, that there is a pestilence in plenty, as well

as in famine.—Take heed therefore, that this sudden elevation, bringeth not upon thee plethoric diseases of indolence—a languid love of sleeping by the fire—a dropsical corpulence, and a vitiated refinement of appetite.[1]

Material pleasures—like carpets, cushions, combs, and "exquisite viands"—were a matter of pride among eighteenth-century Britons, who were well aware of their nation's growing prosperity. At the same time, however, many worried about the potential for such pleasures to corrupt. Anxiety about luxury, fueled by the rise of a consumer society and modern fashion, shaped satirical attacks on pets as violations of gender boundaries, but concerns about luxury and pet keeping focused even more strongly on the implications for class relations. As consumer goods became available to a wide swath of society, and as these goods increased in variety and number, Britons were divided about whether these changes were beneficial or dangerous.

Luxury was a topic of immense importance in the eighteenth century, but its meaning was hotly contested. The malleability of the term made it both useful and problematic. There was a long tradition of condemning luxury as sinful on the grounds that it resulted from an individual's rejection of his or her divinely ordained place in the social hierarchy.[2] In the early eighteenth century, however, Bernard Mandeville articulated a new position in his famous *Fable of the Bees*, claiming that expenditures on sinful pleasures might support commerce and employment to the benefit of society as a whole.[3] As Maxine Berg and Elizabeth Eger argue, "After Mandeville, luxury was increasingly seen in terms of economic advantage," and the debate over luxury "fundamentally turned on problems of defining the term."[4] If it was impossible to agree about what constituted a luxury, it was equally impossible to pinpoint the moral effects of luxury on individuals or societies. Berg and Eger identify an emerging discourse that emphasized a sort of moderate luxury—the availability of new consumer goods to members of the middling sort—as an economic benefit that lacked the moral problems inherent in older ideas of luxury. Yet they also acknowledge that this view "developed in continuing dialogue with critics of luxury who feared that it was at the root of national social problems."[5]

When eighteenth-century writers deployed the concept of luxury, then, they did so to support a variety of agendas. If luxury represented the perilous decadence of a society on the verge of collapse, it was everyone's responsibility to avoid indulging in luxury. But those who viewed luxury as an engine of economic expansion and civilization could also see it in terms of a moral agenda. Even as it became a common complaint that it was impossible to distinguish the serving girl from her mistress, the plight of the poor remained a significant problem. If the poor needed assistance, an obvious way to address that problem was through taxes on luxuries, which would enable the entire society—even those who could not afford to purchase the luxuries themselves—to benefit from luxurious consumption. Yet such ideas did not solve the central problem: what, exactly, was a luxury?

By tracing how debates about pets intersected with the discourse of luxury, we can see how Britons struggled to define the concept, and why the idea of luxury was as problematic as it was useful. Pets were often used as a means of attacking the elite for lavish expenditures; pets were an example of "wasting" precious resources (money and food) on needless conspicuous consumption. They were inexcusable luxuries. At the same time, the poor could also be criticized for indulging in the luxury of pet keeping when they could not afford basic necessities, thus demonstrating their inability to manage their limited funds and suggesting that perhaps they deserved their poverty. But the new discourse that saw moderate luxury as a social good opened the way for a new attitude toward pets. No longer did their status as unnecessary consumer goods automatically imply immorality. This possibility was enhanced, moreover, by broader changes in attitudes toward pet keeping as the practice became more widespread. Although the view of pet keeping as a luxury persisted, ideas about humanity toward and love for animals increasingly meant that pets ceased to be perceived merely as a drain on resources.

Thus, throughout the century, debates over pets served as a way for individuals to consider questions of the rights and wrongs of class relations: ideas about pets and human-animal hierarchies intersected with ideas about eighteenth-century social hierarchies and reflected differing definitions of luxury. Writers employed contrasts between affection for pets and for people to make claims about social responsibility, juxtaposing love of animals with neglect of servants and the poor. Such criticisms were aimed largely at the elite, but they were complicated by the limited sympathy most commentators had for servants and poor people. One response, ironically, was to present working animals as loyal servants, alternatives to both useless pets and lazy human workers. Another strand of thinking about the relationship between class and emotional attachment to animals arose with the humane movement in the last decades of the eighteenth century, which connected care for animals with care for "inferior" human beings, and drew on class as a means of identifying cruelty with the "vulgar." By emphasizing that abuse was characteristic of the lower classes, advocates could implicitly position their readers as members of an elite who would want to identify with the kindness of their fellow humanitarians. Yet those who would deny animal companionship to the poor were also increasingly presented as cruel and inhumane. All of these conflicts regarding interactions across status and species boundaries came together in the century-long debate over whether to institute a tax on dog ownership. This debate reveals both the continuities and the changes in perceptions of the relationship between pet keeping and social status as they evolved over the course of the century.

≈   ≈   ≈

Pets were helpful in thinking through class relations, particularly because of the ways in which their roles resembled and diverged from those of servants. Because maintaining pets and servants required disposable income, both functioned as indicators of social status. Both might be portrayed as useless luxuries—especially when they seemed to be present in excessive quantity or to be kept purely for ostentatious display. The visual link often made in satirical prints between lapdogs or exotic pets and liveried manservants, especially black servants, was no coincidence.[6] Pets and servants were also subordinate to their masters or mistresses, who could acquire or dismiss them at will. But pets and servants might at the same time seem to have strongly opposed interests, competing for affection and material rewards from those same masters and mistresses.
In this view, pets wasted food and money that should have been better used, particularly to care for the poor. Those who chose to keep pets were doubly guilty of failing to understand their obligations to God and to other humans.

Indeed, it was the competition for food that made pets particularly useful for critics of luxurious consumption. Unlike other (inanimate) luxuries, pets remained a drain on resources over time, and in a nation that still experienced widespread hunger as a very real problem, pets literally seemed to be taking food from the mouths of the needy. Thus Jonas

Hanway complained of the pet owner's callous disregard for human suffering: "The costly chicken is ordered for the CAT or DOG, by her who never thinks of giving a morsel of bread to relieve the hunger of a MAN."[7] Just as fashionable individuals' love for their pets could demonstrate their failure to direct their affection to more worthy (human) objects, so could pet keeping demonstrate a broader failure to establish a well-ordered household that offered paternalistic care to social inferiors.

We can see these ideas at work in the print *Summer*, from the late 1770s (fig. 28). As we saw in the previous chapter, satires against fashionable femininity often connected women's pet keeping with their misplaced priorities, and such associations were equally potent in critiques that linked pet keeping to failures of empathy toward humans. In *Summer*, a woman and her sweating husband promenade near White Conduit House (a tavern and pleasure garden in Islington that catered to the middling sort). Next to them, a page boy in livery struggles to carry a shawl, walking stick, pattens—one of which he has just dropped—and a spaniel. The outsized burden the boy must carry, with the dog struggling in his arms, shifts the satire's primary agenda from feminine fashion to class. The Islington location anchors the couple in the middle or lower middle class, implicitly presenting the fashionable accoutrements of liveried servant and pet dog as evidence of social climbing. Just as White Conduit House imitates more exclusive pleasure gardens, so the dog parodies the stereotypical fashionable woman's tiny lapdog. The squirming dog becomes a living testament to the woman's casual indifference to her servant's plight, and that indifference in turn reveals her as unworthy of genuine elite status.

Satires of fashionable women's misplaced love were often expressed from the point of view of the men they spurned. The same cannot be said of critiques relating to the treatment of servants. Such critiques could not extend to a full embrace of the servants' viewpoint, which would represent an inversion of the social hierarchy. Thus, while the contrast between pampered pets and abused servants might reveal household disorder, the solution could not be to place servants in the privileged position of pets.

Fig. 28 After John Collet, *Summer*, ca. 1779.
Mezzotint, hand-colored, 35.5 × 25.2 cm.
Courtesy of the Lewis Walpole Library, Yale
University, 779.01.01.04+.

Printed for & Sold by CARINGTON BOWLES

SUMMER.

at N.º 69 in S.t Paul's Church Yard, LONDON.

From the Original Picture by John Collet in the possession of Carington Bowles.

Published as the Act directs.

393

The difficult balance entailed in these competing impulses is particularly visible in two satires that employ pet keeping as a means of demonstrating a failure of class relations: Francis Coventry's *Pompey the Little*, discussed in detail in chapter 3, and Henry Mackenzie's story of "Mrs. Sensitive."

As we have seen, *Pompey the Little* engaged with questions of gender and fashion, but the work's satire also extended to class, particularly in the section devoted to Lady Tempest. When Pompey arrives at her house, Lady Tempest reveals her infatuation with him by letting him share her dinner: "he received many dainty Bits from her fair Hands, and was caressed by her all Dinner-time, with more than usual Fondness. The Servants winked at one another, while they were waiting, and conveyed many Sneers across the Table with their Looks; all which had the good Luck to escape her Ladyship's Observation." The sexual innuendo that we have seen at work in other parts of *Pompey* is also present here, but Coventry then takes the scene in a different direction. Once they are safely on their own, the servants give "Vent to their Thoughts with all the scurrilous Wit and ill-manner'd Raillery, which distinguishes the Conversation of those parti coloured Gentlemen." The "elderly fat" housekeeper chimes in with horror at providing "*such Creatures with Christian Victuals.*" Next, the lady's maid, "a saucy, forward, affected Girl, of about Twenty" who is responsible for caring for Lady Tempest's many pets, launches into a lengthy complaint about dogs' being "nasty poisonous Vermin." The footman and coachman echo these comments.[8] Later, when Pompey runs away in St. James's Park, a frantic Lady Tempest sends her servants to scour the park for him, but they do nothing, instead sitting in the kitchen or alehouse and mocking her for being so upset.[9] While other parts of the book play with gender norms, this section of the narrative reveals Lady Tempest's character flaws through her relationships to her dog and her servants.

A 1786 piece in Henry Mackenzie's periodical the *Lounger* presents a similar scenario. "Barbara Heartless" writes a letter to the editor complaining about her current position in the household of "Mrs. Sensitive." Barbara is responsible for caring for Mrs. Sensitive's extensive collection of pets, including "three lap-dogs, four cats, . . . a monkey, a flying squirrel," along with many birds, "a dormouse in a box, a set of guineapips [*sic*] in the garret, and a tame otter in the cellar."[10] Mrs. Sensitive dotes on these animals—Barbara's job itself attests to that—but cares nothing for the humans in her household. As Barbara complains, "her feelings are only made for brute creatures, and don't extend to us poor Christians of the family." Mrs. Sensitive weeps over her dead husband, but rumor has it that she treated him badly, and she has ordered her servants never to allow beggars near her. Worst of all, she has cut off her husband's family; one impoverished godson who was living with her was turned out because he hit "Fidele [a lapdog], who was stealing his bread and butter."[11] The three servants are nearly starved so that Mrs. Sensitive can spend more money on food for the animals, while she urges on her human attendants the virtues of vegetarianism.

In both *Pompey the Little* and Barbara's letter to the *Lounger*, the reader is ostensibly given the opportunity to hear the servants' point of view first-hand. We witness the waste inherent in Lady Tempest's provision of human food to her animals; in the case of Mrs. Sensitive, the problem extends so far that the servants are reduced to a meager diet of vegetables. We also see her reject her own needy godson. From this perspective, pets are filthy freeloaders, literally gobbling up resources ("Christian Vict-uals") that would be better spent on humans. But in both cases the servants themselves are also explicitly depicted as lazy and ignorant. Indeed, the narrator in *Pompey* explains that he includes the dining scene in order to show all masters and mistresses that they must not give their servants any reason to ridicule them, lest they be mocked all over lower-class London.[12] Barbara's surname, Heartless, suggests that she could use some of her employer's sensitivity, and her words reveal her lack of education and thoughtfulness. Mrs. Sensitive's "greens and water don't agree with my feelings at all," she says, "but quite to the contrary, that there is such a grumbling about me.—And as for people being changed into birds and beasts, I think it is Heathenish, and downright against the Bible."[13] While most eighteenth-century readers would have agreed with her regarding both vegetarianism and metempsychosis, Barbara remains a caricature.

As these examples demonstrate, satirists juxtaposed the treatment of servants and pets to play with ideas about class and relations between social superiors and inferiors. By using pets to show the misguided priori-ties of their wealthy owners, Coventry and Mackenzie were able to avoid creating too much sympathy for servants.[14] The servants could be igno-rant, coarse, and lazy, even as their masters were presented as foolish, callous, and wasteful. Pets could serve this function because they appeared to be self-evidently pointless, and thus anything they consumed was by definition wasted. Because their owners expended emotional and material resources on them, moreover, they could embody a much stronger moral critique than would be possible if the satirists focused purely on the ill treatment of servants or the poor. Pets enabled satirists to contrast extreme devotion to animals with lack of compassion for other human beings, both family and outsiders. They thus implied the ideal relationships that should exist within the social hierarchy by demonstrating the total failure of these relationships, thanks to the inclusion of another species in this hierarchy.[15] Bad mistresses found themselves with bad servants; more care would lead to a more orderly household. The fundamental goal was to demonstrate the dangers of abdicating one's paternalistic responsibility toward social inferiors. Ultimately, then, even though these works appear to present the viewpoint of lower-class individuals, both the problem and the solution lie with their employers.

If satires like Coventry's and Mackenzie's sought to uphold paternalism and household order by mocking its absence, children's literature, with its goal of creating the upstanding masters and mistresses of the future, used animals to offer a much more forthright picture of idealized class relations.[16] Children's stories present a more sympathetic, but also a more distant, view of servants and the poor. The satires depicted the risks of a disordered household; children's literature offered an orderly world in which both human and animal inferiors were kept in their proper place. Sarah Trimmer's *Fabulous Histories*, for instance, includes a tale of children saving slices of bread to feed songbirds, who have come to expect the treats daily. Their mother, Mrs. Benson, gently admonishes them that "it is not right to cut pieces from a loaf on purpose for birds, because there are many children that want bread, to whom we should give the preference. Would you deprive a poor little hungry boy of his breakfast, to give it to the birds?"[17] The children resolve instead to save all the crumbs from their meal and to ask the servants to save crumbs when they serve at meals. It is unclear how simply refraining from feeding their bread to birds helps the poor; Trimmer does not show the family providing leftover bread as charity. But she does emphasize the importance of respecting animals while recognizing that care for them must be subordinate to one's duty toward other humans. Thus Mrs. Benson praises the children for their "humane behaviour" but reminds them "not to suffer it to gain upon you to such a degree, as to make you unhappy, or forgetful of those, who have a superior claim to your attention: I mean poor people;

always keep in mind the distresses which they endure, and on no account waste any kind of food, nor give to inferior animals what is designed for mankind."[18]

Later in the book, Trimmer returns to the relationship between pet keeping and class obligations, this time portraying pet keeping as a moral failure of the elite. The story of the birds and the bread crumbs relies on the assumption that material resources are limited; a robin's gain must necessarily be a poor boy's loss. In this second story, Trimmer applies a similar model, suggesting that the distribution of affection is also a zero-sum game. Mrs. Benson takes her children to visit Mrs. Addis, who has forsaken all human ties in her obsession with her pets, which include exotic birds, a monkey, a lapdog, and a cat. Trimmer presents Mrs. Addis as a monster who keeps the cat in a doll's cradle, while her own daughter is left upstairs in rags. The Benson family is further horrified to witness Mrs. Addis firing a servant on the grounds that the servant has made her parrot sick. Finally, on their way home, they meet a beggar woman who has been denied alms by the Addis household. The beggar has been told that there is no money for alms because it has all been spent on the animals, and while she is absorbing this news she witnesses the delivery of a rabbit and a fowl to feed the cat and dog. The Bensons, of course, provide the charity themselves, and the entire story is clearly designed to teach the lesson that putting pets before people is an immoral luxury.[19] As is clear in the discussion about feeding songbirds, Trimmer was not opposed to caring for animals, and elsewhere the book offers strong praise of dogs and equally strong criticism of animal abuse. But there must be a bright line, in Trimmer's view, between affection for animals and the luxurious overindulgence in such affection that seemed to characterize pet keeping. Just as critics of material luxuries worried that the masses must suffer when a minority indulged in lavish expenditure, so too, it seemed, did love for useless pets necessarily imply a dearth of affection for more useful human companions.

≈   ≈   ≈

The implied opposition in Trimmer's work between loving pets, which wasted a limited store of human affection, and a benevolent attitude toward animals in general was rooted in the assumption that working animals were free from the faults of their "useless" counterparts. There was little connection, in this view, between the pampered existence of

Pompey the Little or Mrs. Addis's cat in its cradle, and the useful roles played by animals in many areas of daily life. The presumed difference had its parallel in attitudes toward humans, as in eighteenth-century debates about how many servants were "necessary" or about how to differentiate between the truly needy and "sturdy beggars." The distinction between the valuable working animal and the useless—and therefore worthless—pet was even enshrined in law. As Erica Fudge has pointed out, "In the early modern English law there are three categories of animal: *ferae naturae*, wild animals; *domitae naturae*, domestic animals; and recreational animals, whose lack of a Latin name represents their lack of status in the face of the law."[20] Crucially, only the first two categories of animal had monetary value. Thus when pet owners indulged their animals at the expense of other humans, they were valuing something literally worthless above a priceless human life. But this apparently straightforward distinction between the valuable working animal and the worthless pet led to problems of its own, problems most visible in the case of dogs.

The special role of the dog in human life was universally acknowledged. Buffon and his followers understood that it must have been the earliest animal to be domesticated, with spectacular consequences. "Without the assistance of the dog," Buffon asked,

> how could man have conquered, tamed, and reduced the other animals into slavery? How could he still discover, hunt down, and destroy noxious and savage beasts? For his own safety, and to render him master of the animated world, it was necessary to form a party among the animals themselves, to conciliate by caresses those which were capable of attachment and obedience, in order to oppose them to the other species[.] Hence the training of the dog seems to have been the first art invented by man; and the result of this art was the conquest and peaceable possession of the earth. . . . The dog, ever faithful to man, will always maintain a portion of this empire; he will always preserve a degree of superiority over the other animals.[21]

The superiority of the dog was evident to Buffon precisely because dogs assisted humans in enslaving other species. This passage, moreover, was one of those most frequently appropriated in other works about animals.[22] If humankind's survival depended on animal subjugation, then the dog was the willing animal accomplice. Samuel Jackson Pratt's poem

"Defence of our Attachment to Animals," from 1801, shows how the idea of canine slavery could be presented positively. The dog, said Pratt, is "Thro' life the same, in sunshine and in storms, / At once his Lord's protector and his guide, / Shapes to his wishes, to his wants conforms, / His slave, his friend, his pastime, and his pride."[23] In Pratt's view, the dog was both "protector and guide," helping the human contend with the dangerous world, but the animal's greatest virtue lay in its malleability. The dog was admirable because it conformed to the wishes of its master; "slave" and "friend" are presented as easily compatible concepts.

Those who glorified dogs as admirable slaves were, of course, emphasizing their utility to humans. Yet, as we have seen, the rhetoric of animal slavery was deeply problematic, and this willing service to humans could also be understood as a sign of distasteful servility (hence Alexander Pope's disdainful comparison between fawning dogs and courtiers).[24] The contradictions inherent in thinking about dogs are evident in Buffon's remarks on the hound, which he described as the most domestic of all dogs: "The gentleness, docility, and even the timidity of the hound, are proofs of his great degeneration, or rather of the great perfection he has acquired by the long and careful education bestowed on him by man."[25] Degeneration or perfection? It was this question, about the effects of domestic life on dogs, that was at the heart of the difficulty. William Smellie echoed Buffon in noting that silky hair and "pendulous ears" increased with domestication, and that those hanging ears were "the most certain mark of domestic servitude and of fear." But Smellie went further than Buffon in tracing the unpleasant implications of canine slavery. When under "the dominion of man," said Smellie, the dog "is converted into a mean, servile, patient, and parasitical slave."[26]

One response to this problem of canine servility was to redefine the very idea of the dog as slave. In this view, the problem of slavish corruption arises when the dog becomes *too* domestic, when the degeneration proceeds so far that the dog becomes nothing but a parasite. And the quintessential example of such an animal was the lapdog, a beast that seemed to have been intentionally bred so as to render it incapable of providing any real service to humans. The traits that made most dogs so noble were eliminated in the lapdog, leaving only the worst characteristics of meanness and servility. Samuel Ward thus noted in his natural history that the pug dog "appears to be a useless animal, and to want that fidelity that this tribe generally possess. It is entirely domestic, and will never follow its master to any considerable distance."[27] Georg Christian Raff remarked with disgust that some dogs' native "intelligence and attachment" were destroyed because of their owners' treatment: "some are so fat and unweildy [sic] that they can scarcely move: and it is clear, they are fed only for the pleasure taken in having them. The same may be said of lap-dogs and other small dogs."[28] Thomas O'Brien MacMahon, whose diatribe against lapdogs and women appeared in the previous chapter, did not condemn the animals only because they served their mistresses as sexual substitutes. The lapdog was characterized by "meanness, petulance, sloth, adulation, and cowardice," but it won the affection of its mistress by fawning upon her. Lapdogs, he concluded, fed women's lust for power by behaving with repellent servility: "These creatures, by the *attention* they pay, and the *obedience* they render their owners, flatter their *pride* extremely, especially if the proprietors of them happen to be *females*, who, being conscious of *less force* than the other sex, more eagerly grasp at everything, that may contribute to form, or cherish in them, an idea of their own *importance*."[29]

But this view of the danger of the utterly useless lapdog also implied another solution to the problem raised by the servile canine: the idea of the dog not as slave but as willing servant. Thus Sarah Trimmer placed a telling comment in the mouth of Mrs. Benson as she condemned Mrs. Addis's pet mania: "the lap-dop [sic] is, I am sure, a miserable object, full of diseases, the consequences of luxurious living. How enviable is the lot of a spaniel that is at liberty, to be the companion of his master's walks, when compared with his!"[30] Trimmer's spaniel is the "companion" of its master, at "liberty" to roam, in contrast to Mrs. Addis's lapdog or Ward's treacherous and "domestic" pug. The solution to the problem of luxurious pethood was utility, and some thought that even a small dog might find some way to serve. In Aikin and Barbauld's story "The Little Dog," for instance, "a very little Dog" is concerned that, unlike the other animals, he can be of no use to his master; he cannot carry burdens, provide food, or offer protection. Fido's mother assures him that as long as he shows love to his master, the master will love him in return. Yet the story does not end there; seemingly unwilling to suggest that such affection really is service enough, the authors have Fido warn his sleeping master of an imminent building collapse, thus saving his life. The apparently useless pet turns out to be useful after all, and to find his greatest fulfillment in service to his master. Moreover, Aikin and Barbauld make the analogy to humans explicit in their moral: "The poorest man may repay his obliga-tions to the richest and greatest by faithful and affectionate service—the meanest creature may obtain the favour and regard of the Creator him-self, by humble gratitude, and stedfast [*sic*] obedience."[31] The right form of servitude in this presentation transforms the dog from slave into com-panion, thus radically altering Buffon's vision of the working dog as slave. Ironically, in this vision, it is by working for humans that the dog wins its liberty. Both canine and human service become an opportunity rather than a burden.

This alternative to the image of domestication as slavery even emerged in the field of natural history. Buffon himself presented a vision of domestication as a mutual relationship, not merely one of domination and subjection, alongside his insistence on animal slavery. He used this relationship as evidence for his belief in the enormous gulf between apes and humans. Because apes could not be domesticated, he argued, they must be

> farther removed from man than most other animals: For docility implies some analogy between the giver and the receiver of instruc-tion. It is a relative quality, which cannot be exerted but when there is a certain number of common faculties on both sides, that differ only between themselves, because they are active in the master, and passive in the scholar. Now, the passive qualities of the ape have less relation to the active qualities of man than those of the dog or ele-phant, who require no more than good treatment to communicate to them the delicate and gentle sensations of faithful attachment, voluntary obedience, grateful service, and unreserved devotion.[32]

If domestication could mean slavery, it could also involve "delicate and gentle sensations," which for Buffon seemed to involve true emotion and thus turned servitude into "grateful service." Similarly, domestication appeared to be a positive force for man and beast when he compared birds to quadrupeds: "Our influence is smaller on the birds than on the quadrupeds, because their nature is more different from our own, and because they are less submissive and less susceptible of attachment. . . . As their instincts are totally unrelated to our own, we find it impossible to instil our sentiments; and their education is merely mechanical. . . . What comparison between the attachment of a dog, and the familiarity of a canary bird; between the understanding of an elephant, and the sagacity of an ostrich?"[33] In this account, domestication is less the assertion of power in a master-slave relationship than it is a system of mutual affection and understanding. The dog's "attachment" here is a far cry from its "degeneration" and slavery in Buffon's earlier discussion.

This vision of domestication reconfigured animal subjugation from a relationship of raw power to one of paternalistic care. And this model was, not coincidentally, analogous to that which was supposed to guide relationships between humans in the social hierarchy of eighteenth-century Britain. The idea of willing animal servitude thus fulfilled two useful functions. First, it ameliorated the disturbing implications created by the idea of animal enslavement. Second, and even more important, it reinforced the values of social order and paternalism. The utility of this model may account for the strong presence of animals in eighteenth-century literature for children. Not only did these books inform their juvenile readers about how to engage with animals, but they also upheld a reassuring vision of society for their middle- and upper-class adult readers (who would after all be the ones purchasing the books).[34] Proper relations with both animal and human servants would, they promised, be good not only for the future masters and mistresses of Britain but for those who served them as well. A monument to Robert Mossend, a servant who died in 1744, may be the quintessential example of this vision: Mossend's "Spaniel [was] of true English kind," the epitaph reads, "Who's gratitude inflam'd his mind / This servant in an honest way / In all his actions copy'd Tray."[35]

Crucially, however, this model of happy servitude had no room for companionship for its own sake, and it was rare to see a positive depiction of pet keeping in scientific or moral works. The idea of grateful service built on mutual understanding dealt with the problem of animal slavery while maintaining a species hierarchy and insisting on the difference between humans and animals. It thus denied the most threatening aspect of pets—the fact that their owners treated them like humans. The practice of pet keeping continued to expand throughout the eighteenth century, and growing numbers of people were willing to imagine a world in which they had a meaningful bond with their animals. But this cross-species friendship had to take place outside the bounds of the discourse of servitude.

One critical factor that helped make pet keeping more acceptable was the rise of the anticruelty movement.[36] As we have seen, anticruelty advocates became significantly more numerous and vocal in the later eighteenth century. Those favoring humane treatment of animals did not all share the same agenda: some were most concerned about animal labor, others criticized traditional entertainments like bullbaiting, and still others lamented the use of animals in scientific experiments. Their motives also differed. Moral arguments about self-discipline and time management coexisted uneasily with sentimental appeals on behalf of suffering beasts. Nevertheless, those who advocated kindness to animals often focused attention on the lower classes, as they were ostensibly the people most likely to abuse animals.[37] In Hogarth's famous series *The Stages of Cruelty*, for instance, the boy tormenting animals in the first stage (who progresses in later scenes to further abuse and even murder) is wearing a badge on his jacket that identifies him as a ward of St. Giles parish (fig. 29).[38] As in this print, in which abuse is presented as a form of entertainment for idle wastrels, cruelty was often linked to popular disorder and idleness: the poor, it was thought, abused animals out of ignorance, but also because they had the opportunity to do so. Eliminating idleness and encouraging labor discipline would create a more moral population of poor people who would no longer have either the opportunity or the inclination for abuse.[39]

Just as the humane movement was influenced by abolitionism, so, too, did many of the assumptions behind the movement reflect ideas about race and civilization that emerged in the period. The more civilized an individual or society, in this view, the more humane. Abuse of animals was itself a sign of animality; education and politeness fostered the ability to experience sympathy for lesser beings even as they increased the distance between humans and other living beings. Although anticruelty advocates presented different arguments for the kind treatment of animals and offered differing solutions to the problem of abuse, they generally shared the belief that lower-class people were much more likely to abuse animals because, ironically, they were closer to being animals themselves. Critics of the movement were quick to point out the unwillingness of humanitarians to acknowledge the existence of animal cruelty among the upper classes, despite elite participation in hunting, cockfighting, and

While various Scenes of sportive Woe,
    The Infant Race employ,
And torturd Victims bleeding shew
    The Tyrant in the Boy.
Design'd by W. Hogarth   Published according to Act of Parliament Feb.1.1751.

Behold! a Youth of gentler Heart,
    To spare the Creature's pain,
O take, he cries—take all my Tart!
    But Tears and Tart are vain.

Learn from this fair Example—You
    Whom savage Sports delight,
How Cruelty disgusts the view,
    While Pity charms the sight.
    Price 1ˢ.

Fig. 29 William Hogarth, *First Stage of Cruelty*,
1751. Etching and engraving, 380 × 320 mm.
Courtesy of the Lewis Walpole Library, Yale
University, 751.02.01.03.1+, box 200.

other abusive activities. But for anticruelty advocates, such behavior was a
much smaller problem than the failure of these elites to set a good example for their social inferiors. They assumed that their audience would
consist of those with the ability to influence public opinion and popular

behavior, and they appealed to their readers' self-perception as members of the moral as well as social elite. In January 1762, for instance, a correspondent to the *Gentleman's Magazine* noted that "the season of the year is now approaching, when the lower sorts of people throw at cocks, a custom which cannot be reflected upon by any humane person without horror." His insistence that this was a tradition observed solely by the "lower sorts" was typical.[40]

While such remarks undoubtedly reveal the class assumptions behind much of the anticruelty movement, the discourse of humanitarianism was more complicated than might at first appear. Another letter to the *Gentleman's Magazine* provides insight into this complexity. "Humanus" offered a long list of abuses perpetrated against animals, from children pulling the wings off flies to cockfighting. That some enjoyed these activities while "speculative individuals" abhorred them was, he said, a demonstration of "the difference between cultivated and uncultivated minds"; these abuses were "a fruitful source of high gratification to the illiterate and vulgar bulk of mankind."[41] Obviously, the letter reflects the class assumptions behind much anticruelty rhetoric. But the final reference to the "vulgar bulk of mankind" also demonstrates the weight carried by the term "vulgar" in arguments for humanitarianism, where it was commonly employed in distinguishing between supporters and opponents of the movement. By identifying those who opposed the movement as "vulgar," activists offered a much broader definition of the elite, and they also created the opportunity to group wealthier opponents of the movement with lower-class animal abusers. The flexibility of the word "vulgar"—which in the later eighteenth century encompassed ideas not only of class but also of ordinariness, common opinion, and lack of taste—made it enormously useful. In this schema, wealthy individuals who abused their beasts were part of the vulgar majority, while less wealthy, but more sensitive, humanitarians could form a new elite that depended not on socioeconomic status but on access to sympathy with nonhuman beings.

We can see these ideas in Pratt's *Liberal Opinions*. Pratt defined his "liberality" of opinion by contrast with others: "There is a deplorable illiberality in the affections of the vulgar: narrowly bigotted to one mean set of notions, and confirmed by the ungenerous maxims that have been inculcated in the early periods of life, they seldom, or never, rise to a single sentiment, which reflects dignity either on the head or heart; and the feelings of above half mankind are totally guided by the most contracted, and partial prejudices." Pratt congratulated himself for his very different views: "I have the fortitude to think, and judge for myself—I look on the animal world as very nearly connected with me; and thus publicly declare myself the sincere well-wisher of every living thing."[42] Although he began with a general condemnation of the narrow-mindedness of the "vulgar," the statement that followed made a direct connection between "liberal opinions" and a love of the "animal world." For Pratt, however, "the vulgar" was not simply a socioeconomic category; even the servant class had its own subset of ranks, with varieties of tenderness. In a discussion of cruelty to horses, he concluded, "It is an happiness . . . consistent with the delicate prosperity of the female nature and situation . . . that their pursuits and pleasures entirely lay in such parts of the town, as make shocking spectacles [of abuse] not very frequent, if we compare them with the more busy parts of the city.—There is—I cannot but perceive—a civilization of address, an urbanity of demeanour amongst the very chairmen of St. James's, which we shall in vain look for in the messengers of Whitechapel, and the porters of Thames-street."[43] Even the servants in the tonier neighborhoods were, he suggested, better bred and thus kinder to animals than their counterparts in rougher areas. Here we can begin to see the utility of the rhetoric of "vulgarity." If "the very chairmen of St. James's" have a degree of "civilization," then humanitarianism can simultaneously be achievable by all and a marker of status.

John Lawrence made a similar point as he explained his hope that his treatise in favor of humane treatment would meet with a positive reception because of the improving morals of his society at every level: "Even the lowest class of the people of this country have become much more mild and rational in their manners, and more humane in their treatment of brute animals (however defective still) than in former times. The savage sports have long been upon the decline." Nevertheless, Lawrence insisted that a key step against cruelty would be "for all people of property . . . to punish the brutal tyranny of profligate servants in the most exemplary manner"; if they did so, "the morals of servants would in time be amended, and our feelings would not be so frequently harrowed up with those disgusting spectacles which are now so common."[44] Lawrence sought to encourage and chide at the same time, and a focus on class differences helped his cause. By emphasizing the power of elites over their social inferiors, he sought to appeal to his primary audience. At the same time, however, he wanted to stress the potential for all classes of people to engage in humanitarian behavior. Later in the treatise, he employed yet more careful social distinctions, relating his attempt to convince an acquaintance—"one of the rich vulgar"—to stop beating a horse.[45] The offender in this case was wealthy but still "vulgar" enough to engage in the behavior Lawrence abhorred. In some instances, Lawrence thus carefully detailed class position, but in others he left it ambiguous in order to appeal to the widest part of the audience. In the end, he implied, humanitarianism was not the sole purview of rich or poor, but only the vulgar inflicted cruelty on animals.

This rhetoric of "vulgarity" in humanitarian arguments was useful precisely because it appealed to class interests while also suggesting that humanitarianism could transcend class. The relationship between humanitarianism and the discourse of sensibility can be seen, for example, in the sentimental novel. Both anticruelty advocates and sentimental novelists constructed their ideal audience as a special minority, uniquely capable of seeing the world without the restrictions of social norms and established practices.[46] Both thus implicitly presented the vision of an elite that existed beyond the standard categories of status, even as they appealed to their audiences' desire for status. The role of class in these humanitarian works was thus more complicated, and potentially less restrictive, than might at first appear.

≈   ≈   ≈

It may seem nevertheless that the eighteenth century was dominated by a fairly simple distinction between valued and valuable working animals, who were worthy of their masters' affection, and useless, worthless pets. Even the humane movement focused on working animals, and the abuse of pets was still far in the future as a subject of concern for anticruelty advocates. Most of this book has addressed the ways in which writers and artists condemned pets and their owners; indeed, it would be reasonable for the reader at this point to envision the eighteenth century as very distant from our own pet-loving culture. But the moralists whose words and values informed the critiques of pet keeping were protesting what they saw as disturbing trends in their society. Even as they fought a rearguard action, pet ownership was increasing and becoming more socially acceptable among all ranks. To see this change in action, let us now turn to another area of conflict in the eighteenth century: the question of whether there should be a tax on dogs.[47] The debate over a dog tax might seem far removed from depictions of pampered lapdogs, suffering humans, and abused horses, but in fact it was rooted in many of the same questions and concerns.

The idea of taxing dogs first emerged in the 1730s, and the issue came up in pamphlets and parliamentary bills for the rest of the century, until a tax was finally passed in 1796. Some advocates saw the tax as a simple and efficient means of dealing with problems in the existing game laws.[48] But many proponents emphasized the moral aspect of the tax, stressing that it would help eliminate a wasteful luxury. In fact, the law that finally passed was explicitly presented as a luxury tax, albeit a very different kind of luxury tax from the one most advocates sought.

Like discussions of servants and pets, debates about a dog tax thus took place at the intersection of the highly fraught concepts of class and luxury. The very meaning of "luxury" was rooted in assumptions about class; what was a necessity for one person might be a luxury for another. In a society that still generally believed that wealth could not be gained in one area without a loss in another, many people thought that luxurious consumption must have a negative impact on society as a whole, and despite the new argument about the positive economic benefits of luxury, the moralistic view dominated debates about pet keeping. For most of the century, proponents of a tax on dogs constructed dog ownership as a luxury, with the explicit goal of limiting the practice; they directly addressed the problem of competition for resources between pets and lower-class humans, albeit in a very different way from the satires and children's literature discussed above. Taxing dogs, they hoped, would lead to a reduction in the canine population and thus free up precious resources. But the issue of luxury created a variety of new problems in turn. If dogs were a luxury, then for whom? And what distinguished a useful, working dog from a useless luxury?

While writers like Coventry and Trimmer focused on the pets of the wealthy, most tax proponents made clear that their interest was in reducing the number of dogs owned by poor people, on the assumption that dogs were luxuries for the poor. Some writers insisted that a dog tax would reduce the number of people who needed economic relief by forcing them to forego the expense of caring for dogs. Edward Barry suggested that, in addition to a tax on dogs, there should be regulations requiring that overseers of the poor law refuse assistance to anyone who kept a dog.⁴⁹ Indeed, the parishioners of Eccles voted unanimously in 1774 to deny poor relief to any dog-owning paupers.⁵⁰ Behind such ideas lay the assumption that charity was being wasted on the undeserving poor, who were spending what little they had to support a useless animal—a luxury. Writers like Barry thus justified their desire to minimize their own contributions to poor relief with a moral argument. Thomas Gilbert offered a slightly different scheme, but to similar ends. He proposed replacing the Elizabethan poor law entirely with a new set of laws— including taxes on dogs, alehouses, and those who used toll roads on Sundays—aimed at improving the morals and work habits of the nation. He recommended that county officials use the revenue from these taxes to build hospitals and facilities to house and educate poor children; whatever remained could go to the government in compensation for the income it would lose because of an expected reduction in the number of alehouses.⁵¹ Gilbert's proposal thus made explicit another aspect of the luxury-based argument in favor of taxing dogs: it would be a sort of "sin tax" akin to other methods of discouraging immoral behavior and idleness.

Although not everyone presented the tax as a penalty on misguided dog owners, many did suggest that the poor starved themselves in order to feed their dogs. Wasting limited resources on undeserving animals reflected their inability to set sensible priorities. In one sense, then, the dog tax could be seen as saving the poor from themselves, as well as saving the pocketbooks of their betters. This view of the lower orders was common. As early as 1710, Daniel Hilman referred to the "poor Wretches that cannot maintain their Families, [but] must have their Dog or two after them, tho' they know they are maintain'd to the prejudice of their Betters. It springs from a sort of beggarly Pride, or desire to live at the publick Charge, and I think a Man ought to be call'd as much to account how his Dogs live, as how he lives himself."⁵² Roughly eight decades later, George Morland's painting *The Miseries of Idleness* (fig. 30) depicted a dog competing for a bone with a boy in rags, in the hovel of a wastrel and his overdressed wife.⁵³ Sarah Trimmer agreed that "no person should keep Dogs who cannot afford to feed them, or who have no use for them. At present there are certainly too great a number of these animals, and it would be an act of mercy to drown them when puppies, rather than to let them live and suffer the miseries to which many are exposed through the poverty of their keepers."⁵⁴

Fig. 30 George Morland, *The Miseries of Idleness*,
before 1790. Oil on canvas, 31.6 × 37.3 cm.
Scottish National Gallery.

These ideas were widely employed by tax proponents. William King
insisted that even when food was scarce, laborers and beggars wasted it
on dogs. "This is one of the Inconveniencies, which arise from suffering
all Men to have full and free Liberty to keep as many of these useless
Animals as they please," he said, "even tho' they want Bread for the
Support of their Families."[55] In 1791, George Clark also complained that

dogs consumed the low-quality grains and offal that would otherwise feed the poor, thus creating scarcity and raising the price of food. Moreover, "the poor themselves join in promoting this evil" by keeping dogs and feeding them "part of the poor child's dole." Even when children were not deprived, dogs consumed food that might otherwise go to support "more useful animals" like pigs.[56] A correspondent to the *Times* agreed that a dog consumed as much food as a child but suggested that poor children voluntarily shared their food with dogs: "the cur and the child know but one platter or porringer, whenever the parent is not within observation. Hence, the consumption of what should be the proportion of a child, and not of a dog, out of a poor man's earnings."[57]

Even those who entertained a more positive attitude toward the poor could suggest that a dog tax would help the lower orders set more sensible priorities. Charles Varlo acknowledged the affection that poor people could feel for dogs but denied that it was sufficient reason for allowing them to keep animals they could not afford. Poor people with dogs had three choices, he claimed: to starve the dogs, to let them loose to worry sheep, or to feed the dogs the "bread and butter" that would otherwise go to their children. Despite the seemingly obvious option, many a poor man chose to keep "a dog for his children to play with" rather than, for instance, a pig that would feed them all. "I may be asked, why, cannot a poor man see these follies himself? I answer, no; because fore-cast does not always get the better of folly in this, no more than in every other degree in life; there is a natural tenderness and indulgence, in every parent towards their children, as well as in ladies for their lap-dogs; pardon the comparison."[58] Varlo presented himself as sympathetic to the poor, but he agreed with the dominant view that they could not be trusted to determine their own financial destinies. Like ladies who overindulged their lapdogs, indigent parents would bow to the demands of their children, even when doing so went against everyone's best interests.

While poor people's financial irresponsibility thus made a tempting target for advocates of the dog tax, the rhetoric of luxury and morality could be used in other ways to criticize the rich as well as the poor, just as writers like Trimmer and Mackenzie criticized wealthy pet owners for neglecting the needs of their inferiors. After analyzing the irresponsibility of the poor, for instance, Charles Varlo took the wealthy to task. He avoided criticizing well-off dog owners directly, admitting that they could easily afford the twenty shillings a year he calculated it cost to feed an average dog. "But, though such things be not felt by people in affluence yet, be assured, it hurts the public in general," for such behavior increased the demand for victuals and thus also their price—"and a half-penny, or a farthing in a pound, in either meat or bread, is very sensibly felt by the lowest sort of people."[59] Varlo's claims were echoed by many people who saw the large kennels of the wealthy as virtual theft from the poor. In a 1757 letter to the *Gentleman's Magazine*, "Colonus" complained about the rich landowner who overfed his dogs while the poor went hungry: "What large wooden or stone troughs or trays have I seen filled with the soup of the best meat in the shambles, given to dogs, while the poor starveling tenant, with a longing eye, would have rejoiced to have joined in the banquet!"[60] The *Public Advertiser* agreed; dogs were "an article of luxury, confined to the higher ranks, and what is worse, the victuals they consume would serve to feed thousands of poor families.—When one views a magnificent dog-kennel rearing its proud turrets in the neighbourhood of industrious poverty, what an idea must he form of the benevolence and public spirit of our nobility!"[61] In this view, it was not the luxurious living of the poor that was the problem, but the conspicuous consumption of the rich.

Such ideas not only located the source of society's ills away from the poor; they also targeted different dogs. Edward Barry proposed taxing sporting dogs at a lower rate than other breeds because his explicit goal was to reduce the population of nuisance dogs, which he believed were owned primarily by the lower orders. Sporting dogs were workers, not luxuries. Others disagreed with this classification. For some, all hunting dogs were worthy of taxation because they, like horses "kept for diversion," were luxuries. One writer suggested on these grounds that packs of dogs should be taxed at several pounds annually, and that each sporting dog should cost its owner a guinea or more per year. The author was careful to point out that such an approach would prove no burden to the poor, who were already prohibited by the game laws from keeping sporting dogs.[62] Thomas Gilbert also singled out hunting dogs for special taxation in his proposal, which, as we have seen, was intended to reduce luxury and vice.[63] The Member of Parliament John Dent drew on these ideas when, introducing the 1796 bill that eventually led to the passage of a tax, he insisted that dogs epitomized the luxurious self-indulgence of the wealthy at the expense of the poor. He cited examples of gentlemen who spent £400–800 each year on grain to feed their dogs, noted the massive expense of packs of foxhounds (he estimated the annual cost at £1,000–2,000), and insisted that the bread of the poor was in effect stolen to feed the dogs of landowners. Speaking in favor of Dent's bill, Edmund Lechmere agreed that the tax should be enforced on the wealthy: "He trusted it would be of service to the public at large, and particularly to the poor at this time of scarcity. Gentlemen who kept a pack of fox hounds, ought to be compelled to pay high for them."[64] In this view, hunting was a form of entertainment for the privileged, as deserving of taxation as other luxuries. If some tax proponents hoped that it would deter the poor from wasting their money on dogs they could ill afford, men like Lechmere wanted to use the same method to achieve the opposite goal. Treat sporting dogs like the expensive accoutrements they are, these men argued, and tax their owners accordingly.

Behind these discussions lay basic questions about dog ownership: was a dog a luxury or a necessity? Under what circumstances was it acceptable to own a dog? Many of those who argued in favor of a tax believed that dogs were, by and large, luxuries and could thus be taxed like other luxuries. George Clark made the case explicitly; luxuries were the only legitimate objects of taxation, he said, "and that the keeping of Dogs is generally a species of luxury no one will attempt to deny. The fact is notorious, that there are more Dogs kept in this country from fancy, or for pleasure, than from necessity." Although they "are no doubt faithful domestics and cheerful companions," he added, "this by no means makes them necessaries."[65] But questions about the circumstances under which a dog owner might be excused from paying the tax reveal the difficulty of determining just where luxury ended and necessity began. Clark, for instance, proposed that exemptions could be provided for people who were obliged to own dogs; in all other cases, however, dogs were as legitimate subjects of taxation as horses, houses, and hats, all of which were taxed.[66] William King argued similarly that certain groups of dog owners should be exempt from the tax. He offered to excuse all owners of land worth £10 a year, as well as "Tanners, Curriers, Fellmongers, Butchers, and the like," whose trades required a dog. Everyone else, and all those who owned more than one dog, would be subject to the tax.[67] Others suggested that it was not the type but the number of dogs that transformed dog ownership from necessity to luxury. "Publicola," writing to the *Gentleman's Magazine* in 1762, argued that a single dog in each household should be taxed at a mere shilling, which he suggested would be within most people's financial reach; "farmers, shepherds, or even cottagers" could also justify the ownership of one dog. But more than one dog "may, I think, very well be put upon the foot of luxury; the proper subject of a tax even in times of profound peace"—and he believed that each additional dog should be taxed at three or even four times the initial rate.[68]

The arguments for a luxury tax succeeded in 1796. By then there was already a well-established practice of taxing luxuries, from manservants to hair powder. Given the specific circumstances of the moment—widespread food shortages, anxieties about rabies, and a government interested in raising revenue wherever it could be found—the tax won sufficient support for passage.[69] But presenting a tax on dogs as a luxury tax created as many problems as it solved, and there were deep divisions over how to define a dog as a "luxury." John Dent's bill failed; shortly afterward, Parliament did pass a tax, but it was structured very differently from his original proposal. The parliamentary debates over Dent's bill reveal these divisions and thereby explain why the tax assumed the peculiar form it finally did.

The specific definition of a "luxury" dog in the 1796 act was shaped by both long- and short-term factors. Dent argued that all dogs were luxuries, robbing the poor of desperately needed food in a time of severe shortage. But his bill was not approved. Influenced by larger cultural currents that had transformed ideas about pets and other animals by the end of the eighteenth century, the tax that ultimately passed was based on a radically altered notion of the dog as a luxury. George Clark was already responding to such cultural shifts in 1791, when he exclaimed against "false principles of humanity, and absurd or ridiculous attachments" in favor of the "sacrifice of private interest to public good." A dog tax, he insisted, "has nothing but false impressions of tenderness, absurd and ridiculous attachments, or sordid self-interest, to oppose it." It was perfectly clear "that Dogs are, upon the whole, pernicious and destructive animals."[70] By the 1790s, however, such views were in the minority. Two distinct but related changes directly affected the dog tax debates: the rise of the anticruelty movement and a new appreciation for the strong emotional connections people could feel to their pets.

By the time of the 1796 parliamentary debates over the dog tax, rhetoric insisting on humane treatment of animals was widespread, even if little had been accomplished in practice. In this context, the claim that the lower orders wasted their food on dogs could be modified to suggest that they intentionally deprived their animals of food and imposed other cruelties on them. It was but a short step from complaining about the poor giving their children's food to the dogs, to suggesting that the poor also starved their dogs. Barry, for instance, argued that most dogs were owned by the poor, and that those unfortunate animals were "all but starved, through the indigence, and the cruelty, of their owners!" This was a terrible fate for a species known for its "fidelity, docility, and great affection." A tax that would prevent poor people from owning dogs would thus benefit the dogs, given that the poor were notoriously abusive to animals:

> They . . . evince a peculiar tyranny of temper, in their savage correction of such animals as are entrusted to their care, particularly of horses; they delight in barbarous sports, and their very children take pleasure in torturing dumb creatures! It is not, God knows, to offend the poor, because they are poor, that I have made these painful remarks, but to silence such accusations as these, that are made with too much truth, against the majority of them, that I avail myself of every opportunity of circulating this friendly hint, that by more becoming and humane manners, they may induce their friends, and well wishers, to plead in private, as well as in public, with fewer objections, and much better success in the delightful cause of charity![71]

A tax on dogs, Barry thus argued, would not only help society; it would actually help dogs. Ironically, he went on to emphasize that his goal was the extermination of dogs in order to reduce their numbers, but he insisted that allowing the poor to own dogs was simply a license for abuse.[72]

Yet if tax supporters presented poor dog owners as engaging in cruelty, more MPs spoke against Dent's bill than for it, some of whom saw the legislation itself as promoting cruelty. They had some reason for these views, given the publicly articulated hope of tax proponents like Barry and Dent himself that it would lead to the mass destruction of dogs. What, the MPs wondered, would be the effect of such officially sanctioned murder? According to some, the dog tax would have a dangerous effect on the morals of the nation, heightening class antagonism and inuring the population to violence. Such arguments drew on the increasingly common idea that cruelty to animals was a step on a slippery slope to cruelty and barbarism against other humans (a view also implicit in Hogarth's *Stages of Cruelty*).[73] Thus, in the parliamentary debate, John Courtenay contrasted "the caresses, the playfulness, and the fidelity of dogs [which] endeared them to us" with the dangers posed by their widespread extermination: "To accustom the people to look with hard-hearted indifference on the murder of these faithful animals, would debase their moral feelings."[74] Henry Penton similarly worried that "the hanging of dogs would familiarize the people to barbarity"—barbarity that might well be directed at their social superiors. He remembered an incident from his own childhood when he witnessed a park keeper killing "a favourite spaniel belonging to him as a boy, and cutting the animal's head off with a hatchet. Had he had the hatchet in his hand, and had the park-keeper been in his power, at that time, he could not say what might have been the consequence. How, then, could the House say, that the poor man placed in a similar situation would not be actuated by similar feelings?"[75] While tax proponents argued that allowing poor people to keep dogs was a license for cruelty, opponents suggested that the bill itself actually legislated animal abuse and perhaps even encouraged worse behavior.

The 1796 parliamentary debates also reflected the second major change in thinking about animals that took place in the late eighteenth century. Increasingly, caring for animals came to be seen as a sign of moral virtue, rather than weakness, for people of all social classes, and the humane movement's distinction between "the vulgar" and those sympathetic to animals reinforced this new vision. By the 1790s, attempts to deny poor relief to paupers who owned dogs had become controversial. While the *Gentleman's Magazine* in 1774 had reported without comment on the Eccles vote to deny poor relief to dog owners, in 1791 it condemned a meeting at which the Ipswich town council approved the same policy: "We are sorry," the magazine remarked, "that such an order should disgrace the resolutions of a humane and sensible people. The most deplorable object, forsaken by all his fellow-creatures, finds friendship and consolation in his *faithful* dog."[76] Here, charity opposed the arguments about needless waste and luxury; and the remark about "a humane and sensible people" captured two of the new keywords about the desired relationship between humans and animals.

Parliamentary opposition to the proposed tax reflected these new attitudes toward the practice of pet keeping—attitudes apparent in William Windham's argument against the bill. Windham accepted the notion of a tax on sporting dogs "because they were a kind of luxury, and their owners could afford to pay." But he regarded the idea of a tax on all dogs, explicitly intended to lead to their mass extermination, as deeply offensive. There were certainly times when dogs were nuisances, "but he should have been loth to have avenged himself upon the whole of the species, in consequence of a little temporary inconvenience." Windham insisted that dogs consumed much less than others had estimated; and far from taking food away from the poor, they ate garbage that would otherwise become a greater problem than the dogs themselves. More important for Windham than such practical considerations, however, was the emotional attachment between man and dog:

> With the poor the affection for a dog was so natural, that in poetry and painting it had been constantly recorded, and in any sort of domestic representation, we scarcely see a picture without a memorial of this attachment. If the rich man feels a partiality for a dog, what must a poor man do, who has so few amusements? He would be destitute without one. A dog was the companion of his laborious hours, and when he was bereft of his wife and children it filled up the dreary vacuity. It was a well-known fact that Alexander Selkirk, upon whose narrative the story of Robinson Crusoe was founded, sought the society of every animal upon the desart island, except those which he was obliged to kill for food. That was his greatest satisfaction; and a dog afforded a similar satisfaction to the poor. Would the House, then, sacrifice that honest, that virtuous satisfaction?

Windham believed that estimates of the problems caused by poaching and sheep worrying had been exaggerated, but whatever their extent, such problems were outweighed by the pleasure the poor received from their dogs.[77] Richard Brinsley Sheridan similarly argued in favor of the emotional connection between poor people and their dogs. If the lower orders loved their pets so much that in times of extreme scarcity they were willing to share with them what little food they had, then "what was the conclusion, but that they would rather deprive themselves of some of the necessaries of life, than lose their faithful companions."[78] "Dogs," echoed John Courtenay, "had always been the friends of man. They were celebrated in the writings of every poet; and in the Scriptures too, for they must all have read of Tobit's dog."[79]

Such arguments reflected a major change in attitudes toward pets over the course of the eighteenth century. If much of the discourse surrounding pet keeping continued to reflect the legal distinction between valuable working animals and worthless pets, an alternative view was gaining ground along with the spread of pet keeping itself. A moralizing story from the period, for instance, reveals a very different perspective on "useless" animals. A boy and his father give a shilling to a crippled soldier and are immediately accosted by "a sorry beggar woman," who scolds them for wasting their charity on a man who will spend it on gin and his dog. "A beggar keep a dog!" she cries. "What's that but robbing other people, who deserve assistance?" But when the boy recounts the incident to his sister, she is outraged not by the soldier's dog but by the beggar woman's attitude: "no wonder if a soldier, exposed to all kinds of weather, should now and then drink a little gin, which he knows will warm him; and perhaps his dog was his last best friend, and the steady companion of all his bad days."[80] Notably, the story does not suggest that the dog serves any useful purpose, even protection. Instead, it emphasizes the dog's value as a "steady companion" and loyal friend. Henry Mackenzie's *Man of Feeling*, the quintessential example of the sentimental novel, similarly includes scenes in which a dog provides crucial emotional support for the poor; a popular print from the era depicts a famous vignette in the novel in which the hero assists a beggar and his faithful dog (fig. 31).[81]

It was this view that the *Gentleman's Magazine* presented in arguing against denying poor relief to dog owners, and that Windham expressed in his critique of the dog tax as an attack on the poor. The argument that the poor should lose their dogs because they did not *need* dogs is rejected here in favor of the recognition that an emotional bond with a pet could itself be an important aspect of human experience. Opponents of the bill thus mustered a range of arguments at the intersection of class and emotion. To support a tax that would lead to the extermination of the canine population would be the worst sort of ingratitude, rewarding fidelity with death, removing one of the few pleasures the poor could afford, and coarsening the moral sentiments of the entire population.

Although such arguments reflected a paternalism that also fed Windham's opposition to the abolition of bullbaiting,[82] what is most significant about these views is the rhetoric in which they were expressed. Concerns about cruelty or the emotional bonds between people and pets were

Fig. 31   Henry Kingsbury, after John
Kitchingman, *The Beggar and His Dog*, 1775.
Mezzotint, 603 × 456 mm. The British
Museum. © The Trustees of the British
Museum. All rights reserved.

virtually absent from discussions of a dog tax throughout most of the century, but they dominated the 1796 parliamentary debates, while other interests, such as game law reform, vanished. These changes make sense only in the broader context of a transformation in the representation of animals, and their relationship to humans, in eighteenth-century society.

The dog tax was passed in May 1796. In its final form, however, it represented a compromise advocated by the prime minister, William Pitt. Dent had sought a tax of 2s. 6d. on every dog except guide dogs for the blind, hoping that such a tax would drastically reduce the canine population. His efforts resulted in widespread ridicule, earning him the permanent nickname "Dog Dent" and, according to Robert Southey, causing people to send him "some hundred dead dogs packed up as game" after the tax was passed.[83] Pitt agreed that a tax was a good idea but insisted that the law should distinguish between the poor and the wealthy, so that the latter would pay much more.[84] Whereas Dent and other tax proponents advocated legislation explicitly to target the dogs of the poor and to encourage the mass killing of dogs, the final bill accommodated the moral and emotional arguments of Dent's opponents. All people who kept dogs that could be used for sport, as well as all those who owned two or more dogs, were charged five shillings per dog. In cases where there was just one dog and it was not a hunting dog, only those already subject to house or window taxes had to pay, and that tax was limited to three shillings per dog. Instead of contributing to poor relief, as most early advocates had suggested, the revenue was applied to the government's sinking fund, set aside to repay the national debt.[85] Pitt had transformed the legislation from a measure aimed at local problems of poverty and poaching to a tax like those on other luxury consumer goods, and applied it to the needs of a government at war.

This final legislation thus embodied a number of important priorities. By focusing on dogs used for sport, it implicitly endorsed the notion that a tax on dogs should be a luxury tax. Taxing sporting dogs was aimed at the wealthy, who could most easily afford to pay for their diversions. By defining sporting dogs as luxuries, the law also undermined the traditional definition of sporting dogs as working dogs. Hunting, by the end of the century, was firmly established as recreation rather than a means of obtaining food. The provision about multiple dogs drew on a different aspect of the luxury argument—one dog might be a necessity, but more represented an indulgence. The specific structure of the act thus reflected the distinction present in its closest analogue, the tax on manservants. Both were unusual in addressing living beings rather than objects. And both accepted that the same individual (human or canine) might be either a luxury or a necessity, depending on the specific role of that individual. The idea of dog as servant thus survived, but in a radically different form from that envisaged by Sarah Trimmer and her like. Most important, by distinguishing between households that paid other taxes and those that did not, the law embodied Pitt's concern that the poor should be sheltered from the tax. The bill protected the right of the poor to own dogs, either for work or for the pure pleasure of emotional companionship, and, significantly, it did not distinguish between those two functions.

Supporters of a dog tax thus triumphed, in the obvious sense that a tax was passed. But given their justifications for such a law, theirs was a limited victory, even a pyrrhic one. Most supporters of a tax had argued on two grounds. First, the lower orders had no legitimate reason to own a dog; any poor person who kept a dog was either sacrificing himself (or his children) for a ridiculous attachment or had nefarious reasons for doing so. Indigent dog owners were either fools or poachers. Second, the tax would actually benefit the population at large by increasing the food supply while reducing rabies.[86] This second argument depended, of course, on the presumption that the tax would lead to a massacre of the canine population, as dog owners would choose to kill their animals rather than pay taxes on them. Since most tax advocates also wanted to include a clause enabling anyone to confiscate and kill a dog not properly licensed and to use the carcass for his own purposes, they assumed that this provision would add to the number of dogs destroyed. Some of them even recalculated the projected tax revenue downward to reflect the presumed decimation of the dog population.[87] In its final form, however, the tax actually supported the views of the vocal minority who wanted a levy on the pastimes of the elite. It enabled the poor to keep dogs without penalty while taxing the hunting dogs of the landed elite at a higher rate than other breeds. Ultimately, the government endorsed the view that dog ownership was a luxury for some, but not for all. Ironically, in the eyes of the law, the dogs of the wealthy were luxuries, while for poor people, dogs—even "useless" pets—were necessities that they could not live without.

~ ~ ~

The outcome of the dog tax debates, at the close of the eighteenth century, demonstrates the complex influence of class on ideas about animals in general and pet ownership in particular. For much of the century, the concept of immoral luxury drove the arguments; pets symbolized misplaced expenditure by both rich and poor. Critics of the wealthy argued that pet keepers effectively stole food from the poor to feed their pets, and that their love of animals made them incapable of proper care for their social inferiors. Critics of the poor claimed that they were wasting precious time and money on animals instead of focusing on feeding themselves and their families. Animal ownership, in these views, could be justified only if the animal made a legitimate economic contribution to the household. Such a contribution ennobled the animal, enabling it to fulfill its God-given destiny. Proper domestication allowed for real relationships between humans and animals while maintaining the hierarchy of species in which humans were always on top.

Even as this perspective continued to be widely expressed throughout the century, however, actual human-animal relations were changing. Pet keeping was becoming more widespread and more socially acceptable, partly because luxuries were no longer seen as inherently immoral. Pets might be luxuries for some, meriting taxation that would benefit the whole society, but that need not define them as a social evil. The rhetoric of sensibility and opposition to cruelty both reflected and influenced changes in attitudes toward pets and their owners. While the humane movement primarily identified the lower classes as the perpetrators of animal abuse, the discourse of caring sentiment versus vulgarity left open the possibility that all people might construct a more loving relationship with animals.

To recognize this change is not to suggest that the actual conditions of life improved for most animals. But it does offer a window into the transformation that increasingly put pets at the center of Britain's national identity, as symbols of a broader humanitarianism. If loving and caring for animals was a sign of moral superiority in a wealthy individual, it was equally so for the lower classes. Indeed, as the parliamentary debates of 1796 make clear, trying to prevent the poor from keeping pets might even lead to class unrest—a prospect that seemed especially dangerous during the 1790s, a time of economic hardship and of revolution across the English Channel that might potentially strike even closer to home. Pet keeping had shifted from a fundamentally indefensible behavior to one that seemed to offer a bulwark of social harmony.

5 ⟿ PETS AND THEIR PEOPLE

In December 1712, Lady Isabella Wentworth suffered a devastating trag-
edy when Pug, her pet monkey, died. Lady Wentworth was heartbroken.
Pug had been a part of her household for more than seven years[1] and was
a favorite among the large collection of animals with whom she shared
her residence. In a letter to her son Thomas, she wrote that Pug was "the
darling of . . . all" her pets, and she admitted, "God forgive me, there is
some that bears the name of a Christian, that I could have rather had
died."[2] In her grief, she commissioned two death portraits of the monkey,
one "large and the other in miniature," and she buried the beloved animal
in her garden.[3]

While Pug lived, Lady Wentworth frequently wrote about the monkey,
who was, she thought, a truly superior simian. Comparing Pug to another
pet monkey, she said proudly, "mine is very pert, and full of diverting
tricks, . . . the eyes of mine sparkles like two diamonds, and is perter than
ever you see her, and fuller of tricks—but it must be when she has a mind
to it, not else."[4] She was equally proud of how well the monkey got on
with her many other animals, including an assortment of dogs and a parrot. When her dogs had puppies, she reported, Pug helped to care for
them: "there is not in all Twickenham a better nurse than Pug," she wrote
in 1709; "she is the fondest creature of the four puppies that ever was

seen, kisses them and covers them up with a Blanket. It is a very pretty diverting sight to see her."[5]

Lady Wentworth's correspondence provides a rare glimpse of the quotidian interactions of human and pet in the early eighteenth century. In one letter, for instance, she remarked that she was disappointed she could not bring Pug and her favorite dog with her on a day trip to her son's country house, since they both used to love running in the garden—"but I never dare trust Pug without a string."[6] In another letter, Lady Wentworth provided a vivid image of the monkey at home: "Pug is grown very tame, . . . and has a long rope and can go out of one room into another. She is now got upon my shoulder, pulled off all my head clothes, and [is] very busy looking my head [i.e., grooming for vermin]." In short, she concluded, "there is more variety of diversions in my room, than in any one in this town."[7] Two years later, Lady Wentworth returned to the pleasure that the animal gave her: "Sure Pug is prettier than ever, and much better humored than ever. Sue [Lady Wentworth's maid] can do anything with her. When we are alone, we let her loose for an hour or two, keep the windows and doors shut, and she is highly delighted." She added apologetically, "dear soul forgive all this stuff: [your] minutes are all more precious than to be interrupted with such stuff," but she obviously wanted to share this important aspect of her life with her son.[8]

Pug's death, then, was a terrible blow to Lady Wentworth. When Thomas sent his condolences, she responded with a lengthy, detailed, and obviously heartsick description of Pug's last hours, describing her attempts to nurse the monkey as well as Pug's peaceful expression in death.[9] After Thomas, in a misguided attempt to fill the void, offered her his own monkey, she thanked him but declined: "I must confess myself so great a fool I cannot love with moderation, and losing my other pretty fool I shall kill this with too much care."[10] Despite such acknowledgment of her grief, however, Lady Wentworth obviously felt defensive about expressing this emotion. "I must confess I did love it very much and I was foolishly fond of it," she admitted. "But I hope you do but jest; you cannot think me so great a fool, as to pine and make myself sick for the loss of it." On the contrary, "knowing the world to be very censorious, . . . I went out every day," lest anyone suggest that she stayed home to grieve, even though she was in fact suffering from "a great cold."[11]

Her fears were certainly well founded in the case of her daughter-in-law Anne, who found nothing but amusement in Lady Wentworth's loss.

Anne wrote to Thomas on the same day that Lady Wentworth sent word of Pug's demise,

> I think I ought not to have write so long a letter to you today for I am sure you'll have a very long one from Lady Wentworth with very great lamentation, for her monkey is dead. I have been as little merry as I could since [then], for Lady W was so much troubled about it that she was really angry if I laughed; and you may believe it could be no affliction to me to make me melancholy, and I could not cry for my life. The day it died I expected Lady W to dinner and she neither came nor sent [word], and I stayed dinner for her some time; but she would not so much as see me that day. But what is the most extraordinary thing is she has two of its pictures drawn since 'tis dead, one large and the other in miniature.[12]

For Anne, grieving for a monkey was ridiculous and the idea of commissioning portraits pure nonsense. Even Thomas appears to have joined in the teasing, for later in January Lady Wentworth complained, "indeed never was there two so much alike as your spouse and self; for did you not ask me in what manner Pug died in, and now you *laugh at me*, for repeating it."[13] Pug had been a loyal companion for years, but Lady Wentworth found little sympathy even from those closest to her.

Pug had always been a source of conflict between Lady Wentworth and Anne, who seems to have come to terms with her mother-in-law's many dogs but could not abide the monkey. When Thomas acquired one of his own shortly before Pug died, Lady Wentworth said she was "sorry you have got a monkey, for your poor dumbs [i.e., dumb animals] are not very happy and my Lady [Anne] loves them not at all." More details of their fraught relationship followed: "You need never fear; my monkey never came near her here. I kept [it] in my own closet, my Lady was very civil to it, but it never came in my Lady's way, but when she came on purpose to see it. . . . And for Pug's stinking, it's wholesomer than sweets," she added, perhaps revealing one source of the conflict. Finally, she concluded, "he never is in any room but my own, and I am never better than when I am diverted with that and the rest of my dumbs, for I hate cards and tables, and old people must have some diversion. Mistress Godfrey has a monkey, and Lady Duchess of Southampton, and they are fonder, if possible, than I am."[14] The defensive tone in her reference to other women's pets reveals her self-consciousness about Pug's role in her life. And the tension throughout her letters about Pug, which alternated between relishing the details of daily life with the monkey and self-consciously dismissing her great affection, was typical of Lady Wentworth's writing about all her pets. The animals were an enormously important part of her life, yet she was aware that even her beloved son did not fully understand why she cared for them so much.

≈   ≈   ≈

Much of the evidence regarding eighteenth-century pet keeping consists of writing *about* pets and their owners, and much of that writing was deeply critical—an attitude reflected in Lady Wentworth's embarrassment. Pet keeping seemed to many observers to be a symptom of the problems of a society they feared might be on the verge of collapse. The very economic and imperial success that helped make pet keeping possible on a large scale seemed to some to presage decadence and decline. Fashionable women with their lapdogs, apes dressed in footmen's livery, imprisoned songbirds trilling for the amusement of their captors, all could be seen as embodying the worst forms of human self-indulgence in a society that had lost its moral bearings. Yet over the course of the century attitudes toward pets were changing. "Useless" pets no longer represented exclusively the capriciousness of people with high incomes and low taste; instead, they could be seen as a comfort for those who might have no material resources of their own. Thus we see Gertrude Savile escaping the torment of her family by retreating to her room, where she took refuge in solitude and needlework: "That, and my Cat all my pleasure."[15] Companionship and affection from animals might be valuable to those who had little means as well as to those with money to burn; what is most significant is that British society increasingly recognized that pets could represent worthy sentiment as well as embarrassing self-indulgence.

Direct information about nonelite pet ownership is regrettably scarce; lower literacy rates, the expense of paper and postage, and the tendency to confine writing to "important" subjects mean that little firsthand documentation of pet keeping survives from those outside the economic and literary elite. The pet owners from whom we will hear directly in this chapter thus come from a fairly narrow social stratum. However, the existing evidence suggests that pet keeping was becoming much more widespread as well as more socially acceptable over the course of the century. As noted in chapter 1, the sheer number of animals for sale increased dramatically, and those animals represent only a small fraction of the much greater number acquired without the exchange of money. The 1796 parliamentary debates over the dog tax presented estimates of dog ownership in England in the hundreds of thousands or even millions, and revealed much greater acceptance of pet keeping among the poor. Visual evidence supports this perception. Over the course of the century, for example, birds in cages become ubiquitous in prints depicting poor households. John Bull had his loyal dog, and over time, as he became increasingly associated with the middle class, his household was shown with both a dog and a cat to demonstrate the simple comfort of his life. One of the most telling of such images used the loss of such animals to demonstrate the collapse of British values in the face of wartime conscription. James Gillray's 1793 print *John Bull's Progress* begins with "John Bull Happy": the corpulent family man dozes by his fireside, accompanied by a sleeping dog and cat, while his two children feed a caged bird. After he goes off to war, his newly impoverished family is forced to pawn all their household goods, including the (now empty) birdcage. At the final "John Bull's Glorious Return," when he arrives home, gaunt and maimed, his horrified family is sitting in a ruined hovel devoid of furniture, food, and pets.[16] Pet keeping, in this vision of Britain at its best and worst, was no longer the purview of privileged, overindulged women. Instead, it had become a sign of solid prosperity—not decadence but coziness—and to have to give up a pet was a cruel loss.

Part of the shift in attitude was related to changes in thinking about animals. Humane attitudes were often fostered by pet keeping, as becomes clear in one of the earliest publications that consistently advocated kindness to animals, the *Tatler*. A 1709 issue of that periodical begins with a letter from a country friend of Isaac Bickerstaff, the *Tatler*'s fictional editor; the correspondent explains that during hard winters, he takes care of the local songbirds by opening the windows in the morning and putting out food for them. But his son has been attacking and tormenting the birds, to his father's horror. Bickerstaff's response praises the letter writer and then transitions seamlessly from humanitarianism to pets: "For my own Part, I am excluded all Conversation with the Animals that delight only in a Country Life, and am therefore forced to entertain my self as well as I can with my little Dog and Cat. They both of 'em sit by my Fire every Night, expecting my coming Home with Impatience;

and at my Entrance, never fail of running up to me, and bidding me welcome, each of 'em in his proper Language." The dog and cat, he says, were brought up together and have adopted each other's manners, and he takes such great pleasure in playing with them that it makes him realize "how much Reason and Instinct are capable of delighting each other."[17] And while in another issue of the *Tatler* Joseph Addison mocked a woman seeking a physician for her dog, he admitted that men also could show enormous affection for their hunting hounds, and he concluded that "these voluntary Friendships between Animals of different Species, seem to arise from Instinct."[18] Animals might not be worthy of human medical care, but it was entirely natural to seek "Friendship" outside our kind.

The *Tatler* commentaries assumed the distinction between reason and instinct that was so important to ideas about human uniqueness. The dominant discourse regarding human-animal relations presented an enormous gulf between humans and animals, but by the end of the century that discourse was beginning to change in two major ways. First, the idea of human superiority, when combined with a more benevolent view of nature, led to an increasing emphasis on the responsibility humans had toward the animal world—the need to care for rather than merely exploit animals. Cartesian notions of the animal as machine to be exploited survived into the late eighteenth century, but almost exclusively as straw men to be knocked down. Thus William Smellie, in his *Philosophy of Natural History* (1790), remarked that "the notion that animals are mere machines, is perhaps too absurd to merit refutation"—before going on to engage in just such a refutation. Like other writers, he accepted that no animal had the "mental powers" of humans, but he argued that they had feelings, intelligence, art, and language; animals were no more machines than were "children, savages, and ignorant men."[19] Second, there was a growing emphasis on the possibility of sympathy reaching across the species boundary. If humans were unique in their ability to reason, the thinking went, then there was an even more important bond of feeling that crossed species. As Jeremy Bentham famously insisted at the end of the century, it was not reason but the shared capacity for suffering that mattered.[20]

Among those who were more interested in interspecies similarities than differences was David Hume, who in his *Treatise of Human Nature* (1739–40) insisted that just as anatomists used animal dissection to understand human anatomy because of comparable physical structures, so it made sense to see parallel behaviors as resulting from similar impulses.

Thus, he claimed, animals and humans shared passions such as pride, and he cited birds, horses, and hounds as engaging in competitive behavior based on pride. "The *causes* of these passions are likewise much the same in beasts as in us," he added, "making a just allowance for our superior knowledge and understanding." Animals could not understand morality, family, or property, but they did have passions rooted in the abilities or qualities of the body, such as speed, beauty, and strength.[21] Animals also experienced love and hatred, which could cross species lines to enable, for instance, dogs to love their masters (and be loved in return). And they could communicate their passions to one another, which meant, Hume emphasized, that they could experience "*sympathy*."[22] For Buffon, who was as usual not entirely consistent in his views, the absence of reason meant that the affection of dogs for their masters was no different from that of a child for its toy, since neither was based in reason—the only true foundation of friendship.[23] But Buffon was much more eloquent in painting the mutual affection of man and dog in his paeans to domestication than he was in dismissing its similarity to "real" friendship, and ideas like Hume's helped people see the connections between themselves and other animals even as they maintained human uniqueness. As Samuel Jackson Pratt put it, animals "have not reason, but they have *something* that does the business of reason so well, that man is very often put to the blush, and is almost ashamed of the privilege that sets him at the top of the scale. The fact is—brutes are as sensible of insults done to each other as men."[24]

Together, these developments in both the number of people keeping pets and assumptions about the possibility of meaningful cross-species interaction meant that the British experienced a sea change in attitudes toward pets and their owners over the course of the eighteenth century. One way to trace this shift is through the visual culture of the period. As we have seen, a pervasive motif in satirical prints connected pet keeping to the ridiculousness and immorality of fashion. But a countervailing trend emerged in the second half of the century, one that turned from satire to sentiment and glorified the emotional attachments between humans and animals. The liminal status of pets, on the border between human and animal, proved to be a boon in a new cultural movement that applauded humans' ability to connect to the natural world. Pets hinted at the possibility that sympathy—the ability to place oneself mentally in another's situation and understand what that individual is feeling—might extend beyond our own species. And that possibility in turn opened up the equally alluring idea that humans might be able to understand not only the character of a species but the individual character of a single animal, and be understood in return. Buffon's idea of domestication as mutual understanding and consent might extend to a deeper connection, made possible by an intimate bond between one person and one animal. The pet would move even further over the threshold between animal and human, while making it possible for the human to move closer to the animal world in a way that confirmed, rather than endangered, his or her humanity.

Portraits and "fancy pictures" of people and pets both reflected and helped construct these new attitudes. A new sense of animal subjectivity encouraged the spread of portraits of pets as individuals in their own right. Creating a rich visual language of mutual understanding and harmony, images of people with their pets offered a new representation of human-animal relationships. Those with female subjects drew on the associations of femininity and pet keeping, but they transformed those associations into positive ones. Instead of a dangerous sexuality, they constructed a mood of safe and sentimental eroticism. Instead of misplaced affection, they presented love of pets as one more outlet for women's "natural" maternal care. Thus, along with the satirical attacks on feminine fashion, represented through the presence of the useless, sensual lapdog, we can see the development of an alternative tradition that applauded the affection of girls and women for their animals. The imagery of sensibility also offered a new model of masculinity, one that celebrated characteristics usually seen as feminine while maintaining masculine norms of self-control and status-consciousness.

Such images both helped create and reinforced new attitudes toward the practice of pet keeping, not only in British society as a whole but among pet owners themselves. To see this process at work, it is necessary to look at real pet owners. The correspondence of Lady Isabella Wentworth from the early years of the century reveals a woman whose affection for her animals seems strikingly familiar to our own pet-loving culture, but who was also uncomfortably aware of how ill matched her feelings were to those of most of her contemporaries. Later in the century, pet owners could be much less self-conscious. Natural history offered one model for representing pet keeping; by couching discussions of pets in terms of scientific inquiry, the problematic aspects of emotional bonds with animals could be mitigated, and the potential risks of effeminacy limited. The works of William Cowper and Gilbert White are examples of this sort of self-representation. But this was not the only option. In the letters of one of the most famous pet owners of the late eighteenth century, Horace Walpole, we can trace both affection for pets and a changing relationship toward the dominant culture. Notably, Walpole emphasized not only his love for his own pets but also his abhorrence of animal abuse; the rise of the humane movement created an avenue for discussing animals as something other than workers, vermin, or meat, and it provided a context in which pet owners could situate their own pet-keeping practices.

In images that celebrated the bond between pets and their owners, and in the correspondence of pet owners themselves, we see the development of modern pet keeping. Rather than mere parasitic consumers distracting their owners from human need, pets might be seen as valuable creatures capable of reducing human suffering. Rather than representing a failure of genuine human feeling, pets might reveal the deep humanity and sympathy of their owners for all living beings. Far from substituting for "real" attachments, pets, in many people's eyes, came to seem both capable and worthy of affection. Pets might embody that most human of emotions: love.

～   ～   ～

Images of people and animals were transformed by the emergence of sensibility as a major aesthetic and literary movement at midcentury. The ethos of sensibility was a reaction against the values of reason and self-discipline, offering instead a heightened interest in "the faculty of feeling" and glorifying "an innate sensitiveness or susceptibility."[25] It drew on many of the characteristics traditionally seen as dangerously feminine, particularly the direct, spontaneous outpouring of emotion, and an intense sense of kinship with suffering creatures—both human and animal. But by embracing rather than condemning such behavior, sensibility created a new framework in which to view femininity in general and the relationship between femininity and pet keeping in particular.[26] These changes in turn had significant implications for masculinity and its relationship to pet keeping.

Growing belief in the possibility of emotional engagement with an animal correlated to the increasing visual presentation of animals as sentient beings, not merely as objects of human exploitation or inquiry. Animals have always been represented in art, but, as Karen Raber puts it, in the eighteenth century they moved "from margin to center—becoming a subject, not an object in art."[27] No longer mere generic representations or allegories for human characteristics, animals were increasingly represented as individuals as the eighteenth century unfolded. One aspect of this change was the growing subgenre of animal portraiture, from which humans were entirely absent. Such portraiture was distinct from traditions of painting animals in hunting scenes (or dead animals in still life). It drew on natural history, which in the eighteenth century increasingly emphasized the accurate depiction of animals drawn from life. George Edwards, for instance, prided himself on creating detailed images that relied not on previous representations but on his own empirical observation, his access, ideally, to living animals rather than preserved specimens.[28] Naturalists were, moreover, increasingly aware of the difficulties of relying even on animals held in menageries or other exhibitions as specimens, given the effects of their confinement in unnatural conditions.[29] But that awareness also indicates a critical way in which animal portraiture diverged from natural history: whereas naturalists sought to achieve the most representative portrayal, an image that would encompass general characteristics, in portraiture it is the *individual* animal—and thus its subjectivity—that matters.

One of the first species to win such attention was the horse. Given the close bonds between horses and their masters, and horses' function as elite status symbols, it is unsurprising that they would emerge as important subjects in animal portraiture. George Stubbs is only the most famous of the artists who created images of horses that celebrated their individual identity.[30] But dogs were another major subject of portraiture, and, significantly, such images often did not portray them working; as with human subjects, they were posed in idealized landscapes or interiors that paralleled those used in human portraits. As Madeleine Pinault Sørensen notes, "English artists specialized in this genre," and Stubbs painted individual dogs as well as horses.[31] Thomas Gainsborough is justly famous for his portraits of dogs, including *Tristram and Fox* (traditionally assumed to be a portrait of his own two dogs) and *Pomeranian Bitch and Puppy* (fig. 32).[32] In the latter, a portrait of pets belonging to the composer Carl Friedrich Abel, both animals are lively and alert, presented in the type of wooded landscape Gainsborough often used for his human subjects. They fill the frame, and the top of the picture is cut off just above

Fig. 32   Thomas Gainsborough, *Pomeranian*
Bitch and Puppy, ca. 1777. Oil on canvas,
832 × 1118 mm. Tate. © Tate, London, 2015.

the dog's head, bringing the viewer down to eye level with the animals.
The older dog looks off to the viewer's left, head and ears erect, as if
responding to something just outside the frame. Her puppy leans close to
its mother while taking a tentative step toward the viewer, curious but
hesitant. Gainsborough takes pains to present the texture of the dogs' hair
(just as he does with the hair of elegant women in his portraits); the difference between that of the full-grown bitch and her pup is clearly visible.
This is a portrait produced with the same loving care that Gainsborough
employed in his images of humans—including Abel himself.[33]

Because these portraits were produced and commissioned by humans,
their very existence reveals a growing interest in animal subjectivity. They
were designed to capture an animal's personality, a goal requiring the
assumption that animals *have* personalities. Such a goal was perhaps made
easier by the nature of eighteenth-century portraiture, which sought to
capture a "good likeness" but differentiated that goal from producing a
strictly accurate representation. A portrait that idealized its subjects,

removing blemishes or smallpox scars, could be seen as a good likeness because it captured the sitter's inner personality or character. In this context, pets were especially well suited to portraiture, their individual personalities evident to their owners and worthy of preservation. Animal portraiture thus emerged as a distinct genre in the eighteenth century because of a confluence of multiple trends: a growing fascination with accurate representation of the natural world, most notable in natural histories; an increasing willingness to perceive animals and humans as sharing personality traits (recall Hume's insistence on animal passions); and changing views of pet keeping as something to be celebrated rather than condemned, thanks to the impact of the culture of sensibility. All of these characteristics emerged as well in images showing people with their pets.

Because satires equating femininity and pet keeping were so widespread, the impact of sensibility is particularly prominent in images of girls and women. Satirical imagery did not disappear; indeed, the fashionable excesses of the 1770s and 1780s proved fertile ground for satirists. But the growing ideal of sensibility provided an alternative way of thinking about the traditional associations between women and pets, transforming the human-pet relationship from something seen as a perversion of love into one based on genuine feeling. Rejecting the charge that women loved their pets with an emotional intensity that should be reserved for men, the notion of sensibility suggested that affection for animals implied an open heart and the possibility of even greater love for a deserving human companion. Rather than neglecting children, girls and young women in these images rehearsed their future maternal responsibilities through the care of their pets. No longer were animals seen as competition for humans in a zero-sum emotional game.

The visual imagery influenced by the culture of sensibility thus drew on existing associations between femininity and pet keeping while changing the meaning of those associations. The concept of sexual perversion that played such an important role in satires, for instance, became instead an innocuous form of sentimental eroticism. We can see these new connotations in such prints as *The Fond Doves*, in which two young women lean close to each other, observing a pair of billing doves they have freed from a cage.[34] The print creates a visual pun between the pet birds and the women, relying for its mildly erotic effect on the similarity of pose between the birds and the humans and the question of which figures are the "fond doves" of the title. In *The Rival Favourites* (fig. 33), an attractive

THE RIVAL FAVOURITES.

Published Feb.y 4.th 1788 by Rob.t Sayer no Fleet Street London

Fig. 33   *The Rival Favourites,* 1788. Mezzotint,
hand-colored, 35.3 × 25.2 cm. Courtesy of the
Lewis Walpole Library, Yale University,
788.02.04.03+.

woman gestures toward a bird perched on her upraised right hand as she gazes at a cat on the table before her. The title of the image suggests that the woman is torn between two suitors, but the use of animals moves the image into the realm of sentiment rather than satire, transforming her from a coquette into an innocent.

Other prints rely on similar associations but play with the theme of innocence in danger. *Pretty Miss a Sleep* (fig. 34) shows a young woman who has nodded off while feeding her pet bird, which stands next to her on a tray of seeds. A cat has climbed up and seems poised to pounce on the bird. Here, the threat is displaced from human men onto the woman's pets, thus creating a visual association between the woman and the bird while transforming the scene into one of sentimental charm rather than real peril. *The Amorous Thief, or The Lover's Larceny* makes a similar connection. In this print, a young man has bribed a maid to give him access to a sleeping girl, whom he leans in to kiss. The sleeping woman holds a string attached to a squirrel; as she dozes, it climbs into a basket to bite into a peach.[35] The pet both heightens her femininity and echoes the danger of getting caught napping—both man and squirrel are stealing because the young woman has failed to maintain proper vigilance. As with *Pretty Miss a Sleep*, however, the image is more sentimental than moralizing; it draws on established notions of feminine weakness and fragile female chastity while transferring them into a setting of safe domesticity. In neither case is anything really at stake.

Another trope, which gathered strength with the growing emphasis on "natural" female chastity, presented feminine pet keeping in the context of maternity rather than sexuality. While many satirical prints and critics of pet keeping presented female pet owners as bad mothers who neglected their human children, this alternative saw the urge to "mother" animals as a natural and charming outgrowth of the maternal instinct. One of the most direct representations of the relationship between pet keeping and maternity appears in a print, probably from the 1770s,[36] called *Preserving the Young* (fig. 35). A young woman looks coyly at the viewer as she holds two tiny puppies to her bosom, implying her figurative responsibility as nursing mother. The puppies' actual mother stands on a table next to her, its forelegs resting on the woman's arm as it gazes adoringly at the puppies. With a heavily anthropomorphized expression, it appears to be smiling, indicating its approval of the young woman's maternal role. In this image, maternity is doubled, both canine and

Fig. 34   Pretty Miss a Sleep, 1771. Mezzotint, 15 ×
11.2 cm. Courtesy of the Lewis Walpole Library,
Yale University, 771.10.03.04.

human playing similar roles. Yet the title also implies that the woman is
performing a uniquely human function in "preserving the young"; she
does not actually suckle the puppies, but she is preserving them from the
drowning that was the fate of many litters. The print thus simultaneously

Preserving the Young

Fig. 35   *Preserving the Young*, ca. 1793. Mezzotint.
Courtesy of the Lewis Walpole Library, Yale
University, 793.00.00.73.

emphasizes and disguises the boundaries between humans and animals; the young woman's action at once depends upon and conceals species difference, while her maternal feelings bridge that gap.

In the more humorous *Miss Sukey and Her Nursery*, John Raphael Smith portrays a woman dosing a swaddled cat with the contents of a steaming bowl; its medicinal qualities are indicated by the vial and other implements on the table beside her.[37] (The cat looks far from enthusiastic.) A pair of prints from Robert Sayer presents subtler images of maternal care, showing young women cuddling animals.[38] In *Lady with a Dog*, the spaniel licks at her lips as if kissing her; she holds its paw and smiles down on it. The subject of *Lady Caressing a Rabbit* looks out at the viewer as the rabbit nuzzles the large flower she has pinned to her bosom. In both cases, the images play with the combination of erotic and maternal elements, and both naturalize the relationship between the woman and her pet. Whereas satires presented the blurring of species boundaries as dangerous and unnatural, the boundary-crossing characteristics of pets in images like these become a source of pleasure and an opportunity for humans to get closer to nature.

Young girls at play with pets were even easier to accommodate within the realm of sensibility. The development of sentimentalism coincided with a related trend that presented childhood as worthy of special attention and celebration.[39] Images that present positive representations of girls with pets can thus be seen as the counterparts of the children's literature (which also often featured pets) that spread rapidly in this period. Like the images of adult women, such portrayals often implicitly praised this behavior as an extension or foreshadowing of their natural maternal role. In George Romney's famous 1777 portrait of the Clavering children, for instance, Thomas Clavering is shown holding the leash of an adult dog as it jumps up toward him, and he gazes directly at the viewer; his sister, by contrast, looks affectionately and modestly down at the puppy she clasps in her arms.[40] The action and direct gaze of the boy contrast strongly with the demure and maternal pose of the girl, enacting the gender roles that the period insisted were their natural destinies.[41]

These ideas translated easily to the popular "fancy pictures" of the period. In the print *Jump Pussey*, we see a young girl making a hoop of her arms for a cat to jump through.[42] Her sweet smile and focus on the cat presents her as a teacher; rather than teasing the cat, she is fulfilling her natural duty to teach in a way that she will, presumably, follow through on

MISS THOUGHTFUL.

Printed for Carington Bowles, at his Map & Print Warehouse, N° 69 in S.t Paul's Church Yard, London. Published as the Act directs 20 Jun. 1775.

Fig. 36   *Miss Thoughtful,* 1775. Mezzotint, 350 ×
251 mm. Courtesy of the Lewis Walpole
Library, Yale University, 775.06.20.01+.

as a mother of young children. A portrait of Lady Charlotte Williams,
issued as a print under the title *Miss Thoughtful*, shows the young girl tilting
her head to look carefully up at the viewer (fig. 36). Her flowered cap,
long hair, and loose gown and sash combine to create an effect of studied
naturalness. In her arms she holds a small dog, which drapes its forepaws
over her right arm. It, too, looks out at the viewer, mirroring the gaze of

the girl. Both figures combine innocence with vulnerability and caution; the girl's care of her dog becomes a way of telegraphing her personality, not frivolous and playful but "thoughtful." Far from being mutually exclusive, then, pet keeping and motherly love could be seen as mutually reinforcing.

The distinguishing feature of pets—their presence inside the home— also made them particularly useful in connection with a representative tradition that offered the household as a distinct realm of feminine authority and accomplishment. Thus in *The Good Oeconomist's*, a print after Watteau's painting *Occupation selon l'Age*, we see an elderly woman with a distaff, a younger woman mending, and two young girls playing at their feet.[43] A girl sits in the foreground with her back to the viewer, holding a kitten that looks out of the frame over her shoulder. Playing with the kitten is her "occupation," and her connection to the animal is visually represented as akin to the maternity revealed through the multiple generations in the picture. Domestic care, in this view, was a natural extension of girlish pet keeping. Moreover, the transformative effect of sensibility extended beyond girls and women to include the entire family, presenting cozy domesticity as the height of contentment. Sentimental paintings and prints, which were enormously popular in the later eighteenth century, reflected this trend. Genre paintings by artists like Francis Wheatley and George Morland, for instance, not only provided them a steady income but were the source of many popular engravings. As James Christen Steward explains, "the markers of domestic tranquility" in these paintings included "the peaceful relationship of a family and their animals (the ubiquitous dog notably at rest) in a rural setting, with a child at its center."[44] Steward's comment about the dog being "notably at rest" also reflects the sentimental ideal; dogs in such images are presented not as workers but as members of the family, participating in the affective bonds of husband, wife, and happy children.

The culture of sensibility was arguably most important in creating a verbal and visual discourse of emotion, closeness to nature, and humane feeling that applied to men as well as to the women who were traditionally associated with such traits. The great novel of sensibility was Henry Mackenzie's *The Man of Feeling* (1771), not *The Woman of Feeling*; sensibility transcended age, sex, and even species. Along with it came a new celebration of men's open display of emotion. Readers wept along with Harley, the hero of *The Man of Feeling*, as the character listened to tales of woe from reformed prostitutes, the elderly, and the destitute. The stories nested within the narrative frame enabled readers to experience sympathy—to imagine themselves in the characters' place—the emotional impact doubling as they experienced not only their response to the stories but also Harley's. This narrative structure, in which Harley's emotional reactions are described in order to model the reader's intended response, presented with especially strong effect a new ideal celebrating the defiance of masculine traditions. Because animals were so closely linked to femininity and nature, moreover, they offered especially potent illustrations of the new ideal at work. Defying older values that would dismiss affection for animals as effeminate and weak, the open display of such affection served as shorthand for the new masculine sensibility.

Writers who participated in the artistic and literary fashion for sensibility were aware that its dominant mode conflicted with traditional masculinity. We see that conflict in Samuel Jackson Pratt's six-volume miscellany *Liberal Opinions* (1775–77).[45] In one story, "Benignus" describes being so moved by his nurse's touching story of animal feeling that he can never again hurt a fly and even feels terrible eating meat. But when he relates the same story to his fellow schoolboys, it has no effect, and they continue to "delight in slaughter, death, and massacre. . . . I tell them it is cruel,—and they treat me with derision—nay, several *grown-up people* join the laugh against me, and say, that I was designed for a girl."[46] The anonymous "Ode on the Death of a Spaniel," inspired by the death of Horace Walpole's dog, which was killed by a wolf during an Alpine crossing, takes a similarly defensive tone: "Scorn not my tears, ye Great, ye Vain, / . . . With gen'rous Pride I speak; for know, / If I but see an Insect's Woe, / My pitying Soul can weep. . . . The smallest Animal sustains / As sharp, as agonizing Pains, / As when a Giant dies."[47] As Maureen Harkin has noted, the "man of feeling" was presented as ill suited to thrive in modern society; in Mackenzie's novel, the hero suffers a series of indignities and is repeatedly fleeced owing to his too-trusting nature.[48] Indeed, one significant dimension of the sensibility presented in sentimental literature was that it was highly stylized and thus could not function as a model for real social relations.[49] Yet writers like Pratt and Mackenzie were hugely popular, and the expression of sensibility became part of the literary toolbox available for writers even as it became increasingly distrusted by the literary elite.[50] Ironically, then, sensibility represented a popular ideology that defined itself against popularity, and a model of behavior explicitly acknowledged as impractical.[51]

But the cult of sensibility did help move compassion and an emotional relationship with nature into the mainstream, making such bonds laudable rather than problematic even for those who bore no resemblance to the socially awkward misfits who were the usual heroes of sentimental literature. Ebenezer Sibly, for instance, argued in the introduction to his compilation of natural history that the study of the natural world was beneficial in creating "the refined and vivid pleasures of the imagination." Even more important, however, was the positive view of nature it inculcated. The "sensibilities of the mind" created through natural history led to humanitarian behavior, he claimed: "an equal and extensive benevolence is called forth into exertion; and having felt a common interest in the gratifications of inferior beings; we shall be no longer indifferent to their sufferings, or become wantonly instrumental in producing them."[52] Such ideas of sentimental benevolence and kindness to "inferior beings" were not universally held, of course. But sensibility helped make emotional attachments to animals—even "useless" pets—socially acceptable, to the point that, by the end of the century, celebrating the bond between a man and his dog had become the norm rather than the exception. Recall William Windham, who famously opposed laws against bullbaiting, nevertheless offering a parliamentary speech against the dog tax on the grounds that it would destroy one of the few sources of pleasure and affection for a poor man.[53] Sensibility enabled pet keeping to move out of the stereotypical dressing rooms of fashionable women and into the heart of British identity.

In this context, portraiture influenced by sensibility imbued male subjects with traits traditionally associated with femininity without presenting the sitters as effeminate. Pets in such portraits were no longer merely symbolic; instead, they demonstrated the possibility of sympathy that crossed the species boundary. At its best, this portraiture presented both human and animal sitters as recognizable individuals. As Diana Donald has argued, "the dogs in eighteenth-century portraits were not necessarily representatives of particular social types of owners, nor simply standard accessories. They were real animals, who went for their own 'sittings' with the painter, and were 'portrayed' in the full, rounded sense normally applied to humans, with all their idiosyncrasies of character and physique.

Rather than merely enhancing the appearance of the sitter, they assumed a quasi-independent or complementary role."[54]

All of these characteristics come together in Gainsborough's 1770 portrait of Henry, third duke of Buccleuch (fig. 37). Painted a year before the publication of Mackenzie's novel, the portrait can be seen as one of the quintessential works of masculine sensibility. The duke looks out at the viewer with a compassionate gaze, head tilted to his right and a slight smile playing on his lips. The sober colors of his apparel signal both modesty and status; similarly, the half-hidden insignia of the Order of the Thistle reveals his rank while implying that Buccleuch has chosen modestly to conceal it.[55] The position of the viewer, slightly below the sitter, allows Buccleuch to embody the "condescension" so valued among the eighteenth-century elite: the ability to put one's social inferiors at ease. The soft brown of the Duke's hair echoes the browns of the natural landscape, suggesting that he is at one with his surroundings. But it is the presence of the terrier that makes the portrait so arresting. The dog is a fully realized individual in this painting, so much so that we could describe this as a double portrait.[56] This is not merely a dog as a symbol of loyalty, but a portrait of a relationship in which emotion is reciprocated. Desmond Shawe-Taylor says of this portrait that "a comical-looking dog is a familiar emblem of good nature,"[57] but this dog is more than an emblem. We can see in the image the visual counterpart to Buffon's encomium on true domestication as a relationship of mutual understanding and affection. If Buccleuch expresses benevolent condescension, it is toward the human spectator rather than his canine companion. While the duke looks directly at the viewer, the dog gazes slightly off to the side, alert but with its own interests. As Diana Donald notes, the dog's gaze is "deliberately parallel to, but differentiated from, that of the accompanying human; its *individual consciousness* registered."[58] Situated on a hillock, the dog is elevated so that its body is at the level of the duke's torso, suggesting equal importance; this dog does not fawn at his master's feet. Buccleuch's arms wrap his dog in a warm embrace, hands clasped near the animal's face, while the terrier places one paw over its master's wrist in response; the affection, the painting suggests, is mutual. And the visual echoes go further: the halo of hair around the top of the dog's head, its ears jutting out to the side, mirrors the shape of the duke's hair, with its flip of curls by the ears; man, dog, clothing, and landscape all share similar

Henry Duke of Buccleugh,
Knight of the most Ancient and Noble Order of the Thistle.

Fig. 37   John Dixon, after Thomas Gains-
borough, *Henry Scott, 3rd Duke of Buccleuch,* 1771.
Mezzotint, 455 × 329 mm. National Portrait
Gallery. © National Portrait Gallery, London.

painterly technique.[59] This truly is a case of a person resembling his pet. The portrait thus has comic elements, but Gainsborough is not mocking either Buccleuch or his dog.

As Shawe-Taylor suggests, many of the elements of the portrait, particularly the pose, might be construed as feminine. We can see just how feminine if we compare it to the portrait of Charlotte Williams (*Miss Thoughtful*) discussed above. She, too, looks out at the viewer with a slight tilt of the head and a gentle smile. Her arms similarly cradle a curly-haired dog, and the dog's paw drapes over her arm just as the duke's terrier's does. Her dog, too, looks out of the frame with an alert gleam in its eyes. In its typical portrayal of a young girl mothering her lapdog, this picture easily made the transition to a fancy picture of generic sentimentality. When it is juxtaposed with the Gainsborough portrait, it becomes clear how easily the latter can be seen as distinctly feminizing in its presentation of the duke. Indeed, Shawe-Taylor also argues that "the way the Duke cuddles [the dog] suggests almost a child's affection for his pet."[60] Yet there are also crucial differences between the two images. While the duke is situated slightly above the viewer, Miss Williams, as befits a child, is viewed from above and looks up at us. The three-quarter-length presentation heightens our awareness of her small stature, which in turn highlights the diminutive dimensions of the lapdog in her arms. The size of the duke's dog, larger than the one in the Williams print, removes it from the problematic territory of the feminine lapdog. Even the suggestion of a real friendship helps add a masculine weight to the Buccleuch portrait from an eighteenth-century perspective; while the young girl plays at the role of mother with infant, the Gainsborough painting implies a friendship of equals.

Although I am arguing that the Buccleuch portrait is meant to be taken seriously, the comic aspects should not be discounted. Moreover, sensibility was a performance, with a set of aesthetic and behavioral rules that easily lent themselves to mockery. Mackenzie's own depiction of "Mrs. Sensitive," who brags about her "delicate sensibility" but starves her servants, reveals how vulnerable the ideal was to criticism and satire even in its own time.[61] Similarly, the humane movement was attacked by those who perceived its class biases, and it is true that the rhetoric of humanitarianism and sentimentalism did not necessarily create improved conditions for most animals. But what these ideas did do was to open up a space in which individuals could present themselves in new ways, and in which pet keeping could be seen from a new perspective. Satires against pets as the purview of fashionable, shallow women did not go away, but there arose an alternative vision in which pet keeping could become a way of identifying oneself with qualities that were highly valued. Gainsborough's portrait of Buccleuch offers a representation that is identifiably masculine while also embodying many characteristics traditionally associated with femininity.

It is notable, moreover, that the specific pose adopted in the portrait—the affectionate embrace of an animal—appears in many other images as well. At first glance, it might seem that the pose is typically feminine. In Joshua Reynolds's famous portrait of Miss Jane Bowles, for instance, the pose reveals girlish femininity and affection for an uncomfortable-looking dog.[62] But another Reynolds portrait, of Lady Charles Spencer, adds an element of ennobling heroism to both dog and woman, making it much less the sort of saccharine image associated with the sentimental prints and relating it more closely to Buccleuch's portrait.[63] Henry Raeburn's *Boy and Rabbit* (fig. 38), an image that could easily drift into the sentimentalism of the Bowles portrait, instead creates a tone of solemn dignity that presents the boy's protective gesture as one worthy of emulation.[64]

Reynolds's portrait of George Selwyn and his pug Raton emphasizes more of the humor implicit in the dog-human parallel, granting equal dignity to both man and pug—a comparison that would be particularly notable given the pug's "slightly disreputable" reputation. Yet the portrait is well known in part because Raton had his own sittings with Reynolds, so important was it to Selwyn that the image capture both likenesses with equal accuracy.[65] Both dogs and men reveal distinct personalities in these images, again implying the individuality of animal as well as human sitters. Holding their pets, the sitters in all these images also create a physical bond that reproduces and reinforces the emotional bond.

Portraits like these celebrate the possibility of blurring the boundary between human and animal. Many of them contain humorous elements, but unlike the satirical images discussed in chapter 3, they do not question the intelligence or good sense of their pet-loving subjects. Instead, where humor is present, as in the portraits of Selwyn and Buccleuch, the images suggest that the sitters are in on the joke, even as they take their animals seriously. This self-awareness is one reason why such images remain in the realm of acceptable masculinity.

Fig. 38   Henry Raeburn, *Boy and Rabbit,* ca. 1814.
Oil on canvas, 1030 × 793 mm. Royal Academy
of Arts, London.

The conventions of sensibility thus paved the way for a new presentation of the relationship between pets and their owners, by transforming
the boundary-crossing nature of the pet from a liability into an asset. Far
from threatening traditional feminine roles, pets could be constructed as
a safe means for girls and young women to test their future roles as wives

and mothers. And for men, sensibility offered the vision of sympathy across the species boundary to enable a friendship of equals between man and beast. While the fashion for weeping publicly over the death of a fly—or a tragic heroine like Clarissa Howe—faded fairly quickly, furthermore, the bond between men and their pets survived as a legitimate venue for masculine feeling.

~   ~   ~

Literary or visual evidence of the changing ways in which pet owners conceived of and presented their relationships with their animals is particularly valuable given the rarity of sources that provide firsthand views of pets. But the surviving personal writings of pet owners add another dimension to the perceptions of human-animal relations created by artistic works or social commentary. Through a close reading of the correspondence of four individuals—Lady Isabella Wentworth, William Cowper, Gilbert White, and Horace Walpole—we can see the roles pets played in their owners' lives. Pets were family members, entertaining companions, and objects of scientific study. The enormous affection that all four people had for their animals remained constant, yet the varied concerns evident in these sources reflected the changing social attitudes toward pets over the course of the century.

We begin with Lady Isabella Wentworth (ca. 1646–1733), whom we witnessed lamenting poor Pug at the start of this chapter. Widow of the baronet Sir William Wentworth, by the time her extant letters begin, around 1705, she was living in straitened circumstances, relying on an annual income of £200 paid her by her eldest surviving son, Thomas, Earl of Strafford.[66] Thomas was a military officer and diplomat whose career meant that he spent much of his time on the Continent, and it is in Lady Wentworth's twice-weekly letters to him that the record of her experiences exists. Her life revolved around the activities of her children—particularly Thomas, her "dearest and best of children," as she addressed him in almost every letter—and her animals.[67]

Because so many of Lady Wentworth's letters survive, spanning more than twenty years, we can trace her relationships with her pets over time; the correspondence contains perhaps the most extensive documentation of pet keeping in the early eighteenth century. Along with her monkey and multiple dogs, she also owned a parrot and at least one cat; her letters are packed with descriptions of her animals' antics, joyful news of their offspring, and the occasional burst of grief at a death. The family correspondence also reflects the attitudes of those around her, most notably her daughter-in-law Anne, Lady Strafford. While Thomas kept many dogs himself and briefly owned a monkey,[68] Anne was obviously no animal lover. Lady Wentworth's comments and Anne's own letters reveal the tension between the elderly woman's great affection for her pets and her awareness that she was vulnerable to criticism on this score. Yet the correspondence is valuable precisely because it is one of the rare sources in which a pet owner engages in an extended discussion of her animals and what they meant to her. Lady Wentworth's animals were, above all, essential to her conception of the family. As part of her household, they were literally family in the eighteenth-century sense of the word, meaning all those—related or not—who lived under one roof. And they were equally important in the way they helped her construct and maintain her sense of her human family in the face of geographical distance, change, and conflict.

Despite the gap between Lady Wentworth's feelings for her pets and the attitudes of her son and daughter-in-law, pet keeping was an important area through which she sought to forge bonds with Thomas. Both she and her son kept many animals, and sharing news about her pets provided her with the rare topic of interest to them both. Moreover, Thomas frequently brought his dogs with him on trips back to England, leaving them behind in her care.[69] She saw this as an important responsibility and a meaningful way to connect to her distant son.

We can trace both the acquisition of one such dog and the meaning Lady Wentworth attached to her pets through her discussions of Pearl, who was to become a particular favorite. Pearl first appears in a 1710 letter. Responding to Thomas's suggestion that he send Pearl to England, Lady Wentworth insisted, "I would by no means have you part with your pretty Pearl till you come yourself, and then you will see my Gallant [another dog] and the rest are as well looked to as your Pearl."[70] This initial remark, with its emphasis on her reliability as a caregiver, reveals a theme that would dominate much of her writing about her animals. Not only were they companions, but they were also representatives of larger familial ties. One of the most important roles that discussing pets played for Lady Wentworth was that it served as a conduit to her son. His career kept him away from England for extended periods, and his political ambitions and apparent lack of interest in her life made it difficult for her to find a connection with him. Because they both kept pets, however, animals provided her with something they had in common. Even more crucially, her pets became surrogates for her relationship with Thomas; caring for them was, in a way, caring for him.

Pearl arrived in England in 1711, when Thomas came home to marry Anne Johnson in September of that year. He returned to the Continent almost immediately after the marriage, leaving Pearl (and his wife) behind. Pearl quickly became a favorite. In late October, Lady Wentworth wrote a letter explicitly connecting her affection for the animal with her love for her son: "Pretty dear Pearl is in my lap, and brisker than ever. . . . I must confess I am heartily glad Lady Strafford is not fond of dogs, for it would have gone hard with me to have parted from this [one], for sure nothing ever was so pretty of a dog—and, you will say, nor so silly as I, to trouble you with so much nonsense; but coming from so faithful a heart, and so entirely yours, . . . you cannot but forgive it."[71] Pearl was, for Lady Wentworth, a living representation of Thomas and his love for her. Her remarks about Anne reveal the anxiety that Lady Wentworth must have felt about the presence of this new woman in his life. Because Anne was "not fond of dogs," the link created by Pearl was an aspect of their relationship that the new wife could not share. Lady Wentworth's reliance on her animals as a conduit to Thomas is also visible in a note she wrote him shortly after the birth of his first child, a daughter, also named Anne. When Lady Strafford joked that the baby had replaced Pearl in Lady Wentworth's affections, she retorted, "indeed I do dote on dear Lady Anne [the baby], but my love is not one jot lessened to Pearl, for as Lady Anne is the prettiest child I ever see, so is Pearl the prettiest dog was ever seen."[72] Both were precious to her for similar reasons, even though only one of them was human.

Lady Wentworth thus used her animals to strengthen her ties with her human family, but she also constructed her household of "dumbs"—dumb, or mute, animals—as a family in itself. This family, unlike its human counterpart, was entirely loving and harmonious. Thomas was nearly forty when he finally married, and his first child was not born until 1713; Lady Wentworth spent many years worrying that he might never produce an heir.[73] While her lack of grandchildren was a source of enormous frustration, however, she could rely on the fecundity of her dogs. Each new litter of beautiful puppies—and to Lady Wentworth they were always beautiful—filled her with pride and happiness. She kept track of canine lineage with the care of a true aristocrat. Even more significantly, however, she offered a portrait of her human-animal household as a site of domestic bliss.

Over the years of the correspondence, a pattern emerges in which Lady Wentworth established a lineage for her animals, consistently tying that lineage back to Thomas. Just as she desperately hoped that the family line would continue through her eldest son, so she conceived of her dogs in terms of their ancestry. An early favorite was Fubs, almost certainly a gift from Thomas. When Fubs died in 1708, one of her puppies, Flert, became the new favorite. Flert's offspring in return received special notice, and in 1710 Lady Wentworth proudly announced the arrival of "a young Fubs, puppy of Flert and Gallant, prettier than [Flert], and just the temper of her grandmother Fubs."[74] Even in her last extant letters, written when she was about eighty years old, she continued to bring up the family dogs and their ancestry.[75] Moreover, her interest in animal lineage carried over to her interactions with humans. Portraiture was an important means through which aristocrats proclaimed their heritage, and the Wentworths were typical in commissioning many family portraits. But Lady Wentworth went further. When she hired an artist to do crayon drawings of a daughter and a granddaughter, she happily announced, "I made him put in Pearl to one and Poll [her parrot] to another."[76] The family ties multiply here; the portraits show the human family, but by including the animals, Lady Wentworth was implicitly inserting them into that human kinship network. Her decision to commission two death portraits of Pug similarly reveals her willingness to apply human traditions to her animal family.

Through the lineage of her pets, with its parallels to the Wentworths' elite heritage, she presented the animal family as part of a network of kin spanning time, employing the social values of birth and status. But Lady Wentworth also presented her pets in terms of an ideal household, a model of domestic bliss that looked inward rather than outward. She painted word portraits of cozy gatherings by the family hearth: "I am sure could you but see my fireside, you would laugh heartily, to see Fubs upon a cushion, the cat on another, and Pug on another, lapped up (all but her face) in a blanket."[77] Later letters continued the same theme: "Pug is prettier than ever and daily more diverting and Poll you would be much pleased to hear her speak just like a Christian and a very pretty voice."[78] This domestic emphasis accounts in part for the enthusiasm with which she greeted the arrival of puppies. Thus she reported that Pug acted as "nurse" when Fubs had puppies, while Fubs played the affectionate mother. In one letter, for instance, she announced that "nothing is more happy than Pug, I could not be more pleased had I you with me, than she is with all the puppies about her, and the carefullest nurse that ever was seen."[79] Lady Wentworth's juxtaposition of her happiness with this animal family against her longing to see her son reveals how she associated human and animal family ties. Giving the puppies away then became a traumatic event because it destroyed the natural family: "Fubs is in some trouble for yesterday she parted with her last little one, but it is as great a trouble to Pug for she was infinitely fond of it."[80]

Lady Wentworth's animals were not mere amusements to her, but instead provided a crucial source of emotional fulfillment in her life. Indeed, pets were her primary source of companionship, particularly after Thomas married. She insisted on traveling with them as she would with other family members. After Thomas established an estate at Twickenham, she took her pets with her on seasonal visits there; Anne noted with amusement that the coach arrived carrying Lady Wentworth's maid with "all the dumbs."[81] Even on short trips, the animals were gathered up and brought along. In 1712, for instance, Lady Wentworth left Twickenham to spend several nights in her London lodgings, bringing all her pets with her. "I should be dead without them," she explained.[82] A week later, back in Twickenham, she again shared a room with "all my dumbs, which I confess I could not come without."[83]

At home or traveling, Lady Wentworth seems to have spent much of her time alone with her animals. The antics of her monkey, the chatter of her parrot, and the affection of her dogs must have helped fill many lonely hours at a time when she had few outside amusements; her handwriting and spelling reveal a relative unfamiliarity with the written word, while her straitened financial situation, along with her advanced age, kept her from many of London's diversions. Her letters reveal a domestic life with pets at its center, as in this letter to Thomas from 1707: "I live like a nun, see nobody. Miss Pug, Fubs and I, sat two hours this morning in the wilderness and my boy [a servant] played of his viol, and set all the birds a-singing, had you but been there I should not have envied the Queen."[84] In March 1713 she wrote, "Pearl is in my lap and Poll [the parrot] upon a chair by, talking and laughing heartily. . . . It's very pretty to see Poll walk amongst all the dogs, and they never offer to come near her."[85] A little later she continued the same theme, writing that Poll "is extremely diverting, and wonderfully fond of me. If I come home never so l[ate] it will speak to me, and nothing can be prettier than to see it walk about the room."[86]

As we have seen, much eighteenth-century criticism of pet keeping was aimed at women who kept animals, particularly large numbers of them, as Lady Wentworth did. In these critiques, pets represented fashionable consumption, demonstrating the wastefulness and frivolity of fashion. Yet Isabella Wentworth's pets were not an example of such consumption but an alternative to it. Thus she remarked, "to please myself, I had rather have them than so many fine jewels. I would not part with one of them for never so much."[87] Shortly thereafter she reiterated the idea: "I am not fickle, nor with one dog I would not part. . . . I should never be easy to part with any one of my dumbs."[88] Several months later she announced that she could not take on a new animal because it would mean getting rid of one of her old ones, and "I would not for never so much, lose one dog or my parrot. There is not one I can part with."[89]

Lady Wentworth's attachment to her pets was based in part on her sense that they returned her affection, and her choice of favorites seems to reflect this sense of mutual devotion. Her love of Fubs, the first favorite to appear in the correspondence, is a case in point. "I can love no dog like Fubs," she wrote, "who . . . keeps close to me, and lies by me here in my closet."[90] Lady Wentworth admitted that she was terrified of losing Fubs in London: "whenever she is out of sight, and especially if a dog happens to be shot, then I am out of my wits till I see her."[91] In 1707, she was horrified to find that Fubs had "slipped her collar" and run away. Fortunately, a servant was able to run after and recapture the dog.[92] When her favorite became ill in November 1708, Lady Wentworth was extremely concerned: "poor pretty Fubs is very bad, groans sadly, and is lame of all her feet."[93] A few days later, the final blow came when Fubs died; Lady Wentworth was heartbroken. "God forgive me for it; I can not help being more than I ought concerned," she wrote.

> I shall never love any thing of that kind a quarter so well again: I had rather lost a hundred pound, nay all the rest of my dumbs I would have given to have saved poor charming Fubs. Never poor wretch had a harder death; as it lived so it died, full of love, leaning its head in my bosom, never offered to snap at any body in its horrid

torture but nuzzled its head to us. . . . It vomited up a great deal of blood, when it was dead I had it opened, and one of its guts, one part of it, was quite rotten; and those that see it, say it must be some kick it had. God forgive me, if I could tell who it was, I would be revenged of them. Sure of all its kind there never was such a one nor never can be: so many good qualities, so much sense, and good nature, and cleanly and not one fault. But few human creatures had more sense then that had, did never no harm, . . . did use to carry my gloves or handkerchief after me, when I went to or from dinner, and often my workbasket. . . . I could write a quire of paper in her commendations. I have buried her in this garden, and there is a stone laid at her head.[94]

Only Pug's death in 1712 inspired a similar outpouring of grief, and in both cases Lady Wentworth self-consciously admitted that she was more upset than she ought to have been, while nevertheless insisting that the animals were worthy of real mourning. Given the enormously important role that her pets played in her life, her grief was understandable. They were not humans, yet they provided her with love and companionship to an extent that her human family often did not. It was not the case that Lady Wentworth was too shallow or stupid to understand true human affection, as critics of pet owners so often suggested. Rather, animals provided her with a level of emotional contact that her human family often denied her, while simultaneously helping to cement the human ties that she did have.

We can see Lady Wentworth's pets, then, as an extension of her family—another sort of kinship, like that of blood or marriage. The more her connections to her family diminished, as children grew up, married, and relied increasingly on their new relations, the more important her animal family became. This is not to imply that she perceived her animals as children, or that her affection for her pets was a mere substitute for human love. Although we have no letters from her early years, the evidence suggests that she had always been an animal lover. Nor was there necessarily a conflict between human and animal affection; on the contrary, Lady Wentworth viewed her love for her pets and her love for her son as mutually reinforcing.

As much as Lady Wentworth saw her animals as a means of reaching out to her son, however, she and Thomas had very different attitudes toward their pets: they disagreed fundamentally about the nature of the human-animal boundary. For Thomas and most other people of the era, the boundary was absolute, and no animal life could have anything like the value of a human. But it was impossible for Lady Wentworth to differentiate so clearly between her love for her pets and her feelings for human family members. She was self-conscious about her own attitude—hence her attempt to downplay her grief when her favorites died. Yet she could not help criticizing her son for treating his pets as radically different, and inferior, beings. While her animals were purely for companionship, Thomas was keen to train his to do tricks. One immediate consequence of adopting his dogs, Lady Wentworth admitted, was that she allowed them to forget their training. Though she seemed apologetic about this, she saw his methods as cruel. "I pity your poor dog," she wrote in March 1712, "for what torture has that poor creature suffered to be brought to do all these trick[s]."[95] Shortly thereafter she added, "I pity poor Folly I fear he has a sad life . . . but indeed I had rather you would beat me than any of my dumbs. It would break my heart to have them ill used."[96] A year later, she wrote that she was glad he had forgiven his own monkey for some transgression, in a comment suggesting that the animal had suffered terribly: "I would not have one of my dogs so beat as he was, I fear, for ten guineas."[97] Although we do not have Thomas's account of these events, there is no suggestion that he expressed regret about his actions. He seems to have regarded his animals primarily as a means to an end, an attitude reflected in the ease with which he gave them away. For Lady Wentworth, by contrast, the animals' feelings were paramount. Her statement that she would prefer he beat her than her pets suggests both the seriousness of her claim and her perception of the power relations at work within the family.

Thomas's marriage allows us another view of Lady Wentworth's relationship with her pets, thanks to Lady Strafford's letters to him.[98] Anne barely tolerated her mother-in-law's large assortment of animals, and she had no sympathy for Lady Wentworth's deep emotional investment. In one brief but telling comment to Thomas, his mother admitted, "I am glad you have got a dog. I was afraid you would never love dogs more because your dear spouse does not."[99] Two years later, after comparing the charms of her pets with those of Thomas's, she again sighed, "I would give a good deal to live to see your Lady fond of dogs and monkeys and birds."[100] That was not to be.

When Anne referred to the animals at all, it was usually with condescending mockery. Two months after their marriage she wrote, "Lady Wentworth is very angry I never tell how Pearl is improved, as she calls it; if growing fat is that, 'tis very much so. Though I think 'tis very well poor Lady Wentworth has them things to divert her when she is at home."[101] In this early letter, we see the conflict between Anne's perceptions and Lady Wentworth's. While her mother-in-law tried anxiously to keep the animals in Thomas's mind as a means of reminding him of her, Anne made little attempt to conceal her scorn. Her patronizing comment that at least the pets entertained the lonely old woman simply dismisses the important role they played in Lady Wentworth's life. A similar dynamic played out when Thomas offered his dog Folly to his mother. She demurred, saying, "I shall never think it possible for any dog to compare to charming Pearl, I never go anywhere without her except to church."[102] In a postscript to the same letter from Lady Wentworth to her son, Anne took the opportunity to turn his feelings for the pet back to herself with a pun on the dog's name: "Lady Wentworth tells me you are very fond of Folly. I am glad of it, believing you will grow fonder than ever of me since Folly has your affection."[103] Whereas for Lady Wentworth the dogs were a valuable connection to her son and a sign of the bonds between them, for Anne they were at best an oddity and possibly even a threat that diminished Thomas's affection for his wife. Pearl remained a source of some tension between the two women, although Anne appears to have grown somewhat fonder of the animal.[104] She even proposed "a match of great consequence" between Pearl and a friend's dog, "but Lady W says if Pearl should die I must find out a habitation for myself in another country. So you are to decide this great affair."[105] Lady Wentworth ultimately insisted that Pearl should not mate, and Anne remarked sarcastically, "I believe 'tis the only thing she ever had the care of she was for keeping single."[106]

It is clear that despite Anne's declarations of affection for Pearl, she neither shared nor understood Lady Wentworth's intense feelings for the dog. When Pearl became sick, Anne remarked that she was "very glad" the dog recovered, but she could not help mocking Lady Wentworth's concern: "'tis not to be expressed the rout Lady W made with it while 'twas sick. She brought it here every day in two little nightgowns made fit for it and its Legs was put into sleeves. . . . I had a great deal to do to keep myself grave, for her affliction was too great for me to Laugh."[107] While

Anne's amusement at the sight of a fat little dog crammed into a dress is understandable, the letter is typical of her inability to empathize with her mother-in-law's concern.

Anne's attitude matched that of most people who discussed pets in the eighteenth century. Pet keeping was, for her and most of her contemporaries, at best an excusable weakness, a diversion for a lonely old woman who lacked other sources of companionship. Lady Wentworth's letters, however, reveal that for at least one pet owner, the animals meant much more. They were family—both important members of her household in their own right and essential links to her distant son. The ambiguous role so disturbing to many observers was a source of comfort to her. And as the century wore on, more and more people adopted Lady Wentworth's position. A dismissive attitude toward grief at a pet's death, or the willingness to beat an animal severely, came increasingly to be seen as signs not of a sensible awareness of human superiority but of a callous disregard for the feelings of nonhuman animals. Ironically, Lady Wentworth—widowed, elderly, and isolated from fashionable society—was ahead of her time.

≈   ≈   ≈

The growing willingness to celebrate rather than condemn human-animal affection was undoubtedly rooted in new values expressed in the culture of sensibility and the humane movement. But an alternative model of masculine pet keeping, which drew on the popularity of natural history, also emerged during the later decades of the century. In the works of William Cowper (1731–1800) and Gilbert White (1720–1793), we see two men presenting their pets to a public audience through the medium of scientific inquiry. White is still known today as a naturalist, but Cowper is most famous as a poet, and juxtaposing the two might at first seem peculiar. Both men, however, published extended discussions of their pets as a means of increasing knowledge about the natural world.

There was precedent for this approach to natural history. Many naturalists, unable or unwilling to travel very far for their research, observed the live pets of friends and family. Buffon used his sister's pet parrot as a source of information on the habits and, more important, the morals of the Jaco or African grey parrot.[108] George Edwards similarly visited menageries in addition to keeping his own pets, including a "green monkey" whose behavior he described in his natural history.[109] Such pets were part of a broader network of information that relied on correspondence, stuffed specimens, and traveling animal exhibitions for an understanding of rare animals to which most naturalists had little or no access.

But naturalists were as interested in domestic animals as they were in exotic species, and Gilbert and Cowper offered their readers information about two much more familiar animals: the tortoise and the hare. Cowper wrote a lengthy description of his three pet hares in a letter to the *Gentleman's Magazine* published in June 1784, which he followed with his famous "Epitaph on a Hare"—actually written in 1783, before the letter to the editor, but published in the same periodical in December 1784.[110] He explained his reason for writing the letter: "Convinced that you despise no communications that may gratify curiosity, amuse rationally, or add, though but a little, to the stock of public knowledge, I send you a circumstantial account of an animal, which, though its general properties are pretty well known, is for the most part such a stranger to man, that we are but little aware of its peculiarities." He went on to explain how he came to acquire his three hares ten years earlier, when, "being much indisposed both in mind and body," he was grateful for the "diversion" offered when a neighbor gave him a three-month-old leveret. Two others quickly followed, and the three (all male) he named Puss, Tiney, and Bess.[111] Cowper described the hares' housing, diet, and behavior, correcting what he saw as erroneous beliefs. But as interested as he was in furthering knowledge about the species in general, he also presented his hares as unique individuals, explaining at length their very different personalities. "Puss was tamed by gentle usage," he wrote; "Tiney was not to be tamed at all; and Bess had a courage and confidence that made him tame from the beginning." Cowper associated these distinct personalities with distinct "countenances," and he used this idea to suggest a broader implication: it was likely, he thought, that despite their apparently homogenous features, "among a thousand of them no two could be found exactly similar; a circumstance little suspected by those who have not had opportunity to observe it."

In this scientific guise, Cowper presented the details of his domestic life with his animals, explaining, for example, that their daily meals consisted of bread "cut into small squares," along with "shreds of carrot" and "rind of apples cut extremely thin." Observing Puss's demonstrative affection after Cowper had nursed him through an illness, he described the hare "licking my hand, first the back of it, then the palm, then every finger separately, then between all the fingers, as if anxious to leave no part of it unsaluted." And when Puss wanted to go outside, "he would invite me to the garden by drumming upon my knee, and by a look of such expression as it was not possible to misinterpret. If this rhetoric did not immediately succeed, he would take the skirt of my coat between his teeth, and pull at it with all his force." In the evening, all three hares would be set free in the parlor, where "they would frisk and bound and play a thousand gambols." Cowper gave an example of their extraordinary ability to observe even tiny changes in their surroundings: "A small hole being burnt in the carpet, it was mended with a patch, and that patch in a moment underwent the strictest scrutiny." And all three animals had "favourites" among human beings; for instance, a miller's "powdered coat had charms that were irresistible." Such details undoubtedly added to the appeal of Cowper's description, which was among his most popular works.[112]

Cowper also used his observations in support of his own pacifism. Given his "intimate acquaintance" with the hares, he assumed that his readers would not be surprised to hear that he abhorred hunting. The sportsman "little knows what amiable creatures he persecutes, of what gratitude they are capable, how cheerful they are in their spirits, what enjoyment they have of life, and that, impressed as they seem with a peculiar dread of man, it is only because man gives them peculiar cause for it." As further support, he offered yet another experiment. He had, he said, recently introduced Puss to a spaniel. Neither animal had previously encountered a member of the other species, and Cowper was gratified to find that Puss was as unafraid as the dog was unaggressive. Reversing the usual assumptions about the natural world, he insisted that there is "no natural antipathy between dog and hare"—what seemed natural was only the result of training and experience. Indeed, the two animals now "eat bread at the same time out of the same hand, and are in all respects sociable and friendly."

Cowper imbued his epitaph for Tiney with the same telling details, recounting many of the facts he had offered in prose in the letter to the *Gentleman's Magazine*. But outside the confines of scholarly rhetoric, Cowper's epitaph was even more open in its affection for an animal that the poet described as "surliest of his kind," who "Was yet a wild jack hare." "Though duly from my hand he took / His pittance every night, / He did it with a jealous look, / And, when he could, would bite." Cowper loved

Tiney despite, or perhaps because of, his ill temper: "I kept him for old service sake, / For he would oft beguile / My heart of thoughts that made it ach [*sic*], / And force me to a smile." The mix of emotion and empirical observation in both works helps account for their enduring popularity. But Cowper's publications were also among the very few that offered a personal description of pets other than dogs. The potential effeminacy of expressing such affection for three androgynously named hares was countered by the scientific language in which it was couched.

There is evidence that Cowper's letter influenced thinking about the interplay of pet keeping and natural history. At least one correspondent was moved to write to the *Gentleman's Magazine* with his own (alas, much less interesting) description of his experience raising pet squirrels.[113] Although we cannot know whether Gilbert White read Cowper's contribution, White's famous *Natural History and Antiquities of Selborne* (1789) was also an epistolary work, drawn from the letters he wrote to the naturalists Thomas Pennant and Daines Barrington. The letters range across a wide variety of topics (White was particularly interested in birds), but his tortoise, Timothy, warrants frequent mention. Timothy first appears in White's records in Ringmer, Sussex, where he[114] lived in the garden of White's aunt, Rebecca Snooke. White's journal contains repeated reference to Timothy's hibernation habits and diet, beginning in 1771 and continuing after Mrs. Snooke's death in March 1780, when White dug him out of his "hybernaculum" and brought him home to Selborne. White first referred to Timothy by name in a journal entry from 1775,[115] and until just before his death in 1793 he continued to record information about the tortoise.

White's discussion of Timothy in the *Natural History* appears in five letters addressed to Barrington, dated between 1770 and 1780, along with an appendix of "More *Particulars* respecting the *Old Family Tortoise* omitted in the *Natural History*." In the first letter, dated from Ringmer in October 1770, White reports that "a land tortoise . . . has been kept for thirty years in a little walled court belonging to the house where I am now visiting." White's initial letter notes that the tortoise hibernated from November to April and traces the animal's changing eating habits over the summer; he concludes that he has heard of another nearby tortoise reputed to have lived to one hundred years old, "an instance of vast longevity in such a poor reptile!"[116] Two years later, he returned to the subject, detailing Timothy's behavior the previous November as he prepared for hibernation. After watching the tortoise laboriously dig a hole in the ground, White remarked that its slow pace was "suitable to the composure of an animal said to be a whole month in performing one feat of copulation." He expressed amusement at Timothy's "extreme timidity . . . with regard to rain," which he likened to that of "a lady dressed in all her best attire, shuffling away on the first sprinklings, and running it's head up in a corner." And finally, he praised the animal's "sagacity in discerning those that do it kind offices: for, as soon as the good old lady [Mrs. Snooke] comes in sight who has waited on it for more than thirty years, it hobbles towards it's benefactress with aukward alacrity; but remains inattentive to strangers. Thus not only 'the ox knoweth his owner, and the ass his master's crib,' but the most abject reptile and torpid of beings distinguishes the hand that feeds it, and is touched with the feelings of gratitude!"[117]

In two further letters, White confined his observations to days when unusually warm weather prompted Timothy to emerge from hibernation early, only to return to "mud and mire" when the cold returned.[118] But his final discussion is the lengthiest, prompted by his acquisition of the tortoise following Mrs. Snooke's death: "I dug it out of it's winter dormitory in *March* last, when it was enough awakened to express it's resentments by hissing; and, packing it in a box with earth, carried it eighty miles in postchaises." White announced happily that he would "now have an opportunity of enlarging my observations on it's mode of life, and propensities," offering some details that he had already noticed. As with his comment about the tortoise's gratitude, he was once more moved to ponder God's hand in the animal's existence: "When one reflects on the state of this strange being, it is a matter of wonder to find that Providence should bestow such a profusion of days, such a seeming waste of longevity, on a reptile that appears to relish it so little as to squander more than two thirds of it's existence in a joyless stupor, and be lost to all sensation for months together in the profoundest of slumbers."[119]

Yet in the appendix on the "Old Family Tortoise," White was more gracious, beginning his observations with the remark, "Because we call this creature an abject reptile, we are too apt to undervalue his abilities, and depreciate his powers of instinct." Timothy, he noted, was intelligent enough to recognize and avoid falling into a ha-ha. And although he was unfamiliar with geometry, he knew how to angle his shell in the autumn to capture as much sunlight as possible. "Pitiable seems the condition of this poor embarrassed reptile; to be cased in a suit of ponderous armour, which he cannot lay aside; to be imprisoned, as it were, within his own shell," but in early June the tortoise engaged in "remarkable" activity, waking up early and attempting to escape the confines of the garden. White speculated that Timothy was motivated by "amorous" impulses, "which transport him beyond his usual gravity, and induce him to forget for a time his ordinary solemn deportment."[120] White's writing, with its combination of careful observation, humor at the animal's expense, and admiration for Timothy's abilities, reflects an attitude similar to Cowper's toward his hares. White was interested in presenting an objective description of the tortoise, one that would benefit other naturalists. Yet he could not help moving from such specific observations to broader speculation about the meaning and purpose of Timothy's existence, and his comments reveal a belief that Timothy had a recognizable personality. Timothy was both a pet and an object of scientific study; if Cowper's remarks lean more toward that of the loving pet owner, White's tend in the other direction. But both impulses remain at play, and it is likely that in both cases the observations are as detailed as they are because of the affectionate interest behind them.

White's journals, moreover, continued to delineate Timothy's activities long after the 1780 letter to Barrington, and these journals were the source for the appendix in the *Natural History*.[121] Once Timothy moved to Selborne, White referred to him almost exclusively by name, whereas in the observations written in Sussex, he was usually just "Mrs Snooke's old tortoise." White weighed the animal every fall and made note of all the plants Timothy ate. He performed other experiments as well, as when he tried immersing the tortoise in water—an experience that left Timothy "much dismayed." "This species seems not at all amphibious," White noted carefully (1 July 1780, 174). A week later, he recorded the texture and color of Timothy's excrement (8 July 1780, 174), and another experiment involved shouting through a "speaking-trumpet" to see if Timothy could hear (there was no apparent response) (17 September 1780, 177).

But White did not see Timothy solely as an experimental subject. When a rainstorm flooded the tortoise's "hybernaculum," White remarked with concern that Timothy "might have been drowned, had not his friend Thomas come to his assistance & taken him away" (28 March 1782, 203).[122] He was equally worried in May 1784, when Timothy disappeared "for more than a week," though this entry was immediately followed by the note that Timothy had turned up in a nearby field (28 May 1784,

242). A few years later, Timothy again escaped in the spring on what White presumed were "pursuits . . . of the amorous kind," before being found after several days "near the upper malt-house" (5 June 1787, 292). A year later, his escape attempts prompted White to confine him to "the brew-house" (4 May 1788, 307). White remained both curious and concerned about the reptile for the fourteen years he lived after acquiring Timothy, and his last entry on the subject came just a few weeks before his own death in 1793 (1 June 1793, 431).

Another side of White's thinking about Timothy emerges in the letters he wrote to his family and friends, among them his niece Molly White. When Timothy escaped in 1784, White wrote his niece that "poor Timothy" was missing. Thomas Hoar, the gardener, he said, was "much discomposed at this elopement," and White quoted from Samuel Butler's *Hudibras* in gentle mockery. "But to be serious," he immediately added, "I should be very sorry to lose so old a domestic, that has behaved himself in so blameless a manner in the family for near fifty years."[123] And when the tortoise was found a week later, White again wrote to inform his niece. His explanation, that Timothy had gone off in search of a mate, was the same one he used in his journal and the *Natural History*. But in the letter to Molly he developed the humor in the situation, writing from the tortoise's point of view. Timothy had imagined "that beautiful females might inhabit those vast spaces, which appeared boundless in his eye. But having wandered 'til he was tired, and having met with nothing but weeds, and coarse grass, and solitude, he was glad to return to the poppies, and lettuces, and the other luxuries of the garden."[124] White's letter to his nephew Samuel Barker about Timothy's emergence from hibernation similarly presents information from the journal and *Natural History* in a more personal tone: "There is somewhat very forlorn and abject in that creature's first appearance after a profound slumber of five months. When a man first rouses himself from a deep sleep, he does not look very wise: but nothing can be more squalid and stupid than our friend, when he first comes crawling out of his hibernacula."[125] White's use of the word "abject" to describe Timothy is consistent across his work, but here the term is tempered by the self-awareness with which White acknowledges that he might not look his best, either, after months of "profound slumber."[126]

But the most extensive presentation of this mixture of humor and affection emerges in a letter White wrote in Timothy's voice to Hester

Mulso, a friend's daughter, in return for a set of verses she had addressed to Timothy. In this long letter, White provided information about Timothy's arrival in the Snooke family as well as details from his life in Selborne. Juxtaposed against the detailed but dry language of the *Natural History*, this letter enables us to glimpse the sympathy that lay behind White's scientific prose. White begins by speculating about Timothy's origins, having the tortoise announce that he was "born in the year 1734 in the Province of Virginia in the midst of a Savanna that lay between a large tobacco plantation and a creek of the sea," where he lived happily before being captured by a "sea-boy" and carried across the ocean. In Chichester he is sold "for half a crown" to Mr. Snooke, who promptly turns him over to Mrs. Snooke, "a benevolent woman, whose humane attention extended to the meanest of her retainers." "Timothy" writes that his current abode with White has the benefit of a much larger living space and abundant food, "but still at times I miss my good old mistress, whose grave and regular deportment suited best with my disposition." White is unfortunately "what they call a *naturalist*" who insists on performing "whimsical experiments, such as feeling my pulse, putting me in a tub of water to try if I can swim, &c." Equally undignified is the semiannual experience of being weighed, when, we learn, Timothy is taken to the grocer and placed on his back in the scale. Even worse is the "contempt shown for my understanding which these *Lords* of the *Creation* are very apt to discover, thinking that nobody knows anything but themselves." For instance, he has heard White express surprise that he knew enough to avoid falling into the ha-ha. But the "greatest misfortune," says the tortoise, is "the want of society of my own kind"; a description of his escape the previous spring follows. He concludes that he feels more "sorrows" than "satisfactions," and appeals at last to Mulso's "sensibility": "Suppose you were to be kidnapped away *to-morrow*, in the bloom of your life, to a land of Tortoises, and were never to see again for fifty years a human face!!!"[127] With this letter, then, we see White engaging in the cross-species sympathy that was so appealing to many people in the late eighteenth century. Although he obviously did not intend his recipient to take the letter too seriously, it nevertheless reveals his ability to relate to Timothy from a perspective outside the realm of scientific inquiry. The affection hinted at in the journal and *Natural History* emerges fully here; the informality and privacy of letters to close friends and family allowed White to exploit an alternative set of epistolary conventions that reveal a different side of his own personality as well as a new view of his tortoise.

Clearly, Timothy was not a typical pet, not only because of his species but because he lived almost exclusively outdoors, and White's interest merged the scientific with the personal. Like Cowper, he accepted that this animal would never become fully tame. Just as Cowper remarked that Tiney, "when he could, would bite," so White understood that it was necessary to confine Timothy in order to keep him from running away. Like Cowper with his hares, White was interested in the general characteristics that might be gleaned from studying Timothy; by weighing the tortoise before and after each hibernation, for instance, he concluded that it was incorrect to say that tortoises keep growing throughout their lives. His many comments about Timothy's diet reflect a similar interest in such basic information. But Timothy was initially purchased as a pet, and neither Ringmer nor Selborne represented his natural habitat. He is one of the few animals in White's journals to be given a name, and the only one who remains a presence throughout the record. Timothy was obviously special, even though White was less explicit than Cowper in publicly expressing the pleasure he gained from an animal's company. White was willing to make the long coach journey from Hampshire to Sussex (battling terrible motion sickness all the way) to collect Timothy when Mrs. Snooke died, and he carefully watched over the animal for the rest of his life.

For both White and Cowper, the mixture of the scientific and the personal provided an outlet for discussing their pets that did not threaten their masculinity. Neither the poet nor the clergyman fit neatly into a masculine ideal of physical toughness or military valor, of course, but the popularity of natural history created an opportunity to engage in close contact with and observation of pets while avoiding the taint of frivolous femininity or conspicuous consumption. If the culture of sensibility embraced the possibility of sympathy across the species boundary, Cowper's and White's work suggested that affection could be compatible with scientific understanding. They accepted and maintained the boundary between human and animal, with minimal anthropomorphism, but this did not prevent them from revealing their emotional involvement. And in the less formal contexts of personal correspondence and poetry, they were able to express a deeper recognition of both the possibilities and limits of interspecies understanding.

Horace Walpole (1717–1797), collector, critic, novelist, and prolific correspondent, was renowned in his own time. His estate at Strawberry Hill, which he purchased in 1748, was a popular destination for people touring the great houses of England, famous not only for its architecture but for the collection of art Walpole amassed within it.[128] He is also perhaps the best-known pet owner of the eighteenth century, partly because of the literary efforts his animals inspired. His cat Selima was memorialized in Thomas Gray's "Ode on the Death of a Favourite Cat, Drowned in a Tub of Goldfishes," and that work in turn inspired other poems.[129] But Selima was not his only pet whose death provided poetic fodder. Walpole's spaniel Tory was eaten by a wolf on the way over an Alpine pass in 1739, and the incident inspired two poetic elegies.[130] Walpole himself wrote an epitaph for his dog Rosette. There were less tragic animal-related works as well; his first favorite dog, named Patapan, was the subject of a series of humorous poems Walpole exchanged with his friend John Chute. He also wrote a satirical fable (based on one by La Fontaine) entitled "Patapan, or The Little White Dog."[131]

But Walpole's pets were not merely playthings that inspired amusing literary confections. He prided himself on his kindness to animals and opposed all sorts of abuse, even activities that might seem to be harmless recreations.[132] His response to the first successful balloon trip in England was that it was unfair to have brought a dog and a cat along for the ride, especially since the balloon had to make a temporary landing to drop off the cat, which was suffering from the cold. Lunardi "had full right to venture his own neck," Walpole complained, "but none to risk the poor cat."[133] Deliberate harm to animals made him absolutely livid. Following a 1760 order by the London council to exterminate all the loose dogs during a rabies scare, he raged that "the streets are a very picture of the murder of the innocents—one drives over nothing but poor dead dogs! The dear, good-natured, honest, sensible creatures! Christ! how can anybody hurt them?"[134] He was even more horrified to hear that opponents of Charles James Fox during the hotly contested election of 1784 had roasted a fox alive, "a savage meanness that an Iroquois would not have committed!—base, cowardly wretches! how much nobler to have hurried to London and torn Mr Fox himself piecemeal!—I detest a country inhabited by such stupid barbarians!"[135]

Walpole's affection for animals was matched by his avowed distrust of his own species. After reading an essay condemning cruelty to dogs, Walpole said that he had "little [hope] of [it] doing any good: humanity is no match for cruelty . . . our race in general is pestilently bad and malevolent."[136] Similarly, he saw hunting as a sign of humanity's unfortunate love of violence. "As it is a persecution of animals, I do not love hunting; and what old writers mention as a commendation, makes me hate it the more, its being an image of war. Mercy on us! that destruction of any species should be a sport or a merit! . . . A hero or a sportsman who wishes for longer life, is desirous of prolonging devastation."[137] Walpole's vision of human-animal relations, then, was one in which animals provided a model for human behavior. Reversing the usual glorification of military valor, he argued for kindness and sympathy as the greatest virtues—virtues that he believed were much more prevalent in the animal world than in the human one. His antagonism toward abuse was imbued with the ideals of sensibility, including the notion that sensibility itself was ill suited to human society.

Yet Walpole was no "man of feeling" isolated from the beau monde; for all his distrust of humanity, he was extremely sociable and kept up an almost constant round of visits, near and far, as well as his extraordinarily voluminous correspondence. He was also keen to manage his own reputation, collecting his letters in preparation for the day when they would be published and even overseeing some of that publication himself. The persona that emerges in his writing, then, is just that: a persona constructed with enormous care. His personal correspondence reflected not a spontaneous outpouring of emotion but an awareness of an audience beyond the individual to whom each letter was addressed. Yet his discussions of his pets in these letters are valuable partly because of that awareness; they expressed his public image, just as a commissioned portrait might. For Walpole, affection for his animals, particularly his three favorite dogs, helped create a bond with his correspondents. The letters show how one pet owner lived with his nonhuman companions—taking them on visits to friends, caring for them when they were sick—in telling details that are rare in eighteenth-century sources. But the letters are also valuable because they demonstrate how pet keeping had come by the end of the century to be not only the stereotypical refuge of frivolous women but also a means of constructing a virtuous self that appealed to men as well as women. The sentimentalism visible in the popular prints and portraits of the later eighteenth century had its counterpart in the language Walpole used to discuss his dogs Rosette and Tonton, which was markedly distinct from that he employed writing about Patapan, his first favorite. The transformation in Walpole's rhetoric—and its remarkable distance from the apologetic tone of Lady Wentworth's letters—reflects the transformation that took place over the course of the century in attitudes toward pet keeping.

Walpole seems to have been an animal lover all his life. In his earliest extant letter, which he later claimed was the first he ever wrote to his mother, he added a postscript in which he announced that he was "very glad to hear . . . that all my cruataurs [creatures] are all wall."[138] When he was a student at Cambridge, he sent a monkey to his cousin in London.[139] But the most abundant evidence of Walpole's pet-keeping habits comes from his adulthood, thanks to the decades' worth of correspondence that has been preserved. His interest was partly aesthetic: his estate at Strawberry Hill was filled with both domestic and exotic animals, and he dotted the landscape with cattle specifically chosen for the effect of their colors against the scenery, along with exotic livestock like Turkish sheep and Chinese pigs.[140] Similarly, the "Po Yang" goldfish pond he built clearly reflected his taste for Orientalism. His animals also provided entertainment. Writing to his cousin about his daily routine in 1761, Walpole said, "All the morning I play with my workmen or animals."[141] We get another glimpse of this routine in a 1765 letter, when he confessed that he stayed out late, slept late, "and by the time I have breakfasted, fed my birds and my squirrels and dressed, there is an auction ready."[142] But it was his dogs, and to a lesser extent his cats, that meant the most to him. He was unabashed in demonstrating his affection for them; on a visit to Paris, for instance, he told George Montagu to "Kiss Fanny and Mufti and Ponto for me when you go [to] Strawberry [Hill]; dear souls! I long to kiss them myself."[143]

The three most important animals in Walpole's life were his dogs Patapan, Rosette, and Tonton. Other dogs were mentioned, sometimes by name, but no other animals played such long-running roles in his letters. They spanned decades of Walpole's life, from the 1740s through the 1780s. All three were gifts from female friends abroad and thus were tangible reminders of these European friendships, a means, like the letters themselves, of keeping distant relationships prominent in the friends' memories. But Walpole also had very different relationships with each of the dogs, relationships that shed light on his changing life and his changing views of pet keeping. While Patapan was used largely as a source of humor among Walpole and his friends, the later dogs brought out a much more personal and emotional response.

Walpole's first favorite, the "little white dog" Patapan, was a Roman spaniel he received while touring Europe in 1741 from his Florentine *cicisbea*, Elisabetta Grifoni.[144] From the beginning, Walpole played up Patapan's "aristocratic" heritage, and the dog's nobility became a running joke among his group of friends. He jested about making royal matches for Patapan and about naturalizing him and making him an English peer.[145] When Patapan sired puppies, Walpole sent one from Venice to his friend Horace Mann in Florence, complete with a mock pedigree outlining the animal's "titles."[146] Walpole also hired the well-known animal painter John Wootton to paint Patapan's portrait, and once again his description of the portrait relied on mock solemnity. "He is to have a triumphal arch at a distance, to signify his Roman birth," he told Mann, "and his having barked at thousands of Frenchman in the very heart of Paris."[147] A few months later, another friend, John Chute, asked, "Is Patapan's picture like? My respects to him; I wish him joy, and pray tell him I hope if he goes to St Paul's, he will insist upon a seat in the choir, opposite to my Lord of London's [i.e., the bishop of London], or in some other distinguished situation suitable to his high blood."[148] A similar mixture of affection and humor emerges in a poem Chute wrote for Patapan, based on Martial's epigram "On Publius's Lap-Dog": "Pata is frolicksome and smart / . . . A jewel for a lady's ear / And Mr Walpole's pretty dear. / He laughs, and cries, with mirth, or spleen, / He does not speak, but thinks, 'tis plain."[149] Walpole replied that "Patapan is so vain with it that he will read nothing else; I only offered him a Martial to compare it with the original, and the little coxcomb threw it into the fire."[150]

This habit of using the dog as a surrogate to express affection was quite common, and Walpole's friends frequently asked after "little Prince Patapan." Because Walpole had no spouse or children, references to Patapan filled part of the space of the letters that would ordinarily contain greetings to or from those human family members. Such references may also have helped create an acceptable avenue for expressing emotions in his intense relationships with other men. For instance, Chute asked Walpole to "Tell dear Patapan I'll kiss him an hour the first time I see him."[151]

Walpole signed off a letter to Mann with the assurance that "Patapan is entirely yours and entirely handsome."[152] In another letter to Mann, he concluded, "I think I have not said anything lately to you from Patapan; he is handsomer than ever and grows fat."[153] The following winter, he again painted a picture of domestic bliss: "I wish you could come on those nights and sit by my fire-side; I have the prettiest warm little apartment with all my baubles and Patapans and cats!"[154] Humor helped cloak the real affection not only between man and beast but between man and man.

As in the reference to his warm fireside, the correspondence also provides glimpses of Walpole's domestic life with his dog. Upon arriving in Paris in 1741, for instance, he wrote to Lord Lincoln, "I have no news to tell you, for I have not seen a soul, having been a good deal confined upon the couch by Mr Patapan's having been asleep in my lap."[155] After returning to England, Patapan continued to accompany Walpole on all his travels. "My packing up and travelling concerns lie in very small compass," Walpole wrote about one such trip; "nothing but myself and Patapan, my footman, a cloak bag and a couple of books."[156] Another homey image appears in a letter of October 1743, when Walpole told Mann, "Patapan is in my lap: I had him wormed lately, which he took heinously: I made it up with him by tying a collar of rainbow ribband about his neck, for a token that he is never to be wormed any more."[157] Despite all this companionship, however, Walpole's response to Patapan's death in 1745 was muted. Writing to Mann, he lamented the death of a mutual acquaintance and then added, "If it would not sound ridiculously, though I assure you I am far from feeling it lightly, I would tell you of poor Patapan's death: he died about ten days ago."[158] He was obviously sorry, but the mock-heroic tone that had dominated their discussions of the animal was ill suited to dealing with a real loss.

If irony was the dominant mode through which Walpole portrayed his relationship with Patapan, the correspondence paints a very different picture of his next favorite, Rosette, who entered Walpole's life in 1767. She was originally intended as a gift from Sir Gilbert Elliot to Madame du Deffand, a French friend and one of Walpole's most devoted correspondents. Walpole was supposed to have been the chaperone for the delivery of the new animal, but Deffand offered to let him keep Rosette, as she already had a dog.[159] Rosette soon became Walpole's constant companion, accompanying him on his travels both within England and abroad.[160] As he wrote to George Montagu before visiting Stowe at the request of

Princess Amalie, "I cannot say that [Rosette] is either commanded or invited to be of this royal party, but have me, have my dog."[161] On another occasion, he took Rosette on a visit to Castle Howard and was particularly pleased with the treatment they both received: "The housekeeper showed me and told me everything, and even was so kind as to fetch Rosette a basin of water, which completed the conquest of my heart."[162] In 1770, Walpole even credited Rosette with heroism when her barking alerted him to a chimney fire. "She saved my life last Saturday night," he wrote to Mann, "so I am sure you will love her too."[163]

When Rosette died, Walpole was more open in his grief than he had been with Patapan. She had become ill on a summer visit to Viscount Nuneham's estate in Oxfordshire. Writing to his host after returning home, Walpole said sadly, "Rosette has suffered dreadfully ever since she was seized at Nuneham; . . . I dare scarce flatter myself with a glimpse of hope!"[164] In a letter to Lady Ossory, he remarked on the beauties of Twickenham but added, "I must quit my joys for my sorrows. My poor Rosette is dying. She relapsed into her fits the last night of my stay at Nuneham; and has suffered exquisitely ever since. You may believe I have too—I have been out of bed twenty times every night, have had no sleep, and sat up with her till three this morning—but I am only making you laugh at me: I cannot help it, I think of nothing else. Without weaknesses I should not be I, and I may as well tell them, as have them tell themselves."[165] After receiving a letter in which she apparently tried to comfort him, he replied, "You don't flatter me, Madam, by being more concerned for me than for Rosette. She is still alive, but I despair of her recovery; however you have so little dogmanity, that I will say no more about her."[166] There was an improvement a few days later, and Rosette struggled on for several more weeks.[167] The experience was all the worse for Walpole since he was also trying to manage his nephew's estate (the nephew, who had inherited the title of Earl of Orford, was mentally ill). Despite Lady Ossory's lack of "dogmanity," Walpole wrote to her again in late October in despair: "In truth I know nothing, think of nothing but my poor nephew's affairs and Rosette. I left her this morning so ill and weak, that I shall not be surprised, though shocked, if I find her dead. Margaret [Walpole's housekeeper] sat up with her the whole night before last; I have sat up half the night many times and raised all the family—well! there ends the last of my favourites!"[168] A few days later, Walpole sent Lord Nuneham news of Rosette's death, admitting that he had spent all his spare time "nursing Rosette—alas! to no purpose." He included an epitaph he had written, based on Pope's *Essay on Man*. The verse's only merit, he told Nuneham, was that it came "from the heart, if ever epitaph did, and therefore your Dogmanity will not dislike it."[169]

Walpole's expression of sorrow at his dog's death was more literary than Lady Wentworth's, but the grief was obviously no less sincere. The many weeks in which he cared for Rosette must have been terribly difficult. But in his references to the "dogmanity" (or lack thereof) of his correspondents, Walpole's tendency to measure human worth in terms of attitudes toward animals emerged once more. Even though Lady Ossory was a good friend, Walpole was willing to criticize her for her lack of feeling. If Lady Wentworth felt obliged to apologize for mourning her pets, Walpole presented his own emotions as a sign of moral worth.

With Tonton, his last favorite, Walpole's presentation of his pet keeping as a sign of moral superiority emerges most strongly. It was only about two weeks after Rosette's death in 1773 that Tonton first appeared in the correspondence, in a letter from Walpole's friend Madame du Deffand, Tonton's original owner.[170] As early as 1774, she raised the idea of bequeathing Tonton to Walpole: "Promise me that if Tonton ends up without a mistress, you will become his master; I am sure you will love him."[171] Walpole seems to have responded angrily to the suggestion, believing that she thought another dog could replace Rosette.[172] Despite his initial dislike of Tonton and his protestations that Rosette was the last of his favorites, however, it is clear that Walpole was lonely without a replacement. In 1779 he complained that he was terribly bored in town, with "no books or papers or dogs or cats to amuse me."[173] It must have been an added blow when his aged cat Harold, who had lived with him for about fifteen years, died the following summer.[174] Madame du Deffand never gave up the idea of leaving Tonton to her friend, and in January 1780 she wrote to him that she had finished her will and had included in it a bequest to him of a snuffbox with Tonton's portrait on it. "I would like to leave you Tonton himself," she added; "I am sure that you would love him and take great care of him. Please take him if you can."[175]

When she died the following October, Walpole did accept both snuffbox and dog, along with her correspondence and other papers, an action he presented as a testament of his affection for his friend.[176] Unfortunately, Tonton's temper, which was famously vicious in Paris, does not seem to have improved after his mistress's death.[177] With a mixture of amusement and exasperation, Walpole reported that as soon as he arrived at Strawberry Hill, Tonton's "despotic" nature emerged: "he began with exiling my beautiful little cat;—upon which, however, we shall not quite agree. He then flew at one of my dogs, who returned it, by biting his foot till it bled; but was severely beaten for it. I immediately rung for Margaret to dress his foot; but in the midst of my tribulation could not keep my countenance; for she cried, 'Poor little thing, he does not understand my language!'—I hope she will not recollect too that he is a papist!" "If I do not correct his vivacities," Walpole promised, "at least I shall not encourage them like my dear old friend."[178] By November he was able to report some progress: "Tonton is perfectly well, and does not bite anybody once in a month."[179] But several years later, Walpole still had to assure Lady Ossory half-jokingly that Tonton's recent nip at her husband's finger was not a sign of rabies.[180] He also confessed to her that Tonton "has a very decent privy purse for his travels" in order to bribe the servants at the homes he visited not to tell their masters about the dog's depredations to their furniture.[181]

Yet Tonton's faults did not keep Walpole from falling in love with his new dog almost immediately. Just a month after bringing Tonton home, he told a friend, "I have gotten a new idol, in a word, a successor to Rosette and almost as great a favourite . . . it is incredible how fond I am of it. . . . I dined at Richmond House t'other day, and mentioning whither I was going, the Duke said, 'Own the truth, shall not you call at home first and see Tonton?' He guessed rightly. He is now sitting on my paper as I write—not the Duke, but Tonton."[182] In another letter, Walpole confessed that after all his years of resisting the lure of the court, he had accepted an invitation to take his dog to visit Princess Sophia. "My father is reported to have said that every man has his price. You see, Madam," he told Lady Ossory, "my dog was *my* vulnerable part. I have resisted bribes for myself—I was not proof against honours for Tonton."[183] The two even seem to have shared a bed.[184] Walpole's affection for the dog also emerges in simple asides in his letters. While reading George Crabbe's *The Library*, he was charmed by the line "that a dog though a flatterer, is still a friend": "It made me give Tonton a warm kiss, and swear it was true."[185] Complaining of the gout on another occasion, he said, "I . . . could walk about my room without a stick, if Tonton did not caper against me and throw me down, for I have no more elasticity in my joints than the tail of a paper kite."[186] Walpole, never impressively strong, was at this time sixty-five and seems to have been no match for his nine-year-old spaniel.

But Tonton could not live forever, and he died on 17 February 1789.[187] Walpole told Lady Ossory that by the time of his death, Tonton was

> stone deaf, and very near equally blind, and so weak that the two last days he could not walk upstairs. Happily he had not suffered, and died close by my side without a pang or a groan. I have had the satisfaction for my dear old friend's [Madame du Deffand's] sake and his own, of having nursed him up by constant attention to the age of sixteen, yet always afraid of his surviving me, as it was scarce possible he could meet a third person who would study his happiness equally. I sent him to Strawberry [Hill] and went thither on Sunday to see him buried behind the Chapel near Rosette. I shall miss him greatly—and must not have another dog—I am too old, and should only breed it up to be unhappy, when I am gone![188]

Lady Ossory offered to give him a replacement, but he again insisted that he was too old and feeble himself to take on a new responsibility. Besides, he wrote, "I have such a passion for dogs, that a favourite one is a greater misery than pleasure; and to give me one is to sow me with anxiety."[189] This time he was true to his word and acquired no new favorites, although he did help look after Tonton's namesake, a dog belonging to his friends Mary and Anne Berry.[190] For all his faults, the original Tonton was, for Walpole, irreplaceable.

Patapan, Rosette, and Tonton were just a few of the many animals with which Walpole surrounded himself throughout his life. His love of animals was both genuine and central to his self-presentation as someone who abhorred human tendencies toward violence. Famously slight in build and effete in mannerism, he used humanity toward the nonhuman part of creation to establish an alternative image of honor and virtue against the traditional masculine values of martial courage and dominance. This self-image only grew stronger as he aged, and its development is visible in the changing ways he talked about his favorite animals. From the mock heroism and imagined pedigree in discussions of Patapan to his unconcealed grief over Tonton's death, Walpole's portrayal of his relationship with his dogs became much more openly emotional over time. He was certainly no Mackenzian "man of feeling," too tender to survive in the polite world: he loved socializing, enjoyed gossip, and was known for his waspish wit. But the values of sensibility nevertheless permeated his self-presentation in relation to animals and provided an opportunity to construct himself in line with the aristocratic but sensitive masculinity represented in the Duke of Buccleuch's portrait.

≈   ≈   ≈

Together, the letters of Isabella Wentworth, William Cowper, Gilbert White, and Horace Walpole reflect the growing acceptance of pet keeping in British society over the course of the eighteenth century. These writers did not turn to pets as a substitute for human affection, nor was pet keeping for them a form of conspicuous consumption. While all four correspondents reveal deep attachments to their animals, however, their presentations of those relationships were shaped not only by their individual personalities but also by their specific historical contexts. Lady Wentworth lacked the discursive framework through which to present her pet keeping in a positive light. Although she perceived her animals in terms of familial relations, she could not entirely convince her human family members, or even herself, that it was acceptable to love them and grieve their loss. Walpole would have recognized in her a kindred spirit despite their differences in social position and personality, but he lived in an era that allowed him to celebrate his own "Dogmanity" and to grieve openly when Rosette and Tonton died.

One of Walpole's close friends was William, Earl of Strafford—the grandson of Lady Wentworth. Like his father, William had a wife named Anne, but her temperament was apparently much closer to Lady Wentworth's than to the elder Lady Strafford's. William and Anne kept a substantial menagerie at their Yorkshire estate, Wentworth Castle.[191] Walpole frequently referred to their collection in his letters, and he called Anne "the lady of the menagerie."[192] Anne was known for her love of animals and her many pets. In a memoir, Lady Louisa Stuart noted that "Lady Strafford delighted in animals of every sort and species; had favourite horses, dogs, cats, squirrels, parroquets, and singing-birds. Nay, I remember to this hour the pleasure it gave me, when a child, to see a couple of tame green lizards, which she kept in a box, let loose to sport and catch flies in the sunshine."[193] According to Stuart, Lady Strafford had epilepsy, which led her husband to shelter her from much traveling or even socializing. This isolation and her childlessness, Stuart implied, fueled Lady Strafford's interest in animals. But social isolation was not essential to spur such interest. Walpole shared her obsession, and their mutual love of nonhuman companions was a central theme in their correspondence and one basis of their friendship. "Tonton begs his duty to all the lambs, and trusts that Lady Strafford will not reject his homage," he wrote to the earl in 1782.[194] Comparing the couple to Adam and Eve in paradise on another occasion, he suggested that their one flaw was their love of fishing: "If Eve [i.e., Anne] has a sin, I doubt [i.e., fear] it is angling; but as she makes all other creatures happy, I beg she would not impale worms nor whisk carp out of one element into another."[195]

When one of the Straffords' animals died, Walpole sent his condolences, adding a typical sentiment about the relative worth of humans: "Sense and fidelity are wonderful recommendations; and when one meets with them, and can be confident that one is not imposed upon, I cannot think that the two additional legs are any drawback. At least I know that I have had friends who would never have vexed or betrayed me, if they had walked on all fours."[196] Lady Wentworth would probably have been astonished at such open expressions of affection for animals, but the correspondence reveals how much attitudes had changed over the course of only a few generations. Love of animals, even "useless" pets, had for many people become a sign of virtue, attractive to men as well as women.

The growing acceptance of pet keeping did not mean that conditions for animals improved greatly over the course of the eighteenth century. Casual violence against animals continued (even Walpole beat his dogs), and many people still believed that nonhuman creation had value only insofar as it was useful to humans. Arguments for humane treatment of animals encountered as much mockery as they did support.[1] It was not until 1822 that the first, very restricted, legislation against cruelty to animals was passed. Where it did exist, compassion for animals was often strictly limited by unspoken assumptions about the relative value of different species; Walpole's desire to end the suffering of bait worms and carp was not high on many humanitarians' agenda.

Nevertheless, British society in 1800 was very different from that of a hundred years earlier, and attitudes toward animals both reflected and fostered broader social change. Throughout the century, pets helped people think through the pros and cons of the emerging society we now call modern Britain. Their status on the border between human and animal, civilization and nature, family member and stranger was both frightening and appealing when traditional ideas about gender, status, and national identity were in tremendous flux. But pets were more than just symbols. For their owners, from Lady Wentworth to Horace Walpole, what mattered most was the intimate emotional bond between human and animal. And as more and more people had the experience of keeping a pet, assumptions about pets' roles as mere accessories or substitutes for "real" affection were also shaken. Older criticisms did not die, but the eighteenth century saw the birth of the modern pet, loved without apology or remorse.

At the same time, pet keeping in the eighteenth century helps us understand the roots of many conflicts and contradictions in present-day attitudes. Today, in the mockery of "cat ladies" or celebrities' "purse dogs," we hear echoes of stereotypes about spinsters and fashionable lap-dogs in the eighteenth century. Nor have we resolved the paradox inherent in conceptualizing animals as living property: if crisis management preparation now requires plans for the evacuation of pets as well as humans in an emergency, it is still common to criticize the poor or homeless for "wasting" their resources on pets. Ideas about the appropriateness of pet ownership continue to be bound up in assumptions about class and gender.

But if eighteenth-century pet keeping sheds light on modern dilemmas, the historical perspective also requires that we recognize the complexities of change in human-animal relations, which resist simple narratives of progress or decline. We can trace some of these complexities if we follow the development of animal welfare and animal rights movements in the nineteenth and twentieth centuries. As we have seen, the humane movement focused from its inception on abuses perpetrated by poor people, rather than on upper-class pastimes like hunting. Moreover, the most common justification for better treatment of animals was that abuse led to immoral *human* behavior. During the nineteenth century, welfare advocates continued to target working people, and humans remained at the center of the movement's agenda.[2] There was little serious questioning of human-animal relations that might lead to a fundamentally different relationship: for instance, concern over the treatment of livestock did not, as a rule, lead to advocacy of vegetarianism. Vegetarianism did increase among humane activists in the late nineteenth century, but it was often lauded for its allegedly purifying effects on human health and the human spirit, rather than its benefits to animals themselves.[3] Shifting concerns in the humane movement also continued to reflect human priorities and interests. Thus livestock and working animals still drew attention in the nineteenth century, but as Britain increasingly defined itself as a nation of pet lovers, the plight of companion animals took center stage. The establishment of the Battersea Dogs' Home in 1860 is one sign of this change of emphasis; as Hilda Kean notes, "Support for the Dogs' home, as for the RSPCA in an earlier decade, was depicted as an indicator of humane feeling."[4]

The development of the animal rights movement in the late twentieth century transformed the terms of the debate; rather than merely ameliorating the suffering of animals, the new wave asked people to consider animal interests or rights as equal to those of humans.[5] In part, however, this new thinking was the result of considering an old problem—the nature of the human-animal boundary. Thus Peter Singer rooted his pioneering book *Animal Liberation* in the argument that the distinction between humans and animals is purely arbitrary: all of the reasons used to justify humans' special status (the possession of reason or speech, for instance) actually exclude some humans and include some animals.[6] What we see in arguments like Singer's is the logical conclusion of the ideas formulated by humane advocates in the late eighteenth century. It is no coincidence that Singer, a utilitarian, is the intellectual heir of Jeremy Bentham, who replaced the ability to reason with the capacity to suffer—shared by humans and animals alike—as the basis for judging our treatment of animals. Singer's interrogation of the human-animal boundary in turn helped to create the modern field of animal studies, and scholars continue to find fruitful avenues of exploration in studying how people struggled to define that boundary in the past. Moreover, shifting from an agenda of "compassion and humanity" to defending animal *rights* has helped scholars illuminate the limitations of the earlier humane movement.[7]

But Singer's intellectual ties to Bentham should also make us question one of the central narratives of animal studies. Many scholars identify the eighteenth century, or the early modern period more generally, as ushering in a regime that divides animals into those we care about (pets and some particularly adorable or exotic species) and those we don't (livestock, lab rats). Such a division is often connected to a split between animals we see and interact with on a regular basis and those removed from our view in factory farming or experimentation. John Berger, for instance, has famously argued that Descartes introduced a "decisive theoretical break" that came to practical fruition with industrialization, which turned animals first into machines of production and then into "raw material."[8] For those who see the rise of pet keeping as the result of urbanization and decreasing contact with animals, pets are thus implicated in the development of the distinctively modern abuses we practice. Our treatment of pets is the exception that proves the rule.[9] But the situation is more complicated than that, of course, not least because pet keeping became a widespread social phenomenon before the advent of industrialization. Further, as Kean points out, even in cities, eighteenth-century people would have had a great deal of contact with livestock and other working animals; urbanization does not automatically imply the disappearance of animals.[10] And while pet keeping may have encouraged thinking that valued some animals more highly than others, this was not a new phenomenon, either; a long tradition classified animals according to their uses to humans and weighed their moral character accordingly.

We should be wary, then, of the temptation to indulge in nostalgia for a lost era of human-animal understanding that may never have existed. Too great an emphasis on the origins of our current treatment of animals risks both assuming a past "golden age" for animals and reading history simply as a narrative of decline.[11] Historical change is a much more complicated process. As Gilbert White demonstrates, seeing an animal as an object of scientific investigation does not necessarily preclude our recognizing the animal as a sentient being capable of both suffering and emotion. Far from exposing the dawn of an era that reduced animals to machines, the study of eighteenth-century pet keeping reveals the enormous complexity of thinking about animals. For some Britons, pets reinforced a comfortable sense of superiority over other species, cultures, and classes. For others, pet keeping led to questioning of all of these hierarchies. Pets might signify wasteful luxury or an admirable elevation of feeling.

I am not arguing that we should replace the narrative of declining conditions for animals with one of progress and improvement; the contemporary abuses that inspire much work in animal studies are all too real. I am suggesting instead that such overarching narratives distract us from focusing on the particular contexts that shape human attitudes toward and treatment of animals. A careful reading of eighteenth-century thinking about pets demonstrates the historical specificity of such thinking. Naturalists explained animal domestication as slavery because slavery was a central part of their economy; both practices seemed corrupt yet essential to society's survival. Satirists associated lapdogs and fashion because pets were in many ways the ultimate consumer good at a time when consumer goods of all kinds flooded the market, with results both exciting and disturbing. The eighteenth century saw the emergence of new social structures and values in Britain: an economy increasingly based on capitalist trade and manufacturing, with a strong rhetoric of rights and liberty. Although the transformation was far from complete by the end of the century, the changes were wrenching, and people often had deeply conflicted thoughts and feelings about them. Pets helped people think through the meaning of these changes because they embodied so many different, sometimes conflicting identities. Their unstable meaning made them uniquely useful in confronting unstable times.

Pets also illuminate the ways in which eighteenth-century responses to seemingly unrelated problems were in fact connected and drew on a common set of intellectual resources. The attempt to identify natural moral characteristics common to all of humanity is one thread that runs through the chapters of this book. This quest took a variety of forms. When considering animal slavery, for instance, writers asked whether a love of liberty was an essential aspect of human—or animal—existence. For those more concerned with luxury and consumption, the focus was on the question of what constitutes immoral wastefulness. And for those affected by the rise of the culture of sensibility, it became increasingly important to include other species in the moral fabric of human life.

Debates about "useful" and "useless" animals reveal another common concern—the role of pleasure in society. The growing emphasis on a benevolent God suggested that his creations were intended to enjoy life on earth, not merely to suffer in the hope of future redemption. From another perspective, Bernard Mandeville suggested that "private vices" might offer "public benefits," in an argument that privileged material comfort over religiously based self-denial.[12] Because pets were quintessentially objects of enjoyment rather than utility, they became surrogates for questions regarding the legitimacy of human pleasure. Was the pleasure gained by possessing an animal an acceptable use of that animal? Was keeping an animal for human entertainment a justifiable reason to deprive it of its liberty? Should poor people, women, or children be prohibited from enjoying such pleasures on the grounds that they would be unable to keep their enjoyment within reasonable bounds? Responses to pet keeping often emphasized the need for moderation and an awareness of social decorum, and these ideas also emerged in other contexts in response to concerns about the seemingly limitless opportunities to pursue pleasure in eighteenth-century Britain.

Yet another common theme was related to national identity: again and again, people expressed their opinions about pets by asking what it meant to be British. For some, then, liberty was not so much a universal characteristic as a distinctively British one, to be contrasted with the slavish French or Africans. Others sought to defy the whims of foreign fashion on the grounds that frugality and moderation were the quintessential British traits: a good English mastiff was what was wanted, not a Bolognese lapdog. And ultimately, some claimed (or hoped) that compassion for animals was itself a defining characteristic of Britishness.

Pets were thus "useful" after all, in that they helped the British work through their most vexing cultural problems. Beyond that role, however, pets, perhaps more than any other animals, encourage us to try to understand the animal mind even as they constantly remind us that we cannot do so. In the era of animal rights, we try to reimagine our relationships with our pets—to think of ourselves as guardians rather than property owners, or to see training them as an activity in which human and animal learn together. We believe that we have ethical obligations to our pets, but we disagree about the nature and extent of those obligations. Pets raise the tantalizing possibility of a human-animal relationship that is meaningful to both animal and human, but we struggle to explain what is "meaningful" to an animal. That problem was just as pressing in the eighteenth century as it is today. When people looked at their pets, the pets looked back; they were not merely symbols but living beings, and the questions they raised were never merely theoretical. As much as they were objects of contemplation and debate, they were also subjects who shaped human lives and values.

Notes

INTRODUCTION

1. See "Hartsdale Pet Cemetery," http://www.petcem.com/.

2. For a discussion of pets that emphasizes the harsh treatment they receive, see Yi-Fu Tuan, *Dominance and Affection: The Making of Pets* (New Haven: Yale University Press, 1984), chap. 6.

3. For an ethical argument against pet keeping on the grounds that it is wrong to treat animals as property, see Leslie Irvine, "Pampered or Enslaved? The Moral Dilemmas of Pets," *International Journal of Sociology and Social Policy* 24, no. 9 (2004): 5–17.

4. [John Aikin and Anna Laetitia Barbauld], *Evenings at Home, or The Juvenile Budget Opened*, 6 vols. (London: J. Johnson, 1792–96), 1:105.

5. Keith Thomas, *Man and the Natural World: Changing Attitudes in England, 1500–1800* (Oxford: Oxford University Press, 1983), 112–17.

6. Tuan, *Dominance and Affection*, 139–41.

7. Oliver Goldsmith, *An History of the Earth, and Animated Nature*, 8 vols. (London: J. Nourse, 1774), 3:285–86.

8. See Marc Shell, "The Family Pet," *Representations* 15 (1986): 121–53.

9. See, e.g., Adrian Franklin, *Animals and Modern Cultures: A Sociology of Human-Animal Relations in Modernity* (Los Angeles: Sage, 1999), esp. chaps. 2 and 5.

10. Erica Fudge, *Pets* (Stocksfield, UK: Acumen, 2008), esp. chap. 2.

11. See Kathleen Kete, *The Beast in the Boudoir: Petkeeping in Nineteenth-Century Paris* (Berkeley: University of California Press, 1994); Harriet Ritvo, *The Animal Estate: The English and Other Creatures in the Victorian Age* (Cambridge: Harvard University Press, 1987); Harriet Ritvo, "The Emergence of Modern Pet-Keeping," in *Animals and People Sharing the World*, ed. Andrew N. Rowan (Hanover: University Press of New England, 1988), 13–31; Katherine C. Grier, *Pets in America: A History* (Chapel Hill: University of North Carolina Press, 2006).

12. Thomas, *Man and the Natural World*, 114.

13. For an argument that pet keeping was already widespread in medieval society, despite sources skewed toward the elite, see Kathleen Walker-Meikle, *Medieval Pets* (Woodbridge: Boydell Press, 2012), esp. 5. Liliane Bodson asserts that "pet-keeping was a widespread and well-accepted phenomenon in classical antiquity." Bodson, "Motivations for Pet-Keeping in Ancient Greece and Rome: A Preliminary Survey," in *Companion Animals and Us: Exploring the Relationships Between People and Pets*, ed. Anthony L. Podberscek, Elizabeth S. Paul, and James A. Serpell (Cambridge: Cambridge University Press, 2000), 27.

14. James A. Serpell, "Pet-Keeping in Non-Western Societies: Some Popular Misconceptions," in Rowan, *Animals and People Sharing the World*, 33–52; Philippe Erikson, "The Social Significance of Pet-Keeping Among Amazonian Indians," in Podberscek, Paul, and Serpell, *Companion Animals and Us*, 7–26.

15. The defining study of the broad context of human-animal relationships remains Thomas, *Man and the Natural World*.

16. See, for example, Erica Fudge, Ruth Gilbert, and Susan Wiseman, eds., *At the Borders of the Human: Beasts, Bodies, and Natural Philosophy in the Early Modern Period* (Houndmills: Macmillan, 1999); Erica Fudge, *Perceiving Animals: Humans and Beasts in Early Modern English Culture* (New York: St. Martin's Press, 2000); Richard Nash, *Wild Enlightenment: The Borders of Human Identity in the Eighteenth Century* (Charlottesville: University of Virginia Press, 2003); Julia V. Douthwaite, *The Wild Girl, Natural Man, and the Monster: Dangerous Experiments in the Age of Enlightenment* (Chicago: University of Chicago Press, 2002); Laura Brown, *Fables of Modernity: Literature and Culture in the English Eighteenth Century* (Ithaca: Cornell University Press, 2001), esp. chap. 6; Laura Brown, *Homeless Dogs and Melancholy Apes: Humans and Other Animals in the Modern Literary Imagination* (Ithaca: Cornell University Press, 2010).

17. Donna Landry, *Noble Brutes: How Eastern Horses Transformed English Culture* (Baltimore: Johns Hopkins University Press, 2008); Louise E. Robbins, *Elephant Slaves and Pampered Parrots: Exotic Animals in Eighteenth-Century Paris* (Baltimore: Johns Hopkins University Press, 2002).

18. Landry, *Noble Brutes*, 10–11. Landry cites Erica Fudge's influential essay, "A Left-Handed Blow: Writing the History of Animals," in *Representing Animals*, ed. Nigel Rothfels (Bloomington: Indiana University Press, 2002), 3–18.

19. In keeping with this awareness, it may seem desirable entirely to avoid using "human" and "animal" as categories, but doing so would be clumsy (forcing repeated references to "nonhuman species," for instance) and would ignore the importance of these categories in early modern thinking. In *The Accommodated Animal: Cosmopolity in Shakespearean Locales* (Chicago: University of Chicago Press, 2013), Laurie Shannon points out that "beast" was the term more often used in cases where we would today use "animal." The relatively infrequent use of "animal" to refer generically to nonhumans is evident in the rest of this book. Nevertheless, it is clear that eighteenth-century thinkers did work with a basic distinction between humans and other species, and "animal" is a convenient shorthand term that is easily recognizable for a modern reader.

20. For an argument that presents a legal theory accommodating this view, see Steve Cooke, "Duties to Companion Animals," *Res Publica* 17 (2011): 261–74.

21. Vicki Hearne, *Adam's Task: Calling Animals by Name* (New York: Knopf, 1986); Donna Haraway, *The Companion Species Manifesto: Dogs, People, and Significant Otherness* (Chicago: Prickly Paradigm Press, 2003). Haraway deliberately refers to training "with" rather than training "of" animals to get at this idea of mutual cooperation and benefit; see her *When Species Meet* (Minneapolis: University of Minnesota Press, 2007), 222.

22. See, e.g., Virginia DeJohn Anderson, *Creatures of Empire: How Domestic Animals Transformed Early America* (Oxford: Oxford University Press, 2004).

23. The classic statement of the problem of interspecies understanding is Thomas Nagel, "What Is It Like to Be a Bat?," *Philosophical Review* 83, no. 4 (1974): 435–50. See also Fudge, *Pets*, chap. 3; Fudge, "Left-Handed Blow," 5–6.

24. Fudge, "Left-Handed Blow," 15. For an extended discussion of this problem, see H. Peter Steeves, "The Familiar Other and Feral Selves: Life at the Human/Animal

Boundary," in *The Human/Animal Boundary: Historical Perspectives*, ed. Angela N. H. Creager and William Chester Jordan (Rochester: University of Rochester Press, 2002), 228–64.

25. For a similar argument, see Christopher Plumb, "Exotic Animals in Eighteenth-Century Britain" (PhD diss., University of Manchester, 2010), 30–31.

CHAPTER 1

1. *Public Advertiser* 7542 (9 January 1759).

2. One of the earliest connections between consumerism and pet keeping—specifically regarding dog and bird breeding—appears in J. H. Plumb, *The Commercialisation of Leisure in Eighteenth-Century England* (Reading: University of Reading, 1973), 10. But Plumb noted that he had "no time to discuss" the matter.

3. Information in this chapter draws on the listings in the *Public Advertiser* (1753 to 1759, and then every five years from 1765 to 1790) and the *Daily Advertiser* (1731, 1744, and 1775).

4. Maxine Berg, *Luxury and Pleasure in Eighteenth-Century Britain* (Oxford: Oxford University Press, 2005), 149, citing Neil McKendrick, "Josiah Wedgwood and the Commercialization of the Potteries," in Neil McKendrick, John Brewer, and J. H. Plumb, *The Birth of a Consumer Society: The Commercialization of Eighteenth-Century England* (Bloomington: Indiana University Press, 1982); Peter Guillery, *The Small House in Eighteenth-Century London: A Social and Architectural History* (New Haven: Published for the Paul Mellon Centre for Studies in British Art by Yale University Press in association with English Heritage, 2004), 35.

5. See P. G. M. Dickson, *The Financial Revolution in England: A Study in the Development of Public Credit, 1688–1756* (New York: St. Martin's Press, 1967); John Brewer, *The Sinews of Power: War, Money, and the English State, 1688–1783* (New York: Knopf, 1989); Bruce G. Carruthers, *City of Capital: Politics and Markets in the English Financial Revolution* (Princeton: Princeton University Press, 1996), chap. 3; Daniel Carey, "An Empire of Credit: English, Scottish, Irish, and American Contexts," in *The Empire of Credit: The Financial Revolution in the British Atlantic World, 1688–1815*, ed. Daniel Carey and Christopher J. Findlay (Dublin: Irish Academic Press, 2011), 1–22.

6. Carey, "Empire of Credit," 4–6. Carey's article usefully outlines the similarities and differences in the financial systems of the individual states within Great Britain.

7. Brewer, *Sinews of Power*. See also, e.g., Patrick K. O'Brien, "The Political Economy of British Taxation, 1660–1815," *Economic History Review* 41, no. 1 (1988): 1–32.

8. Douglass C. North and Barry R. Weingast, "Constitutions and Commitment: The Evolution of Institutions Governing Public Choice in Seventeenth-Century England," *Journal of Economic History* 49, no. 4 (1989): 803–32; Carruthers, *City of Capital*, chap. 5.

9. For a concise discussion of harvests, dearth, and the renewed threat of extreme hunger in 1795–96 and 1800–1801, see Douglas Hay and Nicholas Rogers, *Eighteenth-Century English Society: Shuttles and Swords* (Oxford: Oxford University Press, 1997), chap. 5. See L. D. Schwarz, *London in the Age of Industrialisation: Entrepreneurs, Labour Force, and Living Conditions, 1700–1850* (Cambridge: Cambridge University Press, 1992), especially part III, for a discussion of the difficulties of identifying the relationship between wages and the standard of living.

10. Peter Borsay, *The English Urban Renaissance: Culture and Society in the Provincial Town, 1660–1770* (Oxford: Clarendon Press, 1989); Berg, *Luxury and Pleasure*, 206–19.

11. Mark Girouard, *Life in the English Country House: A Social and Architectural History* (New Haven: Yale University Press, 1978), 136–43, 151, chap. 7.

12. Carl B. Estabrook, *Urbane and Rustic England: Cultural Ties and Social Spheres in the Provinces, 1660–1780* (Stanford: Stanford University Press, 1998), 151–53. It is important to bear in mind that Estabrook emphasizes that these differentiated spaces were characteristic of urban but not rural dwellers. Peter Guillery observes that poor Londoners often lived in a single room, while those on the edge of the middling orders sometimes had only one or two rooms. He notes, however, that "the 'middling sort' family of the early eighteenth century typically had five to eight rooms, in effect a whole house." *Small House*, 30.

13. Amanda Vickery, *Behind Closed Doors: At Home in Georgian England* (New Haven: Yale University Press, 2009), 14–16, 274–76, 293–95; Amanda Vickery, *The Gentleman's Daughter: Women's Lives in Georgian England* (New Haven: Yale University Press, 1998), 206; Girouard, *Life in the English Country House*, 203; Estabrook, *Urbane and Rustic England*, 152.

14. Neil McKendrick, "The Consumer Revolution of Eighteenth-Century England," in McKendrick, Brewer, and Plumb, *Birth of a Consumer Society*, 9–33. For an influential response to the arguments presented in *Birth of a Consumer Society*, see John Brewer and Roy Porter, eds., *Consumption and the World of Goods* (London: Routledge, 1993).

15. Some of the most important work in this area includes Brewer and Porter, *Consumption and the World of Goods*; Vickery, *Gentleman's Daughter*; Vickery, *Behind Closed Doors*; John Styles and Amanda Vickery, eds., *Gender, Taste, and Material Culture in Britain and North America, 1700–1830* (New Haven: Yale Center for British Art; London: Paul Mellon Centre for Studies in British Art, 2006); Elizabeth Kowaleski-Wallace, *Consuming Subjects: Women, Shopping, and Business in the Eighteenth Century* (New York: Columbia University Press, 1997); Margot Finn, "Women, Consumption, and Coverture in England, c. 1760–1860," *Historical Journal* 39 (1996): 703–22; Lorna Weatherill, *Consumer Behaviour and Material Culture in Britain, 1660–1760* (London: Methuen, 1988).

16. John Styles presents a useful overview of changing patterns of consumption in his "Manufacturing, Consumption, and Design in Eighteenth-Century England," in Brewer and Porter, *Consumption and the World of Goods*, 527–54, esp. 535–42. See also Jan de Vries, "Between Purchasing Power and the World of Goods: Understanding the Household Economy in Early Modern Europe," ibid., 85–132. On the consumer goods of the laboring poor, see John Styles, "Lodging at the Old Bailey: Lodgings and Their Furnishing in Eighteenth-Century London," in Styles and Vickery, *Gender, Taste, and Material Culture*, 61–80.

17. For a good account of this process, see Weatherill, *Consumer Behaviour and Material Culture*.

18. John Styles, "Custom or Consumption? Plebeian Fashion in Eighteenth-Century England," in *Luxury in the Eighteenth Century: Debates, Desires, and Delectable Goods*, ed. Maxine Berg and Elizabeth Eger (Houndmills, Basingstoke: Palgrave Macmillan, 2003), 103–15; John Styles, *The Dress of the People: Everyday Fashion in Eighteenth-Century England* (New Haven: Yale University Press, 2007).

19. Berg, *Luxury and Pleasure*, 15.

20. See Sidney W. Mintz, *Sweetness and Power: The Place of Sugar in Modern History* (New York: Penguin, 1985).

21. On the eighteenth-century debates over luxury, see Berg, *Luxury and Pleasure*, 31–37; John Sekora, *Luxury: The Concept in Western Thought from Eden to Smollett* (Baltimore: Johns Hopkins University Press, 1977); Christopher Berry, *The Idea of Luxury: A Conceptual and Historical Investigation* (Cambridge: Cambridge University Press, 1994).

22. David Porter, *The Chinese Taste in Eighteenth-Century England* (Cambridge: Cambridge University Press, 2010). On the production and marketing of South and East Asian goods

to appeal to British consumers, and the creation of British imitations of these goods, see Berg, *Luxury and Pleasure*, chap. 2.

23. Berg, *Luxury and Pleasure*, chap. 8.

24. Thomas, *Man and the Natural World*, 95, 112.

25. Hester Thrale Piozzi to Penelope Sophia Weston, 11 February 1791, in *The Piozzi Letters: Correspondence of Hester Lynch Piozzi, 1784–1821 (Formerly Mrs. Thrale)*, ed. Edward A. Bloom and Lillian D. Bloom, 6 vols. (Newark: University of Delaware Press, 1989–2002), 1:346.

26. Arnaud Berquin, *The Children's Friend*, new corrected ed., 4 vols. (London: J. Stockdale, 1788), 2:141.

27. For works that situate Enlightenment concepts in the realm of material culture and consumer goods, see John Brewer, *The Pleasures of the Imagination: English Culture in the Eighteenth Century* (New York: Farrar, Straus and Giroux, 1997); Dorinda Outram, *Panorama of the Enlightenment* (Los Angeles: J. Paul Getty Museum, 2006).

28. George Edwards, *Gleanings of Natural History, Exhibiting the Figures of Quadrupeds, Birds, Insects, Plants, &c. Most of Which Have Not, Till Now, Been Either Figured or Described*, 3 vols. (London: Printed for the Author, 1758–64), 2:xxx–xxxi.

29. See Vickery, *Behind Closed Doors*, 241–43; Mark Laird and Alicia Weisberg-Roberts, eds., *Mrs. Delany and Her Circle*, exh. cat. (New Haven: Yale Center for British Art; London: Sir John Soane's Museum, in association with Yale University, 2010); David Elliston Allen, "Tastes and Crazes," in N. Jardine, J. A. Secord, and E. C. Spary, eds., *Cultures of Natural History* (Cambridge: Cambridge University Press, 1996), 394–407, reprinted in David Elliston Allen, *Naturalists and Society: The Culture of Natural History in Britain, 1700–1900* (Aldershot: Ashgate, 2001).

30. Horace Walpole to Sir Horace Mann, 6 May 1770, in Walpole, *The Yale Edition of Horace Walpole's Correspondence*, ed. W. S. Lewis, 48 vols. (New Haven: Yale University Press, 1937–83), 23:210.

31. Plumb, "Exotic Animals," 54.

32. This statement is based on my examination of newspaper advertisements from the period.

33. Edwards, *Gleanings of Natural History*, 2:132–33.

34. Ibid., 1:10–11.

35. Ibid., 3:223.

36. Hilda Kean, *Animal Rights: Political and Social Change in Britain Since 1800* (London: Reaktion Books, 1998), 28–31. Kean is particularly concerned to counter Keith Thomas's assertion that the rise of the animal rights movement was linked to the disappearance of animals from everyday life in urban areas.

37. There are no reliable statistics on pet ownership. The only contemporary attempts to quantify pet ownership that I have been able to locate are the statements by advocates of a tax on dogs regarding the number of dogs in England. George Clark estimated in 1791 that there were a million families in England, half of them owning a dog. See Clark, *An Address to Both Houses of Parliament: Containing Reasons for a Tax upon Dogs, and the Outlines of a Plan for That Purpose; and for Effectually Suppressing the Oppressive Practice of Impressing Seamen, and More Expeditiously Manning the Royal Navy* (London: Johnson, 1791), 6. Edward Barry estimated in 1796 that there were 1.6 million houses, with an average of one dog per house. Barry, *On the Necessity of Adopting Some Measures to Reduce the Present Number of Dogs; with a Short Account of Hydrophobia, and the Most Approved Remedies Against It, a Letter, to Francis Annesley, Esq; M. P. for the Borough of Reading, and One of the Trustees of the British Museum, &c. &c.* (Reading: Smart and Cowslade, 1796), 9–10. Charles Varlo estimated the dog population at two million in 1775,

though he was optimistic that half that population would be destroyed in the event of a tax. Varlo, *Schemes Offered for the Perusal and Consideration of the Legislature, Freeholders, and Public in General: Shewing the Many Evils That Might Be Prevented, and the Good That Would Accrue to the Public, Were They Improved, and Enacted into Laws* (London: J. Chapman, 1775), 137. Estimates thus varied enormously, and all three writers admitted that they were only guessing at the numbers. None of them, moreover, distinguished between household pets and hunting or other working dogs.

38. Even among those for sale, it is difficult to ascertain when deliberate breeding took place. Were the "very curious small light cream coloured Barcelona Dogs, and two or three black and white ones" offered at a Soho hairdresser's in 1770 being disposed of from an unwanted litter or intentionally bred for sale? *Public Advertiser* 11058 (12 May 1770).

39. Horace Walpole to Horace Mann, 30 June 1767, *Horace Walpole's Correspondence*, 22:534; Walpole to Mann, 21 January 1767, 22:479; Walpole to Mann, 4 August 1768, 23:40.

40. *Public Advertiser* 6899 (17 November 1756).

41. *Daily Advertiser* 4165 (23 May 1744).

42. Thomas Pennant, *British Zoology*, 4 vols. (London: Benjamin White, 1768), 2:329.

43. Ibid., 2:329–34. Oliver Goldsmith, who repeated Pennant's description of trapping almost verbatim, remarked that he was unsure why the (male) birdsong was so inviting to male wild birds. He speculated that wild females were the first to investigate, followed by their mates "to bear them company." But, he reflected, if this was the case, the females received their due punishment, for all females caught by bird catchers were "indiscriminately killed, and sold to be served up to the tables of the delicate." Goldsmith, *History of the Earth*, 5:304–6.

44. Pennant, *British Zoology*, 2:336, 337.

45. Goldsmith, *History of the Earth*, 5:338.

46. Ibid., 5:341–44.

47. Eleazar Albin, *A Natural History of Birds. Illustrated with a Hundred and One Copper Plates, Curiously Engraven from the Life*, 3 vols. (London: Printed for the Author, 1731), 1:62.

48. Georges-Louis Leclerc, Comte de Buffon, *The Natural History of Birds*, 9 vols. (London: A. Strahan, T. Cadell, J. Murray, 1793), 4:41–42n, citing *Philosophical Transactions* 63, part 2 (10 January 1773).

49. See Plumb, "Exotic Animals," 49–50. For a fictional example of a street vendor selling canaries, see Thomas Holland and John Holland, *Exercises for the Memory and Understanding: Consisting of Select Pieces in Prose & Verse; Together with a Series of Examinations Relative to Arts, Science, and History* (Manchester: George Nicholson, 1798), 18. The story is a translation of one by Arnaud Berquin. See also Lewis Walpole Library, Yale University (hereafter LWL) 812.00.00.59+; F. G. Stephens and M. D. George, *Catalogue of Political and Personal Satires Preserved in the Department of Prints and Drawings in the British Museum*, 11 vols. (London: By order of the Trustees, 1870–1954), catalogue no. 4721 (hereafter cited as British Museum Satires, followed by the catalogue number).

50. *Public Advertiser* 6974 (3 March 1757).

51. See, e.g., *Public Advertiser* 7438 (7 September 1758).

52. *Daily Advertiser* 13740 (3 January 1775).

53. Lady Mary Coke to Lady Anne Strafford, 11 August 1769, in *The Letters and Journals of Lady Mary Coke*, ed. James Archibald Home, 4 vols. (Bath: Kingsmead Reprints, 1970), 3:130–31.

54. Berg, *Luxury and Pleasure*, 260.

55. Helen Berry, "Polite Consumption: Shopping in Eighteenth-Century England," *Transactions of the Royal Historical Society* 12 (2002): 382–88; Berg, *Luxury and Pleasure*, 260–64.

56. Plumb, "Exotic Animals," 50–51. On the Covent Garden market, see Plumb, *Commercialisation of Leisure*, 11n29.

57. Benjamin Martin, *The Young Gentleman and Lady's Philosophy, in a Continued Survey of the Works of Nature and Art; By Way of Dialogue*, 3rd ed., 3 vols. (London: W. Owen, 1781–82), 3:115.

58. *Public Advertiser* 6917 (8 December 1756).

59. *Public Advertiser* 14225 (5 May 1775).

60. *Gazetteer and New Daily Advertiser* 14310 (5 January 1775). A second ad a month later specified that his work applied to "aviaris" as well as libraries, safes, and windows. See no. 14335 (3 February 1775).

61. *Gazetteer and New Daily Advertiser* 14351 (22 February 1775).

62. Plumb, "Exotic Animals," 50–51.

63. *Daily Advertiser* 13761 (27 January 1775).

64. *Public Advertiser* 9789 (3 April 1758).

65. *Public Advertiser* 5856 (4 August 1753).

66. *Public Advertiser* 5884 (6 September 1753).

67. *Public Advertiser* 5921 (19 October 1753).

68. *Public Advertiser* 6013 (4 February 1754).

69. *Public Advertiser* 6133 (26 June 1754).

70. *Public Advertiser* 6492 (7 August 1755). For similar advertisements, see no. 6594 (28 August 1755) and no. 6605 (13 September 1755).

71. *Public Advertiser* 6542 (4 October 1755).

72. See, e.g., *Public Advertiser* 6564 (11 November 1755) and 6610 (3 January 1756).

73. *Public Advertiser* 6705 (23 April 1756).

74. *Public Advertiser* 6758 (26 June 1756) and 6760 (1 July 1756).

75. *Public Advertiser* 6768 (10 July 1756), 6772 (17 July 1756), and 6775 (2 August 1756). This miscellaneous approach continued into 1758, when he was offering exotic birds, a "Macock," and "One of the best English-made Guittars to be sold cheap." No. 7257 (3 February 1758).

76. *Gazetteer and New Daily Advertiser* 11786 (13 December 1766).

77. *Daily Advertiser* 13144 (6 February 1773).

78. See, e.g., *Public Advertiser* 6612 (6 January 1756) and 6775 (2 August 1756).

79. *Public Advertiser* 6870 (26 October 1756).

80. *Public Advertiser* 9792 (6 April 1758).

81. *Public Advertiser* 7214 (10 December 1757).

82. *Public Advertiser* 7257 (3 February 1758).

83. Thomas Pennant, for instance, claimed that bird shops frequently dyed the breasts of female redpolls in order to deceive buyers into thinking they were male. *British Zoology*, 2:313.

84. Plumb, "Exotic Animals," contains extensive information about the location and business practices of menageries, along with an exploration of how visitors would experience them.

85. The first advertisement I have located for "Brookes Manazera" appeared on 15 March 1757, *Public Advertiser* 6984. On Brookes, see Plumb, "Exotic Animals," 56–59.

86. *Public Advertiser* 9800 (15 April 1758).

87. Plumb, "Exotic Animals," 59.

88. On the convergence of science, entertainment, and consumerism, see Simon Schaffer, "The Consuming Flame: Electrical Showmen and Tory Mystics in the World of Goods," in Brewer and Porter, *Consumption and the World of Goods*, 489–526.

89. Lady Mary Coke, entry of 22 February 1767, *Letters and Journals*, 1:159. See also the entry of 27 February 1768, 2:201.

90. Edwards, *Gleanings of Natural History*, 3:222. Based on the address Edwards provides, the establishment was probably the Parrot, later known as Noah's Ark.

91. Thomas Pennant, *Synopsis of Quadrupeds* (Chester: J. Monk, 1771), 144n; for a more elaborate account, see the retitled 1793 edition, *History of Quadrupeds*, 2 vols. (London: B. and J. White, 1793), 1:238n.

92. *Public Advertiser* 6899 (17 November 1756).

93. *Public Advertiser* 7188 (8 November 1757). She remained on display for a long time; see no. 7294 of the same periodical (11 March 1758), no. 7651 (18 May 1759), and no. 7811 (misnumbered) (13 December 1759). The menagerie also offered for viewing "a large Sea-Monster, a Creature called an Half and Half bred from a Lioness and a Foreign wild Cat, being the only one of the same Kind ever seen in England." This establishment was calling itself Bennett's or Bennet's Warehouse by December 1759.

94. Styles, *Dress of the People*, 8.

95. *Public Advertiser* 6969 (25 February 1757) and 6981 (11 March 1757).

96. *Public Advertiser* 7335 (1 May 1758).

97. Plumb, "Exotic Animals," 55.

98. Ibid., 34, 59–60.

99. Samuel Jackson Pratt, *Gleanings in England; Descriptive of the Countenance, Mind and Character of the Country*, 3rd ed., 3 vols. (London: T. N. Longman and O. Rees, 1801–3), 3:446–47.

100. *Public Advertiser* 6970 (26 February 1757).

101. *Public Advertiser* 7246 (21 January 1758) and 7551 (5 March 1759).

102. *Public Advertiser* 11103 (20 July 1770). On the fashion for eating turtles in the later eighteenth century, see Plumb, "Exotic Animals," 76–79.

103. *Public Advertiser* 14274 (30 June 1775). In 1781, Horace Walpole spent £31 19s. 7d. to build a goldfish pond with a pump at Strawberry Hill; see *Horace Walpole's Correspondence*, 33:292n.

104. Albin, *Natural History of Birds*, 2:16, 3:10, 3:7 (misnumbered).

105. *Public Advertiser* 6027 (20 February 1754).

106. *Public Advertiser* 9451 (15 February 1765).

107. *Public Advertiser* 9620 (1 July 1765). Eighteenth-century writers often used a lowercase "l" followed by a period to represent the English pound sterling; thus the grey parrots on offer here are for sale at "1l." (i.e., one pound), eleven shillings, sixpence. I have taken the liberty of changing the l. to the pound symbol (£) to prevent confusion.

108. *Public Advertiser* 7354 (24 May 1758).

109. *Public Advertiser* 6564 (11 November 1755).

110. *Public Advertiser* 7029 (6 May 1757). Others may have disagreed about its value, since it was apparently still on sale several weeks later; see nos. 7056 (6 June 1757), 7067 (20 June 1757), and 7092 (19 July 1757).

111. Albin, *Natural History of Birds*, 1:13.

112. Styles, "Lodging at the Old Bailey," 69; Craig Muldrew and Stephen King, "Cash, Wages, and the Economy of Makeshifts in England, 1650–1800," in *Experiencing Wages:*

Social and Cultural Aspects of Wage Forms in Europe Since 1500, ed. Peter Scholliers and Leonard Schwarz (Oxford: Berghahn Books, 2003), 172–73.

113. Plumb, "Exotic Animals," 61.

114. *Public Advertiser* 6679 (20 March 1756).

115. *Public Advertiser* 6804 (4 September 1756). See also no. 6874 (30 October 1756), offering "two Pair of Carolina Cross Beak Birds . . . at only Half a Guinea a Pair."

116. *Public Advertiser* 9778 (21 March 1758). Thomas Pennant claimed that bullfinches were trained to speak in Frankfurt and then imported to England, which would have been a sensible move only if they could be sold at a relatively high price. Pennant, *British Zoology*, 2:299.

117. Pennant, *British Zoology*, 2:304.

118. Ibid., 2:336.

119. *Public Advertiser* 6594 (28 August 1755).

120. *Public Advertiser* 6599 (5 September 1755), 6600 (6 September 1755), and 6605 (13 September 1755).

121. *Public Advertiser* 6856 (9 October 1756).

122. *Public Advertiser* 6587 (8 December 1755) and 6592 (12 December 1755).

123. *Public Advertiser* 6634 (31 January 1756). By 10 February, the seller was attempting to increase the pressure on potential buyers by announcing that if the parrot did not sell that week, it would be given away. His desperation, however, may be visible in the postscript adding that "The Man who said he was a Dealer, may have it at the Two Guineas and a Half which he bid." No. 6642 (10 February 1756).

124. *Public Advertiser* 7612 (31 March 1759).

125. *Public Advertiser* 6896 (13 November 1756).

126. *Public Advertiser* 7096 (23 July 1757), 7203 (26 November 1757), 7325 (19 April 1758), and 7376 (17 June 1758).

127. *Public Advertiser* 7394 (18 July 1758). The "Parroquet" was discounted to five guineas shortly thereafter; see no. 7412 (8 August 1758).

128. *Public Advertiser* 6610 (3 January 1756). The ad worked; the issue of 6 January (6612) repeated the offer of starlings but noted that the bullfinch had been sold.

129. *Public Advertiser* 7024 (30 April 1757).

130. *Public Advertiser* 7014 (19 April 1757).

131. *Public Advertiser* 6226 (12 October 1754).

132. Berquin, *Children's Friend*, 2:83.

133. I have not found advertisements for any other kind of lost pet; dogs were a special case.

134. *St. James's Chronicle, or British Evening-Post* 5351 (3–5 May 1744).

135. *Daily Advertiser* 50 (1 April 1731).

136. See, e.g., the advertisement for the duke of Richmond's lost dog in the *Daily Advertiser* 43 (24 March 1730 [1731]). Until 1752, Britain remained on the older, Julian calendar, long after continental Europe had moved to the Gregorian calendar still in use today. The Julian, or "Old Style," calendar was twelve days behind the Gregorian (or "New Style") calendar, and its new year began on 25 March. Thus, although the official date of this issue is 1730, it was actually published in 1731. For dates given in the Old Style, I have added the New Style year in brackets.

137. See, e.g., *Daily Advertiser* 132 (6 July 1731).

138. *Public Advertiser* 7966 (21 June 1759), 7968 (misnumbered) (14 July 1759), and 7972 (27 July 1759).

139. Varlo, *Schemes Offered for the Perusal*, 134–35.

140. See Grier, *Pets in America*, 83, on the practice of feeding pets on scraps into the middle of the nineteenth century.

141. Lady Isabella Wentworth to Thomas, Earl of Strafford, 11 April [1712], British Library Additional MS 22225, fol. 126r.

142. See also LWL 804.04.25.02.

143. Estabrook, *Urbane and Rustic England*, 132–33.

144. Bernard L. Herman, "Tabletop Conversations: Material Culture and Everyday Life in the Eighteenth-Century Atlantic World," in Styles and Vickery, *Gender, Taste, and Material Culture*, 56. Herman does not date the specific inventory, but it comes from a group taken between 1725 and 1735 (50).

145. Tobias Smollett, *The Adventures of Sir Launcelot Greaves*, 2 vols. (London: J. Coote, 1762), 1:25; Tobias Smollett, *Humphry Clinker*, ed. Shaun Regan (New York: Penguin, 2008), 68; Frances Burney, *Cecilia, or Memoirs of an Heiress*, ed. Peter Sabor and Margaret Anne Doody (Oxford: Oxford University Press, 2009), 616.

146. Lady Mary Coke to Lady Anne Strafford, 9 September 1766, *Letters and Journals*, 1:47, and the journal entry of 4 July 1771, 3:417. See also the entry of 13 December 1774, 4:444, in which she discusses her plans to have the dog doctor conduct an autopsy on another pet.

147. There has been little scholarship on the history of veterinary care before the modern period, and what exists focuses on livestock. For an overview, see Louise Hill Curth, *The Care of Brute Beasts: A Social and Cultural Study of Veterinary Medicine in Early Modern England* (Boston: Brill, 2010).

148. Sarah Trimmer, *Fabulous Histories. Designed for the Instruction of Children, Respecting Their Treatment of Animals* (London: T. Longman, G. G. J. and J. Robinson, J. Johnson, 1786), 108.

149. See *Gentleman's Magazine* 30 (August 1760), 392.

150. *Public Advertiser* 6386 (10 April 1755).

151. These were probably quite cheap. According to Geoffrey Wills, ". . . Whose Dog Are You?," *Country Life*, 4 April 1974, 804, simple brass collars in the mid-nineteenth century ranged in price from 6d. to 3s.

152. *Daily Advertiser* 173 (23 August 1731).

153. Katharine MacDonogh, *Reigning Cats and Dogs* (New York: St. Martin's Press, 1999), 132.

154. Francis Coventry, *The History of Pompey the Little, or The Life and Adventures of a Lap-Dog*, 1st ed. (London: M. Cooper, 1751), 15.

155. For an example of a monkey chained outdoors, see Coke, Worksop, 19 August 1766, *Letters and Journals*, 1:21.

156. See, e.g., *Tatler* 266 (21 December 1710), in Donald F. Bond, ed., *The Tatler*, 3 vols. (Oxford: Clarendon Press, 1987), 3:343–46; Trimmer, *Fabulous Histories*, 105.

157. See LWL 777.11.10.07+. The most famous such image is probably John Singleton Copley's 1765 portrait of his younger brother with a flying squirrel held by a delicate gold chain. The portrait is in the collection of the Museum of Fine Arts, Boston.

158. *Public Advertiser* 6981 (11 March 1757). On dressing monkeys in human clothing, see Brown, *Homeless Dogs and Melancholy Apes*, 104–5.

159. Trimmer, *Fabulous Histories*, 101. Nancy Carlisle suggests that designing cages like houses might have been a "way of lessening the otherwise cruel act of caging an animal by placing it in a 'home.'" Nancy C. Carlisle, "The Chewed Chair Leg and the Empty Collar: Mementos of Pet Ownership in New England," in *New England's Creatures: 1400–1900, Dublin*

Seminar for New England Folklife; Annual Proceedings, ed. Peter Benes (Boston: Boston University Press, 1993), 139.

160. Lady Mary Coke to Lady Anne Strafford, 12 September 1766, *Letters and Journals*, 1:49.

161. This print was originally produced in the 1770s, probably 1778. This copy is a much later reissue, published no earlier than 1793, when the partnership of Bowles & Carver was first formed.

162. On the classification of birdcage makers, see R. Campbell, *The London Tradesman* (London: T. Gardner, 1747), 245. Illustrations of most birdcages throughout the eighteenth century follow the same basic model. See Carlisle, "Chewed Chair Leg," 130–36. On more elaborate and expensive cages, see Neil Dana Glukin, "Pet Birds and Cages of the Eighteenth Century," *Early American Life* 8 (1977): 38–40.

163. Carlisle, "Chewed Chair Leg," 133.

164. *Exact and Sure Directions How to Dress and Keep Canary-Birds, and to Preserve Them in Health. And Also, How to Use and Keep the New Fashion Bird-Cages* (London: Printed for the Author, n.d. [ca. 1710?]), 15–16. The author was anonymous, but he was located "At the Sign of the *Bird-Cage* in *Long-Acre*, over against the *Black Boy* Ale-House near *Phœnix-Ally*." For another such pamphlet produced by a bird seller, see Plumb, "Exotic Animals," 51.

165. Campbell, *London Tradesman*, 245, partially quoted in Marcellus Laroon, *The Criers and Hawkers of London: Engravings and Drawings by Marcellus Laroon*, ed. Sean Shesgreen (Stanford: Stanford University Press, 1990), 10.

166. Arthur W. J. G. Ord-Hume, "Bird Instruments," in *Grove Music Online,* http://www.oxfordmusiconline.com; Glukin, "Pet Birds and Cages," 41.

167. See also, e.g., LWL 764.00.00.11+.

168. *Public Advertiser* 7462 (27 September 1758). For ordinary bird organs, see, e.g., nos. 7246 (21 January 1758) and 7814 (22 November 1759).

169. Glukin, "Pet Birds and Cages," 41, 40.

170. Buffon, *Natural History of Birds*, 4:167–68.

CHAPTER 2

1. *Gentleman's Magazine* 8 (September 1738), 492.

2. See Londa Schiebinger, *Nature's Body: Gender in the Making of Modern Science* (Boston: Beacon Press, 1993), 99–106; Brown, *Homeless Dogs and Melancholy Apes*, 53–55; Dror Wahrman, *The Making of the Modern Self: Identity and Culture in Eighteenth-Century England* (New Haven: Yale University Press, 2004), 134–35.

3. Samuel Pepys, entry of 25 January 1661, *The Diary of Samuel Pepys*, ed. Robert Latham and William Matthews, 11 vols. (Berkeley: University of California Press, 1970–83), 2:23.

4. Ibid., entry of 25 April 1664, 5:131–32.

5. Ebenezer Sibly, *Magazine of Natural History. Comprehending the Whole Science of Animals, Plants, and Minerals; Divided into Distinct Parts, the Characters Separately Described, and Systematically Arranged*, 14 vols. (London: Printed for the Proprietor, 1794–1807), 4:199–200.

6. Edwards, *Gleanings of Natural History*, 1:55–56.

7. Tuan, *Dominance and Affection*, 142, citing F. O. Shyllon, *Black Slaves in Britain* (London: Oxford University Press for the Institute of Race Relations, 1974), 9. I have been unable to locate the advertisement that Shyllon quotes as evidence of a goldsmith selling collars for both dogs and slaves.

8. Naturalists did not clearly distinguish between the two species until the nineteenth century, generally referring to both in this period as the "ourang-outang."

9. H. W. Janson, *Apes and Ape Lore in the Middle Ages and the Renaissance* (London: Warburg Institute, 1952). Throughout this book I follow the eighteenth-century practice of using "ape" and "monkey" interchangeably. There was general agreement among naturalists that monkeys had tails while apes did not, but this consensus was not universal, and the terms were rarely used with precision.

10. Diana Donald, *Picturing Animals in Britain, 1750–1850* (New Haven: Yale University Press for the Paul Mellon Centre for Studies in British Art, 2007), 29–39.

11. Schiebinger, *Nature's Body*, 78–88; Thomas, *Man and the Natural World*, 129–36.

12. Goldsmith, *History of the Earth*, 4:195–98.

13. James Burnett, Lord Monboddo, *Of the Origin and Progress of Language*, 6 vols. (London: T. Cadell, 1773–92), 1:271–74; see also 1:289; and see Monboddo's *Antient Metaphysics, or The Science of Universals*, 6 vols. (London: T. Cadell, 1779–99), 3:41–42.

14. Wahrman, *Making of the Modern Self*, 136–38.

15. Donald, *Picturing Animals in Britain*, 104–9. For a discussion of the tradition emphasizing human uniqueness before the eighteenth century, see Thomas, *Man and the Natural World*, 30–41.

16. Pennant, *Synopsis of Quadrupeds*, v.

17. Ibid., 94n.

18. Georges-Louis Leclerc, Comte de Buffon, *Natural History, General and Particular, by the Count De Buffon, Translated into English*, trans. William Smellie, 2nd ed., 9 vols. (London: W. Strahan and T. Cadell, 1785), 8:40–41.

19. Ibid., 8:66; see also 8:96.

20. Buffon, *Natural History of Birds*, 6:64–65. Buffon, like most other naturalists, believed that orangutans had the same organs of speech as humans. The ape's inability to talk was thus not the result of simple anatomical differences. See Robert Wokler, "Tyson and Buffon on the Orang-utan," *Studies on Voltaire and the Eighteenth Century* 155 (1976): 2301–19.

21. Goldsmith, *History of the Earth*, 4:187, 192–93, 249–51.

22. Ibid., 4:203–4.

23. R[ichard] Brookes, *A New and Accurate System of Natural History*, 2nd ed., 6 vols. (London: T. Carnan and F. Newbery, 1772), 1:111–12.

24. [Charles Taylor], *Surveys of Nature, Historical, Moral, and Entertaining, Exhibiting the Principles of Natural Science in Various Branches*, 2 vols. (London: C. Taylor, 1787), vol. 2, part 3, 112 (pagination starts over in each part of the volume).

25. [Edward Augustus Kendall], *Keeper's Travels in Search of His Master* (London: E. Newbery, 1798), 65–67.

26. Sibly, *Magazine of Natural History*, 2:4–5.

27. Johann Caspar Lavater, *Essays on Physiognomy; For the Promotion of the Knowledge and the Love of Mankind*, trans. Thomas Holcroft, 3 vols. (London: G. G. J. and J. Robinson, 1789), 2:195–202 (quotations on 196, 197).

28. [Aikin and Barbauld], *Evenings at Home*, 3:2–12 (quotations on 2, 4, 7–8, 9, 12).

29. For a concise summary of this view, see Thomas, *Man and the Natural World*, 17–25.

30. For the French debates on these issues, see Robbins, *Elephant Slaves and Pampered Parrots*, 186–205.

31. See Oliver Goldsmith's introduction to Brookes, *New and Accurate System of Natural History*, 1:xviii.

32. Ibid.

33. Goldsmith, *History of the Earth*, 2:326–27.

34. Buffon, *Natural History*, 4:61.

35. Ibid., 7:398.

36. Ibid., 7:435.

37. *Beauties of Natural History, or Elements of Zoography* (London: Richardson and Urquhart, 1777), 32–33.

38. [Henry Baker], *The Universal Spectator*, 3rd ed., 4 vols. (London: Dr. Browne, R. Nutt, T. Astley, A. Millar, and J. Ward, 1756), 2:184–87 (quotation on 186).

39. Foucher d'Obsonville, *Philosophic Essays on the Manners of Various Animals; with Observations on the Laws and Customs of Several Eastern Nations*, trans. Thomas Holcroft (London: John Johnson, 1784), 91.

40. François Le Vaillant, *New Travels into the Interior Parts of Africa, by the Way of the Cape of Good Hope, in the Years 1783, 84, and 85*, 3 vols. (London: G. G. J. and J. Robinson, 1796), 3:35–37.

41. [John Gregory], *A Comparative View of the State and Faculties of Man, with Those of the Animal World* (London: J. Dodsley, 1765), 11–12.

42. Ibid., 14–15. As examples of civilized people's tendency to deform their bodies, he offered both Chinese foot binding and European women's tightly laced stays (30–32).

43. William Smellie, *The Philosophy of Natural History*, 2 vols. (Dublin: William Porter, 1790), 1:310. For Smellie's contact with Gregory, see *Oxford Dictionary of National Biography*, s.v. "Smellie, William."

44. Georg Christian Raff, *A System of Natural History, Adapted for the Instruction of Youth, in the Form of a Dialogue*, 2 vols. (London: J. Johnson, G. G. and J. Robinson, 1796), 1:84–85.

45. William Fordyce Mavor, *Natural History, for the Use of Schools; Founded on the Linnæan Arrangement of Animals; with Popular Descriptions in the Manner of Goldsmith and Buffon* (London: R. Phillips, 1800), 26–27.

46. See Harriet Ritvo, "Learning from Animals: Natural History for Children in the Eighteenth and Nineteenth Centuries," *Children's Literature* 13, no. 1 (1985): 72–93.

47. Trimmer, *Fabulous Histories*, 68–69.

48. [Aikin and Barbauld], *Evenings at Home*, 4:149–51.

49. See Aaron Garrett, "Francis Hutcheson and the Origin of Animal Rights," *Journal of the History of Philosophy* 45, no. 2 (2007): 243–65.

50. For a discussion of the relationship between sensibility and the spread of pet keeping, see chapter 5.

51. For a subtle reading of the complexities of humanitarianism, see Karen Halttunen, "Humanitarianism and the Pornography of Pain in Anglo-American Culture," *American Historical Review* 100, no. 2 (1995): 303–34.

52. Jeremy Bentham, *An Introduction to the Principles of Morals and Legislation* (Oxford: Clarendon Press, 1907), 311n.

53. On the rise of the movement against animal cruelty, see David Perkins, *Romanticism and Animal Rights* (Cambridge: Cambridge University Press, 2003); Aaron Garrett, ed., *Animal Rights and Souls in the Eighteenth Century*, 6 vols. (Bristol: Thoemmes Press, 2000); Keith Tester, *Animals and Society: The Humanity of Animal Rights* (London: Routledge, 1991); Robert W. Malcolmson, *Popular Recreations in English Society, 1700–1850* (Cambridge: Cambridge University Press, 1973), 118–57; Thomas, *Man and the Natural World*, 143–91. For a critique of claims as to the significance of this movement, see Emma Griffin, *England's Revelry: A History of Popular Sports and Pastimes, 1660–1830* (Oxford: Oxford University Press for the British Academy, 2005), 115–22.

54. Thomas Young, *An Essay on Humanity to Animals* (London: T. Cadell, Jun. and W. Davies, 1798), 2.

55. See, for example, James Walvin, *England, Slaves, and Freedom, 1776–1838* (Jackson: University Press of Mississippi, 1986). The historiography of the antislavery movement is vast. For a useful overview, see Christopher Leslie Brown, *Moral Capital: Foundations of British Abolitionism* (Chapel Hill: University of North Carolina Press for the Omohundro Institute of Early American History and Culture, 2006), 1–30. Many scholars have noted the connections between the movement against cruelty to animals and the antislavery movement. A recent example is Markman Ellis, "Suffering Things: Lapdogs, Slaves, and Counter-Sensibility," in *The Secret Life of Things: Animals, Objects, and It-Narratives in Eighteenth-Century England*, ed. Mark Blackwell (Lewisburg: Bucknell University Press, 2007), 92–113. On antislavery images that compared slaves to suffering animals, see Marcus Wood, *Blind Memory: Visual Representations of Slavery in England and America, 1780–1865* (New York: Routledge, 2000), 114–16, 271–76.

56. Wahrman, *Making of the Modern Self*, 185–89; Markman Ellis, *The Politics of Sensibility: Race, Gender, and Commerce in the Sentimental Novel* (Cambridge: Cambridge University Press, 1996), 13–14; John Mullan, *Sentiment and Sociability: The Language of Feeling in the Eighteenth Century* (Oxford: Clarendon Press, 1988), 18–56.

57. Pratt, *Gleanings in England*, 2:342.

58. John Oswald, *The Cry of Nature, or An Appeal to Mercy and Justice, on Behalf of the Persecuted Animals* (London: J. Johnson, 1791), 3–5.

59. Humphry Primatt, *A Dissertation on the Duty of Mercy and Sin of Cruelty to Brute Animals* (London: R. Hett, 1776), 137–38.

60. Ibid., 11–12.

61. Perkins points out that it was thus possible to support the humane treatment of animals without accepting any form of social radicalism, and that in fact "the analogy of animals to subordinate social groups suggested that inequality was natural." *Romanticism and Animal Rights*, 108.

62. John Lawrence, *A Philosophical and Practical Treatise on Horses, and on the Moral Duties of Man towards the Brute Creation*, 2 vols. (London: T. N. Longman, 1796–98), 1:83–84.

63. Pratt, *Gleanings in England*, 3:240–43.

64. Brown, *Moral Capital*, 33–101; Walvin, *England, Slaves, and Freedom*, 107–8; Ellis, *Politics of Sensibility*, 49–86.

65. For a reading of pet keeping in colonial America that sees pets as providing "unconscious validation of [the] right to have slaves," see Sarah Hand Meacham, "Pets, Status, and Slavery in the Late-Eighteenth-Century Chesapeake," *Journal of Southern History* 77, no. 3 (2011): 521–54.

66. See Christine Kenyon-Jones, *Kindred Brutes: Animals in Romantic-Period Writing* (Burlington, Vt.: Ashgate, 2001), 79–94; Perkins, *Romanticism and Animal Rights*, 16–19, 89–103; Malcolmson, *Popular Recreations*, 119–57; Griffin, *England's Revelry*, 114–40, 223–49.

67. Young, *Essay on Humanity to Animals*, 178–80.

68. On the long tradition of comparing animals and slaves, see Catherine Osborne, *Dumb Beasts and Dead Philosophers: Humanity and the Humane in Ancient Philosophy and Literature* (Oxford: Clarendon Press, 2007), esp. 128–32; Aaron Garrett, "Francis Hutcheson and the Origin of Animal Rights"; Perkins, *Romanticism and Animal Rights*, 25, 104–8; Kenyon-Jones, *Kindred Brutes*, 39–43; Thomas, *Man and the Natural World*, 44–45. For a modern animal rights argument about the parallels between animals and slaves, see Marjorie

Spiegel, *The Dreaded Comparison: Human and Animal Slavery*, rev. and exp. ed. (New York: Mirror Books, 1996).

69. Richard Steele, *Tatler* 245 (November 2, 1710), 3:256.

70. Thomas Brown, "To Madam *de V*—Upon Sending her a Black, and a Monkey," and "To the Same. Upon the Death of her Monkey," in *The Works of Mr. Thomas Brown, Serious and Comical, in Prose and Verse*, 5th ed., 4 vols. (London: Sam Briscoe, 1720), 1:329, 331.

71. Le Vaillant refers to Kees only as "a monkey, of that kind commonly known at the Cape under the name of *Bawians* [i.e., baboon]." François Le Vaillant, *Travels from the Cape of Good-Hope, into the Interior Parts of Africa, Including Many Interesting Anecdotes*, trans. Elizabeth Helme, 2 vols. (London: William Lane, 1790), 1:140, hereafter cited parenthetically in the text. For species identification, see Jurgens Meester, "Le Vaillant's Mammal Paintings," in J. C. Quinton and A. M. Lewin Robinson, eds., *François Le Vaillant, Traveller in South Africa, and His Collection of 165 Water-Colour Paintings, 1781–1784*, 2 vols. (Cape Town: Library of Parliament, 1973), 2:2–3. A watercolor illustration of Kees is reproduced at 2:78. There are several variants of Le Vaillant's name: he was born simply "Vaillant"; today he is best known as a pioneer of ornithology, in which field he is usually referred to as "Levaillant." I follow his own and his contemporaries' practice in using "Le Vaillant."

72. Matthys Bokhorst, "François Le Vaillant: His Life and Work," in Quinton and Lewin Robinson, *François Le Vaillant*, 1:12.

73. See, e.g., Sibly, *Magazine of Natural History*, 2:74–85. The original French editions came out in 1789 and 1794.

74. For the influence of Rousseau on Le Vaillant's thinking, see Bokhorst, "François Le Vaillant," 1:11, 22; Meester, "Le Vaillant's Mammal Paintings," 2:22–23.

75. For other examples of Le Vaillant's use of Kees as a taster, see *Travels from the Cape of Good-Hope*, 2:278–79; 2:433, and *New Travels into the Interior Parts of Africa*, 2:148–49.

76. See also Le Vaillant, *New Travels into the Interior Parts of Africa*, 1:19, hereafter cited parenthetically in the text.

77. On these encounters, and Le Vaillant's identification of the various tribes he met, see Margaret Shaw, "Hottentots, Bushmen, and Bantu," in Quinton and Lewin Robinson, *François Le Vaillant*, 1:127–51. Today, the term "Hottentot" is widely considered offensive—"Khoikhoi" is the more accurate and preferred name—but in this text I employ the terminology used by Le Vaillant.

78. Ian Glenn, "Primate Time: Rousseau, Levaillant, Marais," *Current Writing: Text and Reception in Southern Africa* 18, no. 1 (2006): 65; Ian Glenn, "Introduction," in François Le Vaillant, *Travels into the Interior of Africa via the Cape of Good Hope*, trans. and ed. Ian Glenn, with Catherine Lauga Du Plessis and Ian Farlam (Cape Town: Van Riebeeck Society for the Publication of South African Historical Documents, 2007), i–lviii.

79. See Shaw, "Hottentots, Bushmen, and Bantu," 128.

80. See, for example, *Travels from the Cape of Good-Hope*, 1:160–61, on the misrepresentations of Hottentots by other writers: "Worthy injured people! whom so many have taken pleasure to represent as unnatural monsters, devouring each other, an infant might lead ye! Peaceful Hottentots! behold with disdain those harsh invaders who first reduced to slavery, then basely traduced and placed ye on a level with the brutes."

81. This implication is especially powerful given that Le Vaillant's criticisms of the baboon's faults echo those often attributed to "Hottentots" and other native Africans, and would have brought to the minds of eighteenth-century readers other stories about travelers who considered apes more effective servants than native Africans. See, e.g., Goldsmith, *History of the Earth*, 4:230–31.

82. See Quinton and Lewin Robinson, *François Le Vaillant*; Glenn, "Introduction," xi–xxxiv.

83. Goldsmith, *History of the Earth*, 5:23. See also, for example, Buffon, *Natural History of Birds*, 1:29; Pennant, *British Zoology*, 2:335; *A New Moral System of Natural History, or the Beauties of Nature Displayed; In the Most Singular, Curious, and Beautiful, Quadrupeds, and Birds*, vol. 6 of *The Historical Pocket Library; or, Biographical Vade-Mecum*, 6 vols. (Bath: S. Hazard for G. Riley, 1789), 113.

84. Goldsmith, *History of the Earth*, 5:23.

85. Ibid., 5:333.

86. Mavor, *Natural History*, 253–54. See 257 for similar comments about the bullfinch.

87. Buffon, *Natural History of Birds*, 4:51–52.

88. Raff, *System of Natural History*, 2:112.

89. For a detailed description of the practice, see Pennant, *British Zoology*, 2:332–33.

90. See *Gentleman's Magazine* 22 (November 1752), 523.

91. Albin, *Natural History of Birds*, 1:61.

92. Raff, *System of Natural History*, 2:106.

93. [Edward Augustus Kendall], *The Sparrow* (London: E. Newbery, 1798), 148.

94. Thomas Percival, *A Father's Instructions; Consisting of Moral Tales, Fables, and Reflections Designed to Promote the Love of Virtue, a Taste for Knowledge, and an Early Acquaintance with the Works of Nature*, new ed. (London: W. Osborne, T. Griffin, H. Mozley and Co., 1796), 3.

95. Harriet Ventum, *Surveys of Nature: A Sequel to Mrs. Trimmer's Introduction; Being Familiar Descriptions of Some Popular Subjects in Natural Philosophy, Adapted to the Capacities of Children* (London: John Radcock, 1802), 11–12.

96. See for example, Berquin, "The Linnets," in *Children's Friend*, 3:155; [Kendall], *Sparrow*, 37–38.

97. Berquin, *Children's Friend*, 3:153–54.

98. Anna Laetitia Barbauld, "Epitaph on a Green-Finch," in Holland and Holland, *Exercises for the Memory and Understanding*, 119–20.

99. Buffon, *Natural History of Birds*, 4:300.

100. Albin, *Natural History of Birds*, 1:61.

101. Samuel Ward, *A Modern System of Natural History*, 12 vols. (London: F. Newbery, 1775–76), 7:95.

102. Pennant, *British Zoology*, 2:313. For other eighteenth-century views that birds benefited from being caged, see Ingrid H. Tague, "Dead Pets: Satire and Sentiment in British Elegies and Epitaphs for Animals," *Eighteenth-Century Studies* 41, no. 3 (2008): 295–96.

103. On canary breeding and importation, see chapter 1.

104. [Edward Augustus Kendall], *The Canary Bird: A Moral Fiction. Interspersed with Poetry* (London: E. Newbery, 1799), 89–143.

105. Sarah Trimmer, *An Easy Introduction to the Knowledge of Nature, and Reading the Holy Scriptures. Adapted to the Capacities of Children* (London: Printed for the Author, 1780), 76.

106. Trimmer, *Fabulous Histories*, 31–32.

107. Percival, *Father's Instructions*, 177–78.

CHAPTER 3

1. Aileen Ribeiro, *Dress and Morality*, new ed. (Oxford: Berg, 2003), 113.

2. See, for example, David Kuchta, *The Three-Piece Suit and Modern Masculinity: England, 1550–1850* (Berkeley: University of California Press, 2002); G. J. Barker-Benfield, *The*

Culture of Sensibility: Sex and Society in Eighteenth-Century Britain (Chicago: University of Chicago Press, 1992); Berry, *Idea of Luxury*; Sekora, *Luxury*.

3. For classic statements regarding Christian views of humanity's relationship to the natural world, see Thomas, *Man and the Natural World*, 17–25; Lynn White Jr., "The Historical Roots of Our Ecologic Crisis," *Science* 155, no. 3767 (1967): 1203–7.

4. Trimmer, *Fabulous Histories*, 70.

5. Quoted in Edward Topsell, *The Historie of Foure-Footed Beastes* (London: William Iaggard [Jaggard], 1607), 164.

6. Ibid., 172.

7. Quoted in Goldsmith, *History of the Earth*, 3:272–74.

8. Ibid., 3:285.

9. Ibid., 3:290, 289.

10. Quoted in Ronald Paulson, *Popular and Polite Art in the Age of Hogarth and Fielding* (Notre Dame: University of Notre Dame Press, 1979), 50.

11. [Sir Richard Phillips], *The Rational Brutes, or Talking Animals* (London: Tegg and Dewick, for Vernor and Hood, 1799), 89–90.

12. Ibid., 91–92.

13. For a definition of the "fancy picture" and the popularity of children as subjects in the genre, see Martin Postle, *Angels and Urchins: The Fancy Picture in Eighteenth-Century British Art*, exh. cat. (Nottingham: Djanogly Art Gallery; Lund Humphries, 1998), introduction and chap. 2; for Postle's discussion of this painting, see 69 (cat. no. 27).

14. Julius Bryant notes that this is the most popular painting in the collection at Kenwood House, probably because most viewers read the painting this way. Julius Bryant, "The Dark Side of the Kitten: A Wright of Derby for Kenwood," *Apollo* 144, no. 418 (1996): 18–19.

15. See Judy Egerton, *Wright of Derby*, exh. cat. (New York: Metropolitan Museum of Art; London: Tate Gallery Publications, 1990), 54, 136 (cat. nos. 17 and 71); Susan L. Siegfried, "Engaging the Audience: Sexual Economies of Vision in Joseph Wright," *Representations* 68 (1999): 47.

16. For discussions of this painting that present readings similar to my own, see Siegfried, "Engaging the Audience," 47–49; Julius Bryant, *Kenwood: Paintings in the Iveagh Bequest* (New Haven: Yale University Press, 2003), 408–12 (no. 101); Leslie Reinhardt, "Serious Daughters: Dolls, Dress, and Female Virtue in the Eighteenth Century," *American Art* 20, no. 2 (2006): 48–49. On the eroticism of fancy pictures of girls with cats, see Postle, *Angels and Urchins*, 68–69 (cat. nos. 26–28).

17. Jodi L. Wyett, "The Lap of Luxury: Lapdogs, Literature, and Social Meaning in the 'Long' Eighteenth Century," *Literature, Interpretation, Theory* 10 (2000), 282. On fashionable ladies' love of lapdogs, see also Thomas, *Man and the Natural World*, 107–8; Theresa Braunschneider, "The Lady and the Lapdog: Mixed Ethnicity in Constantinople, Fashionable Pets in Britain," in *Humans and Other Animals in Eighteenth-Century British Culture: Representation, Hybridity, Ethics*, ed. Frank Palmeri (Aldershot: Ashgate, 2006), 31–48, esp. 39–44; Brown, *Homeless Dogs and Melancholy Apes*, chap. 3; Ellis, "Suffering Things," esp. 96–102.

18. See *The Dog Barber*, Lewis Walpole Library, Yale University (hereafter LWL), Bunbury Coll. 779.3.29.1.2.

19. Catherine Molineux, "Hogarth's Fashionable Slaves: Moral Corruption in Eighteenth-Century London," *English Literary History* 72 (2005): 495–520; Kuchta, *Three-Piece Suit*, chap. 5; Ingrid H. Tague, *Women of Quality: Accepting and Contesting Ideals of*

Femininity in England, 1690–1760 (Woodbridge: Boydell Press, 2002), chap. 2. On the dominance of French fashions, see Aileen Ribeiro, *Dress in Eighteenth-Century Europe, 1715–1789*, rev. ed. (New Haven: Yale University Press, 2002).

20. Many such caricatures and satires appeared in the 1770s and 1780s, a period when such fashions were especially widespread. See Paul Langford, *A Polite and Commercial People: England, 1727–1783* (Oxford: Clarendon Press, 1989), chap. 12; Ribeiro, *Dress and Morality*, 111–13.

21. For an early example that associates the towering headdress with an excess of pets, see *The French Lady in London* (1770), LWL 770.11.20.01+.

22. Ribeiro, *Dress and Morality*, 115.

23. LWL 777.00.00.10+.

24. See Molineux, "Hogarth's Fashionable Slaves," for a discussion of Hogarth's use of black slaves in his images to address "the harmful effects that he perceived in his fellow Londoners' desire for foreign goods" (495).

25. See Ribeiro, *Dress and Morality*, 114.

26. The joke was repeated in at least two more prints, in 1777 and 1786, LWL 777.01.01.02+ and LWL 786.05.16.02+.

27. Stephens and George, *Catalogue of Political and Personal Satires*, no. 5383 (hereafter cited as British Museum Satires, followed by catalogue number). This was a common theme in many verbal satires as well, along with some ostensibly serious newspaper reports.

28. LWL 785.07.11.01+ and LWL 786.01.01.05+.

29. British Museum Satires, 7108.

30. The phrase is Jonas Hanway's, from *A Journal of Eight Days Journey from Portsmouth to Kingston upon Thames; through Southampton, Wiltshire, &c.* (London: H. Woodfall, 1756), 70. Laura Brown uses it as the title and central theme of chap. 3 in *Homeless Dogs and Melancholy Apes*; see esp. 77–79.

31. Thomas O'Brien MacMahon, *Man's Capricious, Petulant, and Tyrannical Conduct Towards the Irrational and Inanimate Part of the Creation, Inquired into and Explained* (London: G. Riley, 1794), 12–13.

32. [Hanway], *Journal of Eight Days Journey*, 71.

33. Wyett, "Lap of Luxury," 286–90; Tague, "Dead Pets," 293–94; Brown, *Homeless Dogs and Melancholy Apes*, 70–77. For a discussion of the erotic symbolism of lapdogs in seventeenth- and eighteenth-century art, see Donald Posner, *Watteau: A Lady at Her Toilet* (New York: Viking, 1973), chap. 6.

34. Pope, *Rape of the Lock*, 3, lines 157–58; 4, lines 119–20. For a discussion of the trio of monkeys, lapdogs, and parrots as particularly significant in eighteenth-century culture, see Brown, *Fables of Modernity*, chap. 6.

35. "Peter Puzzle," letter to the *Guardian* 106 (13 July 1713), in John Calhoun Stephens, ed., *The Guardian* (Lexington: University Press of Kentucky, 1982), 368.

36. Mlle. Fantast in *The Coquet*, act 2, quoted in Braunschneider, "Lady and the Lapdog," 39.

37. Mary Jones, "Elegy on a Favourite Dog, Suppos'd to Be Poison'd. To Miss Molly Clayton," in *Poems by Eminent Ladies*, 2 vols. (London: R. Baldwin, 1755), 1:287.

38. LWL 792.08.01.01.

39. For a similar point about portrayals of women's relationships with their lapdogs in poetry, see Brown, *Homeless Dogs and Melancholy Apes*, 72.

40. Martin Postle, ed., *Joshua Reynolds: The Creation of Celebrity*, exh. cat. (London: Tate Publishing, 2005), 190 (cat. no. 54).

41. William Congreve, *Love for Love*, in *The Complete Plays of William Congreve*, ed. Herbert Davis (Chicago: University of Chicago Press, 1967), 5.1, p. 305.

42. Postle, *Joshua Reynolds*, 190 (cat. no. 54); cf. Joseph F. Musser Jr., "Sir Joshua Reynolds's 'Mrs. Abington as "Miss Prue,"'" *South Atlantic Quarterly* 83 (Spring 1984): 176–92, which sees the gesture and the pose in general as reflecting total innocence.

43. Musser, "Sir Joshua Reynolds's 'Mrs. Abington,'" 181–82.

44. Aileen Ribeiro notes that the painting was altered a few years after Reynolds completed it in order "to give her a higher, more modish coiffure." Ribeiro, "Costuming the Part: A Discourse of Fashion and Fiction in the Image of the Actress in England, 1776–1812," in *Notorious Muse: The Actress in British Art and Culture*, ed. Robyn Asleson, exh. cat. (New Haven: Yale University Press for the Paul Mellon Centre for Studies in British Art, 2003), 108.

45. Musser, "Sir Joshua Reynolds's 'Mrs. Abington,'" esp. 184.

46. *Tatler* 121 (17 January 1710), 2:218–19.

47. British Museum Satires, 8029.

48. LWL 795.09.04.01.

49. On the connections between cats and women, see Katharine M. Rogers, *The Cat and the Human Imagination: Feline Images from Bast to Garfield* (Ann Arbor: University of Michigan Press, 1998), 165–85; and, also by Rogers, *Cat* (London: Reaktion Books, 2006), chap. 4.

50. *Spectator* 209 (30 October 1711), in Donald F. Bond, *The Spectator*, 5 vols. (Oxford: Clarendon Press, 1965), 2:320; Coventry, *History of Pompey the Little*, 1st ed., 90. In one episode in *Pompey the Little*, the eponymous canine lives with an elderly cat named Mopsa, who shares the philosophical tastes of her learned mistress. The humor in the episode relies on the deadpan presentation of their philosophical explorations, which serve not to elevate the intelligence of animals, of course, but to reduce the intellectual aspirations of women to the level of cats and dogs. When Pompey is ejected from the house after he fouls the page of a learned treatise, the satire is complete: the work in question is no more useful to any of the inhabitants than a litter box, but the mistress fails to grasp this basic reality.

51. We can see these connotations and their connection to sexuality at work in a different manner in James Gillray's famous print *The Whore's Last Shift* (British Museum Satires, 5604).

52. See Fudge, *Pets*, 76–87, on the philosophical uses of contrasts between cats and dogs. For an overview of these perceptions of cats from the Middle Ages through the early modern period, see Rogers, *Cat*, chaps. 1–2; Robert Darnton, *The Great Cat Massacre and Other Episodes in French Cultural History* (New York: Vintage, 1985), chap. 2.

53. This statement is based on a comprehensive survey of the Lewis Walpole Library's collection of eighteenth-century prints containing images of pets. See also chapter 1.

54. A variant of the print appeared in 1790 as *Old Tabbies Attending a Favorite Cat's Funeral* (LWL 790.05.10.10+).

55. See *Interested Love* (1793), LWL 793.09.03.01; *An Advertisement for a Husband!* (1803), LWL +803.1.1.1dr.

56. See, e.g., *Piozzi Letters*, 5:397, 6:133, 6:188.

57. LWL 795.03.01.01+.

58. See, e.g., *The Captain's so kind as to thrust in a Note, While old Lady Cuckoo is straining her throat* (British Museum Satires, 4778); *A Quintetto* (ibid., 10200).

59. Another print, from 1810, takes these associations to their logical conclusion. In *The Mischief Making Old Maids' & Gossip's [sic] Arms* (LWL 810.11.12.01+), a monkey dressed in

women's clothing supports the arms, while on the lower left of the shield a cat claws apart a scroll labeled "Reputation, Home, Love, Marriage, Neighbours, Peace, Friendship." It is the cat's evil temper and claws, as well as the association with old maids who keep pet cats, that matter here; all come together in mutually reinforcing signification.

60. See Lisa Berglund, "Oysters for Hodge, or Ordering Society, Writing Biography and Feeding the Cat," *Journal for Eighteenth-Century Studies* 33, no. 4 (2010): 631–45.

61. Tommy Trimmer, *Tommy Trimmer's Historical Account, of Beasts, Reptiles, Fishes, Birds. An Entirely New Edition, Never Before Published. Adorned with Cuts Entirely New* (London: J. Mackenzie, n.d. [ca. 1800?]), 34–35.

62. For a reading of the fop in the early eighteenth century, which usefully distinguishes between accusations of effeminacy and homosexuality, see Philip Carter, "Men About Town: Representations of Foppery and Masculinity in Early Eighteenth-Century Urban Culture," in *Gender in Eighteenth-Century England: Roles, Representations, and Responsibilities*, ed. Hannah Barker and Elaine Chalus (London: Longman, 1997), 32–57.

63. On the role of dancing masters, see Anne Bloomfield and Ruth Watts, "Pedagogue of the Dance: The Dancing Master as Educator in the Long Eighteenth Century," *History of Education* 37, no. 4 (2008): 605–18; Tague, *Women of Quality*, 169–70; Trevor Fawcett, "Dance and Teachers of Dance in Eighteenth-Century Bath," *Bath History* 2 (1988): 27–48. For the career of one well-known early eighteenth-century dancing master (and owner of a pug dog), see Jennifer Thorp, "Mr. Isaac, Dancing-Master," *Dance Research: The Journal of the Society for Dance Research* 24, no. 2 (2006): 117–37, esp. 117–21. On the possibility of social mobility through the acquisition of polite accomplishments, see Lawrence E. Klein, "Politeness for Plebes: Consumption and Social Identity in Early Eighteenth-Century England," in *The Consumption of Culture, 1600–1800: Image, Object, Text*, ed. Ann Bermingham and John Brewer (London: Routledge, 1995), 362–82.

64. The companion print, *Grown Gentlemen Taught to Dance*, which is extant in several different versions, also deploys pets—in this case, cats and dogs—to mock the proceedings. In an early version, cats simply fight in an open violin case; in later versions, dogs and cats square off in postures parodying the dancing master and his pupil. See LWL 767.06.27.01+, 768.08.20.01+, and 768.09.30.01. In these cases, the satire is aimed more at the awkwardness of the students than at the dancing master's questionable masculinity, although his portrayal includes the usual features of mincing steps and ornate dress.

65. Ribeiro, *Dress and Morality*, 111. On criticisms of fashionable men throughout the century, see 97–100, 109–11.

66. See, e.g., *The Exhibition of Wild Beasts. Mankind is fond of looking at their own Likenesses* (LWL 774.10.20.02+).

67. This print is a close variation, with more emphasis on the macaroni-cockatoo pairing, on another print produced a few months earlier by another publisher (LWL 06.25.01.1+).

68. The Walpole Library catalogue refers delicately to both figures as "youths," which would seem to imply that they are both male, but both the print's title and the facial features of the figure on the left suggest otherwise. The ambiguity does, however, highlight the point of the satire, which is the failure of masculinity.

69. LWL 791.03.29.02.

70. For the identification of manliness with sober dress, see Ribeiro, *Dress and Morality*, 100, 111; Kuchta, *Three-Piece Suit*, chap. 5.

71. For more on this long-standing tradition, see Janson, *Apes and Ape Lore*.

72. On dressing monkeys in human clothes, see Brown, *Homeless Dogs and Melancholy Apes*, 104–5. Eighteenth-century people did of course keep female monkeys as pets; my point is simply that eighteenth-century culture gendered monkeys as male, as it did dogs.

73. *Gentleman's Magazine* 3 (February 1733), 86. "Flap" was a term usually applied to giddy or loose women; it is used here to refer to an empty-headed, fashionable young man.

74. LWL 799.08.30.04.

75. For a different reading of the meanings of the monkey in relation to ideas about gender and sexuality, see Brown, *Homeless Dogs and Melancholy Apes*, chap. 4.

76. British Museum Satires, 5204.

77. Ibid., 4615.

78. Ibid., 5946.

79. Bond, *Spectator* 499 (2 October 1712), 4:271.

80. *Lounger* 45 (10 December 1785), in *The Lounger. A Periodical Paper, Published at Edinburgh in the Years 1785 and 1786*, 3rd corrected ed., 3 vols. (Dublin: Printed for Messrs. Colles, Burnet, Moncrieffe, Gilbert, Exshaw, Burton, White, Byrne, H. Whitestone, W. Porter, Heery, McKenzie, Moor, and Dornin, 1787), 2:87.

81. Jonathan Swift's depiction of Gulliver's encounters with the Yahoos is also relevant here. The joke, and the horror for Gulliver, is that he so closely resembles the Yahoos that he is pursued by a lustful female of the species in a parody of stories about apes raping African women. See Brown, *Homeless Dogs and Melancholy Apes*, chap. 1 and 106–7; Brown, *Fables of Modernity*, 236–45; Janson, *Apes and Ape Lore*, 338–89.

82. There are two modern scholarly editions of Coventry's book, one edited by Robert Adams Day and published by Oxford University Press in 1974, the other edited by Nicholas Hudson and published by Broadview Press in Ontario in 2008. I have chosen to cite the eighteenth-century editions (first edition 1751, third edition 1752), because both modern editors combine elements of the original editions to create a single text that varies from both originals.

83. See Nicholas Hudson's introduction to his edition of the book, 10. For recent work on it-narratives, see Blackwell, *Secret Life of Things*; Christina Lupton, "The Knowing Book: Authors, It-Narratives, and Objectification in the Eighteenth Century," *Novel* 39, no. 3 (2006): 402–20; Christopher Flint, "Speaking Objects: The Circulation of Stories in Eighteenth-Century Prose Fiction," *PMLA* 113, no. 2 (1998): 212–26.

84. Coventry, *History of Pompey the Little*, 1st ed., 2–3, hereafter cited parenthetically in the text.

85. Coventry, *History of Pompey the Little*, 3rd ed., 52–53.

86. In another scene, a previous lapdog is used as a pawn in a domestic dispute between the Tempests, and Lady Tempest's affection for her pet implies that she has strayed from her husband in other ways (43–44).

87. Coventry, *History of Pompey the Little*, 3rd ed., 197.

88. In "Lap of Luxury," Jodi L. Wyett connects the collar to the ruff, seeing both as examples employing "the vain, spendthrift woman and her dog" as "common tropes for the evils of eighteenth-century acquisitiveness and luxurious consumption" (283). Laura Brown reads the collar as helping create "an insistent, pervasive, and wholly implicit analogy between the lap dog and the African slave." Brown, *Fables of Modernity*, 260 (see also 260–62).

CHAPTER 4

1. [Samuel Jackson Pratt], *Liberal Opinions, Upon Animals, Man, and Providence. In Which Are Introduced, Anecdotes of a Gentleman. Addressed to the Right Hon. Lady Ch***th. By Courtney Melmoth*, 6 vols. (London: G. Robinson, J. Bew, 1775–77), 1:65–66.

2. Sekora, *Luxury*, 23. On the moral debates over luxury, see also Berry, *Idea of Luxury*.

3. Bernard Mandeville, *The Fable of the Bees, or Private Vices, Public Benefits*, ed. F. B. Kaye (Oxford: Clarendon Press, 1924).

4. Maxine Berg and Elizabeth Eger, "The Rise and Fall of the Luxury Debates," in Berg and Eger, *Luxury in the Eighteenth Century*, 10. See also Berg, *Luxury and Pleasure*, 31–33.

5. Berg and Eger, "Rise and Fall of the Luxury Debates," 14; see also Sekora, *Luxury*, 66.

6. See Tuan, *Dominance and Affection*, chap. 8.

7. [Hanway], *Journal of Eight Days Journey*, 70.

8. Coventry, *History of Pompey the Little*, 1st ed., 47–49.

9. Ibid., 71–72.

10. *Lounger* 90 (21 October 1786), 3:201.

11. Ibid., 3:203–6 (quotations on 203, 204).

12. Coventry, *History of Pompey the Little*, 1st ed., 50–51.

13. *Lounger* 90 (21 October 1786), 3:205–6.

14. For a reading of another satire that implies a critique of both servants and masters, see Janice Thaddeus, "Swift's *Directions to Servants* and the Reader as Eavesdropper," *Studies in Eighteenth-Century Culture* 16 (1986): 107–23.

15. A story in the *Gentleman's Magazine* presents a similar satire, this time involving a poor playwright seeking patronage. Although the playwright is not a servant, the story emphasizes his dependent position and presents an ongoing contrast between his elite audience's care for a lapdog and their complete lack of interest in his work. See *Gentleman's Magazine* 23 (May 1753), 232–33.

16. See Ritvo, "Learning from Animals."

17. Trimmer, *Fabulous Histories*, 5.

18. Ibid., 9. For another example, see *The Children's Friend*, in which a father praises his daughter for forgiving her brother after he loses their beloved pet greyhound: "I know many persons who, for such a trifle, would have turned away an honest servant." The girl is shocked that someone would favor "a creature without reason to a person of our own kind," and her father takes the opportunity to condemn "those who would rather see a poor child suffer hunger or thirst than a favourite dog; who shed tears at the indisposition of a spaniel, and look without pity on the lot of an unhappy orphan abandoned by all the world." Berquin, *Children's Friend*, 2:87.

19. Trimmer, *Fabulous Histories*, 101, 108, 110–12. Ultimately, Mrs. Addis dies alone and unloved.

20. Fudge, *Perceiving Animals*, 125. See also Walker-Meikle, *Medieval Pets*, 2.

21. Buffon, *Natural History*, 4:4–5.

22. See, e.g., [Taylor], *Surveys of Nature*, vol. 2, part 3, 50; [Ralph Beilby], *A General History of Quadrupeds. The Figures Engraved on Wood by T. Bewick* (Newcastle upon Tyne: S. Hodgson, R. Beilby, and T. Bewick, 1790), 281–82; *The Edinburgh Repository for Polite Literature: Consisting of Elegant, Instructive, and Entertaining Extracts, Selected from the Best Ancient and Modern Authors: Principally Designed to Introduce the Youth of Both Sexes to an Acquaintance with Useful and Ornamental Knowledge* (Edinburgh: T. Brown, 1793), 275–76.

23. "Defence of our Attachment to Animals," in Pratt, *Gleanings in England*, 2:344.

24. For a discussion of the traditional associations of "dog" in the English language, see William Empson, *The Structure of Complex Words* (Norfolk, Conn.: New Directions, [1951]), 158–74; Paulson, *Popular and Polite Art*, 49–63.

25. Buffon, *Natural History*, 4:38–39.

26. Smellie, *Philosophy of Natural History*, 2:332–34.

27. Ward, *Modern System of Natural History*, 2:166–67.

28. Raff, *System of Natural History*, 2:215.

29. MacMahon, *Man's Capricious, Petulant, and Tyrannical Conduct*, 11–17 (quotations on 11, 17).

30. Trimmer, *Fabulous Histories*, 107. Trimmer also notes that monkeys and parrots would be happier in their native habitats, and that the cat would rather catch mice than live a life of enforced luxury.

31. [Aikin and Barbauld], *Evenings at Home*, 1:119–24 (quotation on 123–24).

32. Buffon, *Natural History*, 8:74–75.

33. Buffon, *Natural History of Birds*, 1:15. In his description of the Ara parrot (a New World macaw), Buffon praised the animal as unique among birds because "it may be domesticated without being enslaved; . . . it contracts a fondness for the family where it is adopted" (6:156).

34. See Ritvo, "Learning from Animals."

35. Quoted in N. B. Penny, "Dead Dogs and Englishmen," *Connoisseur* 192 (1976): 299.

36. Studies that emphasize the class overtones of the anticruelty crusade and similar movements of the era include Perkins, *Romanticism and Animal Rights*; Malcolmson, *Popular Recreations*, chap. 7; and, for a later period, Ritvo, *Animal Estate*, chap. 3. For the larger context of eighteenth-century ideas about cruelty, see James Steintrager, *Cruel Delight: Enlightenment Culture and the Inhuman* (Bloomington: Indiana University Press, 2004), especially part II.

37. Perkins, *Romanticism and Animal Rights*, 94, points out that because poor people worked most closely with animals, there was a "basis in social fact for [this] widely accepted belief."

38. See Paulson, *Popular and Polite Art*, 4.

39. Malcolmson, *Popular Recreations*, chap. 7; Ian Gilmour, *Riot, Risings, and Revolution: Governance and Violence in Eighteenth-Century England* (London: Pimlico, 1993), 201–2.

40. "A.," letter to *Gentleman's Magazine* 32 (January 1762), 6.

41. "Humanus," letter to *Gentleman's Magazine* 59 (January 1789), 16.

42. [Pratt], *Liberal Opinions*, 1:2–3.

43. Ibid., 160–61.

44. Lawrence, *Philosophical and Practical Treatise*, 1:135, 138.

45. Ibid., 1:140.

46. See Maureen Harkin's introduction to Henry Mackenzie, *The Man of Feeling* (Peterborough, Ont.: Broadview Press, 2005), 30–31; Barker-Benfield, *Culture of Sensibility*, esp. chap. 5; Janet Todd, *Sensibility: An Introduction* (London: Methuen, 1986).

47. For a reading of the dog tax debates similar to the one developed here, see Lynn Festa, "Person, Animal, Thing: The 1796 Dog Tax and the Right to Superfluous Things," *Eighteenth-Century Life* 33, no. 2 (2009): 1–44. Festa addresses the complexities inherent in identifying a living being as a luxury good, and the appeal to sentimental attachment among many opponents of the tax. However, her article is focused primarily on the 1796 parliamentary debates and their aftermath, rather than on the broader context of the debates over the course of the century.

48. See Ingrid H. Tague, "Eighteenth-Century English Debates on a Dog Tax," *Historical Journal* 51, no. 4 (2008): 904–9.

49. Barry, *On the Necessity*, 8. See also *Some Considerations on the Game Laws, Suggested by the Late Motion of Mr. Curwen for the Repeal of the Present System* (London: T. Egerton, 1796), 67–68.

50. *Gentleman's Magazine* 44 (June 1774), 282.

51. T[homas] Gilbert, *Heads of a Bill for the Better Relief and Employment of the Poor, and for the Improvement of the Police of This Country. Submitted to the Consideration of the Members of Both Houses of Parliament* (Manchester: Harrop, 1786), esp. 17.

52. [Daniel Hilman], *Tusser Redivivus: Being Part of Mr. Thomas Tusser's Five Hundred Points of Husbandry; Namely, for the Months of November and December. With Notes. No XI. XII.* (London: J. Morphew, 1710), 4, partially quoted in Malcolmson, *Popular Recreations*, 93; Malcolmson also supplies the author's name.

53. The painting is the pendant to *The Comforts of Industry*, also in the collection of the Scottish National Gallery, in which the only animal presence is a large haunch of meat.

54. Sarah Trimmer, "The Dog," in *The Family Magazine, or A Repository of Religious Instruction, and Rational Amusement,* June 1788, 407.

55. William King, *Reasons and Proposals for Laying a Tax upon Dogs. Humbly Addressed to the Honourable House of Commons* (Reading: D. Henry, 1740), 7–8.

56. Clark, *Address to Both Houses of Parliament*, 13–14.

57. "C.," letter to the *Times* (London), 16 April 1796, 3, col. C.

58. Varlo, *Schemes Offered for the Perusal*, 129–30.

59. Ibid., 134–36.

60. "Colonus," letter to *Gentleman's Magazine* 27 (April 1757), 159.

61. *Public Advertiser* 17617 (23 December 1790).

62. Anonymous letter to *Gentleman's Magazine* 55 (August 1785), 605.

63. Gilbert, *Heads of a Bill*, 16.

64. Both Dent's and Lechmere's remarks can be found in *The Parliamentary History of England, from the Earliest Period to the Year 1803*, vol. 32 (London: T. C. Hansard, 1818), 5 April 1796, cols. 996 and 997, respectively.

65. Clark, *Address to Both Houses of Parliament*, 6–7. See also *Gentleman's Magazine* 55 (August 1785), 605.

66. Clark, *Address to Both Houses of Parliament*, 5–6. The bill he proposed did not list any specific exemptions (17–18).

67. King, *Reasons and Proposals*, 13–16.

68. "Publicola," letter to *Gentleman's Magazine* 32 (January 1762), 21.

69. For the social background, see Tague, "Dog Tax," 902–4.

70. Clark, *Address to Both Houses of Parliament*, 4, 15.

71. Barry, *On the Necessity*, 5–8.

72. Ibid., 12.

73. See Malcolmson, *Popular Recreations*, 137–38; Perkins, *Romanticism and Animal Rights*, 20–22; Steintrager, *Cruel Delight*, chap. 3. For other contemporary connections between abuse of animals and other bad behavior, see Edward Nairne, *The Dog-Tax, a Poem* (Canterbury: Printed for the Author, 1797), 26; Young, *Essay on Humanity to Animals*, 3–5.

74. *Parliamentary History of England*, 25 April 1796, col. 1006.

75. Ibid., col. 1003.

76. *Gentleman's Magazine* 61 (May 1791), 483.

77. *Parliamentary History of England*, 25 April 1796, cols. 1000–1003. Windham's opposition to bills against animal cruelty is well known, and he rehearsed similar ideas in

arguing that the poor would be punished while the pursuits of the wealthy, such as hunting, were allowed to continue. See Kenyon-Jones, *Kindred Brutes*, 81–94; Malcolmson, *Popular Recreations*, 152–54.

78. *Parliamentary History of England*, 25 April 1796, col. 1000.

79. Ibid., 25 April 1796, col. 1006.

80. Holland and Holland, *Exercises for the Memory and Understanding*, 110–11. The story is Arnaud Berquin's and appears in another translation in Berquin, *Children's Friend*, 4:237–41.

81. Mackenzie, *Man of Feeling*, 59–61, 108; Postle, *Angels and Urchins*, 94 (cat. no. 93).

82. Malcolmson, *Popular Recreations*, 166; Kenyon-Jones, *Kindred Brutes*, 81–85.

83. Robert Southey, "Characteristic English Anecdotes and Fragments for Espriella," in *Southey's Common-Place Book, Fourth Series: Original Memoranda, Etc.*, ed. John Wood Warter (London: Longman, Brown, Green, and Longmans, 1851), 417.

84. *Parliamentary History of England*, 5 April 1796, col. 997. See also 25 April 1796, col. 1006.

85. *An Act for Granting to His Majesty Certain Duties on Dogs*, 36 Geo. III c. 124, 19 May 1796, in *The Statutes at Large, From the Thirty-fifth Year of the Reign of King George the Third, To the Thirty-eighth Year of the Reign of King George the Third, Inclusive . . . Being a Thirteenth Volume to Mr. Runnington's Edition, and a Seventeenth to Mr. Ruffhead's* (London: George Eyre and Andrew Strahan, 1798), 415–17. On the sinking fund, see John Ehrman, *The Years of Acclaim*, vol. 1 of *The Younger Pitt* (London: Constable and Co., 1969), 157–58, 267, 270–73.

86. On anxieties about rabies in the dog tax debates, see Tague, "Dog Tax," 903; John D. Blaisdell, "An Ounce of Prevention Causes a Ton of Concern: Rabies and the English Dog Tax of 1796," *Veterinary History*, new ser., 10 (2000–2001): 129–46.

87. Varlo, *Schemes Offered for the Perusal*, 137; Barry, *On the Necessity*, 11. Robert Southey claimed that the tax did indeed cause a massive slaughter of dogs, with the resulting piles of carcasses forcing local authorities to collect and bury huge numbers of abandoned corpses. Southey, "Characteristic English Anecdotes," 417. See also Hester Lynch Piozzi to Penelope Sophia Pennington, 20 [April 1796], *Piozzi Letters*, 2:339–40.

CHAPTER 5

1. References to Pug appear in her earliest extant letters, from early 1705.

2. Letter of 16 December [1712], British Library Additional MS 22225, fol. 199r. Lady Wentworth relied largely on phonetic spelling, which also reflected her Yorkshire accent, and her punctuation was erratic at best. I have modernized the spelling and punctuation of the family correspondence throughout in order to make it more accessible to the modern reader. Unless otherwise noted, all Wentworth correspondence in this chapter is from Lady Wentworth to her son Thomas, Earl of Strafford, and is in the British Library Additional Manuscripts, hereafter cited by date, manuscript number, and folio number(s).

3. Letter of 19 December [1712], ibid., fol. 200v; 30 December [1712], ibid., fol. 207r; Lady Anne Strafford to Thomas, Earl of Strafford, 16 December 1712, MS 22226, fol. 246r.

4. Letter of 12 March [1706], MS 31143, fol. 147r–v. As noted in chapter 1, note 136, until 1752, Britain used the Julian (or "Old Style") calendar, which officially began the new year on 25 March. When a correspondent provides no year, I have added it in brackets with the year taken to begin on 1 January; in the example here, for instance, the Old Style date would be 1705. When a writer provides only the Old Style year, I have added the New Style year in brackets.

5. Letter of 4 July [1709], ibid., fol. 399v.

6. Letter of 4 February [1706], ibid., fol. 136v.

7. Letter of 1 December [1710], ibid., fols. 605v–606r. See also 5 June [1705], ibid., fol. 40r: "Pug is as fond of Bell Skinner as ever she was of me, she looks her head and kisses her, and sits in her lap."

8. Letter of 23 September [1712], MS 22225, fols. 176v–177r.

9. Letter of 30 December [1712], ibid., fols. 208r–209v.

10. Letter of 2 January [1713], ibid., fols. 339v–340r.

11. Letter of 19 December [1712], ibid., fol. 200r.

12. Lady Anne Strafford to Lord Strafford, 16 December 1712, MS 22226, fol. 246r.

13. Letter of [January 1713], MS 22225, fol. 357r.

14. N.d. (ca. September 1712), ibid., fols. 248r–249r. Pug was female, but Lady Wentworth used "he," "she," and "it" interchangeably when discussing her animals.

15. Quoted in Vickery, *Behind Closed Doors*, 188–89.

16. Lewis Walpole Library, Yale University (hereafter LWL), 793.06.03.01+.

17. *Tatler* 112 (27 December 1709), 2:173–77.

18. *Tatler* 121 (17 January 1710), 2:216–19.

19. Smellie, *Philosophy of Natural History*, 1:247–50.

20. Bentham, *Principles of Morals and Legislation*, 311n.

21. David Hume, *A Treatise of Human Nature*, ed. David Fate Norton and Mary J. Norton (Oxford: Oxford University Press, 2000), 2.1.12, "Of the pride and humility of animals," 211–12.

22. Ibid., 2.2.12, "Of the love and hatred of animals," 255–56.

23. See Buffon, *Natural History*, 3:276–78.

24. [Pratt], *Liberal Opinions*, 2:178.

25. Todd, *Sensibility*, 7.

26. For an extensive discussion of the relationship between sensibility and femininity, and the positive effects of the ideals of sensibility on the development of feminism, see Barker-Benfield, *Culture of Sensibility*.

27. Karen Raber, "From Sheep to Meat, from Pets to People: Animal Domestication, 1600–1800," in *A Cultural History of Animals in the Age of Enlightenment*, ed. Matthew Senior (Oxford: Berg, 2007), 89.

28. See, e.g., Edwards, *Gleanings of Natural History*, 1:13, on the "black maucauco": "The print was sketched on the plate from the living animal."

29. See Robbins, *Elephant Slaves and Pampered Parrots*, 65–67.

30. For a recent discussion of Stubbs's famous portrait *Whistlejacket*, see Landry, *Noble Brutes*, 148–61.

31. Madeleine Pinault Sørensen, "Portraits of Animals, 1600–1800," in Senior, *Cultural History of Animals*, 185; Donald, *Picturing Animals in Britain*, 112.

32. *Tristram and Fox*, like *Pomeranian Bitch and Puppy*, is in the Tate collection.

33. Gainsborough's portrait of Abel with his dog is in the Huntington Library collection in San Marino, California.

34. LWL 770.00.00.05+.

35. LWL 777.11.10.07+.

36. Although the Walpole Library dates the print to ca. 1793, the British Museum suggests ca. 1765–75, which seems more likely.

37. British Museum Prints and Drawings Collection, no. 2010,7081.3810.

38. Ibid., no. 2010,7081.3821 and no. 1888,0715.410.

39. This is not to argue that there was a "discovery of childhood" in the eighteenth century or to suggest that parents did not love their children in earlier periods. It is simply to recognize the upsurge in consumer goods aimed at children and the growing presence of children in the visual and print culture of the eighteenth century. See J. H. Plumb, "The New World of Children," in McKendrick, Brewer, and Plumb, *Birth of a Consumer Society*, 286–315; Marcia Pointon, *Hanging the Head: Portraiture and Social Formation in Eighteenth-Century England* (New Haven: Yale University Press, 1993); James Christen Steward, *The New Child: British Art and the Origins of Modern Childhood, 1730–1830*, exh. cat. (Berkeley: University Art Museum and Pacific Film Archive, University of California, Berkeley, in association with the University of Washington Press, 1995); Kate Retford, *The Art of Domestic Life: Family Portraiture in Eighteenth-Century England* (New Haven: Yale University Press for the Paul Mellon Centre for Studies in British Art, 2006), esp. chaps. 3–4.

40. The portrait is in the Huntington Library collection.

41. See Pointon, *Hanging the Head*, 192–93. Pointon presents an extended discussion of the connections between femininity and childhood in eighteenth-century portraiture (177–205).

42. LWL 790.00.00.07.

43. LWL 745.00.00.07+.

44. Steward, *New Child*, 194. Steward also notes that Wheatley's and Morland's works were the source of more engravings than any other artist's.

45. The structure of the first volume, which was ostensibly a collection of manuscripts found in the possession of "Benignus" after his death, is also clearly modeled on Mackenzie's famous work.

46. [Pratt], *Liberal Opinions*, 1:112.

47. "Ode on the Death of a Spaniel," in *Imitations and Translations from the Latin of Mr. Gray's Lyric Odes* (London: J. Dodsley, 1777), 23–24. Edward Burnaby Greene earlier wrote a similar but less overtly sentimental ode. See Greene, "Ode on the Death of a Favorite Spaniel," in *The Latin Odes of Mr. Gray, in English Verse, with an Ode on the Death of a Favorite Spaniel* (London: J. Ridley, 1775), 9–11.

48. See Harkin's introduction to Mackenzie's novel, 30–31.

49. Ibid., 19; Barker-Benfield, *Culture of Sensibility*, 141–44. On the relationship between the limitations of the sentimental novel and the limitations of the abolitionist movement, see Ellis, *Politics of Sensibility*, chaps. 2–3.

50. See Harkin's introduction, 19–21; Todd, *Sensibility*, chap. 8.

51. On the paradox of the culture of sensibility's reliance on both sociability and privacy, see Mullan, *Sentiment and Sociability*.

52. Sibly, *Magazine of Natural History*, 1:iii–iv.

53. *Parliamentary History of England*, 25 April 1796, col. 1002.

54. Donald, *Picturing Animals in Britain*, 111.

55. See Kuchta, *Three-Piece Suit*, 116–21; Desmond Shawe-Taylor, *The Georgians: Eighteenth-Century Portraiture and Society* (London: Barrie and Jenkins, 1990), 71; Michael Rosenthal and Martin Myrone, eds., *Gainsborough*, exh. cat. (London: Tate Publishing, 2002), 182–83. The portrait is in the collection of the Duke of Buccleuch and Queensbury at Bowhill House, Selkirk, Scotland.

56. See Matthew Craske, "Representations of Domestic Animals in Britain," in *Hounds in Leash: The Dog in Eighteenth- and Nineteenth-Century Sculpture*, ed. Jonathan Wood and Stephen Feeke, exh. cat. (Leeds: Henry Moore Institute, 2000), 44.

57. Shawe-Taylor, *Georgians*, 71.

58. Donald, *Picturing Animals in Britain*, 112.

59. Amal Asfour and Paul Williamson, "Gainsborough's Wit," *Journal of the History of Ideas* 58, no. 3 (1997): 496.

60. Shawe-Taylor, *Georgians*, 71.

61. *Lounger* 90 (21 October 1786), 3:200. See chapter 4.

62. The painting is in the Wallace Collection in London. On this portrait and Reynolds's ability to capture his sitter's personality through his social skills, see Richard Wendorf, *Sir Joshua Reynolds: The Painter in Society* (Cambridge: Harvard University Press, 1996), 120–22.

63. The portrait is in the collection of Goodwood House, Sussex.

64. Steward, *New Child*, 187.

65. Craske, "Representations of Domestic Animals," 43–44. The portrait is in the collection of the Earl of Rosebery, Dalmeny House, Scotland.

66. Strafford was awarded the earldom (which had been extinguished upon the death of his cousin) in 1711 upon his marriage to Anne Johnson, the daughter of a wealthy shipbuilder.

67. For biographical information on Lady Wentworth, see Susannah R. Ottaway and Ingrid H. Tague, eds., *Personal Narratives of Ageing*, vol. 8 of *The History of Old Age in England, 1600–1800*, ed. Susannah R. Ottaway and Lynn Botelho, 8 vols. (London: Pickering and Chatto, 2009), 1–5; Ingrid H. Tague, "Aristocratic Women and Ideas of Family in the Early Eighteenth Century," in *The Family in Early Modern England*, ed. Helen Berry and Elizabeth Foyster (Cambridge: Cambridge University Press, 2007), 190–92.

68. See MS 22225, fol. 248r, for reference to his acquisition of the monkey, and fol. 457r for its death.

69. In addition to the clear instance of Pearl, discussed below, there is evidence in the correspondence of several other dogs, including her references to their ties to him, her discussions of their lineage, and a reference to her daughter Betty's acquiring one of his dogs.

70. Letter of 28 July [1710], MS 31143, fol. 524r.

71. Letter of 23 October [1711], MS 22225, fol. 98r–v.

72. Letter of 27 March [1713], ibid., fol. 252v.

73. Tague, "Aristocratic Women and Ideas of Family," 190.

74. Letter of 4 July 1710, MS 22225, fol. 83r.

75. See letter of 24 November [1726], ibid., fol. 496r.

76. Letter of 18 July [1712], ibid., fol. 144r–v.

77. Letter of 14 November [1707], ibid., fol. 57r.

78. Letter of 4 July [1710], ibid., fol. 83r.

79. Letter of 19 January [ca. 1705–6], MS 31143, fol. 126r.

80. Letter of 13 February [1705], ibid., fols. 18v–19r.

81. Lady Anne Strafford to Lord Strafford, 24 June 1712, MS 22226, fol. 163v, and 15 August 1712, fol. 195r.

82. Letter of 8 August [1712], MS 22225, fol. 150r.

83. Letter of 15 August [1712], ibid., fols. 154r–155v.

84. Letter of 12 August [1707], ibid., fol. 24v.

85. Letter of 3 March [1713], ibid., fol. 384v.

86. Letter of 27 March [1713], ibid., fols. 252v–253r.

87. Letter of 2 September [1712], ibid., fol. 165r.

88. Letter of ca. September 1712, ibid., fol. 249r.

89. Letter of 14 April [1713], ibid., fol. 267r.

90. Letter of 24 July (no year given), MS 31144, fols. 148v–149r.

91. Letter of 29 [*sic*] February [1706?], MS 31143, fol. 145v; see also 19 April [1706], fol. 155v.

92. Letter of 1 July 1707, MS 22225, fol. 14r.

93. Letter of 9 November [1708], MS 31143, fol. 227r.

94. Letter of 16 November [1708], ibid., fols. 229r–230r.

95. Letter of 11 March [1712], MS 22225, fol. 240r.

96. Letter of 20 March [1712], ibid., fol. 244r–v.

97. Letter of 17 February [1713], ibid., fol. 370r. Another letter, in which she says she is "glad Pug is well again," may refer to a recovery from the beating; if so, the punishment must have been particularly vicious (3 March [1713], ibid., fol. 384v).

98. Anne was usually left behind in England during Thomas's trips abroad. These long absences account for her many letters to him.

99. Letter of 11 December [1711], MS 22225, fol. 120r.

100. Letter of 17 August 1713, ibid., fol. 321v; see also 10 August [1713], fol. 318v.

101. Lady Anne Strafford to Lord Strafford, 20 November 1711, MS 22226, fol. 26r.

102. Letter of 8 January [1712], MS 22225, fol. 212r.

103. Ibid., fol. 212v (postscript from Anne to Thomas).

104. Lady Anne Strafford to Lord Strafford, 8 February 1712, MS 22226, fol. 290v.

105. Lady Anne Strafford to Lord Strafford, 12 February 1711 [1712], ibid., fol. 81r.

106. Lady Anne Strafford to Lord Strafford, 25 February 1712, ibid., fol. 87. Anne is referring to Lady Wentworth's obsession with finding spouses for her children, which is evident throughout the correspondence.

107. Lady Anne Strafford to Lord Strafford, 8 April 1712, ibid., fol. 136r.

108. Buffon, *Natural History of Birds*, 6:92.

109. Edwards, *Gleanings of Natural History*, 1:10, 2:xii.

110. William Cowper, letter to the editor, *Gentleman's Magazine* 54 (June 1784), 412–14; "Epitaph on a Hare," *Gentleman's Magazine* 54 (December 1784), 935. I have not documented the quotations from the former source with page citations, as they are all drawn from this brief three-page letter, easily accessible to any reader who wishes to consult the June 1784 issue of the *Gentleman's Magazine*.

111. On the tradition of using feminine pronouns for hares, see Perkins, *Romanticism and Animal Rights*, 56.

112. Ibid., 46.

113. *Gentleman's Magazine* 58 (September 1788), 774–76.

114. Although Timothy, whose shell is held at the Museum of Natural History in London, has since been determined to have been female, to avoid confusion I will follow White's gendering of the tortoise as male.

115. Gilbert White, *Gilbert White's Journals*, ed. Walter Johnson (Cambridge: MIT Press, 1971), 108, entry of 7 August 1775: "Timothy, Mrs Snookes' old tortoise has been kept full 30 years in her court before the house, weighs six pounds three quarters, & one ounce. It was never weighed before, but seems to be much grown since it came."

116. Gilbert White, *The Natural History and Antiquities of Selborne, in the County of Southampton: With Engravings, and an Appendix* (London: T. Bensley, 1789), Barrington VII, 135. I am following the convention of identifying the letters by their recipient and number.

117. Ibid., Barrington XIII, 148–49.

118. Ibid., Barrington XVII, 166; Barrington XXXVI, 218.

119. Ibid., Barrington L, 261–62.

120. Ibid., 427–28.

121. See, e.g., White, *Gilbert White's Journals*, 27 May 1780, 172, on Timothy avoiding the ha-ha; see the entry of 17 October 1782, 213–14, on angling his shell toward the sun. White's journals are hereafter cited parenthetically in the text by date and page number.

122. This was Thomas Hoar, a servant who helped manage the garden.

123. White to Molly White, 22 May 1784, in Rashleigh Holt-White, ed., *The Life and Letters of Gilbert White of Selborne*, 2 vols. (London: J. Murray, 1901), 2:121–22.

124. White to Molly White, 12 June 1784, ibid., 2:124.

125. White to Samuel Barker, 17 April 1786, ibid., 2:155–56.

126. See Verlyn Klinkenborg's novel written from Timothy's point of view, which draws attention to and subverts the demeaning adjective. Klinkenborg, *Timothy, or Notes of an Abject Reptile* (New York: Knopf, 2006).

127. "Timothy" to Hester "Hecky" Mulso, 31 August 1784, in Holt-White, *Life and Letters of Gilbert White*, 2:126–29.

128. Walpole initially leased the house in 1747 and bought it outright the following year.

129. See, e.g., Mary Masters, "The Following Upon the Same Occasion, Was Wrote by a Lady, Probably to Selima's Mistress, to Comfort Her for the Loss of Her Favourite," in her *Familiar Letters and Poems On Several Occasions* (London: D. Henry and R. Cave, 1755), 251–53.

130. "Ode on the Death of a Spaniel"; Greene, "Ode on the Death of a Favorite Spaniel." Walpole's pets seem to have been unusually prone to gruesome ends. Another dog, Bettina, died in 1741 after falling off a balcony in Italy. Horace Walpole to Sir Horace Mann, 18 May 1741 NS, *Horace Walpole's Correspondence*, 17:45. "NS" and "OS" in the correspondence refer to "New Style" (dates based on the modern Gregorian calendar) and "Old Style" (dates based on the Julian calendar). The distinction was often necessary in correspondence between Britain and continental Europe so that both sender and recipient could be clear about the specific dates being used.

131. *Horace Walpole's Correspondence*, 13:14.

132. For instance, he praised a new edition of *The Compleat Angler* but expressed his regret that the editor described angling as "so very *innocent* an amusement." Walpole to Sir David Dalrymple, 28 June 1760, ibid., 15:70. Walpole also expressed these sentiments more publicly, as in a 1762 letter printed anonymously in the *Gazetteer and London Daily Advertiser*; see ibid., 40:257. All subsequent citations of letters between Walpole and his correspondents are to *Horace Walpole's Correspondence*, cited by date followed by volume and page number(s).

133. Walpole to Sir Horace Mann, 30 September 1784, 25:528.

134. Walpole to the Earl of Strafford, 4 September 1760, 35:306.

135. Walpole to Sir Horace Mann, 30 March 1784, 25:490.

136. Walpole to Henry Seymour Conway, 28 November 1784, 39:428.

137. Walpole to Lord Strafford, 29 August 1786, 35:387.

138. Walpole to Catherine Walpole, [1725], 36:1.

139. Henry Seymour Conway to Walpole, [31 May 1737], 37:26–27.

140. Walpole to Mann, 5 June 1747 OS, 19:414; Walpole to George Montagu, 15 August 1763, 10:94; Walpole to Charles Hanbury Williams, 27 June 1748, 30:116; Walpole to Henry Seymour Conway, 8 November 1752, 37:347.

141. Walpole to Henry Seymour Conway, 14 July 1761, 38:94.

142. Walpole to Lady Mary Hervey, 11 June 1765, 31:36.

143. Walpole to George Montagu, 12 March 1756, 10:205.

144. See his satirical fable, "Patapan, or The Little White Dog," ibid., vol. 30, Appendix I, in which Walpole's footnotes identify Patapan as "a little Roman dog" (30:287n) and Grifoni as the donor (30:296n).

145. Walpole to Horace Mann, [29 June 1741 NS], 17:76.

146. Mann to Walpole, 21 August [1741 NS], 17:112.

147. Walpole to Mann, 25 April 1743 OS, 18:220–21. He also asked Mann for an Italian motto to accompany the image.

148. John Chute to Walpole, 29 July 1743 NS, 35:41.

149. Chute to Walpole, 1 October 1743 NS, 35:44–46.

150. Walpole to Chute, 12 October 1743 OS, 35:48.

151. Chute to Walpole, 13 February 1742 NS, 35:22.

152. Walpole to Mann, 8 April 1742 OS, 17:392.

153. Walpole to Mann, 10 June 1742 OS, 17:452.

154. Walpole to Mann, 6 January 1743 OS, 18:136.

155. Walpole to Earl of Lincoln, 16 September 1741 NS, 30:18.

156. Walpole to Mann, 16 August 1744 OS, 18:498.

157. Walpole to Mann, 3 October 1743 OS, 18:315.

158. Walpole to Mann, 29 April 1745, 19:39. See also Mann to Walpole, 29 June 1745 NS, 19:59; Walpole to Mann, 25 July 1745 OS, 19:71; Henry Seymour Conway to Walpole, 14 May 1745 NS, 37:192.

159. See Madame du Deffand to Walpole, 16 January and 3 February 1767, 3:212, 225.

160. See Coke, 6 June 1771, *Letters and Journals*, 3:404: "My work was ended & I imagined I shou'd have no company when a Coach came to my door, & out of it came Mr Walpole & his dog." Rosette came with him on a trip to Paris in 1769 and presumably finally visited Madame du Deffand, although Walpole kept her largely confined because he was afraid of a canine "distemper" that was going around. Walpole to John Chute, 30 August 1769, 35:121.

161. Walpole to George Montagu, 1 July 1770, 10:312.

162. Walpole to George Selwyn, 12 August 1772, 30:258.

163. Walpole to Mann, 23 March 1770, 23:200–201.

164. Walpole to Lord Nuneham, 10 August 1773, 35:460.

165. Walpole to Lady Ossory, 9 August 1773, 32:137.

166. Walpole to Lady Ossory, 13 August 1773, 32:139.

167. Walpole to Lord Nuneham, 17 August 1773, 35:463.

168. Walpole to Lady Ossory, 26 October 1773, 32:160.

169. Walpole to Lord Nuneham, 6 November 1773, 35:464–65.

170. Madame du Deffand to Walpole, 17 November 1773, 5:422 ("Je viens de recevoir un billet de M. de Bauffremont, qui me demande si je veux un petit épagneul noir le plus joli du monde, qui n'a que trois mois; je l'ai accepté").

171. Madame du Deffand to Walpole, 1 January 1774, 6:2 ("Promettez-moi que, s'il reste sans maîtresse, vous voudrez bien devenir son maître; je suis sure que vous l'aimerez").

172. Madame du Deffand to Walpole, 17 January [1774], 6:5, and 6 February 1774, 6:13–14.

173. Walpole to Lady Ossory, 3 January 1779, 33:81.

174. Walpole to Lady Ossory, 6 July 1779, 33:108.

175. Madame du Deffand to Walpole, 25 January 1780, 7:201 ("je voudrais vous le laisser lui-même, je suis sûre que vous l'aimeriez et en auriez grand soin. Si cela pouvait être

possible, faites-vous l'apporter"). In a note he later appended to her letter, Walpole wrote, "M. Walpole l'eut, et en eut tous les soins possible."

176. See Jean-François Wiart to Walpole, 22 October 1780, 7:253; Walpole to Thomas Walpole, Strawberry Hill, 26 October 1780, 36:182; Walpole to Lady Ossory, 1 November 1780, 33:235.

177. See, e.g., Madame du Deffand to Walpole, 19 November 1775, 6:238. Walpole to Henry Seymour Conway, 8 September 1775, 39:258; Walpole to George Selwyn, 16 September 1775, 30:265.

178. Walpole to Henry Seymour Conway, 6–8 May 1781, 39:370.

179. Walpole to Thomas Walpole, 11 November 1781, 36:205.

180. Walpole to Lady Ossory, 7 June 1785, 33:464.

181. Walpole to Lady Ossory, 4 July 1781, 33:281.

182. Walpole to William Mason, 22 May 1781, 29:145.

183. Walpole to Lady Ossory, 20 June 1781, 33:276–77.

184. Walpole to Henry Seymour Conway, 30 June 1784, 39:419–20.

185. Walpole to Lady Ossory, 4 September 1781, 33:288.

186. Walpole to Lady Ossory, 25 December 1782, 33:375.

187. Walpole, memorandum, "Book of Visitors at Strawberry Hill, 1784–1796," *Horace Walpole's Correspondence*, 12:265.

188. Walpole to Lady Ossory, 24 February 1789, 34:45.

189. Walpole to Lady Ossory, 28 February 1789, 34:48.

190. Walpole to Mary Berry, 23 June 1789, 11:13.

191. The menagerie was designed by Walpole's friend Richard Bentley at Walpole's instigation. See 35:279–80, 282, 306; 11:65–66; Coke, *Letters and Journals*, 2:108.

192. Walpole to Lord Strafford, 9 August 1759, 35:293; 16 June 1758, 35:289; 6 June 1756, 35:275; 4 July 1757, 35:282; 4 October 1766, 35:320.

193. Lady Louisa Stuart, *Memoir*, in Coke, *Letters and Journals*, 1:xlviii.

194. Walpole to Lord Strafford, 3 October 1782, 35:368.

195. Walpole to Lord Strafford, 3 July 1769, 35:355. Lady Strafford was a keen angler; see Coke, *Letters and Journals*, 2:276–77, 321.

196. Walpole to Lord Strafford, 11 October 1783, 35:377–78.

EPILOGUE

1. The idea of "animal rights" as self-evidently ridiculous was the basis for Thomas Taylor's satire of Mary Wollstonecraft, *A Vindication of the Rights of Brutes* (London: Edward Jeffery, 1792).

2. On the class biases of the humane movement in the nineteenth century, see Ritvo, *Animal Estate*, chap. 3.

3. Kean, *Animal Rights*, 121–28.

4. Ibid., 90. For striking visual evidence of the importance of pets in late nineteenth- and early twentieth-century American animal welfare campaigns, see the National Museum of Animals and Society online exhibition, *Be Kind: A Visual History of Humane Education, 1880–1945*, http://www.bekindexhibit.org.

5. The literature on animal rights today is vast, but much of it is indebted to two early works: Peter Singer, *Animal Liberation*, rev. ed. (New York: Harper Perennial, 2009) (first published in 1975), and Tom Regan, *The Case for Animal Rights* (Berkeley: University of California Press, 1983).

6. Singer, *Animal Liberation*, chap. 1.

7. See Martha Nussbaum, "Beyond 'Compassion and Humanity': Justice for Nonhuman Animals," in her *Frontiers of Justice: Disability, Nationality, Species Membership* (Cambridge: Belknap Press of Harvard University Press, 2006), 325–56. The title refers to John Rawls's claim that animals deserve "compassion and humanity" but cannot be included in theories of justice because of their inability to enter into contracts. Singer himself argues not in terms of rights but in terms of interests and the capacity for suffering, but the phrase "animal rights" has come into common usage to refer generally to the idea that we should not differ in our treatment of animals and humans purely on the basis of species difference. Singer has also been enormously influential for those who do think in terms of rights; Nussbaum, for instance, draws on Singer's idea of sentience as a boundary for determining which species deserve justice.

8. John Berger, "Why Look at Animals?," in his *About Looking* (New York: Vintage, 1991) (first published in 1980), 3–28 (quotations on 11, 13). Laurie Shannon's study of Renaissance thinking, *Accommodated Animal*, argues similarly that Cartesianism destroyed an earlier understanding of animals and humans as participants in a single political order.

9. Berger makes the connection explicit in "Why Look at Animals?," 14–15. For arguments that tie pet keeping to urbanization and industrialization (but not necessarily to large-scale abuse), see Thomas, *Man and the Natural World*; Kete, *Beast in the Boudoir*; Franklin, *Animals and Modern Cultures*, chaps. 2 and 5.

10. Kean, *Animal Rights*, 26–31.

11. My thinking on this subject has been influenced by similar debates over women's history. See in particular Amanda Vickery, "Golden Age to Separate Spheres? A Review of the Categories and Chronology of English Women's History," *Historical Journal* 36 (1993): 383–414.

12. See Mandeville, *Fable of the Bees*. An early version appeared in 1705 as *The Grumbling Hive*, which was then expanded and first published as the *Fable* in 1714.

Bibliography

PRIMARY SOURCES

Manuscripts

British Library
Additional Manuscripts 22225, 22226, 31143, 31144 (Wentworth Family Papers)

Newspapers and Periodicals

Bond, Donald F., ed. *The Spectator*. 5 vols. Oxford: Clarendon Press, 1965.
————, ed. *The Tatler*. 3 vols. Oxford: Clarendon Press, 1987.
The Daily Advertiser.
The Gentleman's Magazine.
The Lounger. A Periodical Paper, Published at Edinburgh in the Years 1785 and 1786. 3rd corrected ed. 3 vols. Dublin: Printed for Messrs. Colles, Burnet, Moncrieffe, Gilbert, Exshaw, Burton, White, Byrne, H. Whitestone, W. Porter, Heery, McKenzie, Moor, and Dornin, 1787.
The Public Advertiser.
Stephens, John Calhoun, ed. *The Guardian*. Lexington: University Press of Kentucky, 1982.

Printed Primary Sources

An Act for Granting to His Majesty Certain Duties on Dogs, 36 Geo. III c. 124, 19 May 1796. In *The Statutes at Large, From the Thirty-Fifth Year of the Reign of King George the Third, to the Thirty-eighth Year of King George the Third, Inclusive . . . Being a Thirteenth Volume to Mr. Runnington's Edition, and a Seventeenth to Mr. Ruffhead's*, 415–17. London: George Eyre and Andrew Strahan, 1798.
[Aikin, John, and Anna Laetitia Barbauld]. *Evenings at Home, or The Juvenile Budget Opened*. 6 vols. London: J. Johnson, 1792–96.
Albin, Eleazar. *A Natural History of Birds. Illustrated with a Hundred and One Copper Plates, Curiously Engraven from the Life*. 3 vols. London: Printed for the Author, 1731.
[Baker, Henry]. *The Universal Spectator*. 3rd ed. 4 vols. London: Dr. Browne, R. Nutt, T. Astley, A. Millar, and J. Ward, 1756.
Barry, Edward. *On the Necessity of Adopting Some Measures to Reduce the Present Number of Dogs; with a Short Account of Hydrophobia, and the Most Approved Remedies Against It, a Letter, to*

Francis Annesley, Esq; M. P. for the Borough of Reading, and One of the Trustees of the British Museum, &c. &c. Reading: Smart and Cowslade, 1796.

Beauties of Natural History, or Elements of Zoography. London: Richardson and Urquhart, 1777.

[Beilby, Ralph]. A General History of Quadrupeds. The Figures Engraved on Wood by T. Bewick. Newcastle upon Tyne: S. Hodgson, R. Beilby, and T. Bewick, 1790.

Bentham, Jeremy. An Introduction to the Principles of Morals and Legislation. Oxford: Clarendon Press, 1907.

Berquin, Arnaud. The Children's Friend. New corrected ed. 4 vols. London: J. Stockdale, 1788.

Brookes, R[ichard]. A New and Accurate System of Natural History. 2nd ed. 6 vols. London: T. Carnan and F. Newbery, 1772.

Brown, Thomas. The Works of Mr. Thomas Brown, Serious and Comical, in Prose and Verse. 5th ed. 4 vols. London: Sam Briscoe, 1720.

Buffon, Georges-Louis Leclerc, Comte de. Natural History, General and Particular, by the Count de Buffon, Translated into English. Translated by William Smellie. 2nd ed. 9 vols. London: W. Strahan and T. Cadell, 1785.

———. The Natural History of Birds. From the French of the Count de Buffon. Illustrated with Engravings; and a Preface, Notes, and Additions, by the Translator. 9 vols. London: A. Strahan, T. Cadell, J. Murray, 1793.

Burnett, James, Lord Monboddo. Antient Metaphysics, or The Science of Universals. 6 vols. London: T. Cadell, 1779–99.

———. Of the Origin and Progress of Language. 6 vols. London: T. Cadell, 1773–92.

Burney, Frances. Cecilia, or Memoirs of an Heiress. Edited by Peter Sabor and Margaret Anne Doody. Oxford: Oxford University Press, 2009.

Campbell, R. The London Tradesman. London: T. Gardner, 1747.

Clark, George. An Address to Both Houses of Parliament: Containing Reasons for a Tax upon Dogs, and the Outlines of a Plan for That Purpose; and for Effectually Suppressing the Oppressive Practice of Impressing Seamen, and More Expeditiously Manning the Royal Navy. London: Johnson, 1791.

Coke, Mary. The Letters and Journals of Lady Mary Coke. Edited by James Archibald Home. 4 vols. Bath: Kingsmead Reprints, 1970.

Congreve, William. The Complete Plays of William Congreve. Edited by Herbert Davis. Chicago: University of Chicago Press, 1967.

Coventry, Francis. The History of Pompey the Little, or The Life and Adventures of a Lap-Dog. London: M. Cooper, 1751; 3rd ed., 1752.

———. The History of Pompey the Little, or The Life and Adventures of a Lap-Dog. Edited by Robert Adams Day. London: Oxford University Press, 1974.

———. The History of Pompey the Little, or The Life and Adventures of a Lap-Dog. Edited by Nicholas Hudson. Peterborough, Ont.: Broadview Press, 2008.

d'Obsonville, Foucher. Philosophic Essays on the Manners of Various Animals; with Observations on the Laws and Customs of Several Eastern Nations. Translated by Thomas Holcroft. London: John Johnson, 1784.

The Edinburgh Repository for Polite Literature: Consisting of Elegant, Instructive, and Entertaining Extracts, Selected from the Best Ancient and Modern Authors: Principally Designed to Introduce the Youth of Both Sexes to an Acquaintance with Useful and Ornamental Knowledge. Edinburgh: T. Brown, 1793.

Edwards, George. Gleanings of Natural History, Exhibiting the Figures of Quadrupeds, Birds, Insects, Plants, &c. Most of Which Have Not, Till Now, Been Either Figured or Described. 3 vols. London: Printed for the Author, 1758–64.

Exact and Sure Directions How to Dress and Keep Canary-Birds, and to Preserve Them in Health. And Also, How to Use and Keep the New Fashion Bird-Cages. London: Printed for the Author, n.d. [ca. 1710?].

Garrett, Aaron, ed. *Animal Rights and Souls in the Eighteenth Century.* 6 vols. Bristol: Thoemmes Press, 2000.

Gilbert, T[homas]. *Heads of a Bill for the Better Relief and Employment of the Poor, and for the Improvement of the Police of This Country. Submitted to the Consideration of the Members of Both Houses of Parliament.* Manchester: Harrop, 1786.

Goldsmith, Oliver. *An History of the Earth, and Animated Nature.* 8 vols. London: J. Nourse, 1774.

Greene, Edward Burnaby. *The Latin Odes of Mr. Gray, in English Verse, with an Ode on the Death of a Favorite Spaniel.* London: J. Ridley, 1775.

[Gregory, John]. *A Comparative View of the State and Faculties of Man, with Those of the Animal World.* London: J. Dodsley, 1765.

[Hanway, Jonas]. *A Journal of Eight Days Journey from Portsmouth to Kingston upon Thames; through Southampton, Wiltshire, &c.* London: H. Woodfall, 1756.

[Hilman, Daniel]. *Tusser Redivivus: Being Part of Mr. Thomas Tusser's Five Hundred Points of Husbandry; Namely, for the Months of November and December. With Notes. No. XI. XII.* London: J. Morphew, 1710.

Holland, Thomas, and John Holland. *Exercises for the Memory and Understanding: Consisting of Select Pieces in Prose & Verse; Together with a Series of Examinations Relative to Arts, Science, and History.* Manchester: George Nicholson, 1798.

Holt-White, Rashleigh, ed. *The Life and Letters of Gilbert White of Selborne.* 2 vols. London: J. Murray, 1901.

Hume, David. *A Treatise of Human Nature.* Edited by David Fate Norton and Mary J. Norton. Oxford: Oxford University Press, 2000.

Imitations and Translations from the Latin of Mr. Gray's Lyric Odes. London: J. Dodsley, 1777.

Johnson, Samuel. *A Dictionary of the English Language.* 2 vols. London: W. Strahan, 1755–56.

[Kendall, Edward Augustus]. *The Canary Bird: A Moral Fiction. Interspersed with Poetry.* London: E. Newbery, 1799.

———. *Keeper's Travels in Search of His Master.* London: E. Newbery, 1798.

———. *The Sparrow.* London: E. Newbery, 1798.

King, William. *Reasons and Proposals for Laying a Tax upon Dogs. Humbly Addressed to the Honourable House of Commons.* Reading: D. Henry, 1740.

Laroon, Marcellus. *The Criers and Hawkers of London: Engravings and Drawings by Marcellus Laroon.* Edited by Sean Shesgreen. Stanford: Stanford University Press, 1990.

Lavater, Johann Caspar. *Essays on Physiognomy; For the Promotion of the Knowledge and the Love of Mankind.* Translated by Thomas Holcroft. 3 vols. London: G. G. J. and J. Robinson, 1789.

Lawrence, John. *A Philosophical and Practical Treatise on Horses, and on the Moral Duties of Man towards the Brute Creation.* 2 vols. London: T. N. Longman, 1796–98.

Le Vaillant, François. *New Travels into the Interior Parts of Africa, by the Way of the Cape of Good Hope, in the Years 1783, 84, and 85.* 3 vols. London: G. G. J. and J. Robinson, 1796.

———. *Travels from the Cape of Good-Hope, into the Interior Parts of Africa, Including Many Interesting Anecdotes.* Translated by Elizabeth Helme. 2 vols. London: William Lane, 1790.

Mackenzie, Henry. *The Man of Feeling.* Edited by Maureen Harkin. Peterborough, Ont.: Broadview Press, 2005.

MacMahon, Thomas O'Brien. *Man's Capricious, Petulant, and Tyrannical Conduct Towards the Irrational and Inanimate Part of the Creation, Inquired into and Explained.* London: G. Riley, 1794.

Mandeville, Bernard. *The Fable of the Bees, or Private Vices, Public Benefits.* Edited by F. B. Kaye. Oxford: Clarendon Press, 1924.

Martin, Benjamin. *The Young Gentleman and Lady's Philosophy, in a Continued Survey of the Works of Nature and Art; By Way of Dialogue.* 3rd ed. 3 vols. London: W. Owen, 1781–82.

Masters, Mary. *Familiar Letters and Poems on Several Occasions.* London: D. Henry and R. Cave, 1755.

Mavor, William Fordyce. *Natural History, for the Use of Schools; Founded on the Linnæan Arrangement of Animals; with Popular Descriptions in the Manner of Goldsmith and Buffon.* London: R. Phillips, 1800.

Nairne, Edward. *The Dog-Tax, a Poem.* Canterbury: Printed for the Author, 1797.

A New Moral System of Natural History, or The Beauties of Nature Displayed; In the Most Singular, Curious, and Beautiful, Quadrupeds, and Birds. Vol. 6 of *The Historical Pocket Library, or Biographical Vade-Mecum,* 6 vols. Bath: S. Hazard for G. Riley, 1789.

Oswald, John. *The Cry of Nature, or An Appeal to Mercy and Justice, on Behalf of the Persecuted Animals.* London: J. Johnson, 1791.

Ottaway, Susannah R., and Ingrid H. Tague, eds. *Personal Narratives of Ageing.* Vol. 8 of *The History of Old Age in England, 1600–1800,* ed. Susannah R. Ottaway and Lynn Botelho, 8 vols. London: Pickering and Chatto, 2009.

The Parliamentary History of England, from the Earliest Period to the Year 1803. Vol. 32. London: T. C. Hansard, 1818.

Pennant, Thomas. *British Zoology.* 4 vols. London: Benjamin White, 1768.

———. *History of Quadrupeds.* (3rd ed. of *Synopsis of Quadrupeds.*) 2 vols. London: B. and J. White, 1793.

———. *Synopsis of Quadrupeds.* Chester: J. Monk, 1771.

Pepys, Samuel. *The Diary of Samuel Pepys.* Edited by Robert Latham and William Matthews. 11 vols. Berkeley: University of California Press, 1970–83.

Percival, Thomas. *A Father's Instructions; Consisting of Moral Tales, Fables, and Reflections Designed to Promote the Love of Virtue, a Taste for Knowledge, and an Early Acquaintance with the Works of Nature.* New ed. London: W. Osborne, T. Griffin, H. Mozley and Co., 1796.

[Phillips, Sir Richard]. *The Rational Brutes, or Talking Animals.* London: Tegg and Dewick, for Vernor and Hood, 1799.

Piozzi, Hester Lynch. *The Piozzi Letters: Correspondence of Hester Lynch Piozzi, 1784–1821 (Formerly Mrs. Thrale).* Edited by Edward A. Bloom and Lillian D. Bloom. 6 vols. Newark: University of Delaware Press, 1989–2002.

Poems by Eminent Ladies. 2 vols. London: R. Baldwin, 1755.

Pope, Alexander. *The Rape of the Lock.* In *The Rape of the Lock, and Other Poems,* ed. Geoffrey Tillotson. Vol. 2 of Alexander Pope, *Poems,* ed. John Butt, 8 vols. New Haven: Yale University Press, 1951–69.

Pratt, Samuel Jackson. *Gleanings in England; Descriptive of the Countenance, Mind and Character of the Country.* 3rd ed. 3 vols. London: T. N. Longman and O. Rees, 1801–3.

[———]. *Liberal Opinions, Upon Animals, Man, and Providence. In Which Are Introduced, Anecdotes of a Gentleman. Addressed to the Right Hon. Lady Ch***th. By Courtney Melmoth.* 6 vols. London: G. Robinson, J. Bew, 1775–77.

Primatt, Humphry. *A Dissertation on the Duty of Mercy and Sin of Cruelty to Brute Animals.* London: R. Hett, 1776.

Raff, Georg Christian. *A System of Natural History, Adapted for the Instruction of Youth, in the Form of a Dialogue.* 2 vols. London: J. Johnson, G. G. and J. Robinson, 1796.

Sibly, Ebenezer. *Magazine of Natural History. Comprehending the Whole Science of Animals, Plants, and Minerals; Divided into Distinct Parts, the Characters Separately Described, and Systematically Arranged.* 14 vols. London: Printed for the Proprietor, 1794–1807.

Smellie, William. *The Philosophy of Natural History.* 2 vols. Dublin: William Porter, 1790.

Smollett, Tobias. *The Adventures of Sir Launcelot Greaves.* 2 vols. London: J. Coote, 1762.

———. *Humphry Clinker.* Edited by Shaun Regan. New York: Penguin, 2008.

Some Considerations on the Game Laws, Suggested by the Late Motion of Mr. Curwen for the Repeal of the Present System. London: T. Egerton, 1796.

Southey, Robert. *Southey's Common-Place Book, Fourth Series: Original Memoranda, Etc.* Edited by John Wood Warter. London: Longman, Brown, Green, and Longmans, 1851.

[Taylor, Charles]. *Surveys of Nature, Historical, Moral, and Entertaining, Exhibiting the Principles of Natural Science in Various Branches.* 2 vols. London: C. Taylor, 1787.

[Taylor, Thomas]. *A Vindication of the Rights of Brutes.* London: Edward Jeffery, 1792.

Topsell, Edward. *The Historie of Foure-Footed Beastes.* London: William Iaggard [Jaggard], 1607.

Trimmer, Sarah. "The Dog." In *The Family Magazine, or A Repository of Religious Instruction, and Rational Amusement,* June 1788, 402–8.

———. *An Easy Introduction to the Knowledge of Nature, and Reading the Holy Scriptures. Adapted to the Capacities of Children.* London: Printed for the Author, 1780.

———. *Fabulous Histories. Designed for the Instruction of Children, Respecting Their Treatment of Animals.* London: T. Longman, G. G. J. and J. Robinson, J. Johnson, 1786.

Trimmer, Tommy. *Tommy Trimmer's Historical Account, of Beasts, Reptiles, Fishes, Birds. An Entirely New Edition, Never Before Published. Adorned with Cuts Entirely New.* London: J. Mackenzie, n.d. [ca. 1800?].

Varlo, Charles. *Schemes Offered for the Perusal and Consideration of the Legislature, Freeholders, and Public in General: Shewing the Many Evils That Might Be Prevented, and the Good That Would Accrue to the Public, Were They Improved, and Enacted into Laws.* London: J. Chapman, 1775.

Ventum, Harriet. *Surveys of Nature: A Sequel to Mrs. Trimmer's Introduction; Being Familiar Descriptions of Some Popular Subjects in Natural Philosophy, Adapted to the Capacities of Children.* London: John Radcock, 1802.

Walpole, Horace. *The Yale Edition of Horace Walpole's Correspondence.* Edited by W. S. Lewis. 48 vols. New Haven: Yale University Press, 1937–83.

Ward, Samuel. *A Modern System of Natural History.* 12 vols. London: F. Newbery, 1775–76.

White, Gilbert. *Gilbert White's Journals.* Edited by Walter Johnson. Cambridge: MIT Press, 1971.

———. *The Natural History and Antiquities of Selborne, in the County of Southampton: With Engravings, and an Appendix.* London: T. Bensley, 1789.

Young, Thomas. *An Essay on Humanity to Animals.* London: T. Cadell, Jun. and W. Davies, 1798.

SECONDARY SOURCES

Allen, David Elliston. *Naturalists and Society: The Culture of Natural History in Britain, 1700–1900.* Aldershot: Ashgate, 2001.

Anderson, Virginia DeJohn. *Creatures of Empire: How Domestic Animals Transformed Early America.* Oxford: Oxford University Press, 2004.

Asfour, Amal, and Paul Williamson. "Gainsborough's Wit." *Journal of the History of Ideas* 58, no. 3 (1997): 479–501.

Barker-Benfield, G. J. *The Culture of Sensibility: Sex and Society in Eighteenth-Century Britain*. Chicago: University of Chicago Press, 1992.

Berg, Maxine. *Luxury and Pleasure in Eighteenth-Century Britain*. Oxford: Oxford University Press, 2005.

Berg, Maxine, and Elizabeth Eger. "The Rise and Fall of the Luxury Debates." In *Luxury in the Eighteenth Century: Debates, Desires, and Delectable Goods*, ed. Maxine Berg and Elizabeth Eger, 7–27. Houndmills, Basingstoke: Palgrave Macmillan, 2003.

Berger, John. *About Looking*. New York: Vintage, 1991.

Berglund, Lisa. "Oysters for Hodge, or Ordering Society, Writing Biography, and Feeding the Cat." *Journal for Eighteenth-Century Studies* 33, no. 4 (2010): 631–45.

Berry, Christopher. *The Idea of Luxury: A Conceptual and Historical Investigation*. Cambridge: Cambridge University Press, 1994.

Berry, Helen. "Polite Consumption: Shopping in Eighteenth-Century England." *Transactions of the Royal Historical Society* 12 (2002): 375–94.

Blackwell, Mark, ed. *The Secret Life of Things: Animals, Objects, and It-Narratives in Eighteenth-Century England*. Lewisburg: Bucknell University Press, 2007.

Blaisdell, John D. "An Ounce of Prevention Causes a Ton of Concern: Rabies and the English Dog Tax of 1796." *Veterinary History*, new ser., 10 (2000–2001): 129–46.

Bloomfield, Anne, and Ruth Watts. "Pedagogue of the Dance: The Dancing Master as Educator in the Long Eighteenth Century." *History of Education* 37, no. 4 (2008): 605–18.

Bodson, Liliane. "Motivations for Pet-Keeping in Ancient Greece and Rome: A Preliminary Survey." In *Companion Animals and Us: Exploring the Relationships Between People and Pets*, ed. Anthony L. Podberscek, Elizabeth S. Paul, and James A. Serpell, 27–41. Cambridge: Cambridge University Press, 2000.

Bokhorst, Matthys. "François Le Vaillant: His Life and Work." In Quinton and Lewin Robinson, *François Le Vaillant*, 1:1–28.

Borsay, Peter. *The English Urban Renaissance: Culture and Society in the Provincial Town, 1660–1770*. Oxford: Clarendon Press, 1989.

Braunschneider, Theresa. "The Lady and the Lapdog: Mixed Ethnicity in Constantinople, Fashionable Pets in Britain." In *Humans and Other Animals in Eighteenth-Century British Culture: Representation, Hybridity, Ethics*, ed. Frank Palmeri, 31–48. Aldershot: Ashgate, 2006.

Brewer, John. *The Pleasures of the Imagination: English Culture in the Eighteenth Century*. New York: Farrar, Straus and Giroux, 1997.

———. *The Sinews of Power: War, Money, and the English State, 1688–1783*. New York: Knopf, 1989.

Brewer, John, and Roy Porter, eds. *Consumption and the World of Goods*. London: Routledge, 1993.

Brown, Christopher Leslie. *Moral Capital: Foundations of British Abolitionism*. Chapel Hill: University of North Carolina Press for the Omohundro Institute of Early American History and Culture, 2006.

Brown, Laura. *Fables of Modernity: Literature and Culture in the English Eighteenth Century*. Ithaca: Cornell University Press, 2001.

———. *Homeless Dogs and Melancholy Apes: Humans and Other Animals in the Modern Literary Imagination*. Ithaca: Cornell University Press, 2010.

Bryant, Julius. "The Dark Side of the Kitten: A Wright of Derby for Kenwood." *Apollo* 144, no. 418 (1996): 18–19.

———. *Kenwood: Paintings in the Iveagh Bequest.* New Haven: Yale University Press, 2003.

Carey, Daniel. "An Empire of Credit: English, Scottish, Irish, and American Contexts." In *The Empire of Credit: The Financial Revolution in the British Atlantic World, 1688–1815,* ed. Daniel Carey and Christopher J. Findlay, 1–22. Dublin: Irish Academic Press, 2011.

Carlisle, Nancy C. "The Chewed Chair Leg and the Empty Collar: Mementos of Pet Ownership in New England." In *New England's Creatures: 1400–1900, Dublin Seminar for New England Folklife; Annual Proceedings,* ed. Peter Benes, 130–46. Boston: Boston University Press, 1993.

Carruthers, Bruce G. *City of Capital: Politics and Markets in the English Financial Revolution.* Princeton: Princeton University Press, 1996.

Carter, Philip. "Men About Town: Representations of Foppery and Masculinity in Early Eighteenth-Century Urban Culture." In *Gender in Eighteenth-Century England: Roles, Representations, and Responsibilities,* ed. Hannah Barker and Elaine Chalus, 32–57. London: Longman, 1997.

Cooke, Steve. "Duties to Companion Animals." *Res Publica* 17 (2011): 261–74.

Craske, Matthew. "Representations of Domestic Animals in Britain." In *Hounds in Leash: The Dog in Eighteenth- and Nineteenth-Century Sculpture,* ed. Jonathan Wood and Stephen Feeke, 40–53. Exh. cat. Leeds: Henry Moore Institute, 2000.

Curth, Louise Hill. *The Care of Brute Beasts: A Social and Cultural Study of Veterinary Medicine in Early Modern England.* Boston: Brill, 2010.

Darnton, Robert. *The Great Cat Massacre and Other Episodes in French Cultural History.* New York: Vintage, 1985.

de Vries, Jan. "Between Purchasing Power and the World of Goods: Understanding the Household Economy in Early Modern Europe." In Brewer and Porter, *Consumption and the World of Goods,* 85–132.

Dickson, P. G. M. *The Financial Revolution in England: A Study in the Development of Public Credit, 1688–1756.* New York: St. Martin's Press, 1967.

Donald, Diana. *Picturing Animals in Britain, 1750–1850.* New Haven: Yale University Press for the Paul Mellon Centre for Studies in British Art, 2007.

Douthwaite, Julia V. *The Wild Girl, Natural Man, and the Monster: Dangerous Experiments in the Age of Enlightenment.* Chicago: University of Chicago Press, 2002.

Egerton, Judy. *Wright of Derby.* Exh. cat. New York: Metropolitan Museum of Art; London: Tate Gallery Publications, 1990.

Ehrman, John. *The Years of Acclaim.* Vol. 1 of *The Younger Pitt.* London: Constable and Co., 1969.

Ellis, Markman. *The Politics of Sensibility: Race, Gender, and Commerce in the Sentimental Novel.* Cambridge: Cambridge University Press, 1996.

———. "Suffering Things: Lapdogs, Slaves, and Counter-Sensibility." In Blackwell, *Secret Life of Things,* 92–113.

Empson, William. *The Structure of Complex Words.* Norfolk, Conn.: New Directions, [1951].

Erikson, Philippe. "The Social Significance of Pet-Keeping Among Amazonian Indians." In *Companion Animals and Us: Exploring the Relationships Between People and Pets,* ed. Anthony L. Podberscek, Elizabeth S. Paul, and James A. Serpell, 7–26. Cambridge: Cambridge University Press, 2000.

Estabrook, Carl B. *Urbane and Rustic England: Cultural Ties and Social Spheres in the Provinces, 1660–1780*. Stanford: Stanford University Press, 1998.

Fawcett, Trevor. "Dance and Teachers of Dance in Eighteenth-Century Bath." *Bath History* 2 (1988): 27–48.

Festa, Lynn. "Person, Animal, Thing: The 1796 Dog Tax and the Right to Superfluous Things." *Eighteenth-Century Life* 33, no. 2 (2009): 1–44.

Finn, Margot. "Women, Consumption, and Coverture in England, c. 1760–1860." *Historical Journal* 39 (1996): 703–22.

Flint, Christopher. "Speaking Objects: The Circulation of Stories in Eighteenth-Century Prose Fiction." *PMLA* 113, no. 2 (1998): 212–26.

Franklin, Adrian. *Animals and Modern Cultures: A Sociology of Human-Animal Relations in Modernity*. Los Angeles: Sage, 1999.

Fudge, Erica. "A Left-Handed Blow: Writing the History of Animals." In *Representing Animals*, ed. Nigel Rothfels, 3–18. Bloomington: Indiana University Press, 2002.

———. *Perceiving Animals: Humans and Beasts in Early Modern English Culture*. New York: St. Martin's Press, 2000.

———. *Pets*. Stocksfield, UK: Acumen, 2008.

Fudge, Erica, Ruth Gilbert, and Susan Wiseman, eds. *At the Borders of the Human: Beasts, Bodies, and Natural Philosophy in the Early Modern Period*. Houndmills: Macmillan, 1999.

Garrett, Aaron. "Francis Hutcheson and the Origin of Animal Rights." *Journal of the History of Philosophy* 45, no. 2 (2007): 243–65.

Gilmour, Ian. *Riot, Risings, and Revolution: Governance and Violence in Eighteenth-Century England*. London: Pimlico, 1993.

Girouard, Mark. *Life in the English Country House: A Social and Architectural History*. New Haven: Yale University Press, 1978.

Glenn, Ian. "Introduction." In François Le Vaillant, *Travels into the Interior of Africa via the Cape of Good Hope*, trans. and ed. Ian Glenn, with Catherine Lauga Du Plessis and Ian Farlam, vol. 1, xi–lx. Cape Town: Van Riebeeck Society for the Publication of South African Historical Documents, 2007.

———. "Primate Time: Rousseau, Levaillant, Marais." *Current Writing: Text and Reception in Southern Africa* 18, no. 1 (2006): 61–77.

Glukin, Neil Dana. "Pet Birds and Cages of the Eighteenth Century." *Early American Life* 8 (1977): 38–41, 59.

Grier, Katherine C. *Pets in America: A History*. Chapel Hill: University of North Carolina Press, 2006.

Griffin, Emma. *England's Revelry: A History of Popular Sports and Pastimes, 1660–1830*. Oxford: Oxford University Press for the British Academy, 2005.

Guillery, Peter. *The Small House in Eighteenth-Century London: A Social and Architectural History*. New Haven: Published for the Paul Mellon Centre for Studies in British Art by Yale University Press in association with English Heritage, 2004.

Halttunen, Karen. "Humanitarianism and the Pornography of Pain in Anglo-American Culture." *American Historical Review* 100, no. 2 (1995): 303–34.

Haraway, Donna. *The Companion Species Manifesto: Dogs, People, and Significant Otherness*. Chicago: Prickly Paradigm Press, 2003.

———. *When Species Meet*. Minneapolis: University of Minnesota Press, 2007.

Hay, Douglas, and Nicholas Rogers. *Eighteenth-Century English Society: Shuttles and Swords*. Oxford: Oxford University Press, 1997.

Hearne, Vicki. *Adam's Task: Calling Animals by Name*. New York: Knopf, 1986.

Herman, Bernard L. "Tabletop Conversations: Material Culture and Everyday Life in the Eighteenth-Century Atlantic World." In Styles and Vickery, *Gender, Taste, and Material Culture*, 37–59.

Irvine, Leslie. "Pampered or Enslaved? The Moral Dilemmas of Pets." *International Journal of Sociology and Social Policy* 24, no. 9 (2004): 5–17.

Janson, H. W. *Apes and Ape Lore in the Middle Ages and the Renaissance*. London: Warburg Institute, 1952.

Kean, Hilda. *Animal Rights: Political and Social Change in Britain Since 1800*. London: Reaktion Books, 1998.

Kenyon-Jones, Christine. *Kindred Brutes: Animals in Romantic-Period Writing*. Burlington, Vt.: Ashgate, 2001.

Kete, Kathleen. *The Beast in the Boudoir: Petkeeping in Nineteenth-Century Paris*. Berkeley: University of California Press, 1994.

Klein, Lawrence E. "Politeness for Plebes: Consumption and Social Identity in Early Eighteenth-Century England." In *The Consumption of Culture, 1600–1800: Image, Object, Text*, ed. Ann Bermingham and John Brewer, 362–82. London: Routledge, 1995.

Klinkenborg, Verlyn. *Timothy, or Notes of an Abject Reptile*. New York: Knopf, 2006.

Kowaleski-Wallace, Elizabeth. *Consuming Subjects: Women, Shopping, and Business in the Eighteenth Century*. New York: Columbia University Press, 1997.

Kuchta, David. *The Three-Piece Suit and Modern Masculinity: England, 1550–1850*. Berkeley: University of California Press, 2002.

Laird, Mark, and Alicia Weisberg-Roberts, eds. *Mrs. Delany and Her Circle*. Exh. cat. New Haven: Yale Center for British Art: London: Sir John Soane's Museum, in association with Yale University, 2010.

Landry, Donna. *Noble Brutes: How Eastern Horses Transformed English Culture*. Baltimore: Johns Hopkins University Press, 2008.

Langford, Paul. *A Polite and Commercial People: England, 1727–1783*. Oxford: Clarendon Press, 1989.

Lupton, Christina. "The Knowing Book: Authors, It-Narratives, and Objectification in the Eighteenth Century." *Novel* 39, no. 3 (2006): 402–20.

MacDonogh, Katharine. *Reigning Cats and Dogs*. New York: St. Martin's Press, 1999.

Malcolmson, Robert W. *Popular Recreations in English Society, 1700–1850*. Cambridge: Cambridge University Press, 1973.

McKendrick, Neil, John Brewer, and J. H. Plumb. *The Birth of a Consumer Society: The Commercialization of Eighteenth-Century England*. Bloomington: Indiana University Press, 1982.

Meacham, Sarah Hand. "Pets, Status, and Slavery in the Late-Eighteenth-Century Chesapeake." *Journal of Southern History* 77, no. 3 (2011): 521–54.

Meester, Jurgens. "Le Vaillant's Mammal Paintings." In Quinton and Lewin Robinson, *François Le Vaillant*, 2:1–24.

Mintz, Sidney W. *Sweetness and Power: The Place of Sugar in Modern History*. New York: Penguin, 1985.

Molineux, Catherine. "Hogarth's Fashionable Slaves: Moral Corruption in Eighteenth-Century London." *English Literary History* 72 (2005): 495–520.

Muldrew, Craig, and Stephen King. "Cash, Wages, and the Economy of Makeshifts in England, 1650–1800." In *Experiencing Wages: Social and Cultural Aspects of Wage Forms in Europe Since 1500*, ed. Peter Scholliers and Leonard Schwarz, 155–80. Oxford: Berghahn Books, 2003.

Mullan, John. *Sentiment and Sociability: The Language of Feeling in the Eighteenth Century*. Oxford: Clarendon Press, 1988.

Musser, Joseph F., Jr. "Sir Joshua Reynolds's 'Mrs. Abington as "Miss Prue."'" *South Atlantic Quarterly* 83 (Spring 1984): 176–92.

Nagel, Thomas. "What Is It Like to Be a Bat?" *Philosophical Review* 83, no. 4 (1974): 435–50.

Nash, Richard. *Wild Enlightenment: The Borders of Human Identity in the Eighteenth Century*. Charlottesville: University of Virginia Press, 2003.

North, Douglass C., and Barry R. Weingast. "Constitutions and Commitment: The Evolution of Institutions Governing Public Choice in Seventeenth-Century England." *Journal of Economic History* 49, no. 4 (1989): 803–32.

Nussbaum, Martha. *Frontiers of Justice: Disability, Nationality, Species Membership*. Cambridge: Belknap Press of Harvard University Press, 2006.

O'Brien, Patrick K. "The Political Economy of British Taxation, 1660–1815." *Economic History Review* 41, no. 1 (1988): 1–32.

Osborne, Catherine. *Dumb Beasts and Dead Philosophers: Humanity and the Humane in Ancient Philosophy and Literature*. Oxford: Clarendon Press, 2007.

Outram, Dorinda. *Panorama of the Enlightenment*. Los Angeles: J. Paul Getty Museum, 2006.

Paulson, Ronald. *Popular and Polite Art in the Age of Hogarth and Fielding*. Notre Dame: University of Notre Dame Press, 1979.

Penny, N. B. "Dead Dogs and Englishmen." *Connoisseur* 192 (1976): 298–303.

Perkins, David. *Romanticism and Animal Rights*. Cambridge: Cambridge University Press, 2003.

Plumb, Christopher. "Exotic Animals in Eighteenth-Century Britain." PhD diss., University of Manchester, 2010.

Plumb, J. H. *The Commercialisation of Leisure in Eighteenth-Century England*. Reading: University of Reading, 1973.

Pointon, Marcia. *Hanging the Head: Portraiture and Social Formation in Eighteenth-Century England*. New Haven: Yale University Press, 1993.

Porter, David. *The Chinese Taste in Eighteenth-Century England*. Cambridge: Cambridge University Press, 2010.

Posner, Donald. *Watteau: A Lady at Her Toilet*. New York: Viking, 1973.

Postle, Martin. *Angels and Urchins: The Fancy Picture in Eighteenth-Century British Art*. Exh. cat. Nottingham: Djanogly Art Gallery; Lund Humphries, 1998.

———, ed. *Joshua Reynolds: The Creation of Celebrity*. Exh. cat. London: Tate Publishing, 2005.

Quinton, J. C., and A. M. Lewin Robinson, eds. *François Le Vaillant, Traveller in South Africa, and His Collection of 165 Water-Colour Paintings, 1781–1784*. 2 vols. Cape Town: Library of Parliament, 1973.

Raber, Karen. "From Sheep to Meat, from Pets to People: Animal Domestication, 1600–1800." In *A Cultural History of Animals in the Age of Enlightenment*, ed. Matthew Senior, 73–99. Oxford: Berg, 2007.

Regan, Tom. *The Case for Animal Rights*. Berkeley: University of California Press, 1983.

Reinhardt, Leslie. "Serious Daughters: Dolls, Dress, and Female Virtue in the Eighteenth Century." *American Art* 20, no. 2 (2006): 32–55.

Retford, Kate. *The Art of Domestic Life: Family Portraiture in Eighteenth-Century England*. New Haven: Yale University Press for the Paul Mellon Centre for Studies in British Art, 2006.

Ribeiro, Aileen. "Costuming the Part: A Discourse of Fashion and Fiction in the Image of the Actress in England, 1776–1812." In *Notorious Muse: The Actress in British Art and*

Culture, ed. Robyn Asleson, 105–27. Exh. cat. New Haven: Yale University Press for the Paul Mellon Centre for Studies in British Art, 2003.

———. *Dress and Morality*. New ed. Oxford: Berg, 2003.

———. *Dress in Eighteenth-Century Europe, 1715–1789*. Rev. ed. New Haven: Yale University Press, 2002.

Ritvo, Harriet. *The Animal Estate: The English and Other Creatures in the Victorian Age*. Cambridge: Harvard University Press, 1987.

———. "The Emergence of Modern Pet-Keeping." In *Animals and People Sharing the World*, ed. Andrew N. Rowan, 13–31. Hanover: University Press of New England, 1988.

———. "Learning from Animals: Natural History for Children in the Eighteenth and Nineteenth Centuries." *Children's Literature* 13, no. 1 (1985): 72–93.

Robbins, Louise E. *Elephant Slaves and Pampered Parrots: Exotic Animals in Eighteenth-Century Paris*. Baltimore: Johns Hopkins University Press, 2002.

Rogers, Katharine M. *Cat*. London: Reaktion Books, 2006.

———. *The Cat and the Human Imagination: Feline Images from Bast to Garfield*. Ann Arbor: University of Michigan Press, 1998.

Rosenthal, Michael, and Martin Myrone, eds. *Gainsborough*. Exh. cat. London: Tate Publishing, 2002.

Schaffer, Simon. "The Consuming Flame: Electrical Showmen and Tory Mystics in the World of Goods." In Brewer and Porter, *Consumption and the World of Goods*, 489–526.

Schiebinger, Londa. *Nature's Body: Gender in the Making of Modern Science*. Boston: Beacon Press, 1993.

Schwarz, L. D. *London in the Age of Industrialisation: Entrepreneurs, Labour Force, and Living Conditions, 1700–1850*. Cambridge: Cambridge University Press, 1992.

Sekora, John. *Luxury: The Concept in Western Thought from Eden to Smollett*. Baltimore: Johns Hopkins University Press, 1977.

Serpell, James A. "Pet-Keeping in Non-Western Societies: Some Popular Misconceptions." In *Animals and People Sharing the World*, ed. Andrew N. Rowan, 33–52. Hanover: University Press of New England, 1988.

Shannon, Laurie. *The Accommodated Animal: Cosmopolity in Shakespearean Locales*. Chicago: University of Chicago Press, 2013.

Shaw, Margaret. "Hottentots, Bushmen, and Bantu." In Quinton and Lewin Robinson, *François Le Vaillant*, 1:127–51.

Shawe-Taylor, Desmond. *The Georgians: Eighteenth-Century Portraiture and Society*. London: Barrie and Jenkins, 1990.

Shell, Marc. "The Family Pet." *Representations* 15 (1986): 121–53.

Shyllon, F. O. *Black Slaves in Britain*. London: Oxford University Press for the Institute of Race Relations, 1974.

Siegfried, Susan L. "Engaging the Audience: Sexual Economies of Vision in Joseph Wright." *Representations* 68 (1999): 34–58.

Singer, Peter. *Animal Liberation*. Rev. ed. New York: Harper Perennial, 2009.

Sørensen, Madeleine Pinault. "Portraits of Animals, 1600–1800." In *A Cultural History of Animals in the Age of Enlightenment*, ed. Matthew Senior, 157–96. Oxford: Berg, 2007.

Spiegel, Marjorie. *The Dreaded Comparison: Human and Animal Slavery*. Rev. and exp. ed. New York: Mirror Books, 1996.

Steeves, H. Peter. "The Familiar Other and Feral Selves: Life at the Human/Animal Boundary." In *The Human/Animal Boundary: Historical Perspectives*, ed. Angela N. H.

Creager and William Chester Jordan, 228–64. Rochester: University of Rochester Press, 2002.

Steintrager, James. *Cruel Delight: Enlightenment Culture and the Inhuman.* Bloomington: Indiana University Press, 2004.

Stephens, F. G., and M. D. George. *Catalogue of Political and Personal Satires Preserved in the Department of Prints and Drawings in the British Museum.* 11 vols. London: By order of the Trustees, 1870–1945.

Steward, James Christen. *The New Child: British Art and the Origins of Modern Childhood, 1730–1830.* Exh. cat. Berkeley: University Art Museum and Pacific Film Archive, University of California, Berkeley, in association with the University of Washington Press, 1995.

Styles, John. "Custom or Consumption? Plebeian Fashion in Eighteenth-Century England." In Berg and Eger, *Luxury in the Eighteenth Century,* 103–15.

———. *The Dress of the People: Everyday Fashion in Eighteenth-Century England.* New Haven: Yale University Press, 2007.

———. "Lodging at the Old Bailey: Lodgings and Their Furnishing in Eighteenth-Century London." In Styles and Vickery, *Gender, Taste, and Material Culture,* 61–80.

———. "Manufacturing, Consumption, and Design in Eighteenth-Century England." In Brewer and Porter, *Consumption and the World of Goods,* 527–54.

Styles, John, and Amanda Vickery, eds. *Gender, Taste, and Material Culture in Britain and North America, 1700–1830.* New Haven: Yale Center for British Art, 2006.

Tague, Ingrid H. "Aristocratic Women and Ideas of Family in the Early Eighteenth Century." In *The Family in Early Modern England,* ed. Helen Berry and Elizabeth Foyster, 184–208. Cambridge: Cambridge University Press, 2007.

———. "Companions, Servants, or Slaves? Considering Animals in Eighteenth-Century England." *Studies in Eighteenth-Century Culture* 39 (2010): 103–22.

———. "Dead Pets: Satire and Sentiment in British Elegies and Epitaphs for Animals." *Eighteenth-Century Studies* 41, no. 3 (2008): 289–306.

———. "Eighteenth-Century English Debates on a Dog Tax." *Historical Journal* 51, no. 4 (2008): 901–20.

———. *Women of Quality: Accepting and Contesting Ideals of Femininity in England, 1690–1760.* Woodbridge: Boydell Press, 2002.

Tester, Keith. *Animals and Society: The Humanity of Animal Rights.* London: Routledge, 1991.

Thaddeus, Janice. "Swift's *Directions to Servants* and the Reader as Eavesdropper." *Studies in Eighteenth-Century Culture* 16 (1986): 107–23.

Thomas, Keith. *Man and the Natural World: Changing Attitudes in England, 1500–1800.* Oxford: Oxford University Press, 1983.

Thorp, Jennifer. "Mr. Isaac, Dancing-Master." *Dance Research: The Journal of the Society for Dance Research* 24, no. 2 (2006): 117–37.

Todd, Janet. *Sensibility: An Introduction.* London: Methuen, 1986.

Tuan, Yi-Fu. *Dominance and Affection: The Making of Pets.* New Haven: Yale University Press, 1984.

Vickery, Amanda. *Behind Closed Doors: At Home in Georgian England.* New Haven: Yale University Press, 2009.

———. *The Gentleman's Daughter: Women's Lives in Georgian England.* New Haven: Yale University Press, 1998.

———. "Golden Age to Separate Spheres? A Review of the Categories and Chronology of English Women's History." *Historical Journal* 36 (1993): 383–414.

Wahrman, Dror. *The Making of the Modern Self: Identity and Culture in Eighteenth-Century England.* New Haven: Yale University Press, 2004.

Walker-Meikle, Kathleen. *Medieval Pets.* Woodbridge: Boydell Press, 2012.

Walvin, James. *England, Slaves, and Freedom, 1776–1838.* Jackson: University Press of Mississippi, 1986.

Weatherill, Lorna. *Consumer Behaviour and Material Culture in Britain, 1660–1760.* London: Methuen, 1988.

Wendorf, Richard. *Sir Joshua Reynolds: The Painter in Society.* Cambridge: Harvard University Press, 1996.

White, Lynn, Jr. "The Historical Roots of Our Ecologic Crisis." *Science* 155, no. 3767 (1967): 1203–7.

Wills, Geoffrey. ". . . Whose Dog Are You?" *Country Life,* 4 April 1974, 804.

Wokler, Robert. "Tyson and Buffon on the Orang-Utan." *Studies on Voltaire and the Eighteenth Century* 155 (1976): 2301–19.

Wood, Marcus. *Blind Memory: Visual Representations of Slavery in England and America, 1780–1865.* New York: Routledge, 2000.

Wyett, Jodi L. "The Lap of Luxury: Lapdogs, Literature, and Social Meaning in the 'Long' Eighteenth Century." *Literature, Interpretation, Theory* 10 (2000): 275–301.

Index

Italic page numbers indicate illustrations.

Abel, Carl Friedrich, 183–84
Abington, Frances, 109–12, 111
abolitionism, 68–71, 89, 153
abuse of animals
  and abolitionist movement, 68–71, 153
  by elite, 153–55
  legislation against, 229
  by lower classes, 153–55, 165, 230
  opposition to (see humane movement)
  suffering as grounds for opposition to, 68–69, 179, 230–31
  Walpole on, 182, 218–19, 264 n. 132
accessories, fashion, pets as, 91–92, 105
accessories for pets
  birdcages, 26, 44, 54, 83–88
  bird organs, 44–48, 47
  chains, 41–42, 43, 244 n. 157
  dog beds, 44, 46
  dog collars, 40–41, 41, 42, 135, 244 n. 151
  housing, 44, 45, 46
  rise of market for, 15
  surviving examples of, 16
Accommodated Animal (Shannon), 267 n. 8
advertising
  cost of pets in, 33–37
  for lost dogs, 36–37, 40, 243 n. 133
  by menageries, 30, 31, 241 n. 85
  by pet shops, 14–16, 21, 26, 28–29
  of pets wanted, 22–23
affection, female, fickleness of, 107–8
affection between humans and animals, 11, 174–228. See also sensibility
  in dog tax debates, 164, 166–70
  in letters of Cowper, 182, 200, 209–12, 214, 217, 227

in letters of Walpole, 182, 200, 218–28
in letters of Wentworth, 174–77, 181, 200–209, 227
in letters of White, 182, 200, 209–10, 212–17, 227, 232
in new framework for femininity, 181, 182, 185–92
in new framework for masculinity, 181, 182, 192–200
vs. other humans, 140–47
recognition of value of, 177, 180–82
as substitute for relations with other humans, 5, 182, 227
in visual culture, 180–81, 182–200
for working animals vs. pets, 4
afterlife for animals, 70
agency of animals, 9
Aikin, John, Evenings at Home, 60–61, 67, 150–51
Albin, Eleazar, 24, 33, 87
Amorous Thief, The (print), 187
angling, 228, 229, 264 n. 132, 266 n. 195
animal(s). See also specific types
  impact on human history, 9
  use of term, 236 n. 19
animal-human boundary. See human-animal boundary
animal-human relations. See human-animal relations
Animal Liberation (Singer), 231, 266 n. 5, 267 n. 7
animal studies, 6–10
  assumptions behind work of, 7–8
  Singer in origins of field, 231
  treatment of animals as focus of, 7–8

Animated Nature (Wicksteed), 91–92, *93*
anthropomorphism, of pet baboon by Le Vaillant, 75, 82
anticruelty movement. *See* humane movement
antiquity, pet keeping in, 235 n. 13
apes
    vs. dogs, intelligence of, 59
    humanoid, definition of, 53
    vs. monkeys, use of terms, 246 n. 9
    similarity to humans, 50–62, 89
art, visual. *See* visual culture

baboons, 54, 73–83
Bank of England, 16–17
Barbauld, Anna Laetitia
    "Epitaph on a Green-Finch," 86
    Evenings at Home, 60–61, 67, 150–51
Barker, Samuel, 215
Barrington, Daines, 212, 214
Barry, Edward, 158–59, 162, 165, 239 n. 37
Battersea Dogs' Home, 230
beast, use of term, 236 n. 19
Beauties of Natural History (anonymous), 64
Beggar and His Dog, The (Kingsbury), 168, *169*
Bennett's (menagerie), 31, 242 n. 93
Bentham, Jeremy, 68, 179, 231
Bentley, Richard, 266 n. 191
Berg, Maxine, 139
Berger, John, 231
Berquin, Arnaud, *The Children's Friend,* 256 n. 18, 259 n. 80
Berry, Anne, 226
Berry, Mary, 226
Bess (hare), 210–11
Bettina (dog), 264 n. 130
bird(s). *See also* exotic birds; *specific types*
    accessories for, 26, 44–48, *47*
    breeding of, 23–24, 32
    cages for, 26, 44, 54, 83–88
    catching of, 23, 240 n. 43
    cost of buying, 33–36
    cost of keeping, 38
    food for, 38, 146–47
    fraud in sale of, 30, 241 n. 83
    individual sellers of, 24–25
    lower class ownership of, 178
    morality of caging, 54, 83–88

    as most common pet, 23
    in pet shops, 26–30
    in satires of fashionable men, 125
    training of, 34, 36, 48, 243 n. 116
    veterinary care for, 40
bird organs, 44–48, *47*
Boarding School Education (print), 122, *123*
Bodson, Liliane, 235 n. 13
Boers, Willem, 74, 78, 80
boundary crossing, pets as, 4–5. *See also* human-animal boundary
Bowles, Jane, 198
Boy and Rabbit (Raeburn), 198, *199*
Brandoin, Michel Vincent, *130*
breeding of pets
    birds, 23–24, 32
    dogs and wolves, 31
    in domestication, 65
    intentionality of, 240 n. 38
Brewer, John, 17
British Empire. *See* imperial growth
Brookes, Joshua, 30–31
Brookes, Richard, 59
Brown, Laura, 252 n. 30, 255 n. 88
Bryant, Julius, 251 n. 14
Buccleuch, Henry Scott, Duke of, 195–98
Buffon, Georges-Louis Leclerc, Comte de
    on affection in animals, 180
    on birds, 48, 57, 84, 87, 151–52, 257 n. 33
    on dogs, 95, 148, 149, 151, 180
    on domestication as mutually beneficial, 151–52, 181
    "Essay on the Degeneration of Animals," 63
    on human-animal boundary, 56–57, 61–62, 151
    Natural History, 12
    Natural History of Birds, 24, 84
    observations on pets by, 209
    plagiarism of works of, 20
    as source for Goldsmith, 12, 63, 95
    on speech as uniquely human, 57, 246 n. 20
Bull, John (character), 178
bullfinches, 34, 36, 87, 243 n. 116
Bum Shop, The (print), 102–4
Burney, Frances, 40
Butler, Samuel, 215

"Caesar and Pompey" (children's story), 19
cages, bird, 26, 44, 54, 83–88
Caius, John, 95, 96
Caldwell, James, *The Macarony Brothers*, 128–29, *130*
calendar, Julian, 243 n. 136, 259 n. 4
call birds, 23
canaries
    breeding of, 23–24, 32
    cost of buying, 34
    morality of caging, 87–88
    for sale in London, 32
    transformation from exotic to common, 23, 52, 92
Canonical Beau, The (Goldar), 108, *109*
cardinals, 21
caricatures. *See* satire
Carlisle, Nancy, 244 n. 159
Cartesianism, 7–8, 179, 231, 267 n. 8
Case for Animal Rights, The (Regan), 266 n. 5
Cato, Thomas, 26
cats
    vs. dogs, connotations of, 116
    food for, 38
    gendered as female, 116
    old maids associated with, 116–19
    as pets of poverty, 116
    resistance to domestication by, 63–64
    young girls associated with, 98–100, 116
cemeteries, pet, 1
chains, pets kept on, 41–42, *43*, 78–80, 244 n. 157
chastity, female, 187
children, as worthy of special attention, 190, 261 n. 39. *See also* girls
Children's Friend, The (Berquin), 256 n. 18, 259 n. 80
children's literature, as primary source, 11–12. *See also specific works*
Chimpanzee (Scotin), *51*
chimpanzees, 50–52, *51*, 53, 246 n. 8
China, "Oriental" style of imports from, 19
Chippendale workshop, 44
Christianity, on human use of animals, 62, 66–68, 94
Chute, John, 218, 221

civilization
    and abuse of animals, 153
    and domestication, dangers of, 64–66
Clark, George, 160–61, 164, 239 n. 37
class. *See* social class
Clavering, Thomas, 190
clothing. *See* fashion
Cobler's Hall (print), 44, *46*, 245 n. 161
cockatoos, 125
cockfighting, 153–55
Coke, Lady Mary
    on dog beds, 44
    on dog doctors, 40, 244 n. 146
    exotic birds bought by, 24–25
    at menageries, 30–31
collars
    dog, 40–41, *41, 42*, 135, 244 n. 151
    slave, 53, 245 n. 7
Collet, John, *45, 109, 143*
commerce in pets. *See* sale of pets
Commercialisation of Leisure in Eighteenth-Century England, The (Plumb), 237 n. 2
companions, pets as
    as defining characteristic, 4
    recognition of value of, 141, 171, 177
Comparative View of the State and Faculties of Man (Gregory), 65, 247 n. 42
Congreve, William, *Love for Love*, 110
consumerism. *See also* fashion
    eighteenth-century boom in, 15, 17–20
    emergence of culture of, 9–10, 15
    gendered aspects of, 18
    luxury as beneficial to, 139–40
    among non-elite, 18
    in rise of pet keeping, 15, 17–20
consumer revolution, 9–10, 17–18
consumers, pets as, 19, 37–41, 94. *See also* accessories for pets
Copley, John Singleton, 244 n. 157
Coquet, The (play), 107–8
Cork Rump or Chloe's Cushion, The (print), 102, *104*
costs
    of buying pets, 15, 33–37
    of dog collars, 40, 244 n. 151
    of keeping pets, 19, 22, 37–38, 159
Courtenay, John, 166, *167*
Covent Garden (London), bird market in, 26

Coventry, Francis. *See History of Pompey the Little, The*
Cowper, William
    affection for pets in letters of, 182, 200, 209–12, 214, 217, 227
    "Epitaph on a Hare," 210, 211–12
Crabbe, George, *The Library,* 225
Cries of London (Merke), 27
Cross, Harriett, 41
Crotchet, P., *Grown Ladies Taught to Dance,* 120–22, *121*
cultural differences, vs. human-animal boundary, 60

Daily Advertiser (newspaper), 15
dancing masters, 120–23
Dawe, Philip, *A New Fashion'd Head Dress,* 112–13, *113*
death of pets, owners' grief over, 174–77, 205–6, 222–26
Deceitful Kisses (print), 129–31
"Defence of our Attachment to Animals" (Pratt), 148–49
Deffand, Madame du, 222, 224, 226
Dent, John, 162–63, 164, 165, 170
Descartes, René, 7–8, 179, 231
Disagreeable Intrusion, The (print), 114–15
Discovery, The (print), 129
divine spirit, as unique human characteristic, 57
Dixon, John, *196*
d'Obsonville, Foucher, 64
doctors, dog, 38–40, 244 n. 146
Dodd, Daniel, *121*
dogs. *See also* hunting dogs; lapdogs
    advertising for lost, 36–37, 40, 243 n. 133
    advertising for wanted, 22–23
    affection of, for masters, 180
    vs. apes, intelligence of, 59
    beds for, 44, *46*
    vs. cats, connotations of, 116
    classification by use, 7, 95–96
    collars for, 40–41, *41, 42,* 135, 244 n. 151
    cost of keeping, 37–38
    domestication of, 64, 149–52
    fashion trends in breeds of, 92
    food for, 37–38, *39,* 159–62
    gendered as male, 116

houses for, 44
indoor vs. outdoor, 19
as luxuries, 158–59, 163–64, 170–72
in menageries, 30–31
in pet shops, 28
population of, 178, 239 n. 37
portraits of, 183–84, 194–98
as servants, 150–52, 171
as slaves, 149–50
sporting, 162–63, 170
superiority over other pets, 148–49
tax on ownership of (*see* dog tax)
veterinary care for, 38–40
of Walpole, 193, 218–27, 264 n. 130
of Wentworth, 38
wolves bred with, 31
as working animals vs. pets, 4, 7, 40, 96, 162–63, 170
dog tax, 141, 157–72
    elite as target of, 161–63, 171
    exemptions proposed for, 163–64
    lower classes as target of, 158–61, 167–68
    as luxury tax, 158, 159, 163–64, 170–72
    origins of, 158
    parliamentary debates over, 158, 163–71, 178
domestication
    animals' resistance to, 63–64
    critics of, 64–66, 83–84
    as demonstration of human power over animals, 62–64
    of dogs, 64, 149–52
    as moral yardstick, 60
    as mutually beneficial, 151–52, 181
    and slavery, links between, 62–68, 89, 151, 232
domesticity
    in definition of pet, 3–4
    in images of femininity, 192
domestic spaces
    indoor vs. outdoor dogs in, 19
    livestock in, end of, 19
    pets in images of, 192
    wealth's impact on configuration of, 17, 238 n. 12
Dominance and Affection (Tuan), 4
dominion, human, 62, 66–68, 72, 94
Donald, Diana, 194–95

Dressing the Kitten (Wright), 98–100, *99*, 251
  n. 14

East India Company, 21, 24
economy, British, financial revolution in,
  9–10, 16–17
Edwards, George
  Gleanings of Natural History, 21
  at menageries, 31, 242 n. 90
  observation of animals by, 183
  pets of, 209
  plagiarism of images of, 20
  on slave trade, 52–53
Eger, Elizabeth, 139
elite
  abuse of animals by, 153–55
  affection for animals vs. humans among,
    140–47
  humane movement's critique of, 153–57
  menageries aimed at, 30–32
  segregation of servants of, 17
elite, pets of, 11, 138–73
  accessories for, 40–41
  advertising for lost dogs, 37
  exotic pets as status symbols, 52
  food for, 37–38
  servants compared to, 140–41
  sources of information on, 177
  as target of dog tax, 161–63, 171
  treatment of, vs. servants, 140–47
  as waste of resources, 140, 145
Elliot, Sir Gilbert, 222
Elopement, The (print), 114
emotional bonds. *See* affection
Empire, British. *See* imperial growth
Enlightenment, importance of animals in, 6
entertainment
  caged songbirds as, 84, 88
  as defining characteristic of pets, 4
environmental history, animals' role in, 9
"Epitaph on a Green-Finch" (Barbauld),
  86
"Epitaph on a Hare" (Cowper), 210, 211–12
equality for animals, 70, 248 n. 61
Essay on Humanity to Animals (Young), 68
Essay on Man (Pope), 224
"Essay on the Degeneration of Animals"
  (Buffon), 63

Estabrook, Carl, 17, 38, 238 n. 12
Evenings at Home (Aikin and Barbauld),
  60–61, 67, 150–51
exotic animals. *See also specific types*
  cost of buying, 33–36
  diversity of, 14–15, 21, 53
  individual sellers of, 24–25
  in menageries, 30–32
  in natural histories, 20
  rise of availability of, 20–21
  sale of, in London, 16, 21
  slavery linked with, 52–54
  as status symbols for elite, 52
  taxidermy of, 20
  warfare in availability of, 20–21, 52
exotic birds
  breeding of, 23–24
  cost of buying, 33–36
  diversity of, 21
  individual sellers of, 24–25
  in menageries, 30–31
  morality of caging, 87–88
  in pet shops, 26–30
  taxidermy of, 20
exotic imports, impact on fashion and
  consumerism, 19

Fable of the Bees (Mandeville), 139, 233, 267
  n. 12
Fabulous Histories (Trimmer), 67, 146–47,
  150, 257 n. 30
family
  of birds, 86
  pets as part of, 5, 201–6
famine, 17
"fancy pictures," 181, 190–92
fashion, 10, 91–137
  caricatures of (*see* satire)
  in Coventry's *Pompey*, 131–37
  as disposable, 101
  emergence of modern sense of, 92
  exotic imports' impact on, 19
  in headdresses, 101–2
  as luxury, critics of, 92–94
  of men, 97, 120–31
  of modish women, 97, 100–112
  of old maids, 97, 112–19
  pets as accessories in, 91–92, 105

fashion (continued)
    and pets as sexual surrogates, 105–12,
        114, 133–34
    young girls' interest in, 97–100
fashionable goods, pets as, 92, 94
fashionable pets, trends in, 92
favoritism, in definition of pet, 3–4
femininity
    cats associated with, 100
    lapdogs associated with, 100–101,
        138–39
    maternal instinct in, 187–92
    sensibility in new framework for, 181,
        182, 185–92
Festa, Lynn, 257 n. 47
financial revolution in Britain, 9–10, 16–17
fiscal-military state, 17, 18
"flap," 128, 255 n. 73
Flert (dog), 203
flies, 67
Fond Doves, The (print), 185
food for pets, 37–38
    birds, 38, 146–47
    cats, 38
    dogs, 37–38, 159–62
    vs. needs of lower classes, 141–42, 146–47,
        159–62
Footman, The (print), 129
fops, 120, 123
Fox, Charles James, 218
France, fashion in, 101
fraud, in sale of birds, 30, 241 n. 83
freedom. See liberty
friendship
    between animals and humans, 132, 179
    and liberty, relationship between, 62, 83
Fubs (dog), 203–6
Fudge, Erica, 5, 6, 9, 148
    Pets, 5

Gainsborough, Thomas
    Henry Scott, 3rd Duke of Buccleuch, 195–98, 196
    Pomeranian Bitch and Puppy, 183–84, 184
    Tristram and Fox, 183
Gallant (dog), 201, 203
gender
    of cats vs. dogs, 116
    and consumerism, 18

    of Coventry's Pompey, 134–35
    and fashionable men, 97, 120–31
    of monkeys, 128, 255 n. 72
Gentleman's Magazine
    on abuse of animals, 155
    on apes and monkeys, 50, 128
    Cowper's writings in, 210, 211–12
    on dog ownership by elite, 162, 256 n. 15
    on dog ownership by lower classes, 166,
        168
    in dog tax debates, 162, 163–64
gifts, pets given as, 22, 52
Gilbert, Thomas, 159, 162
Gillray, James
    John Bull's Progress, 178
    The Whore's Last Shift, 253 n. 51
girls
    kittens associated with, 98–100, 116
    pet keeping by, 97–100
    sensibility in images of, 190–92
Girouard, Mark, 17
Gleanings of Natural History (Edwards), 21
God
    on human use of animals, 62, 66–68, 94
    in uniqueness of humans, 57, 62
Goldar, John, The Canonical Beau, 108, 109
goldfinches, 34, 48, 87
Goldsmith, Oliver
    on bird catchers, 240 n. 43
    on breeding of canaries, 23–24
    Buffon as source for, 12, 63, 95
    on caged birds, 83–84
    on classification of dogs by use, 7, 95–96
    on domestication, 62–63
    History of the Earth, 23–24
    on human-animal boundary, 55, 56–62
    plagiarism of works of, 20, 61
    terminology of animal slavery used by,
        62–63
    on working dogs, 4, 7
Good Oeconomist's, The (print), 192
Graham Children, The (Hogarth), 46, 47
Gravelot, 51
Gray, Thomas, "Ode on the Death of a
    Favourite Cat," 218
Greene, Edward Burnaby, 261 n. 47
Gregory, John, Comparative View of the State and
    Faculties of Man, 65, 247 n. 42

grief, over death of pets, 174–77, 205–6, 222–26
Grier, Katherine, 5
Grifoni, Elisabetta, 221
Grignion, Charles, *January and May*, 45
Grown Gentlemen Taught to Dance (print), 254 n. 64
Grown Ladies Taught to Dance (Crotchet), 120–22, *121*
Guardian (periodical), 107
Guillery, Peter, 238 n. 12
guinea pigs, 24, *25*

hands, human vs. ape, 58
Hanway, Jonas, 106–7, 141–42, 252 n. 30
happiness, of animals and humans, in Christianity, 67–68
Happy Consultation, The (Roberts), 114, *115*
Haraway, Donna, 8, 236 n. 21
hares, 210–12
Harkin, Maureen, 193
headdresses, 101–2
health care for pets, 38–40
Hearne, Vicki, 8
Henry Scott, 3rd Duke of Buccleuch (Gainsborough), 195–98, *196*
hierarchies. *See also* human-animal boundary
  in British society, 5
  debates over nature of, 8
  humans and animals in, 53
Hilman, Daniel, 159
history, animals' impact on human, 9
History of Pompey the Little, The (Coventry), 131–37
  cats and old maids in, 116, 253 n. 50
  differences in editions of, 255 n. 82
  dog collar in, 40–41
  as satire on fashion and gender, 97, 131–37
  as satire on social class, 144–46
History of the Earth (Goldsmith), 23–24
Hoar, Thomas, 214, 215, 264 n. 122
Hogarth, William, 252 n. 24
  The Graham Children, 46, *47*
  The Stages of Cruelty, 153, *154*, 166
horses, 4, 183

Hottentots
  Le Vaillant on, 80–82, 249 nn. 80–81
  use of term, 249 n. 77
households. *See* domestic spaces
housing for pets, 44, *45, 46*, 244 n. 159
human(s)
  meaning and use of term, 9, 236 n. 19
  "savage" vs. "civilized," 53, 60, 61, 65–66
human-animal boundary, 10, 50–90
  in animal rights movement, 231
  in animal studies, 7–8, 231
  apes' similarity to humans in, 50–62, 89
  Buffon on, 56–57, 61–62, 151
  and caged songbirds, morality of, 54, 83–88
  Cartesianism and, 7–8, 179, 231, 267 n. 8
  in Christianity, 62, 66–68, 94
  in Coventry's *Pompey*, 135–36
  cultural construction of, 7
  domestication and, 62–68
  Goldsmith on, 55, 56–62
  Hume on, 179–80
  Le Vaillant on, 72–83
  Linnaeus on, 8, 55–56, 60
  pets as threat to, 96–97, 108
  vs. racial differences, 60, 62
  and rights of animals, 68–71, 231
  and slavery, debates on morality of, 53–54
  terminology regarding, 236 n. 19
  young girls' understanding of, 97–100
human-animal relations. *See also* affection
  complexities of change in, 230
  as master and slave, 54, 62–63, 66
  possibilities for conceptualizing, 8–9
  as substitutes for relations with other humans, 5, 182, 227
humane (anticruelty) movement
  and abolitionist movement, 68–71, 153
  vs. animal rights movement, 230–31
  differences in agendas of, 153, 230
  in dog tax debates, 164–66
  opposition to, 229
  pets vs. working animals in, 157
  rhetoric of vulgarity in, 155–57
  rights of animals in, 68–71, 230
  rise and development of, 153–57, 182, 230

humane (anticruelty) movement *(continued)*
   and slavery, 54, 62, 68–71
   and social class, 153–57, 230
   vegetarianism in, 230
humanitarianism, natural rights for animals
   in, 68–69
humanoid apes. *See* apes
Hume, David, *Treatise on Human Nature*,
   179–80, 185
hunger, among lower classes, 141–42,
   146–47, 159–61
hunting, opposition to, 211, 219
hunting dogs
   collars on, 40
   kennels for, 44
   as target of dog tax, 162–63, 170
   veterinary care for, 40
   as working animals vs. pets, 4

identity
   national, 233–34
   of pets, fluidity of, 5
   pets' role in defining human, 5
imperial growth, British
   in availability of exotic animals, 52
   in rise of pet keeping, 10, 15, 18–21
industrialization
   and consumer revolution, 18
   and pet keeping, 231
insects, purpose of, 67, 94
instinct, vs. reason, 179
intelligence, in human-animal boundary,
   58–60
irrationality, of fashion, 101, 129
it-narratives, 131–32. *See also History of Pompey
   the Little, The* (Coventry)

James, William, 31, 42
January and May (Grignion), *45*
Jefferson, Thomas, 46
Jimmy Lincum Feadle (print), 126–28
John Bull (character), 178
John Bull's Progress (Gillray), 178
Johnson, Samuel, 3, 96, 100, 118
Jones, Mary, 108
Julian calendar, 243 n. 136, 259 n. 4
Jump Pussey (print), 190–91

Kean, Hilda, 22, 230, 231, 239 n. 36
Keeper's Travels in Search of His Master (Kendall),
   59
Kees (baboon), 54, 73–83, 249 n. 71
Kendall, Edward Augustus, 85–86, 87
   Keeper's Travels in Search of His Master, 59
kennels, dog, 44
Kete, Kathleen, 5
King, William, 160, 163
Kingsbury, Henry, *The Beggar and His Dog*, 168,
   169
kinship, pets' role in defining, 5. *See also*
   family
Kitchingman, John, *169*
kittens, young girls associated with,
   98–100, 116

laborers. *See* lower classes
Lady All-Top (print), 101–2, *103*
Lady Caressing a Rabbit (print), 190
Lady Fashion's Secretary's Office (print), *43*
Lady with a Dog (print), 190
Landry, Donna, 7
lapdogs
   in Coventry's *Pompey*, 131–37
   femininity associated with, 100–101,
   138–39
   purpose of, 95, 96
   in satires of fashionable men, 125–28
   in satires of fashionable women, 101–6
   in satires on social class, 142
   servants compared to, 141
   as sexual surrogates for women, 105–12,
   114, 133–34
   as too domesticated, 149–50
   vs. working dogs, 4
Lavater, Johann, 60
law, English
   abuse of animals in, 229
   dog tax established in, 158, 163–71
   pets as property in, 2
   poor relief in, 159
   working animals vs. pets in, 148
Lawrence, John, 70, 156–57
leashes, 41
Lechmere, Edmund, 163
Leeds Castle (Kent), 40–41, *41, 42*

legislation. *See* law
Le Vaillant, François, 72–83
   critique of domestication by, 64–65, 84
   on Hottentots, 80–82, 249 nn. 80–81
   on morality of pet keeping, 54
   pet baboon of, 54, 72–83, 249 n. 71
   popularity of memoirs of, 73
Liberal Opinions (Pratt), 138–39, 155–56, 193,
   261 n. 45
liberty
   absence of, in slavery, 53–54
   as defining value in British society,
   53–54, 233
   and friendship, relationship between, 62,
   83
Library, The (Crabbe), 225
Lincoln, Lord, 222
Linnaeus, Carl, 8, 55–56, 60
linnets, 84, 88
lions, 63–64
literature, sensibility in, 182, 192–94
livestock
   in domestic spaces, 19
   in humane movement, 230
London
   centrality to animal trade, 16
   domestic spaces in, size of, 238 n. 12
   menageries in, 30–32
   pet shops in, 21, 26, 32
   sale of exotic pets in, 16, 21
Lounger (periodical), 131, 144
Love for Love (Congreve), 110
lower classes
   abuse of animals by, 153–55, 165, 230
   in children's literature, 146–47
   hunger among, 141–42, 146–47, 159–61
   luxury taxes as aid to, 140, 159
   menageries visited by, 31
lower classes, pets of, 11, 138–73
   birds as, 178
   as companions, 141, 171, 177
   cost of, 37, 159
   critics of, 11, 37, 140, 158–61, 171
   dog beds for, 44
   lack of documentation on, 177
   owners' affection for, 166–67
   as target of dog tax, 158–61, 167–68

luxury(ies)
   critics of effects of, 92–94, 138–39
   debate over meaning of, 139–40, 158
   dogs as, 158–59, 163–64, 170–72
   economic benefits of, 139–40
   fashion as, 92–94
   moderate, 139, 140
   morality of, 139–40, 158
   pets as, 2, 30, 140
   rise in demand for, 17
   taxes on, 140, 158, 159, 163–64, 170–72
   transformation into necessities, 18

macaronis, 120, 123–31
Macarony Brothers, The (Caldwell), 128–29,
   130
Macarony Dressing Room, The (White), 125, *126*,
   254 n. 67
MacDonogh, Katharine, 40
machines, animals as, 179, 231
Mackenzie, Henry, 144–46
   The Man of Feeling, 168, 192–93, 197, 261 n.
   45
MacMahon, Thomas O'Brien, 106–7, 150
Mandeville, Bernard, *Fable of the Bees*, 139,
   233, 267 n. 12
Mann, Horace, 22, 221, 222
Man of Feeling, The (Mackenzie), 168, 192–93,
   197, 261 n. 45
masculinity
   of dancing masters, 120–23
   of fops and macaronis, 123–31
   natural history in new framework for,
   209–17
   sensibility in new framework for, 181,
   182, 192–200
material culture, pet accessories in, 16
maternal instinct, 187–92
Mavor, William Fordyce, 67, 84
McKendrick, Neil, 17–18
Meacham, Sarah Hand, 248 n. 65
men. *See also* masculinity
   cats belonging to, 118
   as dancing masters, 120–23
   fashion of, 97, 120–31
   as fops and macaronis, 120, 123–31
   gender norms violated by, 97, 120

menageries, 30–32
  admission charged by, 30, 31
  advertising by, 30, 31, 241 n. 85
  sale of animals at, 30–32
  at Wentworth Castle, 227, 266 n. 191
  vs. zoos, 30
Merke, Henri, *Cries of London,* 27
middle class
  advertising for lost dogs by, 37
  exotic pets owned by, 34
  rise of, 5–6, 17
  in satires on pet keeping, 142
Minshull, Captain, *126*
mirror, monkey as, in satires of fashionable
  men, 125, 128–29
Mischief Making Old Maids' & Gossip's Arms, The
  (print), 253 n. 59
Miseries of Idleness, The (Morland), 159, *160*
Miss Sukey and Her Nursery (Smith), 190
Miss Thoughtful (print), *191,* 191–92, 197
Monboddo, James Burnett, Lord, 55–56
money-back guarantees, 29–30
mongooses, 35
monkeys
  vs. apes, use of terms, 246 n. 9
  chains for, 41–42, 78–80
  gendered as male, 128, 255 n. 72
  individual sellers of, 24
  and knowledge about world, 21
  as pet of Le Vaillant, 54, 72–83
  as pet of Wentworth, 174–77, 200,
    203–4, 206
  in satires of fashionable men, 128–31
  as sexual surrogates for women, 114
Montagu, George, 220, 222–23
morality
  of animal slavery or pet keeping, 54, 63,
    71–72
  of caging songbirds, 54, 83–88
  domestication as yardstick for, 60
  of human slavery, 53–54, 71
  of luxury, 139–40, 158
Morland, George, 192, 261 n. 44
  The Miseries of Idleness, 159, *160*
  Selling Guinea Pigs, 24, *25*
Mossend, Robert, 152
Mrs. Abington as Miss Prue (Reynolds), 109–12,
  111, 253 n. 44

Mulso, Hester, 215–16
Musser, Joseph, 112

names of pets
  as defining feature, 4
  and names of slaves, 53
national identity, 233–34
natural history
  classification of world in, 55
  and menageries, 30–31
  in new framework for masculinity,
    209–17
  popularity of, in rise of pet keeping, 15,
    20
  as primary source, 11–12
Natural History (Buffon), 12
Natural History and Antiquities of Selborne
  (White), 212–16
Natural History of Birds (Buffon), 24, 84
naturalists. *See also specific individuals*
  on caged birds, 83–84
  on classification of apes and monkeys,
    246 nn. 8–9
  on classification of dogs, 95–96
  in debates on morality of slavery, 53–54
  on domestication, 62–63, 232
  images of animals by, 183
  masculinity of, 209, 217
  menageries as sources for, 31
  pets as source of information for, 181–
    82, 209–17
  on prices of pets, 33
  on purposes of animals, 94
  on similarities between apes and humans,
    53, 55
natural rights of animals, 68–69
Nest for Puppies, A (print), 104–6
New Academy for Accomplishments, A (print),
  122–23, *124*
New Fashion'd Head Dress, A (Dawe), 112–13, *113*
newspapers. *See* advertising
Noah's Ark (shop), 33, 242 n. 90
"noble savage," 66
nonhumans, use of term, 236 n. 19. *See also*
  animal(s)
nostalgia, 232
Nuneham, Lord, 223–24
Nussbaum, Martha, 267 n. 7

Occupation selon l'Age (Watteau), 192
"Ode on the Death of a Favourite Cat"
    (Gray), 218
"Ode on the Death of a Spaniel" (anony-
    mous), 193, 261 n. 47
old maids
    cats associated with, 116–19
    satire on fashion of, 97, 112–19
Old Maids at a Cat's Funeral (Pettit), 116–17, 117
Old Maids Occasional Concert, The (print),
    117–18
orangutans, 53, 55–60, 246 n. 8, 246 n. 20
organs, bird, 44–48, 47
"Oriental" style, 19
Ossory, Lady, 223, 224, 225, 226
Oswald, John, 69

padding, in fashion, 102–5
Parliament, debates over dog tax in, 158,
    163 71, 178
Parrot, the (shop), 14–15, 21, 31, 242 n. 90
parrots
    Buffon on speech in, 57
    chains for, 42, 43
    cost of buying, 33–36
    diversity of species, 52
    individual sellers of, 24
    in pet shops, 28, 29–30, 32
    rise in availability of, 52
passions, shared by humans and animals,
    180, 185
Patapan (dog), 218, 220–22, 223, 226
patronage, pets as gifts in, 22
Payne, Thomas, 32
Pearl (dog), 201–2, 208–9
Pennant, Thomas
    on bird catchers, 23, 240 n. 43
    on Brookes, 31
    on bullfinches, 243 n. 116
    on caged birds, 87
    on fraud in sale of birds, 241 n. 83
    on Linnaeus's taxonomy, 56
    on prices of birds, 34
    Synopsis of Quadrupeds, 56
    White's letters to, 212
Penton, Henry, 166
Pepys, Samuel, 52
Perkins, David, 248 n. 61, 257 n. 37

personality of animals
    Cowper on, 210
    in portraits, 184–85, 198
pet(s)
    acquisition of, 22–37 (*see also* sale of pets)
    defining characteristics of, 3–5
    meaning and use of term, 3–5
    population estimates for, 178, 239 n. 37
    vs. working animals, 4, 147–48
pet accessories. *See* accessories
pet keeping
    early opposition to, 2, 4, 37, 48, 94–95
    evolution of attitudes toward, 2, 140–41,
        164–73, 177
    factors contributing to rise of, 9–10,
        15–22
    as filling gap in modern life, 5
    humane attitudes fostered by, 178–79
    modern attitudes toward, 1–2, 229–30,
        231
    modern ubiquity of, 2
    monetary costs of, 19, 22, 37–38, 159
    morality of, debates about, 54, 71–72
    paradoxes of, 1–2, 20, 72, 230
    power relations in, 4, 8
    review of literature on, 3–9
    timing of origins of, 2, 5–6
Pets (Fudge), 5
pet shops, 25–30
    advertising by, 14–15, 21, 26, 28–29
    birds in, 26–30
    diversity of animals in, 14–15, 26–28
    emergence of first, 21, 25–26
    in London, 21, 26, 32
    number of, 25–26
Pettit, John, *Old Maids at a Cat's Funeral*, 116–
    17, 117
Philosophy of Natural History (Smellie), 179
Pilton, William, 26, 241 n. 60
Piozzi, Hester Lynch Thrale, 19, 117
Pitt, William, 170, 171
plagiarism, of natural histories, 20, 61
pleasure, in society, role of, 233
Plumb, Christopher, 26, 31–32, 34
Plumb, J. H., *The Commercialisation of Leisure in
    Eighteenth-Century England*, 237 n. 2
Polite Alderman, The (print), 108–9
Poll (parrot), 203–5

Pomeranian Bitch and Puppy (Gainsborough), 183–84, *184*

Pompey the Little, (Coventry). *See History of Pompey the Little, The*

poor pet owners. *See* lower classes

poor relief, and dog ownership, 159, 166

Pope, Alexander, 135, 149
 Essay on Man, 224
 The Rape of the Lock, 107, 115

population of pets, 178, 239 n. 37

portraits of animals, 12, 183–85
 accessories shown in, 16
 affection between humans and pets depicted in, 181
 personality in, 184–85, 198
 rise of, 183
 subjectivity in, 181, 183, 184–85
 of Walpole, 221
 of Wentworth, 174, 176, 203
 with women owners, 181

possessions, pets as, 1

Postle, Martin, 110

poverty. *See also* lower classes
 cats associated with, 116
 relief for, 159, 166

power relations, in pet keeping, 4, 8

Pratt, Samuel Jackson, 32, 69, 70, 180
 "Defence of our Attachment to Animals," 148–49
 Liberal Opinions, 138–39, 155–56, 193, 261 n. 45

Preserving the Young (print), 187–90, *189*

Pretty Miss a Sleep (print), 187, *188*

pride, animals' experience of, 180

Primatt, Humphry, 69–70

prints. *See also* satires; *specific works*
 affection between humans and pets depicted in, 180–81, 182–200
 birds in poor households depicted in, 178
 pet accessories in, 16
 ubiquity of pets in, 16

property, pets as
 legal status of, 2
 paradox of, 1, 2, 230
 and rights of animals, 8

Public Advertiser (newspaper), 15, 162

public credit and debt, establishment of formal system of, 16–17

Pug (monkey), 174–77, 200, 203–4, 206

Puss (hare), 210–11

Raber, Karen, 183

racial differences, vs. human-animal boundary, 60, 62

Raeburn, Henry, *Boy and Rabbit*, 198, *199*

Raff, Georg Christian, 66–67, 84, 85, 150

Rape of the Lock, The (Pope), 107, 115

Raton (dog), 198

Rawls, John, 267 n. 7

reason
 in fashion, lack of, 101, 129
 sensibility as reaction against value of, 182
 as unique human characteristic, 57–62, 69, 89, 179–80

redpolls, 87

Regan, Tom, *The Case for Animal Rights*, 266 n. 5

Renaissance, importance of animals in, 6

residential spaces. *See* domestic spaces

Reynolds, Joshua, 198
 Mrs. Abington as Miss Prue, 109–12, *111*, 253 n. 44

Ribeiro, Aileen, 253 n. 44

rights of animals
 development of movement for, 230–32, 267 n. 7
 foundational works on, 266 n. 5
 and human-animal boundary, 68–71, 231
 in humane movement, 68–71, 230
 mockery of idea of, 229, 266 n. 1
 natural, 68–69
 and property status of animals, 8

Ritvo, Harriet, 5

Rival Favourites, The (print), 185–87, *186*

Roberts, James, *The Happy Consultation*, 114, *115*

Roman Empire, 52, 94

Romney, George, 190

Rosette (dog), 218, 220–26, 265 n. 160

Rowlandson, Thomas, *27*
 Virginia, 118, *119*

rumps, false, 102–5

sagacity, in human-animal boundary, 58–60

sale of pets, 22–37. *See also* pet shops; *specific types of animals*
 centrality of London in, 16

by individuals, 24–25
at menageries, 30–32
pricing in, 15, 33–37
rise of, 14–15, 178
satires on fashion
alternative images replacing, 181, 185, 198
in Coventry's *Pompey*, 131–37
of dancing masters, 120–23
of fops and macaronis, 120, 123–31
of old maids, 112–19
and pet keeping by women, 107–12, 142
slaves in, 102, 252 n. 24
of women's dress, 101–6
satires on pet keeping
aimed at women, 107–12, 142
alternative images replacing, 181–82, 185, 198
social class in, 141–47
on treatment of servants vs. pets, 141–47
"savage" animals, 62–63
"savage" humans, 53, 60, 61, 65–66
Savile, Gertrude, 177
Sayer, Robert, 190
Scotin, Gérard Jean Baptiste, II, *Chimpanzee*, 51
scraps, as pet food, 38
self-discipline
sensibility as reaction against value of, 182
as solution to animal abuse, 153
Selima (cat), 218
Selling Guinea Pigs (Morland), 24, 25
Selwyn, George, 198
sensibility
emergence of ideal of, 11, 68, 182
in humane movement, 68
in literature, 182, 192–94
in new framework for femininity, 181, 182, 185–92
in new framework for masculinity, 181, 182, 192–200
in visual culture, 181–200, 182–200
sentimental novels, 157, 192–94
servants
in children's literature, 146–47
dogs as, 150–52, 171
in elite domestic spaces, 17
humane movement on, 156

outdated fashions given to, 101
pets and working animals compared to, 140–41
in satires, 141–47
tax on, 171
treatment of, vs. pets, 140–47
Seven Years' War, 20–21
sexuality, female
vs. chastity, 187
in Coventry's *Pompey*, 133
of old maids, 112–17
and padding in fashion, 105
and pets as sexual surrogates, 105–12, 114, 133–34
sensibility in reinterpretation of, 185–87
and young girls' interest in fashion, 100
Shannon, Laurie, 7, 236 n. 19
Accommodated Animal, 267 n. 8
Shawe-Taylor, Desmond, 195, 197
Shell, Marc, 4–5
Sheridan, Richard Brinsley, 167
shops, pet. *See* pet shops
Shyllon, F. O., 245 n. 7
Sibly, Ebenezer, 52, 53, 59–60, 194
silver dog collars, 40–41
sin
luxury as, 139–40
pet keeping as, 2, 94, 159
Singer, Peter, *Animal Liberation*, 231, 266 n. 5, 267 n. 7
sin tax, 159
slavery, animal
benefits to humans and animals justifying, 71–72
caging songbirds as, 83–88
in Christianity, 62, 66–68
debates about morality of, 63, 71–72
dogs in, 149–50
and domestication, 62–68, 89, 151, 232
implications for human slavery, 54, 62, 68–71, 89–90
pets as example of, 71–72
terminology of, 62–63, 69
slavery, human
abolitionist movement against, 68–71, 89, 153
corruption of masters in, 66
debates about morality of, 53–54, 71

slavery, human (*continued*)
   and domestication of animals, 62–68,
      89, 151
   and exotic animals, links between, 52–54
   and humane movement, 54, 62, 68–71
   implications of animal slavery for, 54, 62,
      68–71, 89–90
slaves
   in caricatures of fashion, 102, 252 n. 24
   parallels between pets and, 4, 53, 71–72
Smart, Christopher, 118
Smellie, William, 65–66, 149
   Philosophy of Natural History, 179
Smith, John Raphael, *Miss Sukey and Her
     Nursery*, 190
Smith, Thomas, 32
Smollett, Tobias, 38–40
Snooke, Rebecca, 212, 213, 216, 217
social class, 11, 138–73. *See also* elite; lower
     classes; middle class
   in children's literature, 146–47
   of dancing masters, 120
   in dog tax, 141, 157–72
   in humane movement, 153–57, 230
   pets' role in understanding relations
     among, 139–47
   in satires on pet keeping, 141–47
society, British
   changes in, in rise of pet keeping, 17, 19
   hierarchies in, 5
   liberty as defining value in, 53–54, 233
   luxury as beneficial to, 139–40
   pets' role in understanding, 2–3, 12–13,
     229, 232–34
   pleasure in, role of, 233
songbirds
   catching of, 23, 240 n. 43
   morality of caging, 54, 83–88
Sørensen, Madeleine Pinault, 183
souls of animals, 70
Southey, Robert, 170, 259 n. 87
sparrows, 85
Spectator (periodical), 116, 131
speech, as unique human characteristic, 57,
     58, 61, 69, 246 n. 20
Spencer, Lady Charles, 198
sporting dogs. *See also* hunting dogs
   as target of dog tax, 162–63, 170

squirrels
   chains for, 41–42, 244 n. 157
   as fashionable pets, 92
   houses for, 44, *45*
Stages of Cruelty, The (Hogarth), 153, *154, 166*
Steele, Richard, *Tatler*, 3
Steward, James Christen, 192, 261 n. 44
St. James's Chronicle (newspaper), 37
Strafford, Anne, Countess of (wife of
     Thomas)
   marriage of, 202, 262 n. 66
   relationship with mother-in-law, 175–
     76, 201, 202, 204, 207–9
Strafford, Anne, Countess of (wife of Wil-
     liam), 227–28
Strafford, Thomas Wentworth, Earl of,
     200–209
   career of, 200
   earldom of, 262 n. 66
   marriage of, 202, 262 n. 66
   mother's letters to, 174–77, 200–209,
     259 n. 2
   pets of, 176, 201–2, 206–9, 262 n. 69
Strafford, William, Earl of, 227–28
Stuart, Lady Louisa, 227–28
Stubbs, George, 183
subjectivity of animals, growth of interest
     in, 181, 183, 184–85
suffering of animals, 68–69, 179, 230–31
Summer (print), 142, *143*
Supplemental Magazine, The (print), 102–4, *105*
Swift, Jonathan, 255 n. 81
sympathy
   animals' experience of, 180–81
   in children's literature, 86
   definition of, 180
   emergence of ideal of, 11, 179
   in humane movement, 69
Synopsis of Quadrupeds (Pennant), 56

Tatler (periodical), 3, 72, 114, 178–79
taxation
   on dog ownership (*see* dog tax)
   expansion of system of, 17
   on luxuries, 140, 158, 159, 163–64
   on manservants, 171
taxidermy, of exotic birds, 20
Taylor, Charles, 59

Taylor, Thomas, 266 n. 1
theriomorphism, 82
Thomas, Keith, 4, 5, 239 n. 36
Tight Lacing, or Fashion Before Ease (print), 102
time management, as solution to animal abuse, 153
Times of London (newspaper), 161
Timothy (tortoise), 212–17, 263 n. 114
Tiney (hare), 210–12
Tommy Trimmer's Historical Account (Trimmer), 118–19
Tonton (dog), 220, 224–27, 228
Topsell, Edward, 95
tortoises, 212–17
trade in pets. *See* sale of pets
training of animals
    birds, 34, 36, 48, 243 n. 116
    as mutually beneficial, 8, 236 n. 21
Treatise on Human Nature (Hume), 179–80, 185
treatment of animals. *See also* abuse
    in animal rights movement, 230–32
    as focus of animal studies, 7–8
    humane (*see* humane movement)
    vs. humans, 2, 140–47
Trimmer, Sarah, 44, 87–88, 159
    Fabulous Histories, 67, 146–47, 150, 257 n. 30
Trimmer, Tommy, *Tommy Trimmer's Historical Account,* 118–19
Tristram and Fox (Gainsborough), 183
Tuan, Yi-Fu, 53
    Dominance and Affection, 4
turtles, 32
tyranny, domestication as, 63, 65
Tyther, John, 28–30, 33, 34, 36, 241 n. 75

uniqueness of humans. *See* human-animal boundary
Universal Spectator, 64
urbanization, and pet keeping, 5–6, 231–32
utility of animals
    Christianity on, 62, 66–68, 94
    classification by, 7, 95–96, 231–32

Varlo, Charles, 37–38, 161–62, 239 n. 37
vegetarianism, 145, 230
veterinary care, 38–40

Virginia (Rowlandson), 118, *119*
visual culture, animals in, 180–200. *See also* portraits; prints; satires; *specific works*
    in "fancy pictures," 181, 190–92
    as individuals, 183–85, 194–97
    influence of sensibility on, 181, 182–200
    in new framework for femininity, 181, 182, 185–92
    in new framework for masculinity, 181, 182, 192–200
    as subject vs. object, 183
vulgarity, rhetoric of, 155–57

Wahrman, Dror, 55
Walpole, Horace
    on abuse of animals, 182, 218–19, 229, 264 n. 132
    affection for pets in letters of, 182, 200, 218–28
    cats of, 218, 224
    diversity of pets of, 220
    dogs of, 193, 218–27, 264 n. 130
    estate at Strawberry Hill, 218, 220, 264 n. 128
    on exchange of pets, 22
    and menagerie at Wentworth Castle, 227, 266 n. 191
    and "Ode on the Death of a Spaniel," 193, 218
    on taxidermied exotic birds, 20
Ward, Samuel, 87, 149–50
warfare
    and availability of exotic pets, 20–21, 52
    and public debt, 16–17
waste
    in fashion, 101
    food for pets as, 140, 145
Watteau, Jean-Antoine, *Occupation selon l'Age,* 192
wealth
    in configuration of domestic spaces, 17, 238 n. 12
    financial revolution in growth of, 16–17
wealthy pet owners. *See* elite
Wentworth, Lady Isabella
    affection for pets in letters of, 174–77, 181, 200–209, 227, 259 n. 2
    diversity of pets of, 200

Wentworth, Lady Isabella (*continued*)
  food for dogs of, 38
  pet monkey of, 174–77, 200, 203–4, 206
Wentworth, Sir William, 200
Wentworth Castle, menagerie at, 227, 266
  n. 191
Wheatley, Francis, 192, 261 n. 44
Which Is the Man (print), 125–26, *127*, 254 n. 68
White, Charles, *The Macarony Dressing Room*,
  125, *126*, 254 n. 67
White, Gilbert
  affection for pets in writings of, 182,
    200, 209–10, 212–17, 227, 232
  Natural History and Antiquities of Selborne, 212–16
White, Molly, 215
Whore's Last Shift, The (Gillray), 253 n. 51
Wicksteed, James, *Animated Nature*, 91–92, *93*
Williams, Lady Charlotte, 191–92, 197
Wills, Geoffrey, 244 n. 151
Windham, William, 166–67, 168, 194, 258
  n. 77

Wollstonecraft, Mary, 266 n. 1
wolves, 31
women. *see also* fashion; femininity;
    sexuality
  affection of, fickleness of, 107–8
  maternal instinct of, 187–92
  as old maids, 97, 112–19
Wootton, John, 221
working animals. *See also specific types*
  in humane movement, 157, 230
  monetary value of, 148
  vs. pets, 4, 147–48
  servants compared to, 140–41
Wright, Joseph, *Dressing the Kitten*, 98–100,
    99, 251 n. 14
Wyett, Jodi, 100, 255 n. 88

Young, Thomas, 71–72
  Essay on Humanity to Animals, 68

zoos, vs. menageries, 30

Typeset by
COGHILL COMPOSITION COMPANY

Printed and bound by
SHERIDAN BOOKS

Composed in
REQUIEM

Printed on
NATURES NATURAL

Bound in
ARRESTOX

Printed in Great Britain
by Amazon.co.uk, Ltd.,
Marston Gate.